The Qur'ān

The Qur'ān

Translated into English
by Alan Jones

Gibb Memorial Trust
2007

Published by

The E. J. W. Gibb Memorial Trust

Trustees: K. Fleet, C. Hillenbrand, C. D. Holes, G. L. Lewis,
C. P. Melville, J. E. Montgomery, A. H. Morton
Secretary to the Trustees: P. R. Bligh

© Alan Jones 2007

ISBN 978 0 906094 64 8 (h/b)
ISBN 978 0 906094 63 1 (p/b)

A CIP record for this book is available from the British Library

Further details of the E. J. Gibb Memorial Trust and its publications
are available at the Trust's website

www.gibbtrust.org

Printed in Great Britain by
Short Run Press, Exeter

*To my family
past and present*

Contents

Contents

Contents

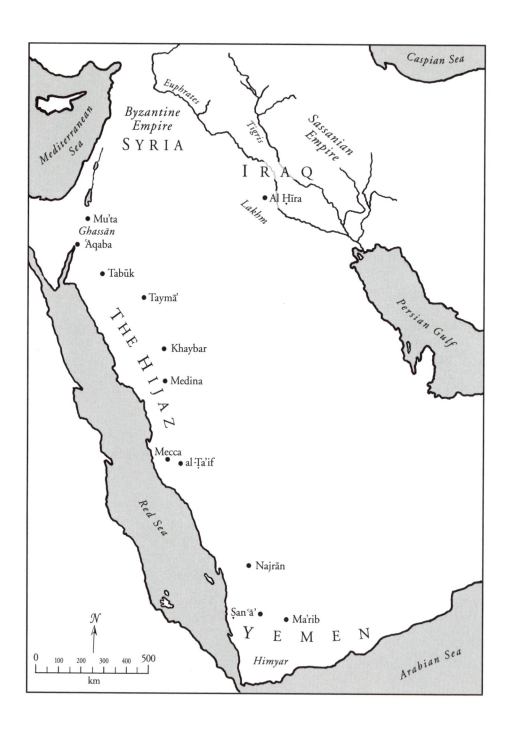

Caspian Sea

Euphrates

Byzantine
Empire

S Y R I A

Mediterranean
Sea

Tigris

Sassanian
Empire

I R A Q

• Al Ḥīra

Lakhm

• Muʾta
Ghassān
• ʿAqaba

• Tabūk

• Taymāʾ

Persian Gulf

THE HIJAZ

• Khaybar

• Medina

Red Sea

Mecca
• • al-Ṭaʾif

• Najrān

N

Ṣanʿāʾ • • Maʾrib

0   100   200   300   400   500

Y E M E N

km

Himyar

Arabian Sea

Introduction

The Qur'ān (often transliterated in English as 'the Koran') is the sacred book of Islam. For Muslims it is the word of God, revealed in Arabic by the archangel Gabriel to the prophet Muḥammad and thence to mankind. Muḥammad lived in the Hijaz region in western Arabia from about 570 to 632 AD, and it is to the Arabian peninsula that we must look for his background.

1. The land and its peoples

(a) The interior and the marches

The deserts and steppes of the Arabian peninsula form a harsh, arid area, which was peopled, despite enormous difficulties, by nomadic Arabic-speaking tribes, who called themselves *bedu*. Over the years the *bedu* had developed great practical skills and complex social organisations to enable them to live in such inhospitable lands. Even so, they would not have managed this without their camels, which could survive quite successfully on the poorest of pasture and on irregular supplies of water. The water came mainly from wells or oases. Rarely there were settlements where there was water, cultivation, trading or in some cases a cultic centre.

The trading settlements were important for the *bedu*. Not only did they facilitate local barter; they sometimes had various commodities that came from abroad. These included wine (from Syria, Iraq and Persia), weapons (spears, etc. from India) and slaves (from Africa).

Some *bedu* tribes lived beyond the confines of the peninsula, but there they came up against groups able to exert authority over them. The north-western, Syrian, march was in the hands of the Ghassānids, who were Arab vassals of the Byzantines; whilst to the north-east the Lakhmids of al-Ḥīra, in what is now southern Iraq, were under the suzerainty of the Sassanians of Persia.

(b) The Yemen

In the south-west the Yemen was quite different from the rest of the peninsula. Its high fertile uplands had long attracted settlers, and it had been the home of successive south-Arabian kingdoms, Minaean, Sabaean (Saba', Sheba) and Himyaritic. After the collapse of the last of these dynasties, the Yemen had fallen under the control of the Abyssinians, about 525 AD. Its population contained various mixed strata, and there were both Himyarite and Arabic speakers. Both Christianity and Judaism had sizable communities of adherents in the Yemen.

(c) The Hijaz

The Hijaz had, and still has, three main settlements: Mecca, Medina and al-Ṭā'if. Muḥammad is thought to have been born in Mecca about 570 AD and he lived there until 622 AD. Mecca is situated in a searingly hot and barren valley ('a valley where there is no sown land' [Q. 14:37]), some 50 miles east of the Red Sea. However, it had the one resource that made life viable: water from a series of wells.

Mecca was a very ancient settlement – the Qur'ān makes Abraham its founder – and was important enough to have been mentioned in classical Greek geographical sources. The name they give it, 'Makoraba', is almost certainly taken, like other Greek names for places in the area, from South Arabian: the Sabaean *mkrb* means 'a sanctuary'. It seems reasonable to infer that the Sabaean word points to Mecca also having acquired a cultic status at an early date.

There was, however, another reason for the interest of the classical writers: long-distance trade. Mecca was a natural stopping place for the caravans that moved goods to and from Syria, the Yemen and Iraq. It also had access to the Red Sea, and there were annual fairs nearby that were centres for local trading.

Recent research has cast some doubt on the importance of Mecca in long-distance trade by the end of the sixth century, and it may well be that the traditional sources overstate the role and wealth of Meccan traders. Nevertheless, the poetry of the period refers to long-distance trade; and the Qur'ān's use of trading phraseology and indeed of ethical ideas based on fair trading points to the importance that such vocabulary had in everyday life in the region. Two good examples are:

> My people, give full measure and full weight in justice.
> Do not defraud the people of their things.   [11:85]

and

> ... He has set the balance,
> That you may not transgress in the balance.
> Perform weighing with justice
> and do not skimp in the balance.   [55:7–9]

However, the most telling piece is to be found in *Sūra* 25. Among the objections made by Muḥammad's Meccan opponents is the following comment in verse 7:

> And they say, 'What is there to this messenger?
> He eats food and walks round the markets.
> Why has not an angel been sent down to him to be a warner with him?'

There is a divine riposte to this in verse 20:

> We never sent any messengers before you [Muḥammad],
> except they ate food and walked around the markets.

The rival settlement to Mecca, al-Ṭā'if, is situated some 45 miles to the south-east. It too was involved in trade and was the centre of a cult, but in one respect it was quite different from Mecca. It lies at a height of nearly 6,000 feet, and it is lush and fertile, renowned for its grain and for its fruit. It is not fanciful to say that its gardens provided earthly examples for many of the gardens of paradise described in the Qur'ān.

Both Mecca and al-Ṭā'if were controlled by single tribes, the Quraysh and Thaqīf respectively. This was not the case at Medina, which was to be Muḥammad's home for the last ten years of his life. Situated some 220 miles to the north of Mecca, Medina (from the Aramaic *medinta* 'area of jurisdiction') was a large, well-populated district, mainly given over to agriculture. Its Arabic and South Arabian name was Yathrib. The double name appears to reflect something of the population mix of the sprawling settlement. It was peopled largely by three Jewish tribes, the Banū l-Naḍīr, the Banū Qaynuqāʿ and the Banū Qurayẓa, and by two Arab tribes, the Aws and Khazraj, who seem to have been relative newcomers. The area was fertile and had plentiful supplies of water. Medina's agricultural prosperity drew the *bedu* to trade there, but not without unease. Malaria was endemic, as it was in most of the settlements (though apparently not in Mecca and al-Ṭā'if).

2. Religion

The religious situation in the area was complex. To the north and east there were large numbers of Christian Arabs in Syria (Monophysites) and in Iraq (Nestorians). In the Hijaz there were communities of Jews at Medina and at settlements on the route to the north, particularly at Khaybar and Taymā'. The Yemen was home to other Jewish communities and to Christians of both Arab and non-Arab origin, particularly at Najrān, said to have been the seat of a 'bishopric' for part of the sixth century; and during the Abyssinian occupation of the Yemen a cathedral was built at Ṣanʿā'. South-western Arabia also witnessed the establishment of several other monotheistic cults, including that of al-Raḥmān 'the Merciful', a name that was to find prominence in the Qur'ān as one of the most favoured epithets of God.

At a more mundane level, idol-worship had developed in various settlements. We are told that in the Hijaz the goddess al-ʿUzzā was particularly venerated by the people of the small settlement of al-Nakhla and by the Quraysh in Mecca, al-Lāt by the people of al-Ṭā'if, and Manāt by the Arabs of Medina. However, amongst the god-figures worshipped, Allāh, 'the god', became recognised as the preponderant, but not all-powerful, deity.

Despite these developments, few of the Arabian *bedu* appear to have had strong religious feelings. Their poetry makes it clear that their basic belief was that Fate ruled their destiny and that sooner or later Fate would bring death. They knew about gods and idols, but there are lines of poetry that show that the gods, even Allāh, were less important to the *bedu* than Fate. However, those who moved into the settlements appear to have identified with the cults there and to have developed some conviction that visiting their idols and performing rituals, including animal sacrifice, might

3

induce the idols to intercede with Fate or even a supreme deity on their behalf. These rituals have something of the appearance of pilgrimage, because the key ceremonies were normally held when the local population was swollen by influxes of visitors to annual fairs, the main purpose of which was trading. Surviving poetry makes it clear that such visitors did take part in the rituals, but it is likely that this was due more to their wish to be seen to be acting at one with the people of the settlements and to be respecting their traditions than to firmly held religious belief.

Though the *bedu* seem to have had little expectation that Fate might be propitiated in this manner, they appear to have sought to avoid its final, fatal appearance in somewhat less formal ways, and recourse to divination and soothsayers (*kāhin*s) was not uncommon.

3. Culture

The culture of pre-Islamic Arabia was centred largely on oral literature. However, the South Arabians had regularly used inscriptions to record matters considered to be of importance; and writing was known and used in the settlements for commercial, contractual and even archival purposes.

In other fields it was a matter of memory. Poetry had the greatest prestige, but later sources also refer to three groups who composed prose literature in Arabic. Most picturesque but least important of these were the soothsayers (*kāhin*s). They had their own form of diction, a highly charged and often cryptic kind of prose, marked by rhythmic clauses and assonance. There were also two types of orators (*khaṭīb*s): tribal spokesmen, with an important role in inter-tribal relations; and itinerants preaching either a religious message or exhorting people to do good. Finally there were story-tellers who told and retold stories and legends of tribal life.

Apart from a few scraps preserved in later Arabic sources, all the *kāhin-* and *khaṭīb*-type material has disappeared; and surviving stories and legends have been recast in the language of later times. There can, however, be no doubt of the influence and importance of these prose forms in providing several types of discourse that were comprehensible over a wide area and were largely, though not entirely, free of dialectal features.

What has survived in a reasonable quantity is pre-Islamic poetry. This is often of the highest quality, for Arabic poetry was at a zenith from 525 to 650 AD. Like story-telling, poetry was part of the fabric of tribal society, and poets were highly esteemed for their ability to sing the praises of the tribe to which they belonged and feared for their ability to satirize or even curse. It was generally believed that each poet was inspired by his own individual inspirational spirit, a *jinn* (synonyms *shayṭān* and *khalīl*).

The survival of considerable amounts of poetry, together with the later use made of it by commentators on the Qur'ān, has tended to divert attention away from the importance of the prose genres in paving the way for the Qur'ān. Yet the briefest comparison will show that poetry and the Qur'ān are not closely linked. Some mordant pieces in the Qur'ān do recall the use of satire in poetry, and expressions of thought sometimes coincide; but the treatment of more important features, such as narrative and homily, is totally different. Moreover, while the Qur'ān has its own strong rhythms, it is only rarely and coincidentally that a Quranic phrase fits one of the metres of poetry. It is true that the Qur'ān depicts Muḥammad as having been accused by some of his Meccan opponents of being a poet, but the way that this claim is rebutted makes it clear that their main assertion was that he was possessed by the *jinn* and not inspired by God. [Q. 44:14, 52:39, 23:25 *etc.*]

4. Muḥammad

Muḥammad was born about 570 AD, a member of the Quraysh tribe that had taken control of Mecca and settled there several generations previously. Tradition has it that his family was respected rather than a rich; that his father, ʿAbdallāh, died before he was born and his mother, Āmina, when he was six; and that after her death he was looked after by his grandfather ʿAbd al-Muṭṭalib and then by his uncle Abū Ṭālib. In general terms this is confirmed by Q. 93:6, 'Did He not find you an orphan and provide you with a home?'

Very little is known of the first forty years of Muḥammad's life, but it is generally agreed that about 595 AD he married Khadīja, a rich widow some years older than himself and that they had several children. Only one of these, his daughter Fāṭima, was to survive him. Muslim tradition pictures Muḥammad engaged in trade and travelling to Syria both before and after his marriage, but this is uncertain.

It would appear that as the years went by Muḥammad turned more and more towards monotheistic meditation, as a number of people in the area were doing. One of the reasons for this was a repugnance for the materialism that had become a feature of life in Mecca. That materialism was a problem is shown by various passages that attack it in the Qur'ān; but the now popular view that this materialism was destroying the social cohesion of the town overstates the case. The strength and tenacity of the Meccan opposition to Muḥammad over a period that was to last for getting on for twenty years would not have been possible in a deeply divided society.

Eventually, around 610 AD, he became convinced that he had been visited by the archangel Gabriel (Jibrīl in Arabic) and had been ordered to preach God's message to the Arabs. After a brief period of uncertainty, when there was no further visitation, he had a similar experience and another revelation. From that time onwards Muḥammad was totally convinced that he was the Messenger of God, and his actions henceforward were based on that unswerving conviction. Occasionally he might have temporized, but his long-term goal never changed. And there were frequent revelations to fortify him in his work.

For a couple of years or so he preached in private to family and friends, converting the majority of them to the new religion. Then in 613 AD he began to preach in public. The response of the majority of Meccans was hostile and was to remain so. As mentioned above, it has recently been fashionable to depict Meccan society as in social and economic decline; but if its long and active resistance to the new religion is an accurate gauge, it was a tough and determined community, bent on preserving its own privileged position, even if it was a bastion of idol-worship in the eyes of the nascent Muslim community.

Muḥammad continued to win over converts, but they were few in number, on average no more than a handful a month; and only occasionally did they include a prominent member of Quraysh. More than once Muḥammad tried to come to terms with the Meccans – the garbled story that has come down to us about the so-called 'satanic verses' being connected with one of these attempts (see Q. 53:19–21). When the Meccans remained implacable, he sent some of the converts to safer territory, certainly as far as the Yemen and possibly to Abyssinia. In 618 AD the situation became even more difficult. First Khadīja died, shortly to be followed by Abū Ṭālib, his uncle, former guardian and head of the family. Abū Ṭālib's successor as head of the family was another of Muḥammad's uncles, 'Abd al-'Uzzā, who happened to be one of his most implacable opponents. The Qur'ān has another name for 'Abd al-'Uzzā: Abū Lahab 'father of the flames':

> The hands of Abū Lahab will perish and he will perish.
> His possessions and gains will be of no avail to him.
> He will roast in a flaming fire.   [111:1–3]

Muḥammad began to consider relocating the new community formed by the believers. In 620 AD he entered into negotiations for a move to al-Ṭā'if, but these failed. The next year, he turned his attention to Medina, which had been in turmoil for a number of years. It appears that the power of the Jewish tribes had collapsed and that the clans of Aws and Khazraj were struggling to take advantage of this. In 616 AD there had been fighting amongst them, culminating in the Battle of Bu'āth. This was followed by a truce of exhaustion. Eventually, just as Muḥammad began to look northwards, the clans began to think of inviting him to Medina as a *ḥakam*, a wise man who would act as an arbiter between the factions. After lengthy negotiations, during which Muḥammad persuaded Aws and Khazraj to accept not only himself but also his whole community, the migration to Medina, the *hijra*, took place, with Muḥammad himself finally arriving there in September 622 AD.

The difficulty that had been faced in establishing the new religion at Mecca is indicated by the number of Emigrants: something over two hundred, followed by some stragglers.

The emigration to Medina was the decisive step in the struggle to establish the new religion, and as such it was later chosen to mark the beginning of the Muslim era. The date is, incidentally, one of the very few in early Islamic history for which there is external corroboration. A papyrus from Egypt bears a double date: year 22 of the *hijra* and a Greek equivalent of April 643 AD.

Most of the Aws and Khazraj converted to Islam, with greater or lesser enthusiasm. The reverse was the case with the Jewish tribes of Medina, on whom Muḥammad had pinned much hope. There were one or two converts from amongst them, but the rest disdainfully rejected his claim to be the messenger of God. They were, however, party to a series of agreements drawn up principally with the clans of Aws and Khazraj that granted some political status in Medina to Muḥammad and the Emigrants. Effective political power remained with the leaders of Aws and Khazraj, a situation that was to alter little until 628 AD. Some of the leaders of Khazraj were politically at some distance from Muḥammad, though they appear never to have challenged his religious claims. These opposition figures were not a cohesive group, but from time to time they caused Muḥammad considerable difficulties, and they are referred to in the Qur'ān as the *Munāfiqūn*, usually, but not entirely appropriately, translated as 'hypocrites'.

At the time, these political difficulties seem to have been less pressing than the new community's economic ones. The Muslims from Aws and Khazraj, now called the *Anṣār* 'Helpers', supported the Emigrants, but the latter still suffered the privations of a displaced group.

As soon as these initial problems in Medina began to ease, Muḥammad once more turned his attention to the Meccans, not merely, it would appear, because of the potential threat they posed, but because it was clear that his long-term aim of spreading his message among the Arabs could not be achieved in the face of Meccan opposition.

There was one conciliatory gesture when the direction to be faced in prayer, the *qibla*, was changed from being towards Jerusalem to being towards the Kaʿba in Mecca. It was, however, more than offset by determined attempts on the part of the Muslims to disrupt Meccan long-distance trading. After several unsuccessful attempts, a small Meccan caravan was intercepted and captured at Nakhla, between Mecca and al-Ṭāʾif. Not long afterwards the Meccans heard that a much larger caravan on its way back from Syria was likely to be attacked. They sent a force of some 1,000 men to protect it. These met some 300 Muslims at Badr, not far from Medina, in a pitched battle in which the Muslims triumphed in March 624 AD.

The victory at Badr, which was to become legendary in the annals of Islam, gave a considerable boost to the standing of Muḥammad in Medina; and when, shortly afterwards, the Muslims clashed with one of the Jewish tribes there, the Banū Qaynuqāʿ, he was able to secure the consent of their Arab protectors, the Khazraj, to the expulsion of the Jewish tribe from the settlement.

On the other side, the Meccans were roused to action by their defeat at Badr, and in 625 AD they mounted a large expedition against Medina. A battle was fought on Mt. Uḥud, one of the outlying parts of the settlement. The Meccans gained the upper hand, and Muḥammad himself was wounded. However, for reasons that are unclear, but possibly logistical, the Meccans failed to press home their advantage. It was to prove a disastrous mistake for them.

Though Uḥud left Muḥammad with theological problems – defeat is not easy to equate with divine support – it does not seem to have affected the political situation in Medina to any great extent. However, the *bedu* tribes to the east became markedly hostile and cut down two small Muslim expeditions. Some months later the second of the Jewish tribes, the Banū l-Naḍīr, who had strong trading links with these *bedu*, clashed with the Muslims. They too were despatched northwards into exile.

It was some two years before the Muslims and the Meccans were to clash again. Both sides tried to consolidate, with the Muslims apparently being more successful despite some initial setbacks.

Then in the spring of 627 AD the Meccans mounted another expedition against Medina. Gathering all the support they could from the *bedu*, they set out to complete the business left unfinished at Uḥud. However, they were baulked by a series of trenches dug at strategic points in Medina, and after a month's ineffective siege they withdrew.

The retreat of the Meccans led to a dark episode at Medina. The last remaining Jewish tribe, the Banū Qurayẓa, was accused of supporting the Meccans. As had been the case with the Banū Qaynuqā' and the Banū l-Naḍīr, the decision about what to do with them lay with their Arab protecting tribe, in this case Aws. The judgement was savage: the men were to be killed and the women and children enslaved. With only a couple of reprieves the sentence was carried out.

The failure of the Meccans to take Medina led to another switch in allegiances among the *bedu*. More importantly, various prominent Meccans began to drop their opposition to the new religion or even to change sides. A masterstroke by Muḥammad in 628 AD accelerated this process. He set out from Medina with a large group of followers to perform the pilgrimage at Mecca. This was to involve modifications to the old pagan rites, but, like the change of the *qibla*, it would put Mecca at the centre of the new religion. The Meccans barred the way, but the confrontation ended in the truce of al-Ḥudaybiya that granted the Muslims the right to make the pilgrimage the next year.

Next year the Meccans did evacuate the city for three days and the Muslims were able to perform a pilgrimage. Before then, however, Muḥammad had led a large expedition and captured Khaybar, the next strategic settlement to the north of Medina. The population of Khaybar was largely Jewish, and included many of those who had already been expelled from Medina. When they resisted, the settlement was taken by force, and those who had resisted were driven out.

The capture of Khaybar was part of a policy of pressure to the north that had started somewhat earlier and was to be pursued vigorously to the end of Muḥammad's life. It was also to lead to expansion northwards into Syria after his death. It appears to have been based on two aims: control of strategic routes and direct contact with northern tribes to convert them to Islam.

The period from the treaty of al-Ḥudaybiya to the death of Muḥammad was one of almost total success, the only reverse being the failure of one of the northern expeditions, to Mu'ta in what is now Jordan, in the autumn of 629 AD. Tribes from various parts of the peninsula began to send delegations to Medina to negotiate allegiance to Muḥammad. His basic condition was always that they should become Muslims. Whether the tribes fully realized at that stage what this meant is open to doubt.

Towards the end of 629 AD an incident took place that led to the Meccans breaking the truce. Thereupon Muḥammad assembled a large expedition and set out to deal with the Meccans once and for all. In the end, there was a negotiated surrender of the city (early January 630 AD).

Important though the capture of Mecca was, the region could not be secured without also winning over the rival settlement of al-Ṭā'if and the Hawāzin, the large tribal confederation in the centre of whose lands al-Ṭā'if lay. At the end of January the Muslims inflicted a crushing defeat on the Hawāzin in a pitched battle at Ḥunayn, not far from al-Ṭā'if; but an attempt to besiege the town itself was as fruitless as the Meccan siege of Medina had been. After only a fortnight the siege was called off, but subsequent negotiations led to the people of al-Ṭā'if also throwing their lot in with the Muslims. Muḥammad then returned to Mecca and performed the lesser pilgrimage (the *'umra*) and afterwards went back to Medina.

He made one final expedition at the end of 630 AD. This was to Tabūk, in furtherance of his northern policy. The size of the expedition, the largest he ever mounted, appears to have enabled him to achieve his main aim, agreements with chiefs as far north as 'Aqaba, in modern Jordan, without major bloodshed.

After his return to Medina, most of Muḥammad's political activities became centred on the lengthy process of negotiating with tribal delegations who now came from increasingly distant parts of the peninsula. Political agreements appear to have been relatively easy to reach, but Muḥammad's main concern remained that the new adherents should become proper Muslims, and it became his practice to send Muslims from Medina back with the delegations to instruct them in the new faith.

Muḥammad left Medina only once more. That was in March 632 AD, when he journeyed to Mecca to perform the Pilgrimage. There are indications that his health was beginning to fail, and in June of that year after a short illness he died. As far as the Arabian peninsula was concerned, he had achieved his goal of bringing the Arabs within the fold of Islam. Most of those outside were to follow shortly.

5. *The Qur'ān*

It is important to remember that the Qur'ān was originally delivered orally. The traditional sources always indicate that Muḥammad recited his message. There is some evidence that towards the end of his life he dictated portions of the Qur'ān to chosen scribes, but there is none that he himself ever made use of written sheets (as others prophets are depicted as doing in *Sūra* 98) or of any other written form.

In the terms of the Qur'ān itself, the recitation *par excellence*, Muḥammad delivered good news and he warned. His role as a preacher is not in doubt (and in this respect it matters little whether or not one accepts the Muslim viewpoint that Muḥammad was the Messenger of God, conveying God's message to his people). It is therefore not unreasonable to view the Qur'ān as a collection of sermons, exhortations, guidance, warnings and pieces of encouragement.

In short, Muḥammad obeyed two apparently very early passages in the Qur'ān. Their importance is indicated in the traditional view that they are the two earliest passages of all. They are:

1. Recite in the name of your Lord who created,
2. Created man from a blood-clot.
3. Recite, for your Lord is the Most Generous,
4. Who taught by the pen,
5. Taught man what he did not know   [96:1–5]

1. You who are wrapped up in your cloak,
2. Arise and warn,
3. And magnify your Lord.
4. Purify your clothes
5. And shun pollution.   [74:1–5]

Form

In the form in which it has come down to us to-day, the Qur'ān is divided into 114 chapters of very unequal length, called *sūra*s. The term *sūra* comes from the Qur'ān itself, but its original meaning is uncertain. The *sūra*s are the working units of the revelation. They are largely composite. All but one (*Sūra* 9, which may well be unfinished) begin with the formula *bi-smi llāhi l-raḥmāni l-raḥīmi* 'in the name of God, the Merciful and Compassionate'; and in 29 *sūra*s this formula is followed by a group of letters of the Arabic alphabet (e.g. *alif*, *lām*, *mīm*, found at the beginning of *sūra*s 2, 3, 29, 30, 31 and 32), whose function is unknown but which seem to be of mystical import.

The text was originally revealed in pieces of varying length, most of them apparently containing a relatively short number of verses (*āyāt*, singular *āya* 'sign'). There are vivid descriptions of Muḥammad's state during a revelation, but, even if they are not apocryphal, they are too brief for us to work out what happened. For example, an account that is traced back to one of his wives, 'A'isha, tells us, 'He was

10

gripped by a spasm, and the sweat ran down him like pearls – and that on a winter's day', but that is all.

The basic revelations then took their places in the working units of the Qur'ān, the *sūra*s. The way in which this happened has never been understood. There are traditions that tell us that at Medina he would dictate to scribes and tell them how to arrange the revelations, sometimes inserting a new revelation into an older passage. A simplified and more pious tradition tells us that Gabriel used to go over the revealed text once a year with Muḥammad and that this happened twice during the last year of Muḥammad's life. Revelations are believed to have occurred over the whole period from the start of Muḥammad's mission in 610 AD to his death in June 632 AD.

Though the Qur'ān was originally delivered orally, in some quite early passages it refers to itself as 'the Scripture', and there is possibly some evidence of pieces being committed to writing by members of the community whilst Muḥammad was still at Mecca. There is no evidence that he used scribes to take down any of the text during the Meccan period, but in the later years at Medina he appears to have had a group of them, to whom he dictated various passages. It is not known what happened after Muḥammad's death to the material written by these copyists; but, as outlined in the section on the text, the scripture moved very quickly towards the form in which we have it today.

It has become traditional to divide the *sūra*s into four or five periods: early Meccan, middle Meccan, late Meccan and Medinan being the most popular schema. Though there is some justification for this, particularly as far as the Medinan period is concerned, it has two serious drawbacks: many of the *sūra*s contain material from at least two periods, and the criteria for classification, particularly for the Middle Meccan and Late Meccan periods, are somewhat vague and impressionistic. Moreover, the groupings by and large ignore the composite nature of the *sūra*s.

The grouping that is most widely known and referred to in the West was drawn up in the nineteenth century by the German scholar Nöldeke. Yet it must be said that it is no real advance on the traditional Muslim dating, on which it is heavily dependent. With the *sūra*s put in numerical order to eliminate some of the pseudo-preciseness, his division of the Meccan *sūra*s is:

Early Meccan: 1, 51–53, 55–56, 68–70, 73–75, 77–97, 99–109, 111–114   (48 *sūra*s)

Middle Meccan: 15, 17–21, 23, 25–27, 36–38, 43–44, 50, 54, 67, 71–72, 76   (21 *sūra*s)

Late Meccan: 6–7, 10–14, 16, 28–32, 34–35, 39–42, 45–46   (21 *sūra*s)

The *sūra*s most commonly agreed to be Medinan are:

2, 3, 4, 5, 8, 9, 22, 24, 33, 47, 48, 49, 57, 58, 59, 60, 61, 62, 63, 64, 65, 66, 98, 110.

(24 *sūra*s)

The order given is again that of the neutral *textus receptus*. Nöldeke and others again have chronological orderings, but while it is true that with some of the Medinan *sūra*s

11

there is quite a good case for relating material they contain to historical events, there is a large number of *sūra*s whose dating remains highly doubtful.

The order of *sūra*s that was adopted as standard appears to have been drawn up precisely to avoid such questions of chronology. The first *sūra* is short but liturgically important. After that the *sūra*s are arranged in rough order of length, from longest to shortest. This puts much of the material that is important for legal purposes early in the arrangement; but it has to be said that many readers find the lack of chronological guidance confusing. This is where an attempted ordering, such as that of Nöldeke set out above, is of some use. However, it should be realized that such a grouping can act only as a rough guide and cannot be refined further. Attempts to put the *sūra*s in an alleged chronological order, such as one finds in the original editions of the translations of Rodwell and Dawood, give a spurious and misleading picture.

One minor matter in which there came to be a certain amount of disagreement was the division of each *sūra* into verses. Verse division and verse numeration do not go back to Muḥammad, but are the work of early scholars, mainly in Iraq, in the second and third centuries of the Islamic era. In some of the longer *sūra*s this divergence is as much as six verses. In most cases the verse divisions are not important, but they have tended to set parameters for our vision of the text; verses tend to be treated as the primary units of the *sūra*, however they are set out.

The name or names given to a *sūra* are again not part of the original text. They are normally taken from some striking word or phrase within the *sūra*.

Content

The central theme of the Qur'ān is the belief in one God, the merciful God who is the Creator of Heaven and Earth and all things and beings therein and whose omnipotence is to be seen everywhere in His signs (*āyāt* [as mentioned above, this word is also used to refer to individual verses of the Qur'ān]). Disobedience will lead to an apocalypse, which will be the prelude to the Day of Judgement. At the Judgement each individual will be judged and the righteous conveyed to Heaven and the unrighteous to Hell. Righteousness requires both belief and general rectitude.

It is clear that from the earliest pieces onwards the message conveyed by Muḥammad was comprehensible enough, but that most of the people of Mecca did not like it. Various passages in the Qur'ān record their objections. In each passage the objections are then set aside with firm conviction and the sermon goes on. A classic example of this comes in a piece near the beginning of *Sūra* 25:

> 4. Those who do not believe say,
> 'This is merely a lie that he has invented,
> and others have helped him with it.'
> They have produced wrong and falsehood.
> 5. And they say, 'Fables of the ancients that he has had written down;
> and they are recited to him morning and evening.'

6. Say, 'He who knows the secret in the heavens and the earth sent it down.
    He is Forgiving and Compassionate.'
7. And they say, 'What is there to this messenger?
    He eats food and walks round the markets.
    Why has not an angel been sent down to him to be a warner with him?
8. Or why is not a treasure bestowed on him,
    or why does he not have a garden
    from which he can eat?'
    And the wrong-doers say,
    'You are merely following a man who is bewitched.'
9. See how they have coined examples for you.
    They have gone astray and cannot find a road.

Polemic of this kind is to be found regularly throughout the Qur'ān. At a later stage one can find the arguments of the Jews and the Christians similarly set aside.

Along with the passages that tell of God and His signs, there are also stories of peoples and prophets. Some of the earliest of these refer to Arabian legends: the destruction of the tribes of 'Ād, Thamūd and Madyan after they failed to respond to the messages of their prophets (Hūd, Ṣāliḥ and Shu'ayb respectively).

As time went on, these stories were afforced by other disaster/punishment stories also to be found in the Old Testament: Noah (Arabic form Nūḥ) and the flood, Lot (Lūṭ) and his people, and Moses (Mūsā) and the Egyptians. In fact, Old Testament stories, often in a guise somewhat different from that in the Bible, dominate much of the narrative that occurs in the Qur'ān. Among the best known are: Adam and Eve; the Fall; the disobedience of Satan; Cain and Abel; Abraham (Ibrāhīm); Isaac (Isḥāq) and Ishmael (Ismā'īl); Jacob (Ya'qūb), Joseph (Yūsuf) and his brothers; Moses, Aaron (Hārūn) and the Israelites; Solomon (Sulaymān) and David (Dāwūd); Jonah (Yūnus) and Job (Ayyūb). By far the most important of these prophetic figures are Moses, the leader who freed the Israelites from the yoke of the Egyptians and led them to the promised land, and Abraham, who, having turned his back on idolatry, built with his son Ishmael the Ka'ba at Mecca as a shrine to the one God. Pharaoh (Fir'awn) is a key figure in many of the stories about Moses, though in the earliest instances in which he is mentioned (85:18 and 89:10) he is no more than the archetype of the wicked king.

There is much less material that recalls the New Testament and Christian apocryphal sources. Apart from the story of Zachariah and the birth of John the Baptist (Yaḥyā) and some references to the Disciples (al-ḥawāriyyūn: they are treated as a group and not named individually), the references are to Mary (Maryam) and, above all to Jesus ('Īsā). The miraculous birth of Jesus is one of the signs of God, and mention is made of his ability to perform miracles such as raising the dead and healing the leper. However, Jesus is basically treated as one in the series of God's prophets, his description as al-Masīḥ 'the Messiah' apparently having little special force. The Qur'ān specifically rejects the doctrine of the Trinity (see, in particular, 5:73). It also denies the crucifixion (4:157) at the beginning of a passage that appears to imply the

13

following sequence of events: apparent death of Jesus, ascension, and then, at some later time, second coming, natural death and general resurrection.

There are some parables, but they are of little significance in comparison with the narrative material. The majority are in effect extended similes very similar to a form used with great success in early Arabic poetry (see, for example, 2:17, 2:19, 16:75, 16:112, 18:45, 24:35, 29:41, 30:28, 39:29, 66:10). For the rare longer parables see 14:24–7 (the good and bad trees); 18:32–44 (the two gardens); 36:13–32 (the unbelieving city); and 68:17–33 (the blighted garden). In addition, *Sūra* 18 includes two stories from the Christian periphery to the north of Arabia: the so-called legend of the Seven Sleepers and extracts from the Alexander romance. There is also material that looks like traditional wisdom literature (*cf.* the material about Luqmān in *Sūra* 31).

The narratives are crucial in underpinning two doctrines that became more prominent as the revelation went on: the first, that God had sent a series of believing Prophets to their peoples over the ages, all conveying the same message; and the second, that Muḥammad was the last in this series of prophets. Linked to this is the doctrine that Muḥammad is the prophet sent to the Arabs in particular and that his message is in Arabic: *lisān ʿarabiyy mubīn* 'clear Arabic language' (16:103, 26:195), *qurʾān ʿarabiyy* 'an Arabic recitation' (12:2, 20:113, 41:3, 42,7; 43:3), *lisān ʿarabiyy* 'Arabic language'(46:12), *ḥukm ʿarabiyy* 'an Arabic judgement' (13:37).

In addition to biblical narrative pieces, there are a number of other parallel passages. From the Old Testament one may cite Q. 24:50 and Deut. 26:17; Q. 53:45 and 49 and 1 Sam. 2:6–7; Q. 53:39–42 and Ezek. 18:20; and, at greater length Q. 17:23–40 and Ex. 20:2–17/Deut. 5:6–21. There are slightly more passages where the parallel is with the New Testament. See, for example, Q. 2:274 and Matth. 6:3–4; Q. 21:20 and Rev. 4:8; Q. 36:53 and 1 Thess. 4:16; Q. 48:29 and Mark 4:29; and, at greater length, Q. 2:49–64 and Acts 7:36–53. However, in none of these passages is there a close verbal relationship. There is more of that in such Semitic sayings as 'an eye for an eye' etc. [Q. 5:45 and Ex. 21:23–7] and 'before the camel will pass through the eye of a needle' [Q. 7:38 and Matth. 19:24]; but it is only in Q. 21:105 'We have written in the Psalms after the Reminder "The earth will be inherited by my righteous servants"' that we have a close parallel: Psalms 37:29 reads 'The righteous shall inherit the land and shall dwell therein forever'. Remarkably the previous verse [Q. 21:104] 'the day We roll up the heavens as a recorder rolls up documents' is a fairly close approximation to part of a quite separate verse [Isaiah 34:4] 'and the heavens shall be rolled together as a scroll'. However, by far the most interesting and instructive parallel is between *Sūra* 12 and Genesis 37–47: the story of Joseph. The Quranic narrative, which includes details from the Midrash as well as Genesis, may at first seem rather sketchy, but as an Arabic narrative it is beautifully judged and effective. It is, incidentally, the only longish *sūra* to be devoted to the telling of a single story.

As has been mentioned, exhortation to belief and rectitude is common from the earliest revelations onwards, but after the *hijra* it became necessary to offer more specific guidance on religious and legal matters. Here one sometimes finds parallels to Talmudic material. See, for example, the note on 5:3.

Three of the five Pillars of Islamic faith (*arkān al-dīn*), witness to the one God (*shahāda*), prayer (*salāt*) and alms-giving (*zakāt*), are mentioned in a fairly general way in Meccan material. Medinan material adds some detail about prayer: that it should be towards Mecca (2:142–50); that there should be ritual purification before prayer (4:43, 5:6), and so on; though the specific requirement to pray five times a day is nowhere mentioned. There is more detail on the two Pillars added in Medina, fasting (*sawm* 2:183–5 & 187) and the pilgrimage (*Hajj* 2:196–200 & 203). There are passages too numerous to mention about fighting the infidel and the sharing of booty. Disturbances within the community are dealt with in passages on retaliation (e.g. 2:178–9, 4:92–3) and on theft (5:38). The practice of usury, clearly disruptive both socially and economically, is dealt with severely (2:275–80, 3:130). There are regulations on bequests and inheritance (2:180–2, 5:106–8) and the assignment of debts (2:282–4). There are fifteen or so passages about marriage, and others about the position of women in society, of which 4:3, 19 and 34 are now thought by many to be problematical. There is regulation of the calendar (9:36–7), and there are ten passages on food and drink. The two main passages commenting on wine are an interesting example of how changes were sometimes gradually introduced, with the latest passage being deemed to abrogate previous ones. *Sūra* 2:219 reads, 'They ask you about wine and *maysir*. Say, "In both these is great sin, but some benefits to the people; but the sin in them is greater than the benefit".' In 5:90–91 this is sharpened to: 'O you who believe, wine, *maysir*, idols and divining arrows are an abomination that is part of the work of Satan. Avoid it, so that you may prosper. Satan only desires to cause enmity and hatred among you through wine and *maysir* and to turn you from remembrance of God and from prayer.'

Style

The views on the style of the Qur'ān that developed within the Muslim community came to centre on what was seen as its uniqueness and inimitability (*i'jāz*). This is an important doctrinal area for Muslims, which largely lies beyond the scope of this translation – though it should be noted that it is the basis of a very traditional view that the Qur'ān cannot be translated. The development of these views limited the extent of the analysis of the stylistic and linguistic context of the Qur'ān. Those who believe that the Qur'ān is the word of God revealed to mankind through the agency of Gabriel and Muḥammad see little point in such questions as 'How was it that seventh century Arabs could understand such apparently unique linguistic material?' However, this is something that needs to be asked, and it is closely borne in mind in the remarks that follow.

Introduction

Stylistically the Qur'ān calls on the four main high-level registers of Arabic that were current in seventh century Arabia: the clipped, gnomic style of the *kāhin*s, the admonitory, exhortative and argumentative style of the *khaṭīb*s, the narrative techniques of the story-tellers and the dramatic style of some poetry. In the Medinan period the verses containing social legislation appear to approximate, at least in part, to the style used in formal agreements.

It is the generally accepted view that much of the earliest material has a vigour which is terse and abrupt and that as time passed the terseness and to some extent the abruptness – and the verve – gradually diminished. The style is thus perceived to have broadened, eventually moving to the diffuse expression of the Medinan material.

One can explain such an evolution of Quranic style as the product of differing mixtures of the registers of the soothsayers, preachers and story-tellers, with the eventual addition of the documentary style.

Whether or not it is accurate to do so is another matter. It all depends on one's view of the importance of one prominent feature found throughout the Qur'ān: assonance. The use of assonance catches both the ear and the eye. Sometimes the assonance changes after a few verses; on other occasions it remains constant through a longish *sūra*; but it is always there. The use of assonance had almost certainly been made popular by soothsayers and preachers, but the scale of its use in the Qur'ān was apparently new and remarkable. It is most striking in early material; but it still has an effective role in the late material at Medina when it is, for example, used to round off legal prescriptions composed largely in a flat documentary style.

The prominence of assonance provided natural landmarks that were used by Muslim scholars to divide the *sūra*s into shorter units. It was perfectly reasonable for them to do so with early Meccan material, when assonance is such a dominant feature, used at fairly short intervals and with considerable rhetorical effect. However, as the revelations went on, assonance became a less prominent feature. There would have been no problem if those dividing the verses had looked for and applied additional criteria. Unfortunately they did not. The result was that they divided material into verses of wildly disparate lengths; and it became standard to say that as the period of the revelation went on the verses got longer and longer.

This inept explanation, built on a circular argument, not only tends to obscure other points of rhetorical focus; it actually masks the underlying style and structure of the Qur'ān.

If one takes just one different criterion and looks at the segments of meaning that make up a verse, the situation is quite different. The basic segments are relatively short, and the end of each is suitable for a pause. Segments are always meaningful but are not necessarily complete sentences. The longer the printed verse, the more syllables there will be. The more syllables there are, the more breaks and segments there will be. That is a simple truism about oral delivery – and oral declamation is at the heart of the matter. Viewed in this way, there is relatively little change of style during the period of the Qur'ān's revelation.

16

It is also the case that problems connected with verse length do not arise in recitation. No reciter recites in paragraphs. He makes breaks at relatively short intervals, putting in a brief pause and then moving on. The pauses are occasioned by the end of a clause or of a sentence or some other noticeable semantic or rhetorical feature.

Three examples of roughly similar length, one thought to be early Meccan, one late Meccan and one Medinan, will show what I mean:

(a)   1.   Glorify the name of your Lord, the Most High,
          2.   Who has created and formed,
          3.   Who has determined and guided,
          4.   Who has brought forth pasturage,
          5.   And then made it withered chaff.
          6.   We shall cause you to recite,
                 so that you do not forget
          7.   Except that which God wills.
                 He knows what is public and what is hidden.
          8.   We shall ease you to ease.
          9.   So remind
                 – if the Reminder is useful.
          10.   He who fears will be reminded;
          11.   But the most wretched will turn aside from it,
          12.   The one who will roast in the great fire,
          13.   In which he will neither die nor live.
          14.   He who purifies himself will prosper -
          15.   Who remembers the name of his Lord and prays.
          16.   But you prefer the life of this world,
          17.   When the world to come is better and more permanent.
          18.   This is in the ancient scrolls,
          19.   The scrolls of Abraham and Moses.
                 [*Sūra* 87: 1–15 are addressed to Muḥammad, 16–19 to the people]

(b)   2.   Is it a wonder for mankind
                 that We have revealed to a man among them [the message],
                 'Warn mankind
                 and bring to those who believe the tidings
                 that they will have a sure footing with their Lord'?
                 The unbelievers say,
                 'This man is a clear sorcerer.'
          3.   Your Lord is God
                 who created the heavens and the earth in six days,
                 then set Himself on the Throne,
                 directing the affair.
                 There is no intercessor unless [He has given] His permission.
                 That is God, your Lord.
                 So serve Him.
                 Will you not be reminded?
          4.   To Him is the return for all of you
                 – the promise of God is true.

He originates creation,
then causes it to return,
so that He may reward with equity
those who believe and do deeds of righteousness.
And those who disbelieve
– they will have a drink of boiling water and a painful punishment
in return for their unbelief.

[10:2–4]

(c)　259.　Or like the one who passed by a settlement
collapsed on its supports:
He said, 'How will God give life to this [settlement]
now that it is dead?'
God caused him to die for a hundred years,
and then brought him back to life.
HE said, 'How long have you tarried?'
He said, 'A day or part of a day.'
HE said, 'No, you have lingered a hundred years.
Look at your food and drink
– it has not spoiled.
Look at your donkey.
[We have done this] to make you a sign for the people.
Look at the bones,
how We set them up
and then clothe them with flesh.'
When it became clear to him, he said,
'I know that God has power over everything.'

[2:259]

The translations given above try to give some indication of segmentation by putting each segment on a separate line. However, a translation cannot give more than an approximation

(a)　because it is impossible to make the translation correspond to the Arabic segments;

(b)　because it is often possible for the Arabic to be divided in more than one way.

Nevertheless, I do not think that I have caused distortion by my divisions. On the contrary, not only do they take us somewhat nearer to oral delivery patterns; they also make it easier to understand the basic flow of the text.

Two further points should be noted. Firstly, those reading the Qur'ān in translation usually find the terse formulation of the early material difficult to follow. In reading this material, it helps if one remembers the oral nature of the revelation. Secondly, it is a point of both content and style that Muḥammad is at the centre of the revelation. In particular, he is the focal point for the dialectic that frequently occurs. Thus it is common to find passages that are introduced by the command 'Say'; and a fair number of these are answers to clauses beginning 'they ask you' or 'they say', frequently referring to Muḥammad's opponents, but sometimes to his followers. See, for example, 17:85:

They will ask you about the Spirit.
Say, 'The Spirit is part of the affair of my Lord;
and you have been given only little knowledge.'

The Text

The basic text used for this translation is that of the Egyptian standard edition, first issued in 1342/1923 and revised in 1381/1960 and subsequently. This is the most widely used text. It had its origins in the Iraqi city of Kūfa in the second century of the Islamic era, and is technically known as the Ḥafṣ recension of the ʿĀṣim reading. Very rarely I have preferred a somewhat more conservative reading that originated in Medina: Warsh's recension of Nāfiʿ's reading. There is a note when I have done so. The notes also refer from time to time to the readings of one of the Companions of the Prophet, ʿAbdallāh Ibn Masʿūd. These readings are treated by Muslim scholars as non-canonical, superseded by the official ʿUthmanic recension some twenty years after the Prophet's death. However, Ibn Masʿūd's readings are occasionally crucial for our understanding of the early history of the text.

By the standards of the sacred books of Judaism and Christianity, the text of the Qur'ān is remarkably well preserved. However, it is not perfectly preserved in the way that many Muslims accept as a matter of dogma. The mere fact that there are seven readings of the text officially promulgated as canonical in 933 AD, some three centuries after the death of Muḥammad, hardly argues for perfect preservation. Before these canonical readings emerged, we can discern two crucial developments. The first was that the Qur'ān was committed to writing in a formal, official way. This effectively curbed the use of variants of a kind common in oral tradition: synonyms, equivalent phrases and the like. Secondly, Arabic script began to develop into the form that it has maintained through the centuries (*a*) with the consistent use of dots to differentiate the consonants fully; (*b*) with the consistent marking of long vowels; and (*c*) with the introduction of clear ways of marking short vowels. Equally important was the shift to writing as the dominant means of scholarship. Whatever may have been the form of their earliest sources, commentators, grammarians and lexicographers all transmitted their knowledge in a written form about a written text. Even Qur'ān recitation has had its own manuals from a relatively early stage.

Sources

Orthodox doctrine renders discussion of the sources of the Qur'ān irrelevant for Muslims: the Qur'ān is the word of God. They are also able to dismiss discrepancies between the Bible and the Qur'ān by recourse to the doctrine that if there are differences between the Jewish, Christian and Muslim versions of the Scripture the Jews and the Christians have mangled the Message and Muslims have not. This doctrinal stance is, however, not without its problems. It is difficult to reconcile the very specific references to, for example, Muḥammad's family [*cf.*, for example, 33:28–33] with the belief that each prophet has received the same message.

For non-Muslims the Muslim standpoint is untenable, and non-Muslim scholars have given much thought to the question of how Muḥammad might have acquired his knowledge of Jewish and Christian scriptures. The most commonly accepted view is that Muḥammad received most of his information about Biblical and post-Biblical stories through informants who talked to him; that this material was digested and meditated on; and that eventually meditation induced Muḥammad to recite. There are two passages in the Qur'ān itself that support this view. The first is Q. 16:103:

> In truth We know that they say, 'It is only a mortal who is teaching him.'
> The speech of the one at whom they hint is foreign,
> whereas this is clear Arabic speech.'

Secondly, there is the passage from *Sūra* 25, quoted above. Verse 6 strongly denies the allegation of fraud, but the question of help is ignored. It should be added that there is some corroboration in *Ḥadīth*, the collected reports of the doings and sayings of the Prophet, that Muḥammad received stories and information from various individuals, including Jews and Christians, and that the material he received from them found its way into Quranic form.

Be that as it may, the question of sources is one where there is an unbridgeable chasm between Muslim and non-Muslim. Tolerance requires us to recognise the chasm and to respect the views of those on the other side, wherever our basic stance may be.

6. The Qur'ān in English

The Qur'ān was first translated into English in 1649 by Alexander Ross, who based his work on the French version of André du Ryer. The first translation directly into English was that of Sale in 1734. This was a remarkable achievement for its time. Since that time there have been four important translations by non-Muslim scholars: Rodwell (1861), Palmer (1880), Bell (1937–9) and Arberry (1955); and there have been over thirty translations by Muslims, mainly from the Indian sub-continent. The most influential translation by a Muslim is undoubtedly that of a British convert, Muhammad Marmaduke Pickthall, which was first published in 1930. The translation of Ross has little interest other than its position as first in the field, but there is something of value in the others I have mentioned, as there is with the fairly recent translation by Majid Fakhry. Given the difficulties associated with translation of the work, all have strengths and weaknesses; but they are all worth consulting, something I would hesitate to say of those that I have not mentioned by name.

7. *Some Notes on this Translation*

The biggest problem for this and any other translation of the Qur'ān is that the text was originally intended to be recited aloud and is highly rhetorical in nature. Recitation frequently gives the text a dimension that does not come across in silent reading, showing up lines of thought that do not stand out clearly when one is perusing the text.

Translators usually tackle this problem by adding to their translations bridging phrases that they normally draw from the numerous, and lengthy, commentaries on the Qur'ān that have been written over the centuries in Arabic. If they do not, they run the risk of being incomprehensible, however accomplished the actual translation. This is shown very clearly by Arberry's *The Koran Interpreted*. The translation is very good, but there is not a single note and virtually no bridging material. In short, there is no interpretation, despite the title. The result is that there are numerous places where Arberry's translation, though technically correct, is almost impossible to follow unless one knows the Arabic well; and if one cannot follow the translation one cannot understand it.

However, Arberry does have a point. Masses of notes lead to the interruption of the flow of reading. After much hesitation I have decided to put most of my notes into a separate volume, my forthcoming Commentary. The notes that remain within the body of the translation are relatively sparse, though in addition there is an introductory note for each *sūra*, mainly intended to give some background material on the contents and possible dating of the *sūra*.

Another difficult problem is the extent to which a translator may legitimately reflect the structure of the original. Arabic and English differ considerably from each other, and one could not be too literal, even if one wished. However, some Arabic structures can be made apparent, and then the translator has to choose between a version that runs smoothly but at some distance from the original and one that gives some indication of the Arabic structure. I have leaned towards the latter, as I believe that in the Qur'ān the structure of the language afforces the message, not least when the language is oblique.

There is a great deal of repetition of vocabulary, and this raises the question of consistency in translation. Consistency has its limits. Take, for example, the phrase *fī l-arḍi*. The basic meaning is 'in the earth', but it can also mean 'in the land' and also 'on earth'. All three translations have to be used. Similarly, the noun *waliyy* is most commonly best translated as 'protector', but sometimes 'friend' is more appropriate and also 'ally' and 'partisan'. Such words and phrases are but the tip of an inevitable iceberg. In addition, there is a considerable number of words that have two or more meanings.

The way modern English has developed poses one considerable problem. It no longer seems possible to use 'thou' and 'thee' for the second person singular pronoun: 'you' is now the standard form; and, unless one uses the non-standard Americanism 'you all' for the plural, there is only one pronoun 'you' to cover the second person masculine singular, feminine singular, dual, masculine plural and feminine plural, all of which occur in the Arabic text of the Qur'ān. The main problem is the need to differentiate between the masculine singular and the masculine plural. Sometimes the context makes this clear, or, as in the case of *Sūra* 102, this can be done in the introductory note to the *sūra*. More frequently the simple 'you' is not clear enough. In such cases I have reluctantly resorted to 'you[s]' for the singular and 'you[p]' for the plural. Much rarer is the ambiguity when God is referred to in the third person. This usually occurs when God is depicted as engaging in rapid conversation. In such cases I have used 'HE said' to refer to God and 'He said' to refer to the person.

Other conventions to note are that I have normally used strict transliteration for Arabic words other than well-known place-names. The transliteration helps those who know Arabic script but can be ignored by those who do not. Names that first came into English through translations of the Bible are given in their traditional form. Finally, square brackets [ ] are used to indicate bridging material.

As indicated earlier, I think that the traditional verse numbering causes some problems with the Arabic. However, I have retained it for reference purposes and to give some indication of where assonance patterns are thought to be. Even so, in quite a few of the long verses I have divided traditional verses into a number of sub-verses, as required by the sense. Numbering of this sort occurs, for example, in *Sūra* 2, where I have divided verse 282 into verses 282, 282a, 282b, 282c and 282d.

8. Background Reading

Richard Bell's *Introduction to the Qur'an* is a very useful book. It was first published by Edinburgh University Press in 1953. This was revised in 1970 by W. Montgomery Watt, and this edition is known as Bell and Watt, *Introduction to the Qur'an*, and is to be readily found in the Edinburgh Paperbacks series.

Recent years have seen the publication of the immensely valuable *Encyclopedia of Qur'an*, edited by Jane Dammen McAuliffe *et al.* [1st Edition, 5 vols, plus index, Leiden, Brill Academic Publishers, 2001–2006].

In addition, there is the *Cambridge Companion to the Qur'an*, also edited by Professor McAuliffe [Cambridge University Press 2006].

There will be a full bibliography in the Commentary. Readers should be aware that a number of major western contributions to Quranic studies are not available in English, in particular Theodor Nöldeke's *Geschichte des Qurāns* and Angelika Neuwirth's *Studien zur Komposition der mekkanischen Suren*, which I refer to as Neuwirth, *Meccan Sūras*.

Sūra 1

This *sūra* is a short prayer, of particular importance in the performance of Muslim ritual prayer (*ṣalāt*). Some early authorities on the Qur'ān omitted it from their collected text, along with *sūra*s 113 and 114. Most prominent of those to do so was ʿAbdallāh ibn Masʿūd, one of the earliest converts to Islam and a devoted companion of the Prophet, whose recitation of the Qur'ān became the one used in the Iraqi garrison town of Kūfa and was replaced with the standard ʿUthmanic text only after great difficulty. Though Ibn Masʿūd excluded this *sūra* from his Qur'ān, a number of variants in it are attributed to him, and he must have fully recognized its liturgical role.

The *sūra* is of uncertain date. At one extreme Bell thinks that it could be as late as 2 or 3 AH, whilst at the other Pickthall believes that 'the fact that it has always, from the very earliest times, formed a part of Muslim worship, there being no record or remembrance of its introduction, or of public prayer without it, makes it clear that it was revealed before the fourth year of the Prophet's Mission (the tenth year before the Hijrah)'. It is conceivable that the last verse is a later modification.

In the first four verses God is spoken of in the third person; in verses 5–7 in the second person singular.

The Opening[1]

1   In the name of the Merciful and Compassionate God.
2.   Praise belongs to God, the Lord of all Beings[2],
3.   The Merciful, the Compassionate,
4.   Master of the Day of Reckoning.
5.   You we serve;
    to You we turn for help.
6.   Guide us on the straight path,
7.   The path of those You have blessed,
    not of those against whom there is anger
    nor of those who go astray.

---

[1] The *sūra* is commonly known by its Arabic name: *al-Fātiḥa*.

[2] It has become standard to translate *ʿālamīn* as 'the worlds' in accordance with the development of the word in Arabic. However, it would appear originally to have meant 'all created beings'.

Sūra 2

This *sūra* is a vast, sprawling multi-facetted piece, a miniature Qur'ān in itself. It is thought to have largely assumed its present form in the second and third years after the Hijra, though it seems likely that some verses come from later in the Medinan period. It takes its name from the cow (*baqara*) mentioned in one of the narratives about Moses (verses 67–71).

In many respects, thanks to the traditional *sūra* order, *Sūra* 2 dominates the rest of the Qur'ān. It is in *Sūra* 2 that those who work through the Qur'ān from the beginning first come across a large number of words, phrases, ideas and constructions; and notes and commentaries inevitably refer to these initial examples, even when the example in *Sūra* 2 comes from a later period than other examples in the *sūras* printed after it in the text (as is the case with all Meccan material).

The *sūra* is most easily divided itself into three major sections, each containing numerous sub-divisions: 1–141; 142–242; and 243–286a.

The first section is largely a mixture of narrative and polemic, which in thrust is little different from late Meccan material. However, those engaged are no longer the Meccans – there is all the Meccan polemic to cater for them – but the opponents of the Muslims in Medina. This emerges at the beginning of the *sūra* where there are successive passages on the believers (verses 2–5), the unbelievers (6–7) and the pretend believers (8–16). Even more specific are the polemical passages addressed not only to the Jews but also to the Christians and, in verse 62, to others. From verse 142 onwards there is a radical change of subject matter. Narratives disappear, and they are replaced by injunctions, ordinances and some prohibitions for the faithful. At first these are interspersed with exhortatory and polemical passages, but from verse 177 to verse 241 they become almost a solid block. In the final part of the *sūra*, they become mixed once more with polemic, parables and a couple of narrative passages, particularly between 245 and 266. Two passages of creed stand out, 255–56 and 284–86, the latter rounded off by the invocation to God that closes the *sūra*.

Amongst the major topics affecting the community are: the *qibla* (142–45, 150); the *Ḥajj* (158, 196–200; 203); *tawḥīd* (163); food (168–69, 172–73); piety (177); retaliation (178–79); bequests (180–82); fasting (183–85, 187); use of possessions (188, 195, 215–17, 219a, 254, 267); fighting (190–93, 215–17, 244); peace (208); women (222–23, 233–35, 240) and divorce (226–32, 241); oaths (224–25); prayer (238–39); alms (263–4, 271); and debts and the witnessing of transactions (280, 282–83a). Major prohibitions include the bribing of judges (188), marriage to infidels (221–21a), and usury (275–76, 278–79).

The length of *Sūra* 2, the rhetoric of some of the polemic, the many passages on social topics, and the fact that all Medinan material builds on Meccan material make

24

difficult reading for those with little or no grounding in Islam. However, the *sūra* has many component passages, and though these are often subtly linked, they offer the reader frequent breaks. Slow reading also helps to highlight the intense and vivid passages that occur throughout the *sūra*, the most famous of which is the 'throne verse' (v. 255).

The Cow

In the name of the Merciful and Compassionate God

1. *Alif, Lām, Mīm.*[1]
2. This is the Scripture
    in which there is no doubt,
    a guidance for those who protect themselves,[2]
3. Who believe in the Invisible[3]
    and perform prayer
    and spend from that which We have provided for them,
4. And who believe in what has been sent down to you[s]
    and what was sent down before you[s]
    and are sure of the world to come.
5. – Those [have] guidance from their Lord;
    those are the ones who prosper.
6. Those who do not believe
    – it is all one for them whether you[s] warn them or not.
    They will not believe.
7. God has set a seal on their hearts and on their hearing,
    and there is a covering on their sight.
    They will have a severe torment.
8. There are some people who say,
    'We believe in God and the Last Day,'
    but they are not believers.
9. They try to deceive God and those who believe,
    but they deceive only themselves;
    but they are not aware.

---

[1] 29 of the *sūra*s of the Qur'ān begin with a cluster of letters (occasionally a single one). They appear to be of mystical import. See the Commentary for further discussion.

[2] This is the original meaning of *ittaqā*. It also came to mean 'fear God', 'be god-fearing' – see, for example, v. 41.

[3] The term *al-ghayb*, which I have normally translated as 'the Invisible', covers a range of meanings, including 'the future', 'the unknowable', 'what people do not know', 'the recesses'.

10. There is sickness in their hearts,[4]
    and God has given them further sickness.
    They will have a painful punishment,
    because they used to lie.
11. When they are told,
    'Do not cause corruption in the land,'
    they say, 'We are putting things right.'
12. Truly they are wreakers of mischief,
    but they do not perceive.
13. When they are told,
    'Believe as the people believe,'
    they say, 'Shall we believe as fools believe?'
    It is they who are the foolish ones,
    but they do not know.
14. When they meet those who believe,
    they say, 'We believe';
    but when they are alone with their satans they say,
    'We are with you[P]; we spoke only in jest.'
15. It is God who mocks them
    and grants them a time to wander blindly in their insolence.
16. Those are the ones who have purchased error
    at the price of guidance.
    Their trading has not profited [them],
    nor are they guided aright.
17. The parallel to them is that of those who light a fire,
    and when it lights up all around them
    God takes away their light and leaves them in darkness, unable to see –
18. Deaf, dumb and blind, they do not return.[5]
19. Or that of a storm-cloud from the sky,
    in which there is darkness and thunder and lightning.
    They put their fingers in their ears at the thunderclaps,
    in fear of death.
    God encompasses the unbelievers.
20. The lightning almost snatches away their sight.
    Whenever it gives them light, they walk in it[6];
    but when it goes dark for them, they stand still.
    If God wished,
    He could take their hearing and their sight.

---

[4] This is a reference to the hypocrites (*munāfiqūn*) – see the Introduction p. 7.
[5] To the light, or to the right path.
[6] The light.

God has power over everything.

21. O people, serve your Lord,
who created you and those who were before you,
so that you may protect yourselves,

22. [God] who made the earth a resting-place for you
and the sky a canopy,
and who sent down water from the sky,
and through it brought forth a provision of fruits for you.
Do not set up rivals to God when you know better.

23. If you[p] are in doubt about what We have sent down to Our servant,
then bring a *sūra* like it,
and call your witnesses apart from God,
if you are truthful.

24. And if you do not
– and you will never be able to –
protect yourselves against the Fire,
whose fuel is men and stones,
which has been prepared for the unbelievers.

25. Give[s] the good tidings to those who believe and do righteous deeds
that they will have gardens
through which rivers flow.
Whenever they are provided with fruit from them,
they say, 'This is what we were provided with before,'
and they will be provided with [fruit of] the same quality.
There they will have pure spouses,
and there they will remain for ever.

26. God is not ashamed to coin a simile
[from] a gnat or what is above it.[7]
Those who believe know that it is the truth coming from their Lord;
but those who do not believe say,
'What did God wish by using this as a simile?'
He leads many astray by it and He guides many by it;
but He leads astray by it only the profligate,

27. Who break God's covenant after He has taken it,
and who sever what God has ordered to be joined
and wreak mischief in the land.
They are the losers.

28. How can you[p] not believe in God,
for you were dead and He gave you life?
Then He will cause you to die,

---

[7] Usually thought to mean 'something bigger'.

and then He will bring you back to life again,
and then you will be returned to Him.

29. [It is] He who created for you[p] all that is on earth.
Then He rose to heaven
and turned it into seven heavens.
He is aware of everything.

30. And [recall] when your[s] Lord said to the angels,
'I am going to put a viceroy in the earth.'
They said, 'Will You put in it someone who will wreak mischief in it and
    will shed blood,
while we glorify You with praise and declare You holy?'
HE said, 'I know what you do not know.'

31. He taught Adam all the names.[8]
Then He put them before the angels, and said,
'Tell me the names of these if you are truthful.'

32. They said, 'Glory be to You.
The only knowledge we have is what You have taught us.
You truly are the Knowing and the Wise.'

33. He said, 'Adam! Tell them their names;'
and when he had told them their names, He said,
'Did I not tell you that I know what is Invisible in the heavens and the earth
and that I know what you disclose and what you have been hiding?'

34. And [recall] when We said to the angels,
'Prostrate yourselves to Adam';
and they [all] prostrated themselves,
apart from Iblīs.[9]
He refused and was haughty and was one of the unbelievers.

35. And We said,
'Adam, dwell in the Garden with your wife,
and the two of you eat in plenty from it
wherever you wish;
but do not approach this tree
lest you become wrong-doers.'

36. But Satan caused them to slip from it
and brought them out of what they were in.
We said, 'Go down [from it], foes of one another.
You will have a habitation on the earth and enjoyment for a time.'

37. Then Adam received words from his Lord,
for He relented towards him.

---

[8] Usually understood as 'the names of all things'.
[9] The name Iblīs is ultimately derived from the Greek ὁ διάβολος 'the devil'.

He is the Relenting and the Merciful.

38.   We said, 'Go down from it, all of you.
If a guidance comes to you from Me [after this],
those who follow My guidance
will have no fear on them nor will they grieve.

39.   But those who do not believe
and who deny the truth of Our signs
– those are the companions of the Fire,
in which they will remain for ever.'

40.   Children of Israel,
remember My blessing which I bestowed on you.
Fulfil [your] covenant with Me
and I shall fulfil [My] covenant with you,
and fear Me,

41.   And believe in what I have sent down,
confirming what is with you,[10]
and do not be the first to disbelieve in it;
and do not sell My signs for a small price,
and fear Me.

42.   Do not confuse falsehood with truth
and do not conceal the truth knowingly.

43.   Perform prayer and pay the *zakāt*,[11]
and bow with those who bow.

44.   Do you[p] order the people to be pious
and you yourselves forget
whilst you recite the Scripture?
Do you not understand?

45.   Seek help through patience and prayer.
It is grievous, save for the humble,

46.   Who think that they will meet their Lord
and that they will return to Him.

47.   Children of Israel,
remember My blessing which I bestowed on you
and how I favoured you over [all] created beings.

48.   Protect yourselves against a day
when no soul will give any satisfaction for any other,
nor will any intercession be accepted from it
nor any equivalent be taken from it,
and they will not be helped.

---

[10] Your scriptures.

[11] Alms, the third pillar of Islam. It is a technical term and so it has been kept in transliteration.

49. And [recall] when We delivered you from the family of Pharaoh
who were afflicting you with evil torment,
slaughtering your sons,
but sparing your women.
In that there was a great trial for you from your Lord;

50. And when We divided the sea for you and saved you
and drowned the family of Pharaoh as you watched,

51. And when We appointed for Moses forty nights;
and then after he [had left you]
you took to yourselves the calf,
being wrongdoers.

52. Then after that We forgave you,
so that you might be grateful.

53. And [recall] when We gave Moses the Scripture and the Salvation,[12]
so that you might be guided aright.

54. And when Moses said to his people,
'O my people, you have wronged yourselves
by taking the calf to yourselves;
so turn towards your Creator and slay yourselves;[13]
that will be better for you with your Creator.'
Then He relented towards you.
He is the Relenting and the Merciful.

55. And when you[p] said,
'Moses, we shall not believe in you
until we see God plainly';
and the thunderbolt took you[p]
as you were watching.

56. Then We raised you after your death,
so that you might be grateful.

57. And We caused the cloud to give you shadow,
and We sent down to you manna and quails:
'Eat the good things which We have provided for you.'
They did not wrong Us,
but they wronged themselves.

58. And [recall] when We said,
'Enter[p] this settlement, and eat plentifully from it
wherever you wish;
but enter [through] the gate in prostration,
and say, "An unburdening".

---

[12] Or 'the Criterion'. There is dispute about the meaning of the Arabic *al-furqān*.
[13] Traditionally understood as 'slay the guilty among you'.

30

We shall forgive you your sins
and give increase to those who do good.'

59.   But those who did wrong substituted another saying
for the one which had been told to them.
So We sent down wrath from heaven on those who had done wrong
because they were reprobates.

60.   And [recall] when Moses asked for water for his people
and We said, 'Strike the rock with your staff,'
and twelve springs gushed out of it;
[and] each people knew its drinking-place:
'Eat and drink God's provision,
and do not cause mischief in the land,
wreaking corruption.'

61.   And [recall] when you^p said,
'Moses, we cannot endure having [only] one kind of food.
Call to your^s Lord for us,
and He will bring forth for us some of what the earth grows:
its greens, cucumbers, corn, lentils and onions.'
He said, 'Do you seek to have what is meaner
instead of what is better?
Go down to Egypt,
for you shall have what you have asked.'

61a.   Humiliation and poverty were stamped upon them,
and they incurred anger from God.
That was because they did not believe in God's signs
and wrongfully slew the prophets,
and that was because they rebelled
and were transgressors.

62.   Those who believe and those who are Jews and the Christians and the Ṣābi'ūn[14]
– those who believe in God and the Last Day and act righteously –
Their reward is with their Lord.
no fear will be upon them nor will they grieve.

63.   And [recall] when We took your^p covenant from you
and raised the mountain above you:
'Take firm hold of what We have given you,
and remember what is in it
so that you might protect yourselves.'

64.   Then after that you turned away,
and but for the bounty and mercy of your Lord to you,
you would have been among the losers.

---

[14] It is not certain who the Ṣābi'ūn (mentioned here and in 5:69 and 22:17) were.

65. You know those of you who transgressed concerning the Sabbath
    and to whom We said,
    'Be you baboons, slinking away.'
66. And We made them an example to their own generation
    and to those that followed them
    and an admonition to those who fear God.
67. And [recall] when Moses said to his people,
    'God commands you to sacrifice a cow.'
    They said, 'Are you making fun of us?'
    He said, 'I take refuge with God from being among the ignorant.'
68. They said, 'Call to your⁵ Lord for us,
    and let Him make clear to us what she is to be.'
    He said, 'HE says, "She is to be a cow
    that is neither old nor immature,
    but one whose age is between these."
    Do as youᴾ are commanded.'
69. They said, 'Call to your Lord,
    and let Him make clear to us
    what her colour is to be.'
    He said, 'HE says, "She is to be a yellow cow
    of bright colour,
    pleasing to those who look [at her]".'
70. They said, 'Call to your Lord
    and let Him make clear to us
    what [kind] she is to be.
    All cattle are much the same to us.
    If God wishes, we shall be guided aright.'
71. He said, 'HE says,
72. "She is to be a cow not broken in
73. to turn over the ground
    nor to water the tilled land,
    [but] kept sound, with no blemish on her".'
    They said, 'Now you have brought the truth.'
    So they slew her – though they almost did not.
72. And [recall] when youᴾ killed a soul
    and disagreed concerning it,
    and God brought out what you were concealing.
73. We said, 'Strike him with part of it.'¹⁵
    Thus God brings the dead to life

---

¹⁵ *i.e.* of the cow.

32

and shows you His signs,
so that you may understand.

74. Then after that your hearts became hardened
and were like stones or even harder;
for there are some stones through which rivers gush
and there are some that are split
so that the water comes from them,
and there are some that fall down
through fear of God.
God is not unaware of what you do.

75. Are you[p] eager that they[16] should believe you
when a party of them used to listen to the words of God
and then change them after they had understood them,
knowingly?

76. And when they meet those who believe,
they say, 'We believe'.
But when they are on their own with one another,
they say, 'Do you[p] tell them what God has revealed to you
that they may use it to dispute with you
in the presence of your Lord?
Do you not understand?'

77. Do they not know that God knows
what they hide and what they make public?

78. Among them are members of the community[17]
who know the Scripture only as vague ideas.
They only guess.

79. Woe to those who write the Scripture with their own hands
and then say, 'This is from God',
so that they may sell it for a paltry price.
Woe to them for what their hands have written.
Woe to them for what they earn.

80. And they say, 'The Fire will touch us only for a few days.'
Say, 'Have you[p] taken a covenant from God
– for God will not break His covenant –
or do you[p] say about God things that you do not know?'

81. No. Those who earn evil and are encompassed by their sin
– those are the companions of the Fire,
in which they will remain for ever.

---

[16] The Jews.

[17] Or else 'the common people'. *Ummī* is normally translated as 'illiterate' or 'uneducated', but this cannot have been the original meaning.

82. And those who believe and do righteous deeds
    – those are the companions of the Garden,
    in which they will remain for ever.
83. And [recall] when We took a covenant from the Children of Israel:
    'Serve only God,
    and [do] good to your parents
    and close relatives and orphans and the destitute;
    and speak good to the people
    and perform prayer and pay the *zakāt*.'
    Then you turned away,
    apart from a few of you,
    turning aside.
84. When We took a covenant from you^p:
    'You shall not shed blood,
    and you shall not expel your own people from your dwellings.'
    Then you confirmed [it],
    and you yourselves bore witness.
85. Then there you were, killing one another
    and expelling a group of you from their dwellings,
    supporting one another against them in sin and enmity.
    If they come to you as captives,
    you ransom them
    – though their expulsion was forbidden to you.
    Do you believe in part of the Scripture
    and not believe in part [of it]?
    What is the reward of those of you who do that
    but shame in the life of this world?
    And on the Day of Resurrection
    they will be sent back to the most severe torment.
    God is not unaware of what you do.
86. These are those who buy the life of this world
    at the cost of the world to come.
    Their torment will not be lightened
    nor will they be helped.
87. In the past We gave Moses the Scripture,
    and after him We caused [other] messengers to follow;
    and We gave Jesus, the son of Mary, the clear proofs,
    and We supported him with the Holy Spirit.
    [Why is it that], whenever a messenger brings
    what your souls do not desire,
    you become haughty
    and some you treat as liars and some you kill?

88. They say, 'Our hearts are uncircumcised.'
    No. God has cursed them for their unbelief.
    Little they believe.

89. When a Scripture comes to them from God,
    confirming what is in their possession
    – and previously they have been seeking victory over those who disbelieve –
    and when what they recognize [as the truth] comes to them
    they do not believe in it.
    The curse of God is on those who do not believe.

90. Evil is what they have sold themselves for:
    disbelief in what God has sent down,
    through envy that God should send down some of His bounty
    to those of His servants whom He wishes.
    They have incurred anger upon anger.
    There is a humiliating torment for the unbelievers.

91. When it is said to them,
    'Believe in what God has sent down',
    they say, 'We believe in what was sent down to us;'
    and they do not believe in what comes after it,
    although it is the truth,
    confirming what is with them.
    Say, 'Why did you kill the prophets of God in former times,
    if you are believers?'

92. In the past Moses brought you the clear proofs;
    but after him you took to yourselves the calf,
    and you were wrong-doers.

93. And [recall] when We took the covenant from you[p]
    and raised the mountain over you:
    'Hold fast to what We have given you and hear.'
    They said, 'We hear and disobey';
    and they were made to drink the calf in their hearts[18] because of their unbelief.

93a. Say, 'Evil is what you are commanded to do by your faith
    – if you are believers.'

94. Say, 'If the last abode with God is yours alone,
    to the exclusion of [other people],
    wish for death, if you speak the truth.'

95. But they will never wish for it
    because of what their hands have forwarded.
    God is aware of the wrong-doers.

96. You will find them the people most eager for life,

---

[18] Pickthall paraphrases neatly, 'worship of the calf was made to sink into their hearts'.

[more eager] than those who associate others with God.
One of them would like to be given a thousand years of life;
but his being given so much life will not remove him from the torment.
God is observer of what they do.

97. Say, 'Who is an enemy to Gabriel?[19]
It is he who brought it[20] down to your[s] heart
with God's permission,
confirming what was before it,
and a guidance and good news for the believers.

98. Who is an enemy to God and His angels
and His messengers and Gabriel and Michael?
God is an enemy to those who do not believe.'

99. In the past We have sent down to you[s] clear signs,
and only the reprobates do not believe in them.

100. How is it that whenever they make a covenant
a part of them cast it aside?
No. Most of them do not believe.

101. And when a messenger comes to them from their Lord,
confirming what they have,
a part of those who have been given the Scripture
throw the Scripture of God behind their backs,
as if they did not know.

102. They follow what the devils recited over the kingdom of Solomon.
Solomon did not disbelieve,

102a. But the devils disbelieved,
teaching the people sorcery
and what was sent down to the two angels in Babylon,
Hārūt and Mārūt.
The two of them did not teach anyone
until they had said,
'We are a temptation;
so do not disbelieve.'
[People] learn from these two how to cause division
between a man and his wife;
but they do not use it to harm anyone
except by God's permission.
They learn what harms them and does not benefit them;
and they know that those who buy it
have no share of happiness in the world to come.

---

[19] The most likely Arabic spelling is Jibrīl, though there are variants.
[20] The Revelation.

Evil is the price for which they sell themselves,
if they did but know.

103. Had they believed and protected themselves,
a recompense from God would have been better,
if they did but know.

104. O you who believe, do not say, 'Regard us',
but say, 'Observe us', and listen.[21]
The unbelievers will have a painful torment.

105. Those of the People of the Scripture who do not believe
and those who associate others with God
do not like any good to be sent down to you[p] from your Lord.
God singles out for His mercy those whom He wishes.
God is possessed of the great bounty.

106. Whatever signs We annul or cause to be forgotten,
We bring better or the like.
Do you[s] not know that God has power over everything?

107. Do you not know that God has sovereignty over the heavens and the earth?
You have no protector or helper apart from God.

108. Or do you[p] wish to question your messenger
as Moses was previously questioned?
Those who exchange belief for unbelief
have strayed from the level way.

109. Many of the People of the Scripture want
to make you unbelievers again
after you have believed,
through envy on their part
after the truth has become clear to them.
Forgive[p] and grant pardon
until God brings His command.
God has power over everything.

110. Perform prayer and pay the *zakāt*.
Whatever good you forward to your souls' account,
you will find it with God.
God is Observer of what you do.

111. They say, 'Only those who are Jews or Christians will enter the Garden.'
These are their own vague ideas.
'Bring your proof, if you tell the truth.'

112. No. Those who surrender their faces to God
and have done good
will have their reward with their Lord.

---

[21] See also 4:46. There is a complex linguistic point in the background – see the Commentary.

There is no fear upon them nor do they grieve.

113. The Jews say,
'The Christians have no ground to stand on,'
and the Christians say,
'The Jews have no ground to stand on.'
– though both recite the Scripture.
Those who have no knowledge[22] speak similarly.
God will give judgement between them on the Day of Resurrection
concerning that about which they used to differ.

114. Who does greater wrong than those who bar access to God's places of worship,
so that His name may not be mentioned in them,
and who strive to destroy them?
They should enter them only in fear.
They will have shame in this world and a great torment in the world to come.

115. God's are the place where the sun rises and the place where the sun sets.
Wherever you[p] turn, there is the face of God.
God is Embracing and Knowing.

116. They[23] say, 'God has taken to himself a son.'
Glory be to Him.
No. He owns whatever is in the heavens and the earth.
All are obedient to Him,

117. The originator of the heavens and the earth.
Whenever He decrees a thing,
He says to it only 'Be', and it is.

118. Those who do not know[24] say,
'Why does God not speak to us?
Why does no sign come to us?'
Those who were before them said similar things.
Their hearts are much alike.
We have made clear the signs for a people who are sure.

119. We have sent you[s] with the truth,
as a bringer of good tidings and as a warner.
You[s] will not be asked about the companions of the Fire.

120. The Jews will not be pleased with you[s]
nor will the Christians
until you follow their creed.

120a. Say[s], 'God's guidance is the [only] guidance'.
If you[s] follow their whims after the knowledge that has come to you,

---

[22] Of Scripture, *i.e.* the pagan Arabs and in particular the Meccans.
[23] The Christians.
[24] The Jews, as in verse 75.

you will have no protector or helper against God.

121. Those to whom We have given the Scripture
and who recite it correctly
– those believe in it.
Those who do not believe in it
– those are the losers.

122. Children of Israel,
remember My blessing which I bestowed on you
and [remember] that I gave you preference over [other] created beings,

123. And protect yourselves against a day
when no soul will make any requital on behalf of another soul,
nor will compensation be accepted from it,
nor will intercession be of any use to it,
nor will they be helped.

124. And [recall] when Abraham was tested by his Lord with certain words,
and he fulfilled them.
HE said, 'I am making you[s] a leader for the people.'
He said, 'And of my seed?'
HE said, 'My covenant does not extend to those who do wrong.'

125. And when We made the house a meeting-place and a sanctuary for the people:
'Take for yourselves Abraham's station as a place for prayer,'
and We made a covenant with Abraham and Ishmael:
'Purify My house for those who visit [it]
and those who cleave to it
and those who bow and prostrate themselves.'

126. And when Abraham said:
'O my Lord make this a secure land
and provide some of its fruits as sustenance
for those of its people who believe in God and the Last Day.'
HE answered, 'And those who do not believe,
I shall give them enjoyment for a little,
then I shall compel them to the torment of the Fire.
How evil is the journey's end.'

127. And when Abraham and Ishmael were raising the foundations of the house;
[He said], 'Our Lord, accept [this] from us.
You are the Hearer and the Knower.

128. Our Lord, make us surrender to You
and make from our seed a community that will surrender to You,
and show us Your rites,
and relent towards us.
You are the Relenting and the Merciful.

129. Our Lord, raise up among them a messenger,

[who is one] of themselves,
who will recite Your signs to them
and will teach them the Scripture and the Wisdom
and will purify them.
You are the Mighty and the Wise.'

130. Who turns away from the religion of Abraham
except those who are foolish?
We chose him in this world,
and in the world to come he will be among the righteous.

131. When his Lord said to him, 'Surrender',
he said, 'I have surrendered to the Lord of created beings.'

132. And Abraham charged his sons with this,
and [so did] Jacob:
'My sons, God has chosen the true religion for you.
Do not die unless you have surrendered [to Him].'

133. Or were you witnesses when death came to Jacob,
when he said to his sons,
'What will you serve after me?'
They said, 'We shall serve your God
and the God of your forefathers,
Abraham and Ishmael and Isaac:
one God. We shall surrender to Him!'

134. Those are a community who have passed away.
They will have what they earned
and you[p] will have what you have earned.
You will not be asked about what they used to do.

135. They say, 'Be Jews or Christians and you will be guided.'
Say[s], 'No. [Be of] the religion of Abraham,
a man of pure faith.[25] He was not one of those who associate others with God.'

136. Say[p], 'We believe in God and in what was revealed to us
and in what was revealed to Abraham, Isaac, Ishmael, Jacob and the tribes,
and in what was given to Moses and Jesus
and in what was given to the prophets from their Lord.
We make no distinction between any of them.
We surrender to Him.'

137. If they believe in the same as you[p] believe in,
they are guided aright.
But if they turn away,
they are surely in schism.
God will suffice you[s] in dealing with them

---

[25] The Arabic is *ḥanīf*, an epithet applied specially to Abraham.

– He is the Hearer and the Knower –

138. [Giving you] God's colouring.
And who gives better colouring than God?
We are His servants.

139. Say^s, 'Do you^p argue with us concerning God,
when He is our Lord and your Lord?
We have our works, and you have yours.
We serve Him alone.

140. Or do you^p say that Abraham, Ishmael, Isaac,
Jacob and the tribes were Jews or Christians?'
Say, 'Do you^p know better, or God?
And who does greater wrong
than those who hide testimony that he has from God?
God is not unaware of what you do.'

141. That is a community that has passed away.
It will have what it has earned
and you^p will have what you have earned.
You will not be asked about what they used to do.

142. The fools among the people will say,
'What has turned them away from the *qibla*[26]
which they used to observe?'
Say, 'To God belong the place where the sun rises and the place where the sun sets.
He guides those whom He wishes to a straight path.'

143. Thus We have made you a moderate community
for you to be witnesses to the people
and for the messenger to be a witness to you.
And We fixed the *qibla* that you used to observe
only to recognize those who would follow the messenger
from those who turn on their heels.
It was a hard thing except for those whom God guided.
But God is not one to see your faith wasted.
God is Gentle and Compassionate.

144. We see you^s turning your face about in the sky,
and so We make you turn
to a *qibla* that will please you.
Turn your^s face towards the Sacred Mosque.
Wherever you^p may be,
turn your faces towards it.
Those who have been given the Scripture

---

[26] The first *qibla*, the direction for the believers to face in prayer, was Jerusalem. The passage here refers to the change in the direction to Mecca.

know that it is the truth from their Lord.
God is not unaware of what they do.

145. Even if you^s bring every sign to those who have been given the Scripture,
they will not follow your^s *qibla*.
You are not a follower of their *qibla*,
nor are they followers of each other's *qibla*.
If you^s follow their whims
after the knowledge that has come to you,
you will in that case be one of the wrong-doers.

146. Those to whom We gave the Scripture
recognize it as they recognize their own sons,
but a part of them conceal the truth
knowingly.

147. It is the Truth from your^s Lord;
so do not be one of those who doubt.

148. Each person has a direction to which he turns.

148a. Strive^p to be foremost in good works.
Wherever you may be, God will bring you all together.
God has power over everything.

149. Wherever you^s come from,
turn your face towards the Sacred Mosque.
It is the truth from your^s Lord.
God is not unaware of what you do.

150. Wherever you^s come from,
turn your face towards the Sacred Mosque;
and wherever you^p may be turn your faces towards it,
so that the people may not have any argument against you^p
– except those of them who do wrong.
Do^p not fear them, but fear Me.
[This is] so that I may complete my blessing to you
and that you may be guided aright,

151. Even as We have sent among you a messenger
[who is] one of you,
who recites Our signs to you
and will purify you and teach you the Scripture and the Wisdom,
and will teach you what you did not know,

152. Remember^p Me and I shall remember you.
Give thanks to Me and do not be ungrateful to me.

153. O you who believe, seek help in patience and in prayer.
God is with the steadfast.

154. Do^p not say of those who are killed in the way of God,
'dead'.

No. They are living, but you do not perceive [that].

155. We shall indeed test you[p]
with some experience of fear and hunger
and loss of possessions and lives and crops;
but give[s] good tidings to the steadfast,

156. Who, when they are beset by misfortune, say,
'We belong to God, and to Him we return.'

157. On those are blessings and mercy from their Lord.
Those are the ones who are rightly guided.

158. al-Ṣafā and al-Marwa[27] are among the waymarks of God.
It is no sin for those who are performing the *Ḥajj* or *'Umra*[28] to the house
to move round the two of them.
Those who do good voluntarily
– God is thankful and knowing.

159. Those who hide the clear proofs and the guidance that We have revealed,
after We have made it clear to the people in the Scripture
– those are cursed by God and by those who curse.

160. That will not be the case with those who repent
and make amends and make [the truth] clear.
Towards those I relent.
I am the Relenting and the Compassionate.

161. Those who do not believe
and who die while they are still unbelievers
– on those is the curse of God and the angels and the people, one and all.

162. They will remain under it for ever.
The torment will not be lightened for them,
nor will they be given respite.

163. Your[p] God is One God;
there is no god except Him,
the Merciful and Compassionate.

164. In the creation of the heavens and the earth
and the alternation of night and day
and the ships that run on the sea with what benefits men
and the water that God sends down from the sky
and revives the earth with it after it has died off
and disperses all kinds of beasts in it,
and in the turning about of the winds and of the clouds
kept under control between heaven and earth

---

[27] al-Ṣafā and al-Marwa are two heights not far from the Ka'ba.

[28] The *Ḥajj*, the greater pilgrimage, can be performed only in the month of Dhū l-Ḥijja; the *'Umra*, the lesser pilgrimage, can be performed at any other time.

– [in all these] there are signs for people who understand.

165. Yet there are some men who adopt rivals
      other than God,
      loving them as [only] God should be loved;
      but those who believe have greater love for God.
      If only those who do wrong might see,
      when they see the torment,
      that all power belongs to God
      and that God is severe in punishment:

166. When those who were followed
      disown those who follow them,
      and they see the doom
      and their cords are severed with them,

167. And those who followed say,
      'If only we might have another turn
      so that we might disown them,
      as they have disowned us!'
      Thus God will show them their works
      as matters of regret for them,
      and they will not come forth from the Fire.

168. O people, eat what is allowable and good in the earth,
      and do not follow the footsteps of Satan.
      He is a persuasive enemy for you:

169. He commands you to do what is evil and improper
      and to say about God what you do not know.

170. When it is said to them,
      'Follow what God has sent down',
      they say, 'No.
      We shall follow what we found our forefathers doing.'
      Even if their fathers had no understanding and were not guided aright?

171. The comparison of those who do not believe
      is like the one who shouts out to what can hear nothing but a shout and a cry:
      Deaf, dumb, and blind, they have no understanding.

172. O you who believe,
      eat the good things that we have provided for your sustenance,
      and be grateful to God, if you worship Him.

173. He has forbidden for you carrion;
      blood; the flesh of the pig;
      and anything that has been dedicated to any other than God;[29]
      but if anyone is compelled,

---

[29] For an expanded list see 5:3.

without wishing [to do so] or [without] transgressing
– it is no sin for him.
God is Forgiving and Compassionate.

174. Those who conceal the Scripture that God has sent down
and purchase with it a paltry gain,
they will eat only the fire in their bellies.
God will not speak to them on the Day of Resurrection
nor will He purify them.
They will have a painful torment.

175. Those are the ones who purchase error at the cost of guidance
and torment at the cost of forgiveness.
How patient they will [have to] be against the Fire.

176. That is because God has sent down the Scripture with the truth.
Those who differ about the Scripture are in distant[30] schism.

177. It is not piety for you[p] to turn your faces
towards the place where the sun rises and where it sets.
Piety [lies in] those who believe in God and the Last Day
and the angels and the Scripture and the prophets;
who give their possessions, for love of Him, to kinsmen,
orphans, the destitute, the traveller and those who ask,
and [give them] for the freeing of slaves;
who perform prayer and pay the *zakāt*;
and those who fulfil their covenant when they have made one;
and those who are patient in adversity, affliction and times of stress.
Those are the ones who are sincere;
those are the god-fearing.

178. O you who believe,
retaliation is prescribed for you concerning the slain:
the free man for the free man;
the slave for the slave;
the female for the female.
For the [killer] who receives some forgiveness
from the brother of [the slain],
prosecution according to what is recognized as proper
and payment to [the brother] in kindness.
That is an alleviation and a mercy from your Lord.
Those who transgress after this will have a painful torment.

179. In retaliation there is life for you[p],
O you who are possessed of understanding,
so that you may protect yourselves.

---

[30] 'Distant' implies 'far-reaching'.

180. Prescribed for you^p,
    when death comes to one of you,
    if he leaves goods,
    are bequests for parents and kinsmen
    according to what is recognized as proper,
    as a duty on those who protect themselves.
181. Whoever changes [the will] after he has heard it[31]
    – the sin of that will rest on those who change it.
    God is Hearing and Knowing.
182. But if anyone fears injustice or sin from a testator
    and makes things right between the two parties,
    no sin will rest on him.
    God is Forgiving and Merciful.
183. O you who believe,
    fasting is prescribed for you,
    as it was prescribed for those who were before you,
    so that you may protect yourselves,
184. For a fixed number of days.
    Those of you who are sick or on a journey,
    a number of other days;
    and, for those who are able to do it,
    there may be a redemption:
    the feeding of a destitute person.
    And those who do better voluntarily,
    it is better for them.
    For you to fast is better for you,
    if you but know.
185. [It is] the month of Ramaḍān,
    in which the Recitation was sent down
    as a guidance to the people
    and as clear proofs of the guidance and of the salvation.
    Let those of you who witness the month
    fast during it.
    Those of you who are sick or on a journey,
    a number of other days.
    God desires ease for you, not hardship,
    and [He desires] you to complete the period
    and to magnify God for having guided you and to be thankful.
186. When My servants question you^s about Me,
    I am near to answer the call of the caller when he calls Me.

---

[31] From the dying person.

So let them respond to Me and let them believe in Me,
so that they may be guided aright.

187. On nights of fasting it is lawful for you
to have intercourse with your wives.
They are a garment for you and you are a garment for them.
God is aware that you were deceiving yourselves
and He has relented towards you and forgiven you.
So now [you may] have intercourse with them.
And seek what God has prescribed for you
and eat and drink
until the white thread is distinct to you
from the black thread at dawn.
Then complete the fast through to the night
and do not have intercourse with them
when you should be at your devotions in the mosque.
Those are God's bounds
– keep well within them.
Thus God makes clear His signs to the people
so that they may protect themselves.

188. Do[p] not consume your possessions amongst you in vanity,
and do not offer it to the judges
that you may sinfully consume a part of the possessions of [other] people,
knowingly.

189. They ask you[s] about new moons.
Say, 'They are appointed times for the people and for the *Hajj*.'

189a. It is not piety to come to your houses from the back.
Piety [lies in] being god-fearing.
Enter[p] your houses through the doors,
and fear God,
so that you may prosper.

190. Fight[p] in the way of God against those who fight you,
but do not be the aggressors
– God does not love aggressors –

191. And kill them wherever you come upon them,
and drive them out of the places
from which they drove you out.
Persecution is worse than killing.

191a. Do not fight them at the Sacred Mosque until they fight you there.
If they fight you, kill them.
Such is the reward of the unbelievers.

192. If they desist
– God is Forgiving and Merciful.

193. Fight[P] them until there is no dissension
     and until the religion is God's.
     Then if they desist,
     let the only enmity be against the wrong-doers.
194. The sacred month for the sacred month,
     sacred things [being subject to] retaliation.
     Those who attack you[P]
     – attack them in the way they attack you.
     Fear God and know that God is with the god-fearing.
195. Spend[P] in the way of God,
     and do not cast yourselves into perdition by your own hands.
     Do good. God loves those who do good.
196. Fulfil[P] the *Ḥajj* and the *'Umra* for God;
     but if you are prevented,
     [give] whatever offerings are feasible.
     Do not shave your heads
     until the offerings have reached their place of sacrifice.
     Those of you who are sick or suffering from an injury to the head
     – there may be a redemption
     in the form of fasting or alms-giving or an offering.
     When you are safe, whoever enjoys the *'Umra* up to the *Ḥajj*
     [shall give] whatever offerings are convenient.
     Those who do not find [any]
     – a fast of three days during the *Ḥajj* and seven when you have returned;
     that is ten complete days in all.
     That is for those whose families are not present at the Sacred Mosque.
     Fear God and know that God is severe in punishment.
197. The *Ḥajj* is in specific months.[32]
     Those who undertake the duty of the *Ḥajj* in them,
     let there be no sexual intercourse or immoral behaviour or wrangling during
          the *Ḥajj*.
     Whatever good you[P] do, God knows it.
     Take provision – though the best provision is piety.
     So fear me, O you who are possessed of understanding.
198. It is no sin for you to seek a bounty from your Lord;
     but when you press on from 'Arafāt,
     remember God at the sacred waymark.
     Remember Him as He has guided you.
     Before that you were among those who were astray.

---

[32] These are most likely to have been the three consecutive months of truce in pre-Islamic times: Dhū l-Qaʿda and Dhū l-Ḥijja and Muḥarram. The crucial period for the *Ḥajj* is the first ten days of Dhū l-Ḥijja.

199. Then press on from where the people press on
and seek God's forgiveness.
God is Forgiving and Merciful.
200. When you have performed your rites
remember God as you remember your forefathers,
or more intensely.
200a. Among the people are some who say,
'Our Lord, give to us in this world.'
They have no share of happiness in the world to come.
201. And among them are some who say,
'Our Lord, give us good in this world
and good in the world to come,
and guard us from the torment of the Fire.'
202. Those will have a portion of what they have earned.
God is swift in reckoning.
203. Remember^p God during fixed days;
but those who hasten on in two days,
there is no sin on them;
and those who delay, there is no sin on them,
for those who are god-fearing.
Fear God and know that you will be rounded up to Him.
204. And among the people are those whose speech about the life of this world
pleases you^s
and who call God to witness what is in their hearts.
Yet they are the most stubborn opponents.
205. And when they turn away,
they strive to make mischief in the land
and to destroy the tillage and the stock.
God does not love corruption.
206. When they are told, 'Fear God',
pride seizes them in their sin.
Their reckoning will be Jahannam
– how evil a resting-place.
207. But among the people are those who sell themselves
in seeking God's approval.
God is gentle towards His servants.
208. O you who believe,
enter the peace, all of you.
Do not follow the footsteps of Satan.
He is a clear enemy to you.
209. But if you slip after the clear proofs have come to you,
know that God is Mighty and Wise.

210. What can they look for
     except that God should come to them in shadows caused by clouds
     together with the angels?
     The matter has been decided,
     and [all] things are returned to God.

211. Ask the Children of Israel how many clear signs we gave them.
     Those who change God's blessing after it has come to them
     – God is severe in punishment.

212. The life of this world has been made to seem fair to those who disbelieve,
     and they mock those who believe.
     Those who fear God will be above them on the Day of Resurrection.
     God makes provision without reckoning for those whom He wishes.

213. The people were one community.
     Then God sent the prophets as bringers of good tidings and as warners;
     and He sent down with them the Scripture with the truth,
     to give decisions between the people about that on which they differed.
     Only those who had been given it differed about it
     after the clear proofs had come to them,
     through outrage amongst them.
     God guided, by His permission, those who believed
     to that truth about which they differed.
     God guides those whom He wishes to a straight path.

214. Or did you^p think that you would enter the Garden
     when the like of what came to those who passed away before you had not
          come to you?
     They were touched by affliction and distress,
     and they were shaken by earthquakes
     till the messenger and those who believed with him said,
     'When will there be help from God?'
     Truly God's help is near.

215. They ask you^s what they are to spend.
     Say, 'Whatever good you^p spend
     should be for parents, close relatives,
     orphans, the destitute and travellers.
     Whatever good you do, God is aware of it.'

216. Prescribed for you^p is fighting,
     though it is something you hate.
     It may be that you hate a thing
     although it is good for you;
     and likewise you may love a thing which is bad for you.
     God knows when you do not know.

217. They ask you^s about the sacred month and fighting in it.³³
Say, 'Fighting in it is grievous;
but turning [people] from God's way
and unbelief in Him
and [turning people away from] the Sacred Mosque
and expelling His people from it is more grievous with God.
Persecution is more serious than killing.'

217a. They will continue to fight you^p
until they turn you away from your religion
if they are able.
Those of you who turn away from their religion
and die as unbelievers
– their works fail in this world and in the next;
these are the companions of the Fire,
in which they will remain for ever.

218. Those who believe
and those who migrate
and those who strive in God's way
– these can hope for God's mercy.
God is Forgiving and Merciful.

219. They ask you about wine and *maysir*.³⁴
Say, 'In both these is great sin,
but some benefits to the people;
but the sin in them is greater than the benefit.'

219a. And they ask you^s about what they should spend.
Say, 'The surplus.'³⁵
Thus God makes the signs clear for you^p,
so that you may reflect

220. On this world and the world to come.

220a. They ask you^s about orphans.
Say^s, 'Setting their affairs right is good.
If you^p mix with them, they are your brothers.
God knows the one who causes mischief
from the one who sets things right.
Had He wished, He could have overburdened you.
God is Mighty and Wise.'

221. Do^p not marry women who associate others with God

---

³³ This verse is believed to refer to an expedition sent by Muḥammad to Nakhla in Rajab of 2 AH / November 623 AD.

³⁴ See the note on 5:90, where both are prohibited.

³⁵ The commentators are not certain of the meaning here.

until they believe.
A bondswoman who believes is better
than a woman who associates others with God,
even if she were to excite your admiration.

221a. Do^P not marry [your women]
to men who associate others with God
until [those men] believe.
A male slave who believes is better
than a man who associates others with God,
even if he were to excite your admiration.
Such people call [you] to the Fire,
whereas God calls you to the Garden and to forgiveness,
by His permission.
He makes His signs clear for the people
so that they may be reminded.

222. They ask you^s about menstruation.
Say, 'It is a vexation.
Withdraw^P from women during menstruation
and do not approach them until they are clean.
When they are clean,
come to them as God has commanded you.'
God loves those who repent,
and He loves those who keep themselves clean.

223. Your^P women are a tillage.
Go to your tillage as you wish,
and send forward [good deeds] for yourselves.
Fear God and know that you will meet Him.
Give^s good tidings to the believers.

224. Do^P not, through your oaths,
make God a hindrance to your being pious and god-fearing
and to your putting things right between the people.
God is Hearing and Knowing.

225. God will not take you^P to task for making slips in your oaths,
but He will take you to task for what your hearts have garnered.
God is Forgiving and Clement.

226. For those who forswear their women
there is a wait of four months;
if they return, God is Forgiving and Merciful.

227. If they decide on divorce
– God is Hearing and Knowing.

228. Divorced women shall wait by themselves for three menstrual cycles.
It is not lawful for them to conceal what God has created in their wombs,

if they believe in God and the Last Day.
In that period their husbands would do better to take them back
if they desire to set things right.

228a. Women have the same rights as obligations in what is recognized as proper,
though men have a rank above them.
God is Mighty and Wise.

229. Divorce is twice;
then retention with humanity
or setting free with kindness.

229a. It is not lawful for you^p to take anything from what you have given them,
except when both fear that they cannot maintain God's bounds.
If you fear that they cannot maintain God's bounds,
there will be no fault for either of them
concerning that by which she redeems herself.
These are the limits of God.
Do not transgress them.
Those who transgress the bounds of God
– those are the wrong-doers.

230. If he divorces her [finally],
she is not lawful to him after that,
until she marries another husband.
If [the latter] divorces her,
it is no sin for the couple to come together again,
if they think that they can maintain God's limits.
These are God's limits.
He makes them clear for a people who understand.

231. When you^p have divorced women and they have reached their term,
retain them properly
or set them free properly.
Do not retain them harmfully so that you transgress.
Whoever does that wrongs himself.

231a. Do not take God's signs in mockery,
but remember God's blessing to you
and the Scripture and the Wisdom that He has sent down to you,
by which He admonishes you.
Fear God and know that God is aware of everything.

232. When you^p have divorced women and they have reached their term,
do not make difficulties about them marrying their [new] husbands
if they have agreed together on the basis of what is recognized as proper.
This is an admonition for those of you who believe in God and the Last Day.
That is purer and cleaner for you.
God knows, when you do not know.

233. Mothers are to suckle their children for two whole years
for those who desire to complete the suckling.
It is the duty of the father
to provide for them and clothe them in the proper manner.
No soul is charged beyond its capacity.
A mother is not to be burdened because of her child
nor the father because of his child.
The [father's] heir has the same responsibility.
If they wish to wean by mutual consent and consultation between the two of them,
it is no sin for them.
If you[P] desire to seek suckling for your children by a wet-nurse,
it is no sin for you
if you hand over what you have given[36] in the way recognized as proper.
Fear God, and know that God is observer of what you do.

234. Those of you who are taken [in death] and leave wives,
the wives shall wait by themselves for four months and ten [days].
When they have reached their term,
there is no fault for you in what they do concerning themselves in the way
that is recognized as proper.
God is informed of what you do.

235. There is no sin for you[P] in what you do publicly or privately about proposals
of marriage to women.
God knows that you will be mindful of them.
But do not make them promises in secret,
without speaking words recognized as proper.
And do not resolve on the knot of marriage
until the prescribed time has reached its term.
Know that God knows what is in your minds, and beware of Him.
And know that God is Forgiving and Clement.

236. It is no sin for you[P] if you divorce women
when you have not touched them or settled any marriage-portion on them;
but make provision for them,
the well-to-do according to his means
and the needy according to his:
a provision in the way recognized as proper,
a duty for those who do good.

237. If you[P] divorce them before you have touched them
but you have already fixed a marriage-portion for them,
[you should pay] half of what you have fixed,
unless they agree to forego it

---

[36] Usually understood as 'you have agreed to give'.

or the one in whose hand is the knot of marriage agrees to forego it.
To forego is nearer to piety.
Do not forget generosity among yourselves.
God is observer of what you do.

238. Be[p] watchful over [your] prayers
and over the middle prayer;[37]
and stand obedient to God.

239. If you[p] are in fear,
[pray] either on foot or mounted;
and when you are safe,
remember God,
as He has taught you the things that you did not know.

240. And those of you who are [about to be] taken in death
and who leave wives
[should make] a bequest to your wives,
a provision for the year [following your death]
without turning them out [of their homes];
but if they leave, there is no sin for you
in what they do concerning themselves
in a way that is recognized as proper.
God is Mighty and Wise.

241. For women who have been divorced
[there must be] a provision
according to what is recognized as proper,
as a duty on the god-fearing.

242. Thus God makes His signs clear for you[p]
so that you may understand.

243. Have you[s] not considered
those who left their dwellings in thousands[38]
In fear of death?
God said to them, 'Die',
and then He brought them [back] to life.
God is bounteous to the people,
but most of the people are not grateful.

244. Fight[p] in the way of God
and know that God is Hearing and Knowing.

245. Who is it that will lend God a fair loan,
that He may multiply it for him many times?
God straitens and is bountiful.

---

[37] Usually considered to be the afternoon prayer, but this is not certain.
[38] This is normally considered to refer to the children of Israel.

To Him you will be returned.

246. Have you^s not considered
the notables of the children of Israel after Moses,
when they said to a prophet of theirs,³⁹
'Raise up for us a king
and we shall fight in the way of God.'
He said, 'Is it possible that,
if fighting is prescribed for you,
you will not fight?'
They said, 'Why should we not fight in the way of God,
when we have been expelled from our dwelling with our children?'
Yet, when fighting was prescribed for them,
they turned their backs,
except a few of them.
God is aware of the wrong-doers.

247. Their prophet said to them,
'God has raised Saul as a king for you.'
They said, 'How can he have sovereignty over us,
when we have a better right to it than him,
since he has not been given any abundance of possessions?'
He said, 'God has chosen him over you
and has given him a generous increase of knowledge and of strength.
God gives His sovereignty to those whom He wishes.
God is Embracing and Knowing.'

248. Their prophet said to them,
'The sign of his sovereignty is that the ark,
in which there is an assurance from your Lord,
will come to you,
and a remnant of that which the family of Moses and Aaron left behind,
borne by the angels.
In that there is a sign for you if you are believers.'

249. When Saul set out with the hosts,
he said, 'God will test you by means of a river.
Those who drink from it are not of [my party],
but those who do not taste it
– and that does not exclude those who scoop up a little in the hand
– are of [my party].'
But they drank from it,
except for a few of them.
When he and those who believed with him had crossed [the river],

---

³⁹ Samuel.

they said,

'We have no power to-day against Goliath and his hosts.'

Those who thought that they were going to meet God said,

'How many a small band has overcome a numerous band by God's permission.

God is with the steadfast.'

250. When they went forth against Goliath and his hosts,

they said, 'Our Lord, pour out on us steadfastness,

make firm our feet,

and give us help against the people who do not believe.'

251. By God's permission they routed them;

and David killed Goliath,

and God gave him sovereignty and wisdom

and taught him some of what He wills.

Had God not driven off some of the people by means of others,

the earth would have become corrupt.

But God is bounteous to created beings.

252. These are the signs of God

which We recite to you^s in truth.

You^s are truly one of those who have been sent.

253. Those messengers

– We have preferred some of them to others.

There are some of them to whom God has spoken,

and some of them He has raised in rank.

253a. We gave Jesus, the son of Mary, the clear signs,

and We supported him with the Holy Spirit.

Had God willed,

those who came after him would not have fought one another,

after the clear signs had come to them.

But they differed,

some of them believing and some not believing.

Had God willed, they would not have fought one another;

but God does what He wishes.

254. O you who believe,

spend some of that which We have given you as provision

before a day comes

on which there will be neither bargain nor friendship nor intercession.

The unbelievers are the wrong-doers.

255. God.

There is no god but Him,

the Living, the Eternal.

Neither slumber nor sleep seize Him.

To Him belongs all that is in the heavens

and all that is on earth.
Who is there who intercedes with Him,
save by His permission?
He knows what is before them and what is after them,
while they encompass none of His knowledge
apart from that which He wishes.
His throne extends over the heavens and the earth,
and He is not tired by guarding them.
He is the Exalted and the Mighty.

256. There is no compulsion in religion.
The right course has become clearly distinguished from error.
Those who reject idols[40] and believe in God
have grasped the firmest handle
which will never be broken.
God is Hearing and Knowing.

257. God is the protector of those who believe.
He brings them out of the darkness into the light.
Those who do not believe
– their protectors are idols.[40]
They bring them out of the light into the darkness.
Those are the companions of the Fire,
in which they will dwell for ever.

258. Have you[s] not considered
the one who disputed with Abraham about his Lord
because God had given him sovereignty?

258a. – When Abraham said,
'My Lord is the One who gives life and causes death,'
he said, 'I give life and cause death.'
Abraham said,
'God brings the sun from the place where it rises in the east.
Bring it from where it sets in the west.'
The unbeliever was confounded.
God does not guide the people who do wrong.

259. Or like[41] the one who passed by a settlement
collapsed on its supports:
he said, 'How will God give life to this [settlement]
now that it is dead?'

---

[40] The Arabic here is *al-ṭāghūt*, a word apparently of Ethiopic origin, that shifts slightly in meaning in the 8 verses in which it occurs. In most it is feminine and would appear to mean 'false gods' or 'idols'; though in 4:60 it is masculine and perhaps means 'the Devil'.

[41] This introduces a parallel to 'the one who disputed' in verse 258.

God caused him to die for a hundred years,
and then brought him back to life.
HE said, 'How long have you tarried?'
He said, 'A day or part of a day.'
HE said, 'No, you have lingered a hundred years.
Look at your food and drink
– it has not spoiled.
Look at your donkey.
[We have done this] to make you a sign for the people.
Look at the bones,
how We set them up
and then clothe them with flesh.'
When it was made clear to him, he said,
'I know that God has power over everything.'

260. And [recall] when Abraham said,
'My Lord, show me how You give life to the dead.'
HE said, 'Do you not believe?'
He said, 'Yes, but to put my heart at ease.'
HE said, 'Take four of the birds,
and incline them to yourself;
then place a part of them on each hill;
then call to them and they will come running to you.
Know that God is Mighty and Wise.'

261. Those who spend their possessions in the way of God
are like a grain that produces seven ears,
in each of which are a hundred grains.
God multiplies for those whom He wills.
God is Embracing and Knowing.

262. Those who spend their possessions in the way of God
and then do not follow up what they have spent
with reproach or vexation
– their reward is with their Lord.
There will be no fear on them nor will they grieve.

263. Kind speech and forgiveness
are better than alms followed by vexation.
God is All-sufficient and Clement.

264. O you who believe,
do not render your alms void by reproach or vexation,
like the one who spends his possessions to make a show to the people
and does not believe in God and the Last Day.
He is like a rock on which is soil,
which is struck by heavy rain, leaving it bare.

They have no power over any of that which they have acquired.
God does not guide people who do not believe.

265. Those who spend their possessions in seeking God's approval and in strengthening their souls
are like a garden on a hill,
which is struck by heavy rain,
and which then yields its produce in double quantity.
If no rain strikes it, there is dew.
God is observer of what you^p do.

266. Would any one of you like to have a garden of palm-trees and vines,
with rivers flowing through it,
with all kinds of fruit in it for him;
and old age has stricken him,
and he has weak offspring;
and a whirlwind containing fire strikes it and it is burnt.
Thus God makes clear [His] signs to you
so that you may reflect.

267. O you who believe,
spend some of the good things you have acquired
and of the things We have brought forth from the earth for you;
and do not have recourse to the bad things to spend
when you would not take them [for yourselves]
without shutting your eyes over them.
Know that God is All-sufficient and Laudable.

268. Satan promises you poverty
and urges you to immorality;
but God promises you forgiveness and bounty from Himself.
God is Embracing and Knowing.

269. He gives wisdom to those whom He wishes.
Those to whom wisdom is given have been given great good;
but only those possessed of understanding are mindful.

270. Whatever expenditure you^p make,
whatever vows you make,
God knows it.
The wrong-doers have no helpers.

271. If you^p make public your alms-giving,
that is excellent;
but if you conceal it and give it to the poor,
that is better for you.
It will atone for some of your evil deeds for you.
God is informed of what you do.

272. Their guidance is not your^s responsibility,

but God guides those whom He wishes.
Whatever good thing you[p] spend,
it is for yourselves,
when you spend only to seek God's face;
and whatever good thing you spend will be repaid to you in full,
and you will not be wronged

273. – [It being] for the poor who are constrained in the way of God
and are unable to travel in the land.
The ignorant man supposes them to be rich because of their abstinence[42]
– but you will know them by their mark:
they do not beg importunately from the people.
Whatever good thing you spend, God is aware of it.

274. Those who spend their possessions by night and day,
secretly [or] openly,
have their reward with God.
There will be no fear on them, nor will they grieve.

275. Those who live on usury
will rise only as does the one who is prostrated by the touch of Satan.
That is because they have said,
'Usury is no different from trading.'
God has made trading lawful,
whilst He has forbidden usury.
Those who receive an admonition from their Lord and desist
– he will have his past [gains],
and his affair [in the future] is with God.
Those who return [to usury]
– those are the companions of the Fire,
in which they will remain for ever.

276. God obliterates usury but makes alms grow.
God does not love every sinful, ungrateful man.

277. Those who believe and do righteously
and perform prayer and pay the *zakāt*,
they will have their reward with their Lord.
There will be no fear on them, nor will they grieve.

278. O you who believe,
fear God and give up the usury that is outstanding,
if you are believers.

279. If you do not,
be apprised of a war against you from God and His messenger.
If you repent, you will have your principal.

---

[42] 'Abstinence': their not asking for alms.

When you do not do wrong, you will not be wronged.

280.   If a man of straitened circumstances is [the debtor]
let [him have] respite to a time that is easier.
For you[P] to remit [the debt] as alms is better for you,
if you did but know it.

281.   Guard yourselves against a day
on which you will be returned to God.
Then every soul will be paid in full what it has earned,
and they will not be wronged.

282.   O you who believe,
when you contract debts with one another for a fixed term,
record it in writing.
Let a scribe record it justly in writing between you.
Let no scribe refuse to write in the way that God has taught him.
Let him write and let the one who has incurred the debt dictate,
and let him fear his Lord, God,
and let him not diminish any of it.

282a. If the one who has incurred the debt is a fool
or weak or unable to dictate,
let his friend dictate justly.

282b. Call[P] two of your men to act as witnesses;
and if there are not two men,
one man and two women from those you are satisfied with as witnesses,
so that if one of the women goes astray
the other can remind her;
and let not witnesses refuse,
whenever they are summoned.

282c. Do[P] not be averse to writing it down,
big or little,
[with] its term.
That is more equitable with God and surer for testimony,
and more likely to stop you being in doubt.

282d. This will not be the case with merchandise in your presence
that you circulate amongst you,
when there is no fault for you not to record it
– but have witnesses when you are trading with one another,
and let not a scribe or witness be harmed.
If you do [harm], that is a sin for you.
Fear God.
God is teaching you.
God is aware of everything.

283.   If you[P] are on a journey and you do not find a scribe,

let there be a pledge taken;
but if one of you trusts another,
let the one who is trusted deliver his trust,
and let him fear his Lord, God.

283a. Do[p] not conceal testimony.
Whoever does so, his heart is sinful.
God is aware of what you do.

284. All that is in the heavens and all that is on earth
belongs to God.
Whether you reveal what is in your minds
or you conceal it,
God will bring you to reckoning for it.
He forgives those whom He wishes
and He punishes those whom He wishes.
God has power over everything.

285. The messenger believes
in what has been sent down to him from His Lord,
as do the believers:
each one believes in God and His Angels
and His Scriptures and His Messengers.
We make no distinction between any of His messengers.
And they say,
'We hear and obey.
[Grant us] Your forgiveness, our Lord.
To You is the journeying.'

286. God charges no soul beyond its capacity;
to its account is what it has earned,
and against its account is what it has merited.

286a. Our Lord,
do not take us to task if we forget or make a mistake.
Our Lord,
Do not lay on us a burden
like that you laid on those who were before us.
Our Lord,
do not lay on us such a burden as we are incapable of bearing.
Pardon us and forgive us and have mercy on us.
You are our Protector
– Give us victory over the people who are not believers.'

Sūra 3

The bulk of this Medinan *sūra* appears to come from the third and fourth years after the *Hijra*. It refers to the Battle of Badr by name in verse 123, and clearly that section of the *sūra* must postdate the battle (March 624 AD). So, too, must verse 13, traditionally thought to refer to Badr. However it is argued that a majority of the verses that appear to have a historical context, in particular 121–24, 152–54, 165–68 and 172–74, refer to the Battle of Uḥud some two years later. (The Battle of Uḥud is never mentioned by name.) This may be justified in the case of verse 122, but, as is not uncommon with Medinan verses referring to historical events, the rhetorical nature of much of the accompanying material means that most details are allusive rather than precise. Such difficulties cause particular problems in the present *sūra* and in *Sūra* 8; and one must be very cautious about looking to historical sources for corroboration – see the Introductory Note to *Sūra* 8.

Unlike the other long Medinan *sūra*s, *Sūra* 3 contains relatively little prescriptive material – and that is mostly brief and general (see, for example, verse 97 on the *Ḥajj* and verses 130–31 on usury). The core of it is polemic of various kinds: some passages aimed at unbelievers, some at Jews and Christians, and one at the hypocrites (*munāfiqūn*) (verses 167–68); and the narratives about contemporary events are set in the midst of such material. There is only one traditional piece of narrative (33–58), most of that being devoted to the story of the birth of Jesus (35–58), and even this is rounded off by a brief polemical passage on the nature of Jesus (59–62). Three hymn-like passages, 1–9, 26–27 and 191–94, offer notable contrast.

The Family of 'Imrān

In the name of the Merciful and Compassionate God

1. *Alif, Lām, Mīm.*[1]
2. God.
    There is no god but Him, the Living, the Eternal.
3. He has sent down to you[s] the Scripture in truth,
    confirming what came before it.
    And He sent down the *Torah* and the *Gospel*,
4. Previously,
    as a guidance for the people;
    and He sent down the Salvation.[2]

---

[1] On the mystical letters see the note on 2:1.
[2] Or 'the Criterion'. See note on 2:53.

4a.   Those who do not believe in the signs of God
       will have painful torment.
       God is Mighty and Able to take revenge.

5.   Nothing in the heavens and the earth is concealed from God.

6.   It is He who forms you^s in the wombs as He wishes.
       There is no god but Him, the Mighty and the Wise.

7.   It is He who has sent down to you^s the Scripture,
       in which are firm signs
       which are the matrix of the Scripture,
       whilst there are others that are like one another.
       As for those in whose hearts is deviation,
       they follow [the verses] that are like one another,
       seeking mischief and seeking its interpretation.
       Only God knows its interpretation.
       Those who are well-grounded in knowledge say,
       'We believe in it. All is from our Lord.
       Only men of understanding are reminded.

8.   Our Lord, do not cause our hearts to deviate
       after You have guided us;
       and give us mercy from Yourself.
       You are indeed the Giver.

9.   Our Lord, You are the gatherer of the people
       to a day about which there is no doubt.
       God will not fail to keep the tryst.'

10.   Those who do not believe
       – their wealth and their children
       will be of no avail to them against God.
       Those will be fuel for the Fire,

11.   As was the case with the family of Pharaoh
       and those who were before them,
       who denied the truth of Our signs.
       God seized them for their sins.
       God is severe in punishment.

12.   Say to those who do not believe,
       'You will be overcome and rounded up into Jahannam
       – an evil resting-place.'

13.   There was a sign for you^p in the two parties that met,[3]
       one party fighting in the way of God,
       another not believing,
       whom they saw with the clearness of the eye to be twice as many.

---

[3] At the battle of Badr.

But God supports with His help those whom He wishes.
In that there is a warning for those possessed of sight.

14. Love of the pleasures that come from women and children
and heaped up hoards of gold and silver
and branded horses and livestock and tilled land
have been made to seem fair to the people.
That is the enjoyment of the life of this world;
but with God is fair resort.

15. Say, 'Shall I tell you^p of something better than that?'
For those who fear God,
there are gardens with their Lord,
through which rivers flow,
in which they will remain for ever;
and there are pure spouses and God's pleasure.
God is observer of His servants,

16. Who say, 'Our Lord, we believe.
Forgive us our sins
and protect us from the punishment of the Fire'

17. – The patient, the truthful, the obedient,
those who spend and those who seek pardon in the mornings.

18. God bears witness that there is no god but Him,
as do the angels and men of learning,
upholding justice.
There is no god but Him, the Mighty and the Wise.

19. Religion with God is Submission.
Those to whom the Scripture has been given
differed only after knowledge came to them,
through outrage amongst themselves.
Those who do not believe in God's signs
– God is swift to the reckoning.

20. If they argue with you^s, say,
'I have surrendered my face to God,
as have those who follow me.'
And say to those who have been given the Scripture
and to those who have not,
'Have you surrendered?'
If they surrender, they will be guided aright;
but if they turn away, your duty is only to convey [the message].
God is observer of His servants.

21. Those who deny God's signs and kill the prophets without right
and kill those people who enjoin justice
– give^s them the tidings of a painful punishment

22. – Those whose works have failed in this world and the next,
    and who have no helpers.

23. Have you[s] not seen those who have been given a portion of the Scripture
    being called to God's Scripture,
    for it to provide a decision between them,
    then a group of them turning away and moving aside?

24. This is because they say,
    'The Fire will not touch us,
    except for a limited number of days.'
    What they have been inventing
    has deluded them concerning their religion.

25. How [will it be] when We gather them
    for a day of which there is no doubt
    and [when] each soul will be paid in full what it has earned
    and they will not be wronged?

26. Say, 'O God, owner of sovereignty,
    You give sovereignty to those whom You wish;
    You take sovereignty away from those whom You wish;
    You exalt those whom You wish;
    and You abase those whom You wish.
    In Your hand is Good.
    You have power over everything.

27. You merge the night into the day and the day into the night.
    You bring forth the living from the dead and the dead from the living.
    You give sustenance to those whom You wish without reckoning.'

28. Let not the believers take the unbelievers as friends
    to the exclusion of believers.
    Those who do that have no connection with God
    though that is not the case if you are protecting yourselves against them.
    God warns you to beware of Him.
    To Him is the journeying.'

29. Say, 'Whether you[p] conceal what is in your breasts or reveal it,
    God knows it,
    [just as] He knows what is in the heavens and on earth.
    God has power over everything.'

30. On the day when every soul will find itself confronted with
    whatever good it has done
    and whatever evil it has done,
    it will wish there to be a distant period between itself and [that day].
    God warns you[p] to beware of Him.
    God is gentle with [His] servants.

31. Say, 'If you[p] love God, follow me

and God will love you and forgive you your sins.
God is Forgiving and Merciful.'

32. Say, 'Obey^p God and the messenger.'
If you turn away,
[remember that] God does not love the unbelievers.

33. God chose Adam and Noah and the family of Abraham
and the family of 'Imrān above all created beings,

34. The seed of one another.
God is the Hearer and the Knower.

35. [Recall] when the wife of 'Imrān said, 'My Lord,
I have vowed to You what is in my belly
as a dedicated [offering].
Accept it from me.
You are the Hearer and the Knower.'

36. When she gave birth to her, she said,
'My Lord, I have given birth to her, a female.'
– And God was well aware of what she had given birth to.
The male is not like the female. –
'I have called her Mary.
I seek protection with You for her
and for her offspring from the accursed Satan.'

37. Her Lord received [the child] graciously,
and caused her to grow with fair growth;
and Zachariah took charge of her.
Whenever Zachariah went into the sanctuary to see her,
he found that she had provisions.
He said, 'O Mary, where does this come from for you?'
She said, 'From God.
God gives provision without reckoning to those whom He wishes.'

38. Zachariah called to his Lord there, saying,
'My Lord, give me a good offspring from Yourself.
You are the Hearer of supplications.'

39. And the angels called out to him
whilst he was standing praying in the sanctuary,
'God gives you^s the good news of John,
confirming a word⁴ from God:
a chief and a chaste man and a prophet from among the righteous'.

40. He said, 'How can I have a son,
when old age has come upon me
and my wife is barren?'

---

⁴ Jesus.

He said, '[It will be] so.
God does what He wishes.'

41. He said, 'My Lord, make a sign for me.'
He said, 'Your sign will be
that you will not be able speak to the people for three days
except by gesture.
Remember your Lord often
and glorify [Him] in the evening and in the morning.'

42. And [recall] when the angels said,
'O Mary, God has chosen you and purified you
and chosen you above the [other] women [among] created beings.

43. O Mary, be obedient to your Lord and prostrate yourself and bow with those
who bow.'

44. That is from the tidings of the Invisible.
We reveal it to you[s],
for you[s] were not with them
when they threw their pens[5]
as to which of them should be guardian of Mary,
nor were you[s] with them when they quarrelled.

45. And [recall] when the angels said, 'O Mary,
God gives you good news of a word from Him,
whose name is *al-Masīḥ*,
Jesus, son of Mary,
illustrious in this world and the next,
and one of those brought near.

46. He will speak to the people in the cradle and in maturity,
and [he is] one of the righteous.'

47. She said, 'My Lord, how can I have a son,
when no mortal has touched me?'
He said, '[It will be] so.
God creates what He wishes.
When He decides on something,
He says to it only "Be", and it is.

48. He will teach him the Scripture and the Wisdom
and the *Torah* and the *Gospel*.

49. And [make him] a messenger to the Children of Israel,
saying, "I have brought you[p] a sign from your Lord.
I shall create for you out of clay
[a shape] like that of a bird,
and I shall breathe into it,

---

[5] Drew lots.

and it shall become a bird by God's permission;[6]
and I shall cure the blind and the leper
and give life to the dead by God's permission;
and I shall tell you what you should eat
and what you should store up in your houses.
In that there is a sign for you, if you are believers.

50. And [I have come] to confirm the *Torah* that there was before me
and to make lawful to you[p] some of that which was forbidden to you.
I bring you a sign from your Lord;
so fear God and obey me.

51. God is my Lord and your Lord.
So worship Him.
That is a straight path".'

52. When Jesus perceived their unbelief, he said,
'Who will be my helpers towards God?'
The Disciples said, 'We are God's helpers.
We believe in God.
Bear witness that we surrender.

53. Our Lord, We believe in what You have sent down.
We follow the messenger.
Register us with those who bear witness.'

54. They schemed,[7] and God schemed
– and God is the best of schemers.

55. And [recall] when God said, 'O Jesus,
I am going to take you
and raise you to Me
and cleanse you of those who do not believe
and set those who follow you above the unbelievers
till the Day of Resurrection.
Then your return will be to Me,
and I shall judge between you
concerning that about which you used to differ.

56. As for those who do not believe,
I shall punish them with a terrible punishment
in this world and the next,
and they will have no helpers.'

57. As for those who believe and do righteous deeds,
He will pay them their wages in full.
But God has no love for wrong-doers.

---

[6] This recalls the passage in the Christian apocryphal work *The Infancy Gospel of Thomas*, 2:3–6.
[7] The Jews.

58.   This We recite to you^s of the signs and the wise reminder.

59.   The parallel of Jesus with God
        is like that of Adam.
        He created him from dust and then said to him, 'Be',
        and he was.

60.   The truth is from your^s Lord;
        so do not be one of those who doubt.

61.   Those who argue with you^s about Him
        after the knowledge has come to you,
        say [to them], 'Come, and we shall call our sons and your sons,
        our wives and your wives,
        our selves and your selves,
        and then we shall pray humbly
        and place the curse of God on those who lie.'

62.   This is the true story.
        There is no god but God.
        God is the Mighty and the Wise.

63.   If they turn away, God is aware of those who wreak mischief.

64.   Say, 'O people of the Scripture,
        come to a word that is common between you and us,
        "We serve only God,
        and we associate nothing with Him
        and we do not take one another as lords
        to the exclusion of God".'
        If they turn away,
        say, 'Bear witness that we surrender.'

65.   O people of the Scripture,
        why do you argue with us about Abraham,
        when the *Torah* and the *Gospel* were only sent down after him?
        Do you not understand?

66.   You are indeed those who argue about that of which you have some knowledge
        but why do you argue about something of which you have no knowledge?
        God knows. You do not know.

67.   Abraham was neither a Jew nor a Christian.
        He was a man of pure faith,⁸ one who surrendered.
        He was not one of those who associate others with God.

68.   The nearest people to Abraham
        are those who followed him and this prophet
        and those who believe.
        God is the protector of the believers.

---

⁸ See the note on 2:135.

69. A party of the people of the Scripture long to lead you astray,
    but they will lead only themselves astray
    – though they will not be aware of it.

70. O people of the Scripture,
    why do you not believe in God's signs,
    when you witness [them]?

71. O people of the Scripture,
    why do you confound the true with the false
    and conceal the truth,
    knowingly?

72. A party of the people of the Scripture say,
    'Believe^p in what has been sent down
    to those who believe at the beginning of the day
    and do not believe at the end of it,
    so that they may return,

73. And believe^p only in him who follows your religion.'

73a. Say^s, 'The guidance is God's guidance:
    ⁹that anyone [can be] given the like of what you^p have been given
    or that they [can] argue with you^p in the presence of their Lord.'

73b. Say, 'Bounty is in the hand of God.
    He gives it to those whom He wishes.
    God is Embracing and Knowing.

74. He singles out for His mercy those whom He wishes.
    God is possessed of enormous bounty.'

75. Among the people of the Scripture are those who,
    if you^s entrust them with a talent,¹⁰
    will pay it back to you;
    and among them are those who,
    if you^s entrust him with one gold coin,
    will not pay it back to you,
    unless you remain standing over him.
    That is because they say,
    'We have no obligation
    to those who are not of our community.'
    They speak lies against God,
    knowingly.

76. [Contrast them with] those who fulfil their covenant and fear God.

---

[9] The thrust of the text is unclear. One traditional explanation is that a phrase such as 'do not believe' has to be understood, but that hardly helps.

[10] 'Talent' seems a suitably vague translation for *qinṭār*, ultimately derived from the Latin *centenarium*. See the Commentary on 3:14. The contrast is with *dīnār*, one gold coin.

God loves the god-fearing.

77.   Those who buy little gain
at the cost of God's covenant and their oaths
– those have no share of happiness in the world to come.
God will not speak to them or look at them on the Day of Judgement,
nor will He purify them.
Theirs is a painful torment.

78.   There is a party of them who twist their tongues with the Scripture,
that you[p] may think it to be from the Scripture
when it is not from the Scripture.
They say, 'It is from God',
when it is not from God.
They speak lies against God,
knowingly.

79.   It is not for any mortal
to be given the Scripture, the Judgement, and Prophecy by God
and then [for him] to say to the people,
'Be servants to me, to the exclusion of God,'
but rather [he should say], 'Be masters
because you have been teaching the Scripture
and have been studying [it].'

80.   He does not order you[p] to take the angels and prophets as lords.
Would He order you not to believe after you had surrendered?

81.   [Recall] when God took the covenant of the prophets,
'Behold, what Scripture and Wisdom I have given you[p].
Later there will come to you a messenger
to confirm what you have.
Behold, you will believe in him
and you will help him.'

81a.   HE said, 'Do you agree and take up My burden on you on that condition?'
They said, 'We agree.'
HE said, 'Then bear witness.
I shall be one of those who witness with you.'

82.   Those who turn their back after that
– those are the reprobates.

83.   Do they desire some religion other than God's,
when all those who are in the heavens and on earth
have surrendered to him,
voluntarily or involuntarily,
and will be returned to Him?

84.   Say, 'We believe in God and what has been revealed to us
and what was revealed to Abraham and Ishmael

and Isaac and Jacob and the tribes
and in what was given to Moses and Jesus
and the prophets from their Lord.
We make no distinction between any of them,
and we surrender to Him.'

85.   Those who seek some religion other than Submission,
it will not be accepted from them
– they will be among the losers in the world to come.

86.   How [can] God guide a people who disbelieved
after they had believed and had borne witness
that the messenger is true
and [after] the clear proofs had come to them?
God does not guide people who do wrong.

87.   Those – their recompense is that the curse of God
and of the angels and of the people,
one and all, will be upon them,

88.   And they will remain in it for ever,
without their punishment being eased from them
and without them having respite,

89.   Though this is not the case with those who repent after that
and make amends.
God is Forgiving and Merciful.

90.   [But] those who disbelieve after they have believed
and whose unbelief has increased,
their repentance will not be accepted.
Those are the ones who go astray.

91.   Those who do not believe and die as unbelievers
– the whole earth full of gold would not be accepted from any one of them,
if he were to [try to] ransom himself with it.
Those will have a painful torment and will have no helpers.

92.   You[P] will not attain piety until you spend some of what you love;
and whatever you spend, God is aware of it.

93.   All food was lawful for the Children of Israel
apart from that which Israel forbade to himself
before the *Torah* was sent down.
Say, 'Bring[P] the *Torah* and recite it,
if you tell the truth.'

94.   Those who invent lies against God after that
– those are the wrong-doers.

95.   Say, 'God speaks the truth.
Follow the religion of Abraham, a man of pure faith.
He was not one of those who associate others with God.'

96. The first house founded for the people was at Bakka,[11]
a blessed [place] and a guidance for created beings.

97. In it are clear signs
– the station of Abraham.
Those who enter it are safe.

97a. It is the people's duty to God to make pilgrimage to [that] house
– for those who can make a way to it,
Those who do not believe – God has no need of created beings.

98. Say, 'O people of the Scripture,
why do you not believe in God's signs,
when God witnesses what you do?'

99. Say, 'O people of the Scripture,
why do you turn from God's way those who believe,
seeking to make it crooked,
when you are witnesses and God is not unaware of what you do?'

100. O you who believe,
if you obey a party of those who have been given the Scripture,
they will turn you back into unbelievers
after you have believed.

101. How can you be unbelievers
when the signs of God are recited to you,
and His messenger is among you?
Those who hold fast to God are guided to a straight path.

102. O you who believe,
fear God with the fear that is due to him
and die only as people who have submitted [to Him].

103. Hold fast to God's rope, all together,
and do not split up;
and recall God's blessing to you:
when you were enemies
and He brought reconciliation to your hearts,
and by His blessing you became brothers;
and you were on the lip of a pit of Fire
and he saved you from it.
Thus God makes His signs plain for you, so that you may be guided.

104. Let there be [one] community from you,
summoning [people] to good and enjoining what is reputable
and forbidding what is disreputable.
Those will be the ones who prosper.

105. Do not be like those who have split up

---

[11] Mecca.

and disagreed after the clear proofs have come to them.
Those will have a severe punishment,

106. The day when some faces become white
and when some faces become black.
As for those whose faces become black:
'Did you disbelieve after you had believed?
Taste the punishment in return for your unbelief.'

107. As for those whose faces become white,
they will be in God's mercy,
in which they will remain for ever.

108. These are the signs of God.
We recite them to you[s] in truth.
God does not want any injustice for created beings.

109. To God belongs all that is in the heavens and on earth.
[All] things are returned to God.

110. You[p] are the best community brought forth for the people.
You[p] enjoin what is reputable
and you forbid the disreputable
and you believe in God.
Had the people of the Scripture believed,
it would have been better for them.
Some of them are believers,
but most of them are profligate.

111. They will harm you[p] only with vexation;
and if they fight you they will turn their backs;
then they will not be helped.

112. Humiliation will be stamped on them
wherever they are found,
unless [they grasp] a rope from God
and a rope from the people.
They have incurred anger from God
and destitution will be stamped upon them.
That is because they used to disbelieve in the signs of God
and slay the prophets without right.
That is because they were rebellious and used to transgress.

113. They are not [all] alike.
Among the people of the Scripture
there is an upright community
who recite the signs of God in the watches of the night
and who prostrate themselves.

114. They believe in God and the Last Day
and enjoin what is reputable

and forbid the disreputable
and vie in good deeds.
These are among the righteous.

115. Whatever good they do,
they will not be treated ungratefully for it.
God is Aware of those who are god-fearing.

116. The riches and children of those who disbelieve
will avail them nothing against God.
They are the companions of the Fire,
in which they will remain for ever.

117. There is a parallel between what they spend in the life of the world
and an icy wind which smites the tillage of a people
who have wronged themselves and destroys it.
God does not wrong them, but they wrong themselves.

118. O you who believe,
do not take intimates from outside yourselves,
who will spare no efforts to ruin you
and love what you are distressed at.
Their hatred has already appeared from their mouths,
and what their breasts conceal is greater.
We have made the signs clear for you,
if you understand.

119. Truly, you^p love them,
but they do not love you;
you believe in the whole of the Scripture,
and when they meet you they say, 'We believe',
but when they are alone, they bite their fingers in anger at you.
Say^s, 'Die^p through your anger.
God is aware of the thoughts in your breasts.'

120. If a piece of good fortune touches you^p,
it is evil in their view;
but if a piece of evil befalls you,
they rejoice at it.
But if you persevere and protect yourselves,
their trickery will not harm you in any way.
God encompasses what they do.

121. [Recall] when you^s left your family in the morning
to place the believers in positions for battle
– and God was Hearer and Knower –

122. When two parties of you were inclined to flag
and God was their protector.
Let the believers put their trust in God.

123. God had already helped you^p at Badr,
when you were humble.
So fear God, that you may be thankful.

124. When you^s said to the believers,
'Is it not sufficient for you^p
that your Lord will reinforce you
with three thousand angels sent down?

125. Of course it is, but if you^p persevere and fear God,
and [the enemy] come against you in the rush they make,
your Lord will reinforce you
with five thousand angels driving on.'

126. God only did this as good news for you^p
and to set your hearts at rest
– victory comes only from God,
the Mighty and the Wise –

127. To cut off a part of those who do not believe
or to prostrate them
so that they might move away disappointed.

128. It is no part of the matter for you^s
whether He relents towards them or punishes them.
They are wrong-doers.

129. To God belongs all that is in the heavens and on earth.
He forgives those whom He wishes
and He punishes those whom He wishes.
But God is Forgiving and Merciful.

130. O you who believe,
do not live on usury,
[receiving the sum lent] multiplied many times.
Fear God so that you may prosper,

131. And protect yourselves from the Fire
that has been prepared for the unbelievers;

132. And obey God and the messenger
so that you may be granted mercy.

133. Vie^p for forgiveness from your Lord
and for a garden as wide as the heavens and the earth,
which has been prepared for those who fear God,

134. Those who spend both in prosperity and in adversity
and who choke back their anger
and who forgive the people.
God loves those who do good,

135. And those who,
when they commit an immoral act or wrong themselves,

remember God and seek forgiveness for their sins
– and who but God can forgive sins –
and do not knowingly persist in what they have done.

136. The reward of these will be forgiveness from their Lord
and gardens through which rivers flow,
in which they will remain for ever.
How excellent is the reward of those who work.

137. Institutions have passed away before you[P].
Travel[P] in the land
and see how was the consequence for those who denied the truth.

138. This is a declaration for the people
and a guidance and an admonition to those who fear God.

139. Do[P] not be faint nor grieve,
for you will have the upper hand if you are believers.

140. If a wound touches you[P],
a similar wound has already touched the people [who oppose you].[12]
These are the turns of fortune
that We deal out in turn amongst the people.
[We do this] that God may know those who believe
and that He may take witnesses from among you
– God does not love the wrong-doers –

141. And that God may prove the believers
and blot out the unbelievers.

142. Or did you[P] reckon that you would enter the Garden,
when God did not yet know which of you strive
and not yet know which are steadfast?

143. You[P] used to wish for death before you met it.
Now you have seen it, staring [it] in the face.

144. Muḥammad is only a messenger.
[There have been] messengers who have passed away before him.
If he dies or is killed,
will you[P] turn on your heels?
Those who turn on their heels do not harm God in any way,
and God will reward the thankful.

145. No soul may die except by God's permission,
according to a fixed record.
Those who desire the reward of this world,
We shall bestow some of it on them;
and those who desire the reward of the world to come,

---

[12] The first half to the sentence is taken to refer to the battle of Uḥud, and the second to the battle of Badr. For a similar sentiment see the first part of verse 165.

We shall bestow some of it on them.
We shall reward the thankful.

146. How many a prophet has there been,
together with whom many myriads have fought.
They did not weaken because of what befell them
nor were they feeble nor did they humble themselves.
God loves those who are steadfast.

147. All that they said was,
'Our Lord, forgive us our sins and our extravagance in our affair.
Make our feet firm
and help us against the people who do not believe.'

148. So God gave them the reward of this world
and the fair reward of the world to come.
God loves those who do good.

149. O you who believe,
if you obey those who disbelieve,
they will turn you back on your heels
and you will come away losers.

150. No. God is your protector.
He is the best of helpers.

151. We shall cast terror into the hearts of those who disbelieve
because they associate with God
that with which He has not sent down any authority.
Their lodging will be the Fire.
How evil is the lodging of the wrong-doers.

152. God made good to you^p His promise
when you were slaughtering them by His leave;
then, when you flagged
and quarrelled with each other about the matter
and you disobeyed,
after He had shown you what you wanted,

152a. There were some of you that desired this world,
and some of you that desired the next.
Then He turned you from them
that He might test you.
Now He has pardoned you.
God possesses bounty for the believers.

153. When you^p were climbing up,
not twisting aside for anyone,
and the messenger was calling you in your rear,
HE rewarded you with grief in return for grief
that you might not be sad

for what escaped you or what befell you.
God is informed of what you do.

154. Then after the grief He sent down security
– a drowsiness that came over a party of you,
whilst a party of you were anxious about themselves,
thinking thoughts about God that were not true
– the notions of the age of ignorance –
saying, 'Have we any part in the matter?'

154a. Say, 'The whole matter is God's.'
They were concealing within themselves
what they would not reveal to you[s],
saying 'Had we any part in the affair,
we would not have been killed here.'

154b. Say, 'Even if you had been in your houses,
those appointed to be slain would have gone forth
to the places where they were to lie.
[All this was] so that God might test
what is in your breasts
and prove what is in your hearts.
God is aware of the thoughts in your breasts.

155. Those of you who turned back
on the day when two hosts met
– it was Satan who caused them to slip
on account of some of what they had earned.
Now God has forgiven them.
God is Forgiving and Prudent.

156. O you who believe,
do not be like those who do not believe
and who say about their brothers
who travel in the land or go on raids,
'Had they been with us,
they would not have died or been slain.'
[This is] so that God may make that a cause of anguish in their hearts.
God gives life and brings death.
God is observer of what you do.

157. If you[p] are killed or die in God's way,
pardon and mercy from God are better
than what they collect.

158. If you[s] die or are killed,
you will be gathered up to God.

159. It was through some mercy from God

that you^s were lenient with them.¹³
Had you^s been rough and hard-hearted,
they would have scattered from around you^s.
Forgive^s them and seek forgiveness for them
and take counsel with them in the affair.
Then when you^s have decided,
put your trust in God.
God loves those who put their trust [in Him].

160. If God helps you^p, none can overcome you;
but if He abandons you,
who is there who can help you after him?
Let those who believe put their trust in God.

161. It is not for any prophet to deceive [the people].
Those who deceive will bring their deceit [with them] on the Day of Judgement.
Then every soul will be paid in full what it has amassed,
and they will not be wronged.

162. Is one who follows God's pleasure
like the one who has incurred God's anger
and whose abode is Jahannam?
How evil is the journey's end [there].

163. They [are set in] degrees with God.
God is observer of what they do.

164. God has been gracious to the believers
when He raised up among them
a messenger from among themselves,
who recites to them His signs
and brings them purity
and teaches them the Scripture and the Wisdom,
although before that they were in manifest error.

165. When a disaster befell you^p,
when you had already inflicted the same twice over,
did you say, 'How is this?'
Say, 'It is from yourselves.
God has power over everything.'

166. What befell you^p on the day when the two hosts met
was by God's permission,
and that He might know the believers;

167. And that He might know those who crept away,¹⁴

---

¹³ This is traditionally taken to refer to the waverers at the battle of Uḥud.
¹⁴ The verb used is *nāfaqa*, from which is derived the technical term *munāfiqūn*, used to denote Muḥammad's opponents among the Arabs of Medina, the Hypocrites.

when they were told, 'Come.
Fight in God's way or defend yourselves.'
They said, 'If we knew [how] to fight,
we would follow you^p.'
On that day they were nearer to unbelief
than they were to belief.
They say with their mouths what is not in their hearts.
God is well aware of what they hide –

168. Those who said of their brothers
whilst they themselves were sitting at home,
'Had they obeyed us, they would not have been killed.'
Say, 'Then avert death from yourselves,
if you speak the truth.'

169. Do^s not reckon those who were killed in God's way as dead:
No! [They are] alive with their Lord.
They have provision [from Him],

170. Joyful at what God has given them from His bounty,
and rejoicing in those who have not [yet] joined them but remain behind
– that there will be no fear on them nor will they grieve.

171. They rejoice in a blessing and bounty from God
and that God does not neglect the wage of the believers,

172. Who answered God and the messenger after the hurt had befallen them.
For those of them who do good and fear God
there is a great reward.

173. – Those to whom the people said,
'The people have gathered against you^p. Fear them.'
[This] increased them in their faith and they said,
'God is sufficient for us.
How excellent a guardian He is.'

174. So they came away with blessing and bounty from God,
no evil having touched them.
They followed God's pleasure.
God is possessed of great bounty.

175. That is only Satan making [people] fear his partisans;
do^p not fear them, but fear Me,
if you are believers.

176. Let not those who vie in unbelief grieve you^s.
They will not hurt God in anything.
God does not wish to assign to them a portion in the world to come.
They will have a mighty punishment,

177. Those who buy unbelief at the price of faith
will not hurt God in anything.

They will have a painful punishment.

178. Let not those who do not believe
think that the respite We grant them
is good for their souls.
We grant them respite that they may increase in sinfulness.
They will have a shaming torment.

179. God is not one to leave the believers in the state
in which you^p are
until He distinguishes the bad from the good.[15]
Nor is God one to inform you of the Invisible.
God chooses those whom He wishes from His messengers.
Believe in God and His messengers.
If you believe and fear God,
you will have a great reward.

180. And let not those who are miserly with the bounty God has given them
think that it is better for them.
No! It is worse for them.
That with which they are miserly
will be hung round their necks on the Day of Resurrection.
God's is the inheritance of the heavens and the earth.
God is aware of what you^p do.

181. God has heard the words of those who have said,
'God is poor, and we are rich.'
We shall record what they have said,
together with their wrongful killing of the prophets.
We shall say, 'Taste the torment of the burning.'

182. That is because of what your^p hands have forwarded
and because God is no wrong-doer to [His] servants

183. – Those who have said, 'God has made a covenant with us
that we should not believe in any messenger
until he brings us a sacrifice devoured by fire.'
Say, 'Messengers have come to you^p before me
with the clear proofs and with what you have described.
Why did you kill them, if you speak the truth?'

184. If they say that you^s lie,
messengers before you^s were said to lie,
who came with the clear signs
and the Psalms and the illuminating Scripture.

185. Every soul will taste death
– and you^p will be paid your reward in full on the Day of Resurrection.

---

[15] *i.e.* until the Day of Resurrection.

Those who are removed from the Fire
and are admitted to the Garden are triumphant.
The life of this world is merely enjoyment of delusion.

186. You will indeed be tried concerning your possessions and your selves
and you will hear much annoyance
from those who were given the Scripture before you
and from those who associate others with God.
If you persevere and fear God
– that comes from determination in affairs.

187. [Recall] when God took the covenant of those who were given the Scripture,
'You^s are to make it clear to the people
and you are not to hide it.'
But they flung it behind their backs
and bought a small gain with it.
Evil is what they purchase.

188. Do not think that those who rejoice in what they have done
and want to be praised for what they have not done
– do not think that they are in a place of safety from the torment:
they will have a painful torment.

189. To God belongs the sovereignty of the heavens and the earth.
God has power over everything.

190. In the creation of the heavens and the earth
and in the alternation of night and day
there are signs for those possessed of understanding

191. – Those who remember God standing and sitting and [lying] on their sides
and who reflect on the creation of the heavens and the earth,
'Our Lord, You did not create this in vain.
Glory be to You.
Preserve us from the torment of the Fire.

192. Our Lord, those whom You cause to enter the Fire,
You have abased them.
The wrong-doers have no helpers.

193. Our Lord, we have heard someone calling [us] to the faith, saying,
"Believe^p in your Lord" and we have believed.

193a. Our Lord, forgive us our sins,
and acquit us of our evil deeds,
and take us with the pious.

194. Our Lord, give us what You have promised us through Your messengers.
Do not shame us on the Day of Resurrection.
You will not break the tryst.'

195. Their Lord has answered them, saying,
'I shall not neglect the work of any of you, male or female.

You are of a kind.

195a. Those who have migrated and have been expelled from their homes
and have suffered annoyance in My way
and have fought and have been killed
– I shall acquit them of their evil deeds
and I shall admit them to gardens,
through which rivers flow,
as a reward from God.
With God is the fair reward.'

196. Do^s not be deluded by the fact that
those who do not believe move to and fro in the land

197. – A little enjoyment and then their lodging is Jahannam.
How evil is the resting-place.

198. But those who fear their Lord will have gardens,
through which rivers flow,
in which they will remain for ever
– hospitality from God.
What is with God is better for the pious.

199. Among the people of the Scripture
there are some who believe in God
and what has been sent down to you^p
and what has been sent down to them,
humble before God,
not purchasing a trifling gain at the cost of God's signs.
The reward of those is with their Lord.
God is swift in reckoning.

200. O you who believe, be patient and vie in patience,
make ready and fear God,
so that you may prosper.

Sūra 4

The *sūra* appears to consist entirely of Medinan material. Much of it is traditionally linked to events that happened in the 4th and 5th years after the *hijra*, and there is no cogent argument against such a view. *Sūra* 4 is a particularly earnest piece, hardly leavened at all by narrative passages. The tone is set by the admonition made in the first verse and by the lengthy injunctions about orphans, marriage and inheritance (2–12a) and about fornication, marriage and divorce (15–25a). The rest of the *sūra* contains its fair share of other injunctions and statements that are often tantamount to injunctions, but it is dominated by polemic: unbelievers in general are frequently attacked, and there are more direct passages against the Jews (46–47, 155–157a (denying the crucifixion of Jesus), 160–161) and the hypocrites (*munāfiqūn*) (61–63, 88, 138–147). Not much effort is expended on Christians, but see 171–172.

It is worth noting that Pickthall begins his introduction to the *sūra* in a way that well reflects traditional Islamic attitudes as he perceived them in the 1930s:

> *An-nisâ*, "Women" is so called because it largely deals with women's rights.

This is not the view of modernists and feminists, who find verses such as 3 and 34 particularly difficult.

Women

In the name of the Merciful and Compassionate God

1. O people, fear your Lord,
   who created you from a single soul
   and who created from it its fellow
   and who spread many men and women from the two of them;
   and fear God,
   through whom you seek rights from one another and from the ties of relationship.
   God is a watcher over you.
2. Give[p] orphans their property;
   and do not substitute the bad for the good,
   nor devour their property in addition to your own.
   That is a great sin.
3. If you[p] fear that you will not act fairly towards those orphans,
   marry such of the women as it seems good to you:
   two, three or four each;
3a. But if you fear that you will not be fair,

one [only] or what your right hands possess.[1]
That is more likely [to ensure] that you will not be unfair.

4. Give[P] the women their dowries as a free gift.
   If they are pleased to give some of it to you,
   consume it in a way that is entirely wholesome.

5. Do[P] not give those of weak intellect your property
   that God assigned to you to maintain for them,
   but provide for them and clothe them from it,
   and speak to them properly.

6. Test[P] orphans;
   and then when they reach [the age of] marriage,
   if you perceive in them rightness [of judgement],
   hand over their property to them;
   do not consume it in extravagance
   or in anticipation of them growing up.

6a. Let those who are rich abstain,
    but let those who are poor consume in the way that is recognized as proper.
    When you[P] hand their property over to them
    call witness over them.[2]
    God suffices as a reckoner.

7. Men have a share of what parents and kinsmen leave,
   and so too do women,
   whether it is little or much
   – a share laid down.

8 When the kinsmen and the orphans and the destitute are present at the division,
  provide[P] for them out of it
  and speak to them properly.

9. Let there be fear on the part of those
   who, if they left weak offspring behind them,
   would be afraid for them.
   Let them fear God and speak in an upright fashion.

10. Those who consume the property of orphans wrongfully
    consume fire in their bellies,
    and they will roast in a blaze.

11. God charges you[P] concerning your children:
    to the male the equivalent of the portion of two females;
    if there are more women than two,
    they get two-thirds of what he leaves;
    [but] if there is only one she gets half.

---

[1] 'What your right hands possess' is a stock phrase for 'slaves' (usually, as here, female).
[2] To witness the transfer.

To each of his parents one sixth of what he leaves,
if he has a child;
but if he does not have a child
and his heir is his father,
his mother gets a third;
but if he has brothers,
his mother gets a sixth
after any bequest he may have made or any debt.
Your[p] fathers and your sons
– you do not know which of them is nearer to benefit for you.
[This is] an ordinance from God.
God is Knowing and Wise.

12. To you[p] is half of what your wives leave,
if they have no child;
but if they have a child,
you get a quarter of what they leave,
after any bequest they may have made or any debt.
They[3] get a quarter of what you leave,
if you have no child;
but if you do have a child
they receive one eighth of what you leave
after any bequest you may have made or any debt.

12a. If a man, or a woman, has no direct heir,
but has a brother or sister,
each of the two gets a sixth.
If there are more than that,
they share in a third
after any bequest he may have made
or any debt that is not prejudicial.
[This is] a charge from God.
God is Knowing and Prudent.

13. These are God's limits.
Those who obey God and His messenger
– He will admit them to gardens,
through which rivers flow,
in which they will remain for ever.
That is the great success.

14. Those who disobey God and His Messenger and transgress His limits
– He will admit them to a fire,
in which they will remain for ever,

---

[3] *i.e.* your wives.

and they will have a humiliating punishment.

15. Those of your^p women who commit indecency
    – call four of you as witnesses against them.
    If [the four] give their testimony,
    confine them in their houses
    until death takes them
    or God appoints a way for them.[4]

16. If two of you commit it,[5]
    punish them both;
    and if they repent and make amends,
    turn from them.
    God is Relenting and Compassionate

17. – But God is only bound to relent
    in the case of those who do evil in ignorance
    and repent shortly afterwards.
    God will relent towards these.
    God is Knowing and Wise.

18. There is no relenting for those who do evil deeds,
    and then, when death comes to one of them,
    he says, 'Now, I repent',
    nor for those who die when they are unbelievers.
    For these We have prepared a painful torment.

19. O you who believe,
    it is not lawful for you to inherit women against their will
    or to coerce them that you may take away part of what you have given them
    unless they commit a flagrant indecency.
    Consort with them properly.
    If you dislike them,
    perhaps you dislike something when God has put much good into it.

20. If you wish to replace a wife by another
    and you have given one of them a large sum,
    take nothing from it.
    Would you take it by calumny and manifest sin?

21. How can you take it after you have come together with one another,
    and they have taken a binding pledge from you?

22. Do not marry women whom your fathers have married,
    except for cases that have happened in the past.
    That is improper behaviour and an abhorrence and an evil way.

---

[4] This conflicts with 24:2–3, which is traditionally thought to be a later revelation and thus to abrogate the present verse.
[5] This is traditionally taken to refer to two men.

23. Forbidden to you^p are:
    your mothers; your daughters; your sisters;
    your paternal aunts; your maternal aunts;
    brother's daughters; sister's daughters;
    [those who have become] your mothers by suckling you;
    your sisters by suckling; your wives' mothers;
    your step-daughters who are in your care,
    born to wives with whom you have consummated marriage;
    but if you have not consummated the marriage,
    it is no sin for you [to marry the daughters];
    the wives of your sons who are from your own loins.
    [It is also forbidden] that you should have two sisters together,
    except for cases that have happened in the past.
    God is Forgiving and Merciful.

24. [Also forbidden] are married women,
    except what your right hands possess.
    [That is] a decree from God for you.

24a. Lawful to you^p is what is beyond those [just mentioned],
    for you to seek with your wealth,
    acting properly and not improperly.
    The wives that you enjoy thereby,
    give them their wages.[6]
    [This is] a duty.
    There is no sin for you in what you may agree with them after [that] duty.
    God is Knowing and Wise.

25. Those of you unable to afford to marry believing chaste women,
    let them marry some of the believing young women
    whom your right hands possess.
    God is well aware of your faith.
    You are of a kind.
    Marry them with the permission of their family
    and give them their wages in the way that is recognized as proper,
    women living in wedlock,
    not in some loose arrangement
    or taking them as 'companions'.

25a. If they commit indecency when they are properly married
    they shall incur half of the punishment for chaste women.
    That is for those among you who fear sin.
    It is better for you to be patient.
    God is Forgiving and Merciful.

---

[6] *i.e.* their dowries.

26. God wishes to make [things] clear to you[P]
    and to guide you by the customs of those who were before you
    and to relent towards you.
    God is Knowing and Wise.
27. God wishes to relent towards you,
    but those who follow their desires
    want you to deviate greatly.
28. God wishes to lighten [things] for you,
    for man was created weak.
29. O you who believe,
    do not consume your property among you in vanity,
    but let there be trading by mutual consent among you.
    Do not kill yourselves.
    God is merciful to you.
30. Those who do that through wrong-doing and aggression,
    We shall roast them in a fire
    – that is easy for God.
31. If you[P] avoid the serious things that you are forbidden,
    We shall remit from you your evil deeds
    and grant you a noble admittance.
32. Do[P] not covet that
    through which God has granted some of you preference over others.
    Men will receive a share of what they have earned,
    and so will women.
    Ask God [for some] of His bounty.
    God knows everything.
33. To everyone We have appointed heirs
    for what parents and close relations leave;
    and those with whom your right hands have made a covenant,
    give them their share.
    God is witness over everything.
34. Men are overseers of women
    because God has granted some of them bounty in preference to others
    and because of the possessions which they spend.
    Righteous women are obedient,
    guarding the invisible
    because God has guarded [them].
    Admonish[P] those women whose rebelliousness you fear,
    shun them in [their] resting-places
    and hit them.
    If they obey you, do not seek a [further] way against them.
    God is Exalted and Great.

35. If you fear a breach between the two of them,
     appoint an arbiter from his folk and one from hers.
     If the two desire to set things right,
     God will bring agreement between them.
     God is Knowing and Informed.
36. Serve^p God and do not associate anything with Him;
     [let there be] kindness to parents;
     to close relatives; to orphans; to the destitute;
     to the neighbour who is related to you;
     to the neighbour who is a stranger;
     to the companion at your side; to the traveller;
     and to those whom your right hands possess.
     God does not love those who are boastful and proud,
37. Those who are niggardly and enjoin avarice on the people
     and hide the bounty that God has bestowed on them
     – We have prepared a humiliating punishment for the unbelievers –
38. And those who spend their wealth to show off to the people
     and who do not believe in God nor in the Last Day.
     Those who have Satan as a comrade
     – he is an evil comrade [for them].
39. What harm would it do them
     if they were to believe in God and the Last Day
     and spend some of that that God has provided for them?
     God is aware of them.
40. God does not do a grain's weight of wrong;
     and if there is a good deed,
     He will double it and give from Himself a great wage.
41. How will it be when We bring a witness from each community
     and We bring you^s as a witness against these?
42. On that day those who have disbelieved and disobeyed the messenger
     will want the earth to be levelled over them.
     They will not conceal any tiding from God.
43. O you who believe,
     do not draw near to prayer when you are intoxicated,
     until you know what you say;
     nor when you are polluted,
     save when you are traversing a way,
     until you have washed yourselves.
     If you are sick or on a journey
     or one of you comes from the closet
     or if you have had contact with women
     and you do not find water,

93

have recourse to clean soil
and wipe your faces and your hands with it.
God is Pardoning and Forgiving.

44. Have you[s] not seen those who were given a portion of the Scripture
purchasing error and wanting you to stray from the way?

45. God is well aware of your[p] enemies.
God is a sufficient protector and helper.

46. Some of those who are Jews
change words from their places[7] and say,
'We hear and rebel',
and, 'Hear [something inaudible]',
and, 'Observe us',
twisting with their tongues and traducing religion.
Had they said, 'We hear and obey',
and, 'Hear', and, 'Regard us',
it would have been better and more upright for them.
But God has cursed them for their unbelief,
and so they do not believe, except a few.

47. O you who have been given the Scripture,
believe in what We have sent down,
confirming what is with you,
before We obliterate faces and turn them on their backs
or curse them as We cursed the men of the Sabbath.
God's command is done.

48. God does not forgive others being associated with Him;
but He forgives anything short of that
to those whom He wishes.
Those who associate others with God
invent great sin.

49. Have you[s] not seen those who consider themselves pure?
No! God purifies those whom He wishes.
They will not be wronged one whit.

50. See[s] how they invent lies about God.
That is sufficient to be a flagrant sin.

51. Have you[s] not seen those who were given a portion of the Scripture
believing in false gods and idols[8]
and saying to those who do not believe,
'These are more rightly guided on the way than those who believe'?

---

[7] The contexts they have in the *Torah*. See 5:13 and 41.

[8] The meaning of *al-jibt*, another word from Ethiopic, is only clear in general terms. On *al-ṭāghūt* see the note on 2:256.

52. Those are the ones whom God has cursed.
    Those whom God curses
    – you^s will not find any helper for them.
53. Or do they have a share in the Sovereignty?
    If that were the case,
    they would not give the people one speck.
54. Or do they envy the people for what God has given them of his bounty?
    In the past We gave the family of Abraham
    the Scripture and the Wisdom
    and We gave them a mighty kingdom.
55. There were some of them who have believed in it
    and some of them who have turned [others] away from it.
    Jahannam is a sufficient blaze.
56. Those who do not believe in Our signs
    – We shall roast them in a fire:
    every time their skins are consumed
    We shall give them [new] skins in exchange,
    that they may taste the torment.
    God is Mighty and Wise.
57. Those who believe and do righteous deeds
    – We shall admit them to the gardens,
    through which rivers flow,
    in which they will remain for ever
    and in which they will have pure spouses,
    and We shall admit them to dense shade.
58. God commands you^p to pay back to their owners things entrusted to you
    and to judge fairly if you judge between the people.
    Excellent is the admonition which God gives you.
    God is Hearing and Observing.
59. O you who believe,
    obey God and obey the messenger and those of you who have authority.
    If you quarrel with one another about anything,
    refer it to God and the messenger,
    if you believe in God and the Last Day.
    That is better and fairer as a course.
60. Have you^s not seen those who say that they believe
    in what has been sent down to you
    and what has been sent down before you
    desiring to take their disputes to the Devil[9],
    when they have been ordered not to believe in him?

---

[9] Here *al-ṭāghūt* is masculine.

Satan wishes to lead them astray into distant error.

61. When it is said to them,
'Come to what God has sent down and to the messenger',
you^s see the hypocrites turning [people] away from you.

62. How [will it be] when misfortune smites them
because of what their right hands have forwarded
and then they come to you^s swearing, 'By God,
we only meant kindness and conciliation'?

63. These are the ones that God knows what is in their hearts.
Turn^s away from them and admonish them
and speak^s to them eloquently about themselves.

64. We did not send any messenger
except that he might be obeyed by God's permission.
Had they come to you^s when they wronged themselves
and sought God's forgiveness
and the messenger had sought forgiveness for them,
they would have found God relenting and compassionate.

65. No, by your^s Lord,
they will not believe
until they make you^s the judge concerning what is in dispute between them,
and then they will not find in their souls any difficulty
in what you^s decide but will submit readily.

66. If We had prescribed for them: 'Kill yourselves'
or 'Leave your dwellings',
only a few of them would have done it;
but had they done what they were admonished to do,
it would have been better and more strengthening for them.

67. In that case We would give them a mighty wage from Our presence

68. And guide them on a straight path.

69. Those who obey God and the messenger
– they are with those whom God has blessed:
the prophets and the loyal ones
and the witnesses and the righteous.
They are fine companions.

70. That is the bounty from God.
God is sufficient as one who knows.

71. O you who believe, take precautions.
Advance in companies or advance all together.

72. Among you are those who loiter
and who say if a misfortune smites you,
'God blessed me when I was not present with them.'

73. But if some bounty from God comes to you,

they would say,

as if there had never been any friendship between you and them,

'Would that I had been with them to achieve a great success.'

74. Let those who sell the life of this world for that of the next fight in the way of God.

Whoever fights in the way of God,

whether he is killed or is victorious,

We shall give him a great wage.

75. Why should you^p not fight in the way of God

and of the oppressed, men, women and children, who say,

'Our Lord, take us out of this settlement¹⁰

whose people are wrong-doers.

Appoint for us from Your presence a protector.

Appoint for us from Your presence a helper'?

76. Those who believe fight in the way of God.

Those who do not believe fight in the way of the Devil.¹¹

Fight the partisans of Satan.

Satan's trickery is weak.

77. Have you^s not seen those who were told,

'Restrain your hands,

perform prayer and pay the *zakāt*'?

But when fighting has been prescribed for them,

Lo, there is a party of them who fear the people

as they fear God, or even more so,

and say, 'Our Lord,

Why have You prescribed fighting for us?

Why have You not given us respite to a near term?'

Say^s, 'The enjoyment of this world is little;

the next world is better for those who fear God.

You^p will not be wronged one whit.'

78. Wherever you^p are, death will overtake you,

even if you^p are in well-built towers.

Yet if something good befalls them,

they say, 'This is from God';

but if something evil befalls them,

they say, 'This is through you^s.'

Say^s, 'Everything is from God.'

What is the matter with these people?

They scarcely understand any tiding.

---

¹⁰ Mecca.

¹¹ It would appear that the meaning of *al-ṭāghūt* here is similar to that in verse 60. The gender of the word here is not obvious from the text.

79. Whatever good befalls you^s, it is from God.
    Whatever evil befalls you^s, it is from yourself.
    We have sent you^s as a messenger to the people.
    God is sufficient witness.

80. Those who obey the messenger obey God.
    Those who turn away
    – We have not sent you^s as guardian over them.

81. They say, 'Obedience',
    but when they go forth from your^s presence,
    a party of them spend the night doing other than what you^s say.
    God records what they do in the night.
    Turn^s away from them and put your trust in God.
    God is sufficient trustee.

82. Do they not ponder on the Recitation?
    Had it been from any other than God,
    they would have found much contradiction in it.

83. If any matter comes to them,
    whether of safety or of fear,
    they spread it abroad;
    whereas, if they were to refer it to the messenger
    and to those who have authority among them,
    those among them able to investigate the matter would know [how to handle] it.
    But for God's bounty and mercy to you^p,
    you would have followed Satan,
    except for a few of you.

84. So fight^s in the way of God.
    You are charged only with yourself.
    Urge on the believers
    – it may be that God will restrain the might of those who do not believe.
    God is stronger in might and in ability to inflict punishment.

85. Those who make fair intercession will have a share of it;
    whilst those who make evil intercession will bear the responsibility for it.
    God has power over everything.

86. When you^p are greeted with a greeting,
    greet with a fairer greeting or return it.
    God takes account of everything.

87. God. There is no god but Him.
    He will indeed gather you^p to the Day of Resurrection,
    about which there is no doubt.
    Who gives truer tidings than God?

88. Why have you^p become two parties concerning the hypocrites,
    when God has turned them on their heads

because of what they amassed?
Do you^p wish to guide those whom God has sent astray?
Those whom God sends astray,
you^s will not find a way for them.

89. They would like you^p to disbelieve as they have disbelieved
and you to be equal [with them].
Do not take allies from among them
until they migrate in the way of God.

89a. If they turn their backs,
take^p them and kill them wherever you find them.
Take neither ally nor helper from among them,

90. Except in the case of those who reach a people with whom you^p have a covenant
or those who come to you too distressed at heart to fight you
or to fight their own people.
Had God wished, He could have given them power over you^p
and they would have fought you.
If they keep aloof from you and do not fight you and offer you peace,
God will not appoint any way for you against them.

91. You^p will find others who wish to be secure from you and from their own people,
but whenever they are returned to temptation,
they are turned on their heads in it.

91a. If they do not keep aloof from you
and do not offer you peace nor restrain their hands,
take them and kill them wherever you find them.
Against these We have given you a clear authority.

92. A believer should not kill a believer,
unless [it happens] by mistake.
Whoever kills a believer by mistake,
must set free a believing slave
and pay blood-money to the victim's family,
unless they remit it as alms.
If the victim is from a people who are hostile to you^p
but is [nevertheless] a believer,
[the recompense is] the freeing of a believing slave.
If he comes from a people with whom you have a covenant,
blood-money is to be handed over to his family
and there must be the freeing of a believing slave.
Whoever does not find [the means for that] must fast for two consecutive months,
a penance from God.
God is Knowing and Wise.

93. Whoever kills a believer wilfully,
his reward is Jahannam,

in which he will dwell for ever.
God will be angry with him
and will curse him
and prepare a terrible torment for him.

94. O you who believe,
when you journey in the way of God,
act with discrimination and do not say to someone who offers peace to you,
'You are not a believer,'
seeking chance gain in the life of this world.
There is abundant booty with God.
You were like that previously,
but God has been gracious to you.
So act with discrimination.
God is informed of what you do.

95. Those of the believers who sit still,
other than those who are suffering some injury,
are not on an equal footing with those who strive in God's way
with their possessions and their persons.
God gives preference in rank to those who strive
with their possessions and their persons,
[placing them] above those who sit still.
God has promised each the fairest reward,
but He bestows a mighty way on those who strive,
in preference to those who sit still:

96. Degrees of rank from Him and mercy and forgiveness.
God is Forgiving and Compassionate.

97. Those who wrong themselves and are taken by the angels
will be asked, 'In what circumstances were you?'
They will say, 'We were oppressed in the land.'
They will say, 'Was not God's land spacious enough for you to migrate in it?'
These – their abode is in Jahannam,
an evil journey's end,

98. Except in the case of the oppressed,
be they men, women, or children,
who cannot devise something and are not guided to a way.

99. These – it may be that God will pardon them.
God is Pardoning and Forgiving.

100. Those who migrate in the way of God
will find many a road to refuge and space in the land;
and those who leave their houses,
emigrating to God and his messenger
and are then overtaken by death,

their wages fall on God.
God is Forgiving and Merciful.

101. When you[p] travel in the land,
it is no sin for you to curtail your prayer,
if you fear that those who disbelieve may do you mischief.
Those who disbelieve are a manifest enemy for you.

102. When you[s] are amongst them
and perform prayer for them,
let a part of them stand with you,
and let them take their weapons.
When they have prostrated themselves,
let them fall to the rear,
and let another party who have not prayed come
and pray with you;
and let them take their guard and their weapons.
Those who do not believe
would long for you to neglect your arms and your baggage
and for themselves to turn on you in one move.
It is no sin for you[p] to lay aside your weapons
if rain impedes you or you are sick.
But be[p] on your guard.
God has prepared a humiliating torment for the unbelievers.

103. When you[p] have performed prayer,
remember God, standing or sitting or reclining on your sides.
If you feel secure, perform prayer.

103a. Prayer is a prescription at fixed times for the believers.

104. Do[p] not be weak in seeking out the people [who oppose you].
If you are suffering,
they suffer just as you do,
but you can hope for what they cannot hope for from God.
God is Knowing and Wise.

105. We have sent down to you[s] the Scripture with the truth,
for you to judge between the people
by that which God has shown you.
Do not be an advocate for the treacherous,

106. And seek[s] God's forgiveness.
God is Forgiving and Merciful.

107. And do[s] not argue on behalf of those who betray themselves.
God does not love those who are treacherous and sinful.

108. They hide themselves from men,
but they cannot hide themselves from God.
He is with them when they spend the night in speech that is displeasing [to Him].

God encompasses what they do.

109. There you are, those who have argued for them in the life of this world!
Who will argue with God on their behalf on the Day of Resurrection
or who will be a trustee for them?

110. Yet those who do evil or wrong themselves
and then seek God's forgiveness
will find God Forgiving and Merciful.

111. Those who amass a sin,
amass it only against themselves.
God is Knowing and Wise.

112. And those who amass an error or a sin
and then cast it on an innocent person
burden themselves with calumny and manifest sin.

113. But for God's bounty and mercy to you^s,
a party of them had intended to lead you astray.
But they will only lead themselves astray
and they will not harm you in any way.

113a. God has sent down to you^s the Scripture and the Wisdom,
and He has taught you^s what you did not know.
God's bounty to you^s is great.

114. There is no good in much of their secret talk,
except in the case of those who enjoin alms-giving
and reputable dealing or setting things right between the people.
Those who do that, seeking God's approval
– We shall give them a great wage.

115. Those who cause a split with the messenger
after [God's] guidance has become clear to them
and who follow [a way] other than that of the believers,
We shall consign them to what they have turned to
and roast them in Jahannam
– an evil journey's end.

116. God will not forgive anything being associated with Him.
He pardons what is less serious than that
for those whom He wishes.
Those who associate anything with God have wandered far astray.

117. Instead of Him they call only to females;[12]
and they call only to a rebellious devil,

118. Whom God cursed, when he said,
'I shall take for myself an appointed portion of Your servants,

119. And truly I shall lead them astray

---

[12] Female idols.

and fill them with desires and give them commands,
and they will cut off [their] animals' ears.
I shall command them
and they will alter God's creation.'
Those who choose Satan as a protector,
to the exclusion of God,
have suffered manifest loss.

120. He makes promises to them and stirs up desires in them;
but Satan promises them only delusion.

121. These – their refuge is Jahannam.
They will find no refuge from it.

122. But those who believe and do righteous deeds,
We shall admit them to gardens,
through which rivers flow,
in which they will remain for ever
– God's promise in truth.
And who can be more truthful in his utterances than God?

123. [These] are not wishes on your^s part or wishes of the people of the Scripture.
Those who do wrong will be requited for it
and will not find for themselves any protector or helper
apart from God.

124. Those who do good works, whether male or female,
and are believers
– they will enter the Garden
and will not be wronged one speck.

125. Who is better in religion than those who surrender their faces to God
and do good and follow the religion of Abraham as a true believer?
God chose Abraham as a friend.

126. To God belongs all that is in the heavens and on earth.
God encompasses everything.

127. They consult you^s about women.
Say, 'God will make a pronouncement concerning them;
and [there is] what has already been recited to you^p in the Scripture,
concerning female orphans
to whom you do not give what has been prescribed for them,
though you desire to marry them,
and concerning oppressed children
that you should act justly in the case of orphans.
Whatever good you do, God is aware of it.'

128. If a woman fears stubbornness or aversion from her husband,
it is no sin for the two of them
to reach an agreement between them.

Peace is good, but souls are oppressed by avarice.
If you do good and protect yourselves,
you will find that God is informed of what you do.

129. You^p will not be able to deal equitably between your wives,
even if you are eager to do so.
But do^p not turn [away from any of them] completely,
so that you leave her like one suspended.
If you put things right and are god-fearing
– you will find that God is Forgiving and Merciful.

130. If the two separate,
God will provide each with sufficiency
from His own abundance.
God is All-embracing and Wise.

131. To God belongs all that is in the heavens and on earth.

131a. We have charged those who have been given the Scripture before you^p
and [We have charged] you to fear God.
If you disbelieve,
[you should remember that] to God belongs all that is in the heavens and the earth.
God is All-sufficient and Laudable.

132. To God belongs all that is in the heavens and on earth.
God is sufficient trustee.

133. If He wishes, He can remove you, O people,
and bring others.
God has power to do that.

134. Those who desire the reward of this world
– the reward of both this world and the next is with God.
God is Hearing and Observing.

135. O you who believe,
be steadfast in justice, witnesses for God,
even if it is against your selves or your parents or your close relatives.
Whether the person be rich or poor,
God is closer to both.
Do not follow whim lest you turn.[13]
If you twist or turn away,
you will find that God is informed of what you do.

136. O you who believe,
believe in God and His messenger
and in the Scripture which He has sent down to His messenger
and in the Scripture which He has sent down previously.
Those who do not believe in God and His angels and His Scriptures and His

---

[13] Turn away from justice.

Messengers and the Last Day
have wandered far astray. *angels – articles of faith*

137. Those who believe, then disbelieve,
then believe, then disbelieve and then increase in unbelief,
God will not pardon them nor guide them to a way.

138. Give[s] the hypocrites the tidings that they will have a painful doom

139. – Those who choose the unbelievers as their protectors
to the exclusion of the believers.
Do they seek glory with them?
All glory belongs to God.

140. He has sent down to you[p] in the Scripture the message
that when you hear God's signs being disbelieved and derided
you should not sit down with them
until they engage in some other talk.
If you do that, you are like them.
God will gather the hypocrites and the unbelievers all together into Jahannam,

141. Those who wait [to see what will happen to] you[p]
and who say if a victory comes to you from God,
'Were we not with you?'
But if the unbelievers get a share,
they say, 'Did we not have mastery in your affairs
and defend you from the believers?'
God will judge between you on the Day of Resurrection;
and God will not grant to the unbelievers a way over the believers.

142. The hypocrites try to deceive God
– but He deceives them.
When they stand for prayer,
they do so lazily, making a show before the people
and remembering God only a little,

143. Wavering between this [and that],
neither to these nor to those.
Those whom God leads astray,
you[s] will not find a way for them.

144. O you who believe,
do not choose the unbelievers as allies
to the exclusion of the believers.
Do you want to give God a clear authority against you?

145. The hypocrites will be in the lowest reach of the Fire.
You[s] will find no helper for them,

146. Except in the case of those who repent and make good
and hold fast to God and devote their religion solely to God.
Those are with the believers.

God will give the believers a great wage.

147. What would God do with punishing you[p]
if you are grateful and believe?
God is Thankful and Knowing.

148. God does not like the public utterance of foul words
– except by someone who has been wronged.
God is Hearing and Knowing.

149. If you[p] do good openly or in secret or pardon an evil
– God is Pardoning and Powerful.

150. Those who do not believe in God and His messengers,
and wish to make a distinction between God and His messengers
and say, 'We believe in part and disbelieve in part',
wishing to choose a way between [this and] that –

151. Those are in truth the unbelievers.
We have prepared for the unbelievers a humiliating torment.

152. But those who believe in God and His messengers
and make no distinction between any of them
– God will give them their wages.
God is Forgiving and Merciful.

153. The people of the Scripture ask you[s]
to bring down a Scripture from heaven for them.

153a. In the past they asked Moses for something greater than that
when they said, 'Show us God plainly.'
A thunderbolt took them because of their wrong-doing.
Then they chose the calf after the clear proofs had come to them.
Yet We forgave them that,
and gave Moses a manifest authority.

154. We raised the mountain over them
in return for their compact
and We told them, 'Enter the gate in prostration';
and We told them, 'Do not transgress the Sabbath',
and We took from them a firm covenant.

155. Because they broke their covenant
and did not believe in God's signs
and killed the prophets without right
and said, 'Our hearts are hardened'

155a. – No, God has set a seal upon them
because of their unbelief,
and they do not believe, except for a few.

156. Because they disbelieved and uttered a great calumny against Mary,

157. And because they said, 'We killed *al-Masīḥ*,
Jesus, the son of Mary, the messenger of God

157a. – They did not kill him nor crucify him,
but it was made to seem so to them.[14]
Those who disagree about him[15] are in doubt about it.[15]
They have no knowledge of it[15]
and only follow conjecture.
Certainly, they did not kill him.

158. No. God raised him to Himself.
God is Mighty and Wise.

159. There is not one of the people of the Scripture
but will truly believe before his death.
On the Day of Resurrection he will be a witness against them.

160. Because of wrong-doing on the part of the Jews,
We have forbidden them good things which had been lawful to them;
and because of their turning many from God's way

161. And their taking usury when they were forbidden to take it,
and their devouring the property of the people in vanity,
We have prepared for those of them who do not believe a painful torment.

162. But those of them who are firm in knowledge
and the believers
believe in what has been sent down to you[s]
and what was sent down before you,
and those performing prayer and paying *zakāt*
and believing in God and the Last Day.
These – We shall give them a mighty wage.

163. We have made revelations to you[s],
as We made them to Noah and the prophets after him,
and as We made them to Abraham and Ishmael
and Isaac and Jacob and the tribes
and Jesus and Job and Jonah
and Aaron and Solomon;
and We gave David psalms;[16]

164. And messengers whom We have told you[s] about before,
and messengers whom We have not told you[s] about;
and God spoke to Moses directly;

165. Messengers bringing good news and bringing warnings
that the people might have no argument against God after the messengers.
God is Mighty and Wise.

166. But God [himself] bears witness

---

[14] Bell points out that this phrase parallels the Gnostic Christian belief that only a *Simulacrum* of Jesus was crucified.

[15] These pronouns may be translated as 'him' or 'it'.

[16] Or, possibly, 'scripture'. The Arabic is indefinite.

about what He has sent down to you[s]
– He has sent it down with His knowledge –
and the angels testify,
though God is sufficient witness.

167. Those who disbelieve and who turn [men] from God's way
– they have wandered far astray.

168. Those who disbelieve and do wrong,
God is not going to forgive them
nor will He guide them to any road,

169. Except the road of Jahannam,
in which they will remain forever.
That is easy for God.

170. O people, the messenger has brought you the truth from your Lord.
So believe.
[That is] better for you.
If you disbelieve
– to God belongs what is in the heavens and the earth.
God is Knowing and Wise.

171. O People of the Scripture,
do not go beyond the bounds in your religion.
Do not say anything but the truth about God.
al-Masīḥ, Jesus, the son of Mary, is truly God's messenger,
and His word, which He cast into Mary,
and a spirit from Him.
So believe in God and His messengers
and do not say, 'Three'.
Desist. [That is] better for you.
God is one God.
Glory be to Him – that He should have a son.
To Him belongs all that is in the heavens and on earth.
God is sufficient trustee.

172. *al-Masīḥ* does not disdain to be a servant to God,
nor do the angels who are stationed near Him.
Those who disdain His service and are haughty
– He will round them up to Himself all together.

173. As for those who believe and do righteous deeds,
He will pay them their wages in full
and give them extra, from His bounty;
and as for those who are disdainful and haughty,
He will inflict on them a painful torment.
They will not find a protector or helper for themselves,
apart from God.

174. O people, a proof has come to you from your Lord.
We have sent down to you a clear light.
175. As for those who believe in God and hold fast to Him,
He will admit them to mercy from Him and to bounty,
and He will guide them to Himself along a straight road.
176. They ask you[s] for a pronouncement.
Say, 'God pronounces for you concerning distant kin:
if a man perishes and has no children,
but he has a sister,
she receives half of what he leaves.
He inherits from her if she has no children.
If there are two sisters,
they get two-thirds of what he leaves.
If there are both brothers and sisters,
the male gets a share equivalent to the share of two [sisters].
God makes things clear for you so that you do not err.
God is Aware of everything.'

Sūra 5

The *sūra* is an amalgam of passages from different times in the Medinan period. Some of these passages appear to come from relatively early in the period: *e.g.* verse 5 and probably verse 3 are unlikely to date from after the time of Muḥammad's break with the Jews (on which see verse 57 *ff.*); whilst others, such as 2a, probably date from the time of al-Ḥudaybiya (628 AD). Further, Bell is probably right in suggesting that the last sentence of verse 2 and its expansion in verse 95 date from after the conquest of Mecca; whilst verse 3b is considered by very many Muslims to be the last verse of the Qur'ān to have been revealed and is traditionally linked with Muḥammad's 'Farewell Pilgrimage' to Mecca in March 632 AD. Even if we consider these last two datings to be doubtful, the present form of the *sūra* must be relatively late. The sequence of passages is complex and difficult to follow, so much so that Bell divides it into over fifty separate pieces. The rapidity of the changes of subject is not dissimilar from that in *Sūra* 9, which may have been put together at more or less the same time, but the mixture of types of material – regulatory mixed with polemic and a leavening of narrative – is akin to that in *Sūra* 2 and, to a lesser extent, that in *Sūra* 4.

The *sūra* is particularly concerned with regulations for the believers, which are set out in various forms: injunctions, affirmations, prohibitions, exceptions, questions and answers, and encouragement to Muḥammad. The polemic is for the most part directed at the Jews and the Christians. The stance towards them varies from tolerance (*e.g.* verses 5 and 69) to condemnation (*e.g.* verse 13: Jews; verses 72–73: Christians).

The Table

In the name of the Merciful and Compassionate God

1.   O you who believe, fulfil your undertakings.
1a.   Permitted to you[P] [as food] is the beast of the herds,
      except those which are about to be recited to you
      – and you must not deem game permissible
      when you are in the pilgrim state.
      God decrees what He wills.
2.   O you who believe, do not profane God's waymarks
      nor the sacred month[1] nor offerings nor garlands

---

[1] This is traditionally understood to mean any of the four sacred months. On these see the note on 9:2. Another interpretation is that it means the season of the *Ḥajj*.

nor those repairing to the Sacred House[2],
seeking bounty and approval from their Lord.
When you leave the pilgrim state, you may hunt.

2a. Let not [your] hatred for a people [that has arisen]
because they barred you from the Sacred Mosque[2]
incite you to commit aggression.
Help one another to righteousness and piety;
but do not help one another to sin and transgression.
Fear God, for God is severe in punishment.

3. Forbidden to you[p] are:
carrion; blood; the flesh of the pig;
anything on which [the name of] any other than God has been invoked;
the strangled; the beaten; the fallen; the gored;
what has been devoured by beasts of prey
– unless you manage to slaughter [it];
whatever has been sacrificed to idols.[3]

3a. Also [it is forbidden] for you divide out by means of divining arrows.[4]
That is an abomination for you all.

3b. To-day those who are unbelievers have despaired of your[p] religion.
Do not fear them. Fear Me.

3c. To-day I have perfected your[p] religion for you
and completed My blessing for you
and have approved Submission[5] as a religion for you.

3d. Those who are forced to sin in a state of hunger,
without premeditation
– God is Forgiving, Merciful.

4. They ask you[s] what is permitted to them.
Say, 'Permitted to you[p] are [all] good things;
and those hunting beasts that you teach,
training them, teaching them what God has taught you
– eat what they catch for you,
mentioning God's name over it
and fearing God.
God is swift to the reckoning.'

5. Permitted to you to-day are [all] good things.
The food of those who have been given the Scripture is lawful for you,
and yours for them.

---

[2] The Ka'ba at Mecca.

[3] For a detailed list of Jewish prohibitions, see *Mishnah, Hullin*, ch. 3 (pp. 517–9 in Danby's translation).

[4] This is a term for a set of arrows used for divination. See also verse 90.

[5] The Arabic is *al-Islām*.

5a.   [Permitted to you in marriage]
     are the chaste women of the believers
     and the chaste women of those who have been given the Scripture before you,
     if you give them their wages[6],
     and if you live with them in wedlock,
     not in some loose arrangement
     or taking them as 'companions'.

5b.   Those who do not believe in the faith,
     their work is in vain,
     and they will be among the losers in the next world.

6.   O you who believe,
     when you rise to pray,
     wash your faces and your hands up to the elbows,
     and wipe your heads and your feet up to the ankles.

6a.   If you are polluted, purify yourselves.
     If you are sick or on a journey
     or one of you comes from the closet
     or if you have had contact with women
     and you do not find water,
     have recourse to clean soil
     and wipe your faces and your hands with it.

6b.   God does not wish to place any difficulty on you,
     but He wishes to make you pure and to complete His blessing on you
     so that you may be grateful.

7.   Remember[p] God's blessing on you
     and the covenant that He took from you,
     when you said, 'We hear and we obey.'
     Fear God.
     God knows [the thoughts] contained in [men's] breasts.

8.   O you who believe,
     be steadfast for God, bearing witness with equity.
     Let not the hatred of any people induce you to act unjustly.
     Act justly
     – that is nearer to fear of God –
     and fear God.
     God is informed of what you do.

9.   God has promised those who believe and do righteous deeds:
     they will have forgiveness and a great reward.

10.   Those who do not believe and deny the truth of Our signs
     – those are the companions of Hell.

---

[6] Dowries.

11. O you who believe,
remember God's blessing to you
when a people intended to stretch their hands towards you.
He restrained their hands from you.
So fear God.
Let the believers put their trust in God.

12. In the past God took a covenant from the Children of Israel.
We raised among them twelve chieftains,
and God said, 'I am with you.
If you perform prayer and pay the *zakāt*,
and believe in My messengers and support them
and make a fair loan to God,
I shall redeem your sins for you,
and I shall cause you to enter gardens
through which rivers flow.
Those of you who do not believe after that
will stray from the level road.'

13. Because of their breaking their covenant,
We cursed them and made their hearts hard.
They change words from their places;[7]
and they have forgotten a part of that by which they were reminded.
You[s] will continue to observe treachery from them
– except for a few of them.
But pardon[s] them and forgive.
God loves those who do good.

14. We also took a covenant from those who say, 'We are Christians';
but they have forgotten a part of that by which they were reminded.
So We have stirred up enmity and hatred among them till the Day of Resurrection,
[when] God will tell them about the things that they have done.

15. O people of the Scripture,
Our Messenger has come to you,
making clear to you much of the Scripture
that you have been concealing
and erasing much.
A light and a clear Scripture have come to you from God,

16. By which God guides those who seek His approval to paths of peace.
He brings them from the darkness into the light by His permission
and guides them to a straight path.

17. Unbelievers are those who say,
'God is *al-Masīḥ*, the son of Mary.'

---

[7] The contexts they have in the *Torah*.

Say, 'Who can exert control over God in any way
if He wishes to destroy *al-Masīḥ*, the son of Mary,
and his mother and all who are on earth?'
God has sovereignty over the heavens and the earth and what is between them.
He creates what He wishes.
God has power over everything.

18. The Jews and the Christians say,
'We are the children of God, the ones He loves.'
Say, 'Then why does He punish you for your sins?
No. You are mortals, of those He has created.
He forgives those whom He wishes
and He punishes those whom He wishes.
God has sovereignty over the heavens and the earth and what is between them.
To Him is the journeying.'

19. O people of the Scripture,
Our messenger has come to you,
making things clear to you after an interval between messengers,
so that you cannot say,
'No bearer of good tidings or warner has come to us.'
A bearer of good tidings and a warner has come to you.
God has power over everything.

20. And [recall] when Moses said to his people,
'O my people,
remember the blessings of God to you
when He placed prophets amongst you
and made you kings
and gave you what He had not given to any one [else] among created beings.

21. O my people,
enter the holy land which God has prescribed for you.
Do not turn your backs, lest you return as losers.'

22. They said, 'Moses, there is in it a people who are men of might.
We shall not enter it until they leave it.
If they leave it, we shall enter.'

23. Then two men whom God had blessed,
from among those who feared [God],
said, 'Go through the gate into their presence.
If you enter through it, you will be victorious.
Put your trust [in God] if you are believers.'

24. They said, 'Moses, we shall never enter it[8]
as long as they are in it.

---

[8] The holy land.

Go[s] with your Lord and the two of you fight [them].
We shall sit here.'

25. He said, 'My Lord, I control only my brother and myself.
Make a separation between us and the people who are reprobates.'

26. HE said, 'It[8] shall be forbidden to them for forty years
while they wander in the land;
and do not grieve for the people who are reprobates.'

27. And recite[s] to them in truth
the tale of the two sons of Adam,[9]
when they offered sacrifices,
and it was accepted from one of them and not from the other.
[The latter] said, 'I shall kill you.'
[His brother] replied, 'God accepts
only from those who are god-fearing.

28. If you stretch out your hand to me to kill me,
I shall not stretch out my hand to kill you.
I fear God, Lord of created beings.

29. I wish you to take on both your sin and my sin
and become one of the companions of the Fire.
That is the recompense of evil-doers.'

30. Then his soul prompted him to kill his brother;
so he killed him, and became one of the losers.

31. Then God sent a crow, which scratched into the earth
to show him how he might hide the corpse of his brother.
He said, 'Woe on me.
Am I unable to be like this crow,
and hide the corpse of my brother?'
And he became one of the repentant.

32. Because of that, We have prescribed for the Children of Israel
that whoever kills a soul,
other than in retaliation for [another] soul
or for corruption in the land,
will be as if he had killed all the people;
and whoever saves one
will be as if he had saved the life of all the people.

32a. Our messengers have come to them in the past with the clear proofs;
but even after that many of them commit excesses in the land.

33. The recompense of those who wage war against God and His messenger
and who wreak mischief in the land
is that they will be slaughtered or crucified

---

[9] Cain and Abel are not named explicitly.

or have their hands and feet cut off on alternate sides
or will be banished from the land.
That is shame for them in this world,
and in the next world they will have a grievous punishment

34. – But this will not be the case with those who repent before you have power
     over them.
     Know[p] that God is Forgiving and Compassionate.

35. O you who believe,
     fear God and seek the means to approach Him
     and strive in His way so that you may prosper.

36. Those who do not believe:
     even if they had all that is on earth and as much again
     to ransom themselves from the punishment of the Day of Resurrection,
     it would not be accepted from them.
     They will have a painful punishment.

37. They will wish to leave the Fire,
     but they will not leave it.
     They will have a lasting torment.

38. The thief, male and female:
     cut off their hands as a recompense for what they have acquired
     – an exemplary punishment from God.
     God is Mighty and Wise.

39. But whoever repents after his wrong-doing and makes amends,
     God relents towards him.
     God is Forgiving and Merciful.

40. Do you[s] not know that God has sovereignty over the heavens and the earth?
     He punishes those whom He wishes
     and He forgives those whom He wishes.
     God has power over everything.

41. O messenger,
     let not those who vie with one another in unbelief grieve you.
     [They are] from those who say with their mouths, 'We believe',
     but their hearts do not believe,
     and from the Jews
     – listeners to falsehood,
     listeners to another people who have not come to you[s],
     moving words from their places,[10] saying,
     'If you[p] are given this, take it;
     if you are not given it, beware.'

41a. Those whom God wishes to test,

---

[10] See verse 13 and note.

you[s] have nothing for them from God.
Those are the ones whose hearts God does not wish to purify.
They will have shame in this world,
and they will have a severe punishment in the next

42. – Listeners to falsehood, living on illegal gain.
If they come to you[s],
[you[s] may] judge between them or turn away from them;
if you turn from them, they will do you no harm;
but if you pass judgement,
judge between them with equity.
God loves those who act fairly.

43. How do they make you[s] judge when they have the *Torah*,
in which is God's judgement?
But even after that they turn away.
Those are not believers.

44. We revealed the *Torah*,
in which there is guidance and light,
by which the prophets who had surrendered [themselves to God] gave
    judgement to the Jews;
as did the rabbis and the learned men
by that portion of God's Scripture they were asked to remember
and to which they were witness.
Do[p] not fear the people.
Fear Me.
Do not sell My signs for a paltry price.
Those who do not judge by what God has sent down
– those are the ungrateful.

45. We prescribed for them in it:[11]
a soul for a soul;
an eye for an eye;
a nose for a nose;
an ear for an ear;
a tooth for a tooth;
and wounds [carry] retaliation.
But whoever remits it as alms-giving,
it will be an expiation for him.
Those who do not judge by what God has sent down
– those are the wrong-doers.

46. We caused Jesus, the son of Mary, to follow in their footsteps,

---

[11] *Cf.* Exodus 21:24–27; Leviticus 24:20–21; Deuteronomy 19:21. Even earlier is the Code of Hammurabi, law 196.

confirming that which [had been revealed] before it in the *Torah*,
and We bestowed on him the *Gospel* in which is guidance and light
– confirming that which [had been revealed] before it in the *Torah*
– a guidance and admonition to those who fear God.

47. Let the people of the *Gospel* judge by what God has sent down in it.
Those who do not judge by what God has sent down
– those are the reprobates.

48. We have sent down to you^s the Scripture in truth,
confirming all the Scripture [that had been revealed] before it,
and a watcher over it.
So judge^s between them by what God has sent down;
and do not follow their whims
away from the Truth that has come down to you^s.

48a. To each one of you We have assigned a path and a way of action.
Had God willed,
He could have made you^p one community;
but [He has not done so]
that He may try you^p in what has come to you.
So be foremost in good works.
You will all return to God,
and He will inform you concerning that about which you differ.

49. So judge^s between them by what God has sent down,
and do not follow their whims;
but beware of them
lest they tempt you away from some of what God has sent down to you.
And if they turn away [from you],
know that God wishes to smite them for some of their sins.
Many of mankind are reprobates.

50. Is it the judgement of the age of ignorance that they are seeking?
Who is better than God in judgement
for a people who are sure?

51. O you who believe,
do not take the Jews and Christians as friends.
They are friends of each other.
Whoever of you makes them his friends is one of them.
God does not guide the people who do wrong.

52. You^s see those in whose hearts is sickness
running amongst them and saying,
'We fear lest a turn of fortune smite us.'
Perhaps God will send victory or some command from Him,
and they will come to regret what they kept secret among themselves,

53. And those who believe will say,

'Are these the ones who swore their most binding oaths
that they were with you[p]?
Their works have failed,
and they have become losers.'

54. O you who believe,
[in the case of] those of you who turn away from their religion,
God will bring [in their stead] a people who love Him and whom He loves,
humble towards the believers,
mighty towards the unbelievers,
striving in the way of God,
not fearing the blame of any blamer.
That is the bounty of God which He gives to those whom He wishes.
God is Embracing and Knowing.

55. Your[p] protector is God –
and His messenger,
and those who believe:
those who perform prayer and pay the *zakāt* and bow down.

56. Those who take as friends God and His messenger and those who believe
– the party of God are the victors.

57. O you who believe,
do not take as friends
those who take your religion in mockery and as a sport,
whether they are from the ones who were given the Scripture before you
or from the unbelievers.
Fear God if you are believers.

58. When you give the call to prayer,
they take it in mockery and as a sport.
That is because they are a people who do not understand.

59. Say, 'O people of the Scripture,
do you blame us
for any reason other than we believe in God
and what has been sent down to us
and what has been sent down previously
and because most of you are reprobates?'

60. Say, 'Shall I tell you of [someone] worse than that for retribution with God?
[It is] the one whom God has cursed and with whom He is angry.
He makes some of them baboons
and some of them pigs
and some the servants of idols.[12]
These are in a worse position

---

[12] See the note on 2:256.

and further astray from the level road.'

61. When they come to you[P], they say, 'We believe',
though they have entered in unbelief and will leave in it.
God is well aware of what they have been hiding.

62. You[s] see many of them
racing into sin and transgression
and into living on illegal gain.
What they have been doing is truly evil.

63. Why do not the rabbis and learned men
forbid them to speak sin and to live on illegal gain?
What they have been doing is truly evil.

64. The Jews say, 'God's hand is fettered.'
[It is] their hands [that] are fettered,
and they are cursed for what they have said.
No. His hands are spread out.
He spends how He wishes.

64a. What has been sent down to you[s] from your Lord
will indeed increase many of them in insolence and unbelief.
We have cast among them enmity and hatred,
till the Day of Resurrection.
Whenever they light a fire for war,
God will extinguish it.
They wreak mischief in the land,
and God does not love those who do mischief.

65. Had the people of the Scripture believed and been god-fearing,
We would have forgiven them their sins
and caused them to enter the gardens of bliss.

66. Had they observed the *Torah* and the *Gospel*
and what was sent down to them from their Lord,
they would have eaten [what was] above them and [what was] below their feet.
Among them there is a moderate community,
but many of them are evil in what they do.

67. O messenger,
proclaim what has been sent down to you from your Lord.
If you do not do that,
you are not delivering His message.
God will protect you from the people.
God does not guide the people who do not believe.

68. Say, 'O people of the Scripture,
you have no base until you observe the *Torah* and the *Gospel*
and what has been sent down to you from your Lord.'
And what has been sent down from your Lord to you[s]

will increase the insolence and unbelief of many of them.
But do not grieve for the people who are unbelievers.

69. Those who believe and those who are Jews
and the Ṣābi'ūn[13] and the Christians
– those who believe in God and the Last Day and act righteously
– no fear will be upon them nor will they grieve.

70. In times past We took a covenant from the Children of Israel
and We sent messengers to them.
Whenever a messenger came to them
with what their souls did not desire,
a number they denied,
a number they killed.

71. They thought that there would be no trial [because of that],
and so they were blind and deaf.
Then God relented towards them,
but [yet again] many of them were blind and deaf.
But God is observer of what they do.

72. Unbelievers are those who say,
'God is *al-Masīḥ*, the son of Mary.'
The *Masīḥ* said, 'Children of Israel,
serve God, my Lord and your Lord.'
Those who associate others with God will be banned by God from the Garden.
The Fire will be their abode.
Evil-doers will have no helpers.

73. Unbelievers are those who say,
'God is the third of the three.'
There is no god but One God.
If they do not desist from what they are saying,
the unbelievers amongst them will be touched by a painful torment.

74. Will they not turn to God and seek His forgiveness?
God is Forgiving and Merciful.

75. The *Masīḥ*, the son of Mary, was only a messenger,
before whom [other] messengers had passed away,
and his mother was an honest woman.
Both used to eat the food [of this world].
See how We make the signs clear for them
– then see how they are involved in lies.

76. Say, 'Do you worship,
to the exclusion of God,
what has the ability neither to harm you nor to help you?

---

[13] See the note on 2:62.

God is the Hearer and the Knower.'

77.	Say, 'O people of the Scripture,
	do not stress anything but the truth in your religion.
	Do not follow the whims of a people
	who strayed previously and led many astray
	and strayed from the level path.'

78.	Those of the Children of Israel who have not believed
	have been cursed by the tongue of David and of Jesus, the son of Mary.
	That was because they rebelled and used to transgress.

79.	They did not restrain one another from disreputable conduct.
	Evil was what they used to do.

80.	You^s see many of them making friends of those who do not believe.
	Evil [for them] is what they have sent on before for themselves,
	because God is incensed with them
	and they will remain for ever in torment.

81.	Had they believed in God and the Prophet
	and what has been sent down to him,
	they would not have taken them as friends,
	but many of them are reprobates.

82.	You^s will certainly find that the people most hostile to those who believe
	are the Jews and those who associate others with God;
	and you will find that those of them who are most friendly to those who believe
	are those who say, 'We are Christians.'
	This is because amongst them there are priests and monks
	and because they are not proud.

83.	When they hear what has been sent down to the messenger,
	you can see their eyes overflow with tears
	because of the truth they recognize.
	They say, 'Our Lord, we believe.
	Write us down among the witnesses.

84.	How should we not believe in God and the truth that has come to us?
	and how should we not desire our Lord to cause us to enter
	with the people who are righteous?'

85.	God will reward them for what they say
	with gardens, through which rivers flow,
	in which they will remain for ever.
	That is the reward of those who do good.

86.	But those who do not believe and deny Our signs,
	those are the companions of the Fire.

87.	O you who believe,
	do not forbid the good things
	which God has made lawful for you,

and do not transgress,

– God does not love transgressors –

88. Eat what God has provided you as allowable and good,

and fear God,

in whom you are believers.

89. God will not take you to task for making inadvertent errors in your oaths,

but He will take you to task for agreements you have made through oaths.

Expiation [for a broken oath] is the feeding of ten destitute people

with the average of the food with which you feed your families

or the clothing of them or the freeing of a slave.

Whoever does not find [the means for that]

should fast for three days.

That is the expiation of your oaths when you have sworn[14]

– but keep your oaths.

Thus God makes His signs clear to you,

so that you may be thankful.

90. O you who believe,

wine, *maysir*,[15] idols and divining arrows

are an abomination that is of the work of Satan.

Avoid it, so that you may prosper.

91. Satan only desires to cause enmity and hatred among you

through wine and *maysir*

and to turn you from remembrance of God and from prayer.

Are you going to desist?

92. Obey God and obey the messenger and beware!

If you turn away,

know that the only duty of Our messenger is the clear conveyance [of Our message].

93. There is no sin for those who believe and do righteous deeds

concerning what they have eaten,

if they are god-fearing and believe and do righteous deeds

and then are god-fearing and believe

and then are god-fearing and do good.

God loves those who do good.

94. O you who believe,

God will indeed test you

in [the matter of] some of the game taken by your hands and your spears,

that God may know who fears Him in the Invisible.

Those who transgress after this will have a painful punishment.

---

[14] *i.e.* sworn an oath and broken it.

[15] *Maysir* was a form of gambling, which had a bad name for involving cheating and drunkenness, though its intent was charitable. See the Commentary.

95. O you who believe,
do not kill game while you are in the sacred state.
If any of you kill [such game] intentionally,
[there must be] recompense
– the like of what he has killed from [his] livestock,
as two men of justice from you decide,
an offering to reach the Ka'ba or expiation:
food for the destitute or the equivalent of that in fasting,
that he may taste the mischief of his action.
God forgives what has happened in the past;
but God will take vengeance on those who repeat [the offence].
God is Mighty and a Wielder of vengeance.

96. Permitted to you[p] are fishing at sea and the food obtained from it,
a provision for you and for travellers;
but forbidden to you is hunting on land
whilst you are in the sacred state.
And fear God, to whom you will be rounded up.

97. God has appointed the Ka'ba,
the Sacred House,[16]
as something that stands for mankind,
together with the sacred months and offerings and garlands.
That is so that you may know
that God knows all that is in the heavens and all that is on earth
and that God is aware of everything.

98. Know that God is severe in punishment,
but that God is [also] Forgiving and Compassionate.

99. The only duty of the messenger is to convey [the message].
God knows what you reveal and what you hide.

100. Say, 'Evil and good are not equal,
though the abundance of the evil may amaze you.'
O you who are possessed of understanding,
fear God, so that you may succeed.

101. O you who believe,
do not ask about things which,
if they are revealed to you,
will trouble you.
Yet if you do ask about them
when the Recitation is being sent down
they will be revealed to you.
God forgives that.

---

[16] See verse 2.

God is Forgiving and Prudent.

102. A people before you asked about them,
but then did not believe in them.

103. God has not appointed any *bahīra* or *sā'iba* or *waṣīla* or *ḥāmī*;[17]
but those who do not believe forge lies against God
– most of them do not understand.

104. When it is said to them,
'Come to what God has sent down and to the messenger',
they say, 'What we found our forefathers practising is enough for us.'
Even if their forefathers knew nothing and were not guided aright?

105. O you who believe, take care of your souls.
Those who have gone astray cannot harm you
if you are guided aright.
You will all return to God,
and He will tell you what you were doing.

106. O you who believe, [let there be] witnessing between you
when death comes to one of you
at the time when bequests are made:
two witnesses, just men from among you,
or two persons from another people
if you are travelling in the land and the misfortune of death befalls you.
You should hold them back after prayer,
and they should swear by God,
If you have doubts,
'We shall not sell it for a price,
even though it were a near relative;
nor shall we hide the testimony of God,[18]
for in that case we should be among the sinners.'

107. But if by chance it is discovered that the two of them merit [the suspicion of] sin,
let two others stand in their place,
the two nearest from those from whom he has demanded his right,
and let them swear by God,
'Our testimony is truer than theirs,
and we have not transgressed,
for in that case we should be among the wrong-doers.'

108. That [makes it] easier for them to give testimony truly
or to be afraid that [other] oaths will be given to a contrary view after their oaths.
Fear God and hear.
God does not guide the people who are reprobates.

---

[17] Names for types of beasts sacrificed at the Ka'ba.
[18] The testimony required by God.

109. On the day when God gathers the messengers and says,
     'What answer were you given?'
     they will say, 'We have no knowledge.
     You are the one who knows fully the things that are hidden.'
110. When God says, 'Jesus, son of Mary,
     remember My blessing to you and to your mother,
     when I strengthened you with the Holy Spirit,
     [enabling you to] speak to the people both in the cradle and in maturity;
     and when I taught you the Scripture and the Wisdom
     and the *Torah* and the *Gospel*;
     and when you were creating from clay
     [shapes] like those of birds,[19]
     by My permission,
     and blowing into them
     and they became birds,
     by My permission;
     and you were curing the blind and the leper,
     by My permission;
     and you were bringing forth the dead,
     by My permission;
     and when I restrained the Children of Israel from you,
     when you came to them with the clear proofs,
     and those of them who did not believe said,
     "This is merely persuasive magic";
111. And when I inspired the Disciples, saying,
     "Believe in Me and in My messenger",
     They said, "We believe; witness that we submit".'
112. And when the Disciples said,
     'Jesus, son of Mary,
     is your Lord able to send a table down to us from heaven?'
112a. He said, 'Fear God, if you are believers.'
113. They said, 'We wish to eat from it,
     and for our hearts to be at rest,
     and [we wish] to know that you have spoken the truth to us
     and to be witnesses to that.'
114. Jesus, the son of Mary, said, 'O God, our Lord,
     send a table down to us from heaven
     to be a festival for us,
     the first of us and the last of us,
     and to be a sign from You.

---

[19] See note on 3:49.

Give us sustenance.
You are the best of providers.'
115. God said, 'I shall send it down to you.
Those of you who do not believe afterwards,
I shall punish them with a punishment
which I do not inflict on any [other] created beings.'
116. And [recall] when God said, 'Jesus, son of Mary,
did you say to the people,
"Take me and my mother as gods
to the exclusion of God"?'
He said, 'Glory be to You.
It is not for me to say what I have no right to.
If I said it, You know that.
You know what is in my soul.
You are the one who knows fully the things that are hidden.
117. I said to them only what You ordered me to say,
"Serve God, my Lord and your Lord".
I was a witness over them as long as I was among them.
When You took me,
it was You who were the watcher over them.
You are witness over everything.
118. If you punish them,
they are Your servants;
if you forgive them
– You are the Mighty and the Wise.'
119. God says, 'This is the day when the truthful will benefit from their truthfulness.
They will have Gardens through which rivers flow,
in which they will remain for ever.
God will be pleased with them and they with Him.
That is the great triumph.'
120. To God belongs the sovereignty of the heavens and the earth and what is in them.
He has power over everything.

Sūra 6

Most Muslim commentators class this as a very late Meccan *sūra*, with some Medinan verses added to it. In general, this seems to be an accurate assessment, though it is doubtful whether the verses traditionally thought to be Medinan (20, 23, 91, 93, 114, 141, 151–53) come from that period. However, there are other verses that are almost certainly Medinan (e.g. 79, 145–46, 161) or contain Medinan modifications. Such revisions reflect the shift in Muḥammad's doctrinal opponents from the idolaters of Mecca to the Jews of Medina. The *sūra* is notable for its strong polemical emphasis, much of it addressed to or through Muḥammad. There is a brief hymn to God at the beginning of the *sūra* (1–3), but after that polemic begins and carries through to the end of the *sūra* with only minor interludes of other material (e.g. 59–61, 95–99) to provide contrast. Even the section of narrative (74–87/8) is relatively short. Much of the polemic is condemnation of the association of others with God, though among other topics is the very difficult passage (138–146) on livestock and their consumption, from which the *sūra* takes its name.

Livestock

In the name of the Merciful and Compassionate God

1. Praise belongs to God,
    who has created the heavens and the earth
    and made darkness and light.
    Yet those who do not believe ascribe equals to their Lord.
2. [It is] He who has created you[P] from clay and then fixed a term
    – and [it is] a term that is stated with Him.
    Yet you[P] still doubt.
3. He is God in the heavens and the earth.
    He knows what you keep secret and what you make public;
    and He knows what you amass.
4. None of their Lord's signs comes to them
    without them turning away from it.
5. They denied the truth when it came to them;
    but news of what they used to scorn will come to them.
6. Have they not seen how many generations We have destroyed before them,
    whom We had established in the land
    to an extent that We have not established you[P];
    and on whom We sent down the sky in torrents

and made the rivers flow beneath them;
and whom We destroyed because of their sins
and created another generation after them?

7. Had We sent down to you[s] a Scripture on parchment
and they could have felt it with their hands,
those who disbelieve would have said,
'This is merely persuasive magic.'

8. They say, 'Why has an angel not been sent down to him?'
Had We sent down an angel,
the matter would have been determined;
and then they would have no respite.

9. Had We made him an angel,
We would have made him a man[1]
and have confused for them what they are confusing.

10. Scorn has been shown to messengers before you[s],
and what they scorned engulfed those of them who mocked.

11. Say, 'Travel[p] in the land
and see how was the consequence for those who denied the truth.'

12. Say, 'To whom belongs what is in the heavens on earth?'
Say, 'To God.
He has prescribed mercy for Himself:
He will gather you[p] together to the Day of Resurrection,
about which there is no doubt.
Those who have lost their souls
– they do not believe.

13. To Him belongs whatever rests in the night and in the day.
He is the Hearer and the Knower.'

14. Say, 'Shall I take as protector someone other than God,
the Creator of the heavens and the earth,
who feeds and is not fed?'
Say, 'I have been ordered to be the first to surrender:
"Do not be one of those who associate others with God".'

15. Say, 'If I rebel against my Lord, I fear the torment of a mighty day.'

16. Those from whom [the torment] is turned away on that day
– God has mercy on them.
That is the clear triumph.

17. If God touches you[s] with harm,
there is no one to remove it but Him;
and if he touches you[s] with good

---

[1] *i.e.* 'fashioned him in the form of a man'. The rhetoric of the verse makes the meaning slightly opaque.

– He has power over everything.

18. He is the One with power over His servants.
He is the Wise and the Informed.

19. Say, 'What thing is more weighty in testimony?'
Say, 'God is a witness between you^p and me.
This Recitation has been revealed to me,
that I may warn by it [both] you^p and all those it reaches.
Do you bear witness that there are other gods
in addition to God?'
Say, 'I do not bear witness.'

19a. Say, 'He is only One God.
I have nothing to do with what you associate with Him.'

20. Those to whom We have given the Scripture
recognize it as they recognize their own sons.
Those who have lost their souls do not believe.

21. Who does greater wrong
than the one who invents a lie against God
or denies the truth of His signs?
The wrong-doers will not prosper.

22. On the day when We round them all up
and then We say to those who associated others with God,
'Where are those whom you asserted were associates [of God]?'

23. Then their only temptation will be to say,
'By God, our Lord, we did not associate others with God.'

24. See^s how they lie against themselves
and how what they used to invent has failed them.

25. Among them are those who listen to you^s,
but over whose hearts We have placed veils,
so that they do not understand it,
and heaviness in their ears.
If they see a sign, they do not believe in it;
and then, when they come to you^s to argue with you,
those who disbelieve say,
'These are nothing but the fables of the ancients.'

26. And they forbid [others] from it^2 and keep their distance from it^2 [themselves].
They destroy only themselves,
but they are not aware.

27. If you^s could see when they are set before the Fire and say,
'Would that we might be returned
that we might not deny the truth of the signs of our Lord

---

^2 Or 'him', *i.e.* Muḥammad.

and might be among the believers.'

28. No! What they were previously concealing will have become clear to them.
Were they to be returned,
they would go back to what they have been forbidden.
They are liars.

29. They say, 'There is only our life in this world.
We shall not be raised.'

30. If you^s could see [them] when they are set before their Lord.
He will say, 'Is this not real?'
They will say, 'Yes, it is, by our Lord.'
He will say, 'Taste the punishment for your persistent ingratitude.'

31. Lost are those who deny the truth of the meeting with God.
Then, when the Hour comes upon them suddenly, they cry,
'Alas for us, for the neglect we have shown about it.'
These bear their burdens on their own backs.
Evil indeed is what they bear.

32. The life of this world is only play and diversion.
The World to Come is better for those who protect themselves.
Do you^p not understand?

33. We are well aware that what they say grieves you^s;
yet they do not think you^s are lying.
But wrong-doers deny the signs of God.

34. Messengers have been thought liars before you^s.
They endured patiently the disbelief and hurt [they suffered],
until Our help came to them.
There is no one who can change God's words;
and you^s have heard some of the tidings of the messengers.

35. If their aversion lies heavy on you^s,
if you^s can seek a hole into the earth or a ladder into the sky
and bring them a sign, [do so]
– Had God willed, He would have brought them together to the guidance.
Do not be one of the ignorant.

36. Only those who hear can respond;
but God will [also] raise the dead
and then they will be returned to Him.

37. They say, 'Why has no sign from His lord been sent down to him?'
Say, 'God is able to send down a sign,
but most of them do not know.'

38. There is no beast in the earth nor bird that flies with its wings
but they are communities like you^p.
We have neglected nothing in the record.
Then they will be rounded up to their Lord.

39. Those who deny the truth of Our signs are deaf and dumb, in darkness.
    God sends astray those whom He wishes,
    and He places on a straight path those whom He wishes.
40. Say, 'Have you^p considered?
    If God's torment comes to you^p or the Hour comes to you^p,
    Will you call on any other than God,
    if you are truthful?'
41. No, it is to Him you^p will call,
    and He will remove that about which you call Him, if He wishes,
    and you will forget what you associate with Him.
42. In the past We have sent³ to communities before you^s,
    and We seized them with distress and tribulation,
    so that they might be humble.
43. If only they had been humble when Our might came to them.
    But their hearts were hard,
    and Satan made what they were doing seem fair to them.
44. Then, when they forgot that about which they had been reminded,
    We opened for them the gate of everything.
    Then, when they rejoiced in what they had been given,
    We seized them unawares, and, lo, they were confounded.
45. And so the last remnant of the people who did wrong was cut off.
    Praise belongs to God, Lord of created beings.
46. Say, 'Have you^p considered?
    If God takes away your hearing and your sight
    and puts a seal on your hearts,
    who is a god other than God to bring it [back] to you?'
    See how We turn the signs about;
    yet they turn away.
47. Say, 'Have you considered?
    If God's torment comes to you suddenly or openly,
    will any be destroyed apart from the people who do wrong?'
48. We send the messengers only as bearers of good tidings and warners.
    Those who believe and make amends,
    there will be no fear upon them nor will they grieve;
49. But those who deny the truth of Our signs
    – torment will touch them because they were reprobates.
50. Say, 'I do not say to you^p,
    "I possess the treasuries of God",
    nor do I know the Invisible.
    Nor do I say to you, "I am an angel".

---

³ Unexpectedly there is no object, such as 'messengers'.

I only follow what is revealed to me.'
Say, 'Are the man who is blind and the man who sees equal?
Will you^p not reflect?'

51.   Warn^s with it[4] those who fear that they will be rounded up to their Lord
    – they have no protector or intercessor apart from Him –
    so that they may protect themselves.

52.   Do^s not drive away those who call to their Lord
    in the morning and the evening, seeking His face.
    No part of their account falls on you^s
    (nor any part of yours on them)
    that you^s should drive them away
    and become one of the wrong-doers.

53.   Thus We have tested some of them by others,
    that they may say, 'Are these the ones among us
    to whom God has been gracious?'
    Is not God well aware of those who are grateful?

54.   When those who believe in Our signs come to you^s,
    say, 'Peace be upon you.
    Your Lord has prescribed mercy for Himself:
    that [in the case of] those of you who do evil through ignorance
    and then repent after it and make amends
    – He is Forgiving and Compassionate.'

55.   Thus We make the signs distinct,
    and [this is] so that the way of the sinners may become clear.

56.   Say, 'I have been forbidden to serve those to whom you^p call
    apart from God.'
    Say, 'I shall not follow your^p whims.
    If I were to do that, I should go astray
    and not be one of those guided aright.'

57.   Say, 'I stand on clear evidence from my Lord,
    and you^p have denied its truth.
    I do not have what you seek to hasten.
    The decision is only with God.
    He recounts the truth.
    He is the best of expounders.'

58.   Say, 'If I had that which you^p seek to hasten,
    the matter would have been decided between you and me.
    God is well aware of the wrong-doers.'

59.   With Him are the keys of the Invisible.
    Only He knows them.

---

[4] 'That message' or the Recitation in general.

He [also] knows what is in the land and the sea.
No leaf falls without Him knowing it,
nor is there a grain in the darkness of the earth
nor anything wet or dry
but it is in a clear record.

60. It is He who takes you[p] by night
and knows what you have done by day.
Then He will raise you in it,
that a stated term may be completed.
Then is your return to Him
– and then He will inform you about what you used to do.

61. He is the One with power over His servants.
He sends watchers over you.
Then, when death comes to one of you,
Our messengers[5] take him
– and they do not neglect [anyone].

62. Then they are returned to God, their true protector.
Truly, His is the judgement.
He is the swiftest of reckoners.

63. Say, 'Who delivers you[p] from the darkness of the land and the sea?
You call to Him humbly and in secret:
"If He delivers us from this,
we shall indeed be among the thankful".'

64. Say, 'God delivers you from this and from every disaster;
yet you still associate others with Him.'

65. Say, 'He is able to send against you a torment from above you
or from beneath your feet,
or to confuse you [by dividing you] into parties
and to make you taste the might of one another.'
See how We turn the signs about,
so that they may understand.

66. Your[s] people have denied its truth, though it is the truth.
Say, 'I am not a trustee over you.'

67. Every tiding has a time when it comes to pass,
and you[p] will know.

68. When you[s] see those who plunge into[6] Our signs,
turn[s] away from them until they plunge into another topic.
If Satan causes you[s] to forget, do not sit,
after the reminder, with the people who do wrong.

69. No part of their account falls on those who protect themselves,

---

[5] Angels.

[6] A fairly common phrase meaning 'to engage in', normally with a pejorative sense.

but it is a reminder, so that they may protect themselves.

70. Leave⁵ alone those who take their religion as a sport and a diversion
and who are deluded by the life of this world.
Remind⁵ through it⁷ lest any soul be delivered to destruction
for what it has amassed.
It has no protector or intercessor apart from God;
and if it offers every equivalent
it will not be taken from it.

70a. Those are the ones who are delivered to destruction
for what they have amassed.
They will have a drink of boiling water and a painful torment,
because they were unbelievers.

71. Say, 'Shall we call on what neither benefits us nor harms us,
to the exclusion of God,
and shall we be turned back on our heels
after God has guided us,
like the one whom the satans have infatuated with the earth
and is bewildered,
although he has companions who call him to guidance,
"Come to us"?'

71a. Say, 'God's guidance is the guidance,
and we have been ordered to surrender to the Lord of all created beings;'

72. And 'Perform prayer and protect yourselves against Him.
He is the one to whom you will be rounded up.'

73. It is He who created the heavens and the earth in truth.
On the day He says 'Be', it is.
His saying is the truth.
His is the sovereignty on the day when there is a blast on the trumpet.
[He is] the Knower of the Invisible and the Witnessed.
He is the Wise and the Informed.

74. [Remember] when Abraham said to his father Āzar,
'Do you take idols as gods?
I see you and your people in manifest error.'

75. Thus We showed Abraham the kingdom of the heavens and the earth,
that he might be one of those with certainty.

76. When the night came down on him, he saw a star.
He said, 'This is my Lord;'
but when it set, he said, 'I do not love things that set.'

77. When he saw the moon rising, he said, 'This is my Lord;'
but when it set, he said, 'If my Lord does not guide me,

---

⁷ The Recitation.

I shall be one of the people who go astray.'

78. When he saw the sun rising, he said, 'This is my Lord. This is greater;'
but when it set, he said, 'O my people, I am quit of what you associate with God.

79. I have turned my face to Him who created the heavens and the earth, as a man
of pure faith,
and I am not one of those who associate others with God.'

80. His people argued with him.
He said, 'Do you dispute with me about God,
when He has guided me?
I do not fear what you associate with Him,
unless my Lord wills something.
My Lord embraces everything in His knowledge.
Will you not be reminded?

81. How should I fear what you have associated with Him,
when you are not afraid to have associated with God
that for which He has not sent down any authority?
Which of the two parties has more right to security
– if you have any knowledge?

82. Those who believe and have not obscured their faith with wrong-doing
– those have security and are guided aright.'

83. That is Our argument.
We gave it to Abraham against his people.
We raise in rank those whom We wish.
Your^s Lord is Wise and Informed.

84. And We gave to him Isaac and Jacob
– each of them We guided.
And We guided Noah previously
and of his seed [We guided] David and Solomon
and Job and Joseph and Moses and Aaron
– thus We recompense those who do good –

85. And Zachariah and John and Jesus and Ilyās
– each one [of them] was of the righteous –

86. And Ishmael and al-Yasaʿ and Jonah and Lot
– each one We preferred over all created beings,

87. And some of their forefathers and their offspring and their brothers;
and We chose them and guided them to a straight path.

88. That is the guidance of God,
by which He guides those of His servants whom He wishes.
Had they associated [anything with Him]
all that they had been doing would have failed them.

89. Those are the ones to whom We gave the Scripture and the Judgement and
Prophethood.

If these people disbelieve in them,
We have already entrusted them to a people who do not disbelieve in them.

90. These are the ones whom God has guided
– so follow their guidance.

90a. Say, 'I do not ask any wage for it.
It is only a reminder to all created beings.'

91. They have not measured God's power properly when they have said,
'God has not sent down anything to any mortal.'

91a. Say, 'Who sent down the Scripture which Moses brought
as a light and a guidance to the people?
You^P put it [on] parchments,
revealing them, but concealing much.
And you were taught what you did not know
– neither you nor your forefathers.'

91b. Say, 'God', then leave them playing in their plunging.

92. This is a Scripture We have sent down, blessed,
confirming what was [sent down] before it,
and for you^s to warn the mother of the settlements[8] and those who are around it.
Those who believe in the next world believe in it,
and they watch over their prayer.

93. Who does greater wrong than the one who invents falsehood against God
or who says, 'Revelation has come to me,'
when nothing has been revealed to him;
or who says, 'I shall send down the like of what God has sent down'?

93a. If you^s could see when the wrong-doers are in the floods of death,
and the angels are stretching out their hands:
'Give^P up your souls.
To-day you are recompensed with the torment of humiliation,
because of your untrue statements about God
and [because] you treated His signs with disdain.'

94. 'Now you have come to Us singly,
as We created you the first time,
and you have left behind your backs all that We bestowed on you.
Nor do We see with you your intercessors,
whom you asserted to be partners with[9] you.
The bond between you has been cut
and what you asserted has failed you.'

95. It is God who splits the grain and the date-stone.
He brings forth the living from the dead

---

[8] Mecca.
[9] The text has 'in'.

and it is He who brings forth the dead from the living.
That is God.
How is it that you^P are embroiled in lies?

96. He splits the sky in the morning,
and He has made the night a rest,
and the sun and moon as a reckoning.
That is the disposing of the Mighty and the Knowing.

97. It is He who has placed the stars for you^P,
for you to be guided by them in the darknesses of land and sea.
We have expounded the signs for a people who know.

98. It is He who has produced you from a single soul.
[Then there is] a lodging place and a place of deposit.
We have expounded the signs for a people who understand.

99. It is He who has sent down water from the sky.
With it We bring forth plants of every kind.
From them We bring forth green shoots;
from them We bring forth grain in clusters;
and from the date-palm, from its spathe, clusters of dates close at hand;
and gardens of grapes and olives and pomegranates,
like one another and unlike one another.
Look^P at their fruits when they bear fruit and at their ripening.
In that there are signs for a people who believe.

100. They make the *Jinn* associates of God,
although He created them,
and they falsely impute sons and daughters to Him,
without any knowledge.
Glory be to Him. May He be exalted high above what they describe

101. – The originator of the heavens and the earth.
How can He have a child when He has no consort,
when He created everything and is Aware of everything?

102. That is God, your^P Lord.
There is no god but Him,
the Creator of all things,
so Worship Him.
He has charge of everything.

103. Sight does not reach Him, but He reaches sight.
He is the Gentle and the Informed.

104. Clear proofs have come to you^P from your Lord.
Those who see clearly
– it is to their own advantage.
Those who remain blind
– it is to their disadvantage.

I am not a keeper over you.

105. Thus We turn about the signs
– [We do so] that they may say,
'You^s have studied',
and that We may make it clear for a people who have knowledge.

106. Follow^s what has been revealed to you from your Lord
– there is no god but Him
– and turn away from those who associate others with God.

107. Had God willed,
they would not have associated others with Him.
We have not made you a watcher over them,
and you^s are not in charge of them.

108. Do not revile^p those to whom they call,
to the exclusion of God,
lest they wrongfully revile God through ignorance.
Thus We have made the deeds of every community seem fair to it.
Then their return is to their Lord,
and He will tell them what they have been doing.

109. They have sworn their most solemn oaths by God
that if a sign comes to them they will believe in it.
Say, 'The signs are with God.'
What will make you^p aware that when [the sign] comes they will not believe?

110. We turn their hearts and eyes about
just as [We did when] they did not believe in it the first time.
We shall leave them wandering blindly in their insolence.

111. Even if We were to send the angels down to them
and the dead were to speak to them
and We were to round up everything against them,
face to face,
they would not be ones to believe,
without God's will.
But most of them are ignorant.

112. Thus We have appointed an enemy for every prophet:
devils from both men and *Jinn*
who suggest fancy speech to one another – a delusion.
Had your^s Lord wished, they would not do so.
Leave^s them alone with what they invent,

113. That the hearts of those who do not believe in the Next World may incline to it,
and be content with it
and that they may gain what they are gaining.

114. Shall I seek any judge other than God,
for it is He who has sent down to you^p the Scripture set out distinctly –

and those to whom We have already given the Scripture
know that it is sent down from your[s] Lord in truth.
Do[s] not be one of those who have doubts.

115. The Word of your[s] Lord is perfect in truth and justice.
There is no one who can change His words.
He is the Hearer and the Knower.

116. If you[s] obey most of those on the earth,
they will lead you astray from God's way.
They only follow surmise.
They only conjecture.

117. Your[s] Lord is well aware of those who stray from His way
and He is well aware of those who are rightly guided.

118. So eat[p] of that over which God's name has been mentioned,
if you believe in His signs.

119. Why is it that you[s] do not eat of that over which God's name has been mentioned,
when He has expounded for you what He has forbidden to you,
unless you are compelled to eat it?
Many lead astray by their whims,
in ignorance.
Your Lord is well aware of the transgressors.

120. Forsake[p] outward and inward sin.
Those who amass sin will be recompensed for what they have earned.

121. Do[p] not eat of that over which God's name has not been mentioned,
for it is abomination.
The devils inspire their friends to dispute with you[p].
If you obey them, you will be people who associate others with God.

122. Is the one who was dead and to whom We gave life and appointed for him a light
by which he could walk among the people
like the one whose likeness is in darkness
from which he cannot emerge?
Thus what they have been doing has been made to seem fair to the unbelievers.

123. And thus We have appointed in every settlement leaders of its sinners,
that they might plot there.
But they only scheme against themselves,
though they are not aware of that.

124. When a sign comes to them they say,
'We shall not believe
till we are given the same as God's messengers are given.'
God is well aware of where to place His message.
Those who sin will be smitten by humiliation with God
and by a severe torment because of their scheming.

125. Whomsoever God wishes to guide,

He expands his breast to Submission;
and whomsoever He wishes to send astray,
He makes his breast tight and narrow,
as though he were engaged in climbing to the sky.
Thus God places abomination on those who do not believe.

126. This is the path of your^s Lord, a straight one.

126a. We have expounded the signs for a people who let themselves be reminded.

127. For them is the abode of peace with their Lord.
He is their Protector because of what they used to do.

128. On the day when He will round them all up:
'O assembly of the *Jinn*,
you have desired many of mankind [as adherents].'
And their friends among mankind will say, 'Our Lord,
we profited from one another,
but now we have reached the term that you set for us.'
He will say, 'The Fire is your abode,
in which you will remain for ever'
– except as God wills.
Your Lord is Wise and Informed.

129. Thus We make wrong-doers friends of one another
because of what they have been amassing.

130. 'O assembly of *Jinn* and men,
did not messengers come to you from among you,
who recounted My signs to you,
and warned of the meeting of this day of yours?'
They will say, 'We bear witness against ourselves.'
The life of this world deluded them,
and they bear witness against themselves
that they were unbelievers.

131. This is because your^s Lord would not destroy the settlements wrongfully,
when their people are unaware.

132. All have ranks according to what they have done,
and your^s Lord is not unaware of what they do.

133. Your^s Lord is the All-sufficient, Endowed with mercy.
If He wishes, He will remove you^s
and cause whatever He wishes to succeed you,
just as He raised you from the seed of other people.

134. What you have been promised is coming,
and you cannot frustrate [it].

135. Say, 'O my people, work according to your station.
I am working [too].
You will come to know to whom will belong the sequel of the abode.

Those who do wrong will not be successful.'

136. They assign to God a portion of the tillage and livestock He has created;
and they say, in their assertions, 'This is God's'
and 'This is for those we associate with Him.'
But what is for those they associate with Him does not reach God,
yet what is for God reaches those they associate with Him.
Evil is their judgement.

137. Thus those whom they associate with God
have made the killing of their children seem fair
to those who associate them with God,
that they may destroy them and confuse their religion for them.
Had God willed, they would not have done it.
So leave them alone with what they invent.

138. And they say, in their assertions,
'These are livestock and tillage that are forbidden,
and only those we wish may eat them'
– livestock whose backs have been forbidden,
and livestock over which they do not mention God's name:
an invention against Him.
He will recompense them for what they used to invent.

139. And they say, 'What is within the bellies of these beasts
is reserved for our males and forbidden to our spouses;
but if it is [born] dead, they may share in it.'
He will recompense them for their description.
He is Wise and Knowing.

140. Those who kill their children in folly,
without knowledge,
are losers.
They have made forbidden what God has provided for them,
an invention against God.
They have gone astray and are not guided aright.

141. It is He who produces gardens,
both trellised and untrellised,
and date-palms and crops of different produce
and olives and pomegranates,
like one another and unlike one another.

141a. Eat^p of their fruit when they fruit,
and give its due portion on the day it is harvested,
and do not be prodigal.
God does not love those who are prodigal.

142. From the beasts [He has produced] some for burden and some for slaughtering:[10]
142a. (Eat[p] what God has provided for your sustenance
       and do not follow the footsteps of Satan.
       He is a clear enemy for you.)
143. Eight paired together:
     two of sheep and two of goats;
143a. (Say, 'Has He forbidden the two males
       or the two females
       or what the wombs of the two females contain?
       Tell[p] me with knowledge, if you are truthful.')
144. Two of camels and two of cattle.
144a. (Say, 'Has He forbidden the two males
       or the two females
       or what the wombs of the two females contain?
       Or were you[p] witnesses when God enjoined this on you?'
       'Who does greater wrong
       than those who invent falsehood against God,
       to lead the people astray, without knowledge.
       God does not guide the people who do wrong.')
145. Say, 'I do not find in what is revealed to me
     anything forbidden to the eater of it,
     unless it is carrion or blood shed
     or the flesh of a pig
     – for that is an abomination –
     or something ungodly killed in the name of some one other than God.
     But whoever is compelled,
     neither desiring nor transgressing
     – your[s] Lord is Forgiving and Compassionate.'
146. For those who are Jews We have forbidden everything with claws;[11]
     and of cattle and sheep We have forbidden the fat of them
     save that carried by their backs, or the intestines,
     or what is mixed with bone.
     We made that their recompense for their insolence.
     We speak the truth.

---

[10] Verses 142a, 143a and 144a appear to be additions to an original Meccan passage, and this may well be the case with 141a, which looks like a bridging verse. In recitation, the interruptions caused by verses 142a, 143a and 144a are much less obvious than when one reads the text.

[11] There has been a tendency among non-Muslim scholars to try to link this verse with passages in Leviticus (ch. 11) and Deuteronomy (ch. 14). I cannot see that *zufur* can be stretched to mean anything other than claws. The only Biblical parallel is the list of birds in Leviticus 11:13–20. Any attempt to take account of hooves seems doomed by the prohibition of the eating of camels in Deuteronomy 14:7, which is flatly contradicted by verse 144 here.

147. So if they say you[s] lie,
     say, 'Your[p] Lord is endowed with great mercy,
     but His might will not be turned back from the people who are sinners.'
148. Those who associate others with God will say,
     'Had God willed, we would not have associated others with Him
     nor would our forefathers,
     nor would we have forbidden anything.'
     Thus those who were before them denied the truth
     until they tasted Our might.
148a. Say, 'Have you[p] any knowledge that you can produce for us?
     You only follow surmise.
     You only conjecture.'
149. Say, 'God's is the clinching argument.
     Had he wished, He would have guided you all.'
150. Say, 'Produce[p] your witnesses who can bear witness that God forbade this.'
     And if they testify, do not testify with them.
     Do[s] not follow the whims of those who deny the truth of Our signs
     and who do not believe in the World to Come
     and ascribe equals to their Lord.
151. Say, 'Come[p] and I shall recite what your Lord has made sacred for you:
     that you associate nothing with him;
     that [you show] kindness to [your] parents;
     that you do not kill your children because of poverty
     – We shall provide for you and them;
     that you do not approach immoral acts,
     whether open or concealed;
     and do not kill the soul that God has made sacred,
     except by right.
     This is what He has enjoined on you,
     so that you may understand.
152. Do[p] not approach the wealth of the orphan,
     save with what is better,
     till he reaches maturity.
     Fill up the measure and the balance, in justice.
     (We do not impose burdens on any soul beyond its capacity.)
     If you[p] speak, be just,
     even though it is a relative [who is involved].
     Fulfil God's covenant.
     This is what He has enjoined on you,
     so that you may be reminded.'
153. And 'This is My path, straight.
     Follow[p] it and do not follow [other] ways

lest they take you away from His path.
That is what He has enjoined on you,
so that you may protect yourselves.'

154. Then We gave Moses the Scripture,
complete for him who had done good,
an exposition of everything
and a guidance and a mercy,
so that they[12] might believe in their meeting with their Lord.

155. This is a Scripture that We have sent down, blessed.
Follow[P] it and protect yourselves,
so that you may receive mercy.

156. Lest you say, 'The Scripture was sent down only to two parties[13] before us,
and we have been heedless of their study.'

157. Or lest you say, 'Had the Scripture been sent down to us,
we would have been better guided than them.'
A clear proof and a guidance and a mercy have come to you from your Lord.

157a. Who does greater wrong than those who deny the truth of God's signs
and turn away from them?
We will recompense with an evil torment
those who turn away from Our signs
because of their turning away.

158. Do they expect anything other than that the angels should come to them,
or Your[s] Lord comes
or one of the signs of your Lord.
On the day when one of the signs of your Lord comes,
belief will not benefit a soul that has never previously believed
or has not amassed some good in belief.
Say, 'Wait[P] – We are waiting.'

159. Those who have divided their religion and become groups
– you[s] have no concern with them.
Their case goes to God.
He will tell them what they have been doing.

160. Whoever brings a good deed will have ten like it;
and whoever brings a bad deed will have only its like.
They will not be wronged.

161. Say, 'God has guided me to a straight path, a right religion,
the community of Abraham, a man of pure faith,
who was not one of those who associated others with God.'

162. Say, 'My prayer and my sacrifice

---

[12] The Jews.
[13] The Jews and the Christians.

and my living and my dying are for God,
Lord of all created beings.

163. He has no associate.
I have been commanded to do this.
I am first of those who surrender.'

164. Say, 'Shall I seek a lord other than God,
when He is Lord of everything.
No soul amasses anything except upon itself.
No laden soul bears the burden of another.
Then your[p] return is to your Lord,
and He will inform you about that over which you differed.'

165. It is He who has appointed you[p] viceroys of the earth
and has raised some of you in rank above others,
to test you by what He has given you.
Your Lord is swift in punishment,
but He is Forgiving and Compassionate.

Sūra 7

This *sūra* is generally taken to be late Meccan, though there can be little doubt that there was some recasting and expansion at Medina, particularly in the latter part of the *sūra* (from 157 onwards). It is notable for its narratives, both of the creation and the fall (verses 10–34) and of the prophets (verses 59–174). These latter deal with Noah, Hūd, Ṣāliḥ, Lot and Shuʿayb (59–102) and then Moses (103–174). It should be noted that the group Noah, Hūd, Ṣāliḥ, Lot, Shuʿayb occurs in that order, but not with the same narratives, in 26:105–191. Also *Sūra* 11:25–95 has the same order of stories, but with a piece about Abraham preceding the story of Lot. Comparison should also be made with the early *Sūra* 54:9–40, which recounts the first four of the stories, followed by a couple of verses on Pharaoh. The narratives of *Sūra* 7 provide the fullest versions of the stories about this key group of prophets, with the exception of Moses, on whom there are additional narratives, with considerably different content, in *Sūra*s 18 and 20. One prophet who is not mentioned in *Sūra* 7 is Abraham.

The narratives are introduced by a passage that moves quickly from the theme of revelation to the role of the prophet and then to warning (1–9); and at the end of the *sūra* the narratives are rounded off by a little bridge piece (175–76) on a nameless failed prophet, which leads into a substantial piece of polemic (177–206).

The Heights

In the name of the Merciful and Compassionate God

1. *Alif, Lām, Mīm, Ṣad.*[1]
2. A Scripture which has been revealed to you[s]
    – let there be no difficulty in your[s] breast because of it –
    for you[s] to give warning through it
    and as a reminder to the believers:
3. 'Follow what has been sent down to you[p] from your Lord
    and do not follow friends to His exclusion.
    Little are you[p] reminded.'
4. How many a settlement have We destroyed,
    on which Our might came by night
    or when they were resting in the heat of the day.
5. All they could cry when Our might came upon them

---

[1] On the mystical letters see the note on 2:1.

147

were the words, 'We were not wrong-doers.'

6. We shall question those to whom messengers were sent
and then We shall question the messengers.

7. Then We shall recount their story to them with knowledge,
for We were not absent.

8. The weighing on that day is the true [weighing].
Those whose balances are heavy
– they are the ones who will prosper;

9. And those whose balances are light
– they are the ones who will lose their souls,
because they have wronged Our signs.

10. We have given you^p position in the land
and appointed means of life for you in it
– but you give little thanks.

11. We created you and then We shaped you
and then told the angels,
'Prostrate yourselves to Adam.'
They [all] prostrated themselves
apart from Iblīs,
who was not one of those who prostrated themselves.

12. HE said, 'What prevented you from prostrating yourself
when I ordered you [to do so]?'

12a. He said, 'I am better than him.
You created me from fire and him from mud.'

13. HE said, 'Go down from it.²
You should not show pride in it.
Leave. You are one of the abased.'

14. He said, 'Give me respite to the day when they are raised.'

15. HE said, 'You are one of those given a respite.'

16. He said, 'Because You have sent me astray
I shall lie in wait for them on Your straight path.

17. Then I shall come to them from before them and from behind them,
from their right hands and from their left hands.
You will not find most of them thankful.'

18. HE said, 'Leave^s it, despised and banished.
Those of them who follow you
– I shall fill Jahannam with you all.'

19. And, 'O Adam, inhabit the Garden,
you and your wife,
and eat wherever you wish;

---

² The Garden of Eden.

but do not approach this tree
lest you be of the wrong-doers.'

20. Then Satan whispered to them
to reveal to them what was hidden from them of their bare bodies,
saying, 'Your Lord has only forbidden you this tree
lest you become angels or become immortals.'

21. And he swore to them,
'I am one of those who give you good advice.'

22. Thus he sent them down by delusion.

22a. And when they tasted the tree
their bare bodies became clear to them
and they began heaping upon themselves some of the leaves of the Garden.
And their Lord called out to them,
'Did I not forbid you this tree
and tell you, "Satan is a manifest enemy for you"?'

23. They said, 'Our Lord, we have wronged ourselves.
If You do not forgive us and have mercy on us,
we shall be among the losers.'

24. He said, 'Go down, each in enmity to the other.
You will have a place to stay on earth
and enjoyment for a time.'

25. He said, 'You will live in it and you will die in it
and you will be brought forth in it.'

26. Children of Adam!
We have sent down to you clothing, to conceal your bare bodies, and fine feathers;
but the clothing of piety – that is better.
That is one of God's signs,
so that they may remember.

27. Children of Adam!
Let not Satan tempt you
in the way that he caused your ancestors to leave the Garden,
stripping them of their clothing to show them their bare bodies.
He sees you, he and his tribe, from where you do not see them.
We have made the satans friends for those who do not believe.

28. When they commit some immoral act, they say,
'We found our forefathers practising it,
and God has ordered us to do it.'
'God does not order immoral acts.
Do you say about God what you do not know?'

29. Say, 'My Lord has ordered justice.
Set your faces straight at every place of worship
and call to him,

devoting your religion solely to Him.
You will return as He originated you.

30. He has guided a part,
but another part has been gripped by error.
They have adopted the satans as friends,
to the exclusion of God,
and they think that they are rightly guided.

31. Children of Adam!
Take your adornment at every place of worship,
and eat and drink and do not be extravagant.
Truly, He does not love the extravagant.

32. Say, 'Who has forbidden the adornment of God
that He has produced for His servants
and the good things of [His] provision?

32a. Say, 'On the Day of Resurrection
these things will be only for those who have believed
during the life in this world.'
Thus We set out in detail Our signs for a people who have knowledge.

33. Say, 'Truly my Lord has forbidden immoral acts,
both open and secret,
and unjust sin and oppression
and your associating with God that for which no authority has been sent down
and your saying about God that which you do not know.'

34. Every community has its term;
and when its term comes,
they cannot put it off for an hour nor advance it an hour.

35. Children of Adam!
If messengers from among you come to you,
recounting My signs to you,
those who are god-fearing and make amends
– there will be no fear on them nor will they grieve.

36. But those who deny the truth of Our signs
and are scornful of them
– those are the companions of the Fire,
in which they will remain for ever.

37. Who does greater wrong than those who invent lies against God
or deny the truth of His signs?
These shall be reached by their portion of the record;
and then, when Our messengers come to them, to take them,
they say, 'Where is that to which you used to call,
to the exclusion of God?'
They reply, 'They have gone astray from us,'

and they bear witness against themselves that they were unbelievers.

38.   HE says, 'Enter the Fire among communities that have passed away before you,
both *Jinn* and men.
Whenever a community enters,
it curses its sister [community];
then, when they have all followed one another into it,
the last of them will say to the first of them,
'Our Lord, these led us astray.
Give them a double torment of the Fire.'
HE says, 'For each there is a double [torment],
but you do not know.'

39.   And the first of them will say to the last of them,
'You have no superiority over us.
So taste the torment for what you have amassed.'

40.   Those who deny the truth of Our signs
and are scornful of them
– the gates of heaven will not be opened for them,
nor will they enter the Garden
until the camel passes through the eye of the needle.[3]
Thus We recompense the sinners.

41.   They will have a resting-place in Jahannam,
and above them coverings.
Thus We recompense the wrong-doers.

42.   But those who believe and do righteous deeds
– We do not charge any soul beyond its capacity.
These are the companions of the Garden,
in which they will remain for ever.

43.   We shall remove whatever rancour is in their breasts,
and the rivers will flow beneath them,
and they will say, 'Praise belongs to God,
who has guided us to this.
Had God not guided us,
we would [never] have been guided aright.
The messengers of our Lord did indeed bring the truth.'
And it will be proclaimed to them,
'This is the Garden for you.
You have been given it as inheritance
for what you used to do.'

44.   And the companions of the Garden will call out to the companions of the Fire,

---

[3] This recalls the New Testament (Matth. 19:24; Mark 10:25; Luke 18:25), but the reference there is to a rich man, not quite the context here.

'We have found what our Lord promised us to be true.
Have you found what your Lord promised you to be true?'
They will say, 'Yes'.
And a crier amongst them will proclaim,
'God's curse is on the wrong-doers,

45. Who bar [men] from God's path
and seek to make it crooked
and who do not believe in the next world.'

46. Between the two groups is a barrier;
and on the heights[4]
are men who recognize each [of them] by their marks;
and they call out to the companions of the Garden,
'Peace be on you! They have not entered it,
though they long [to do so].'

47. And when their eyes are turned towards the companions of the Fire,
they say, 'Our Lord, do not place us with the people who do wrong.'

48. And the companions of the heights
call out to men whom they recognize by their marks,
saying, 'Your gathering [of wealth] has not availed you,
nor the pride you have displayed.

49. Are these the ones you swore God would not reach with mercy?'
[To those given mercy it will be said,]
'Enter the Garden.
There will be no fear on you, nor will you grieve.'

50. And the companions of the Fire call out to the companions of Paradise,
'Pour some water on us
or some of that God has provided for you.'
They reply, 'God has forbidden both of them
to those who do not believe,

51. Who took their religion as diversion and sport
and who were deluded by the life of this world.'
To-day We forget them
as they forgot that they would meet this day of theirs
and as they used to deny Our signs.

52. We have brought them a Scripture,
which We have set out in detail,
based on knowledge,
a guidance and a mercy for a people who believe.

53. Do they expect anything but its interpretation?
On the day when its interpretation comes,

---

[4] This phrase is traditionally linked to the previous one and understood as 'the heights of the barrier'.

those who previously forgot it will say,
'The messengers of our Lord brought the truth.
Have we any intercessors to intercede for us,
or shall we be returned to do other than what we were doing?'
They have lost their souls
and what they were inventing has failed them.

54. Your Lord is God
who created the heavens and the earth in six days,
then set himself on the Throne,
covering the day with the night,
which seeks it swiftly,
with the sun and the moon and the stars subject to His command.
His indeed is the creation and the command.
Blessed be God, Lord of all beings.

55. Call upon your Lord humbly and in secret.
He does not love transgressors.

56. Do not make mischief in the land after it has been put right;
and call on Him in fear and longing.
The mercy of God is something near those who do good.

57. [It is] He who looses the winds as good tidings [running] before His mercy;
then, when they bear heavy clouds
We drive them to a dead land and send down water through them,
with which We bring forth some of every [kind of fruit].
Thus We bring forth the dead,
so that you may be reminded.

58. The good land
– its vegetation comes forth by permission of its Lord;
that which is bad
– it comes forth only scantily.
Thus We turn the signs about for a people who are thankful.

59. In the past We sent Noah to his people.
He said, 'O my people, serve God.
You have no god other than Him.
I fear for you the torment of a mighty day.'

60. The notables of his people said,
'We see you in manifest error.'

61. He said, 'O my people, there is no error in me;
I am a messenger from the Lord of all beings.

62. I convey to you the messages of my Lord
and give you good advice;
and from God I know what you do not know.

63. Do you[P] wonder that a reminder from your Lord has come to you

through a man from among you,
that he may warn you
and that you may protect yourselves
and that you may be given mercy?'

64. But they considered that he was not telling the truth;
so We saved him and those with him in the ship,
and We drowned those who denied our signs.
They were a blind people.

65. To 'Ād [We sent] their brother Hūd.
He said, 'O my people, serve God.
You have no god other than Him.
Will you not protect yourselves?'

66. The notables of his people,
who were unbelievers, said,
'We see you [caught up] in foolishness,
and we think you one of the liars.'

67. He said, 'O my people, there is no folly in me.
I am a messenger from the Lord of all beings.

68. I convey to you the messages of my Lord,
and I am a faithful adviser for you.

69. Do you wonder that a reminder from your Lord has come to you
through a man from among you,
that he may warn you?
Remember when He made you successors after the people of Noah
and gave you generous increase in strength;
and remember God's bounties,
so that you may prosper.'

70. They said, 'Have you come to us
that we should serve God alone
and forsake what our forefathers used to serve?
Then bring us what you promise us,
if you are one of those who tell the truth.'

71. He said, 'Abomination and anger from your Lord have fallen on you.
Do you argue with me about names[5] that you have named,
you and your forefathers,
for which God has sent down no authority?
Wait. I am one of those who will wait with you.'

72. We saved him and those with him by a mercy from Us,
and We cut the last remnant of those who denied Our signs and were not believers.

73. And to Thamūd [We sent] their brother Ṣāliḥ.

---

[5] The names of idols. *Cf.* 12:40 and 53:23.

He said, 'O my people, serve God.
You have no god other than Him.
A clear proof from your Lord has come to you.
This is the she-camel of God as a sign for you.
So let her eat in God's land,
and do not touch her with evil,
lest a painful torment seize you.

74. Remember[p] when He made you successors after 'Ād
and lodged you in the land,
and you took castles in its plains
and hewed the mountains into houses.
Remember God's bounties and do not make mischief,
causing corruption in the land.'

75. The notables of his people, who were haughty,
said to those who were thought weak,
to those of them who believed,
'Do you know that Ṣāliḥ has been sent from his Lord?'
They said, 'We are believers in [the message] with which he has been sent.'

76. Those who were haughty said,
'We do not believe in what you believe in.'

77. So they hamstrung the she-camel
and turned with disdain from their Lord's command;
and they said, 'O Ṣāliḥ, bring us what you promise us,
if you are one of those who have been sent.'

78. So the earthquake seized them,
and in the morning they were prostrate in their dwelling-place.

79. So he turned from them and said, 'O my people,
I conveyed to you the message of my Lord
and I gave you good advice,
but you do not love those who give good advice.'

80. And [We sent] Lot when he said to his people,
'Do you commit such immoral acts
as no created beings committed before you?

81. You approach men in lust rather than women.
You are a people of excess.'

82. The only answer of his people was to say,
'Expel them from your settlement,
for they are a people who would be pure.'

83. So We saved him and his family,
apart from his wife, who was one of those who tarried.

84. We caused a rain to fall on them.
See how was the consequence for the sinners.

85. To Madyan[6] [We sent] their brother Shu'ayb.
     He said, 'O my people, serve God.
     You have no god other than Him.
     A clear proof from your Lord has come to you.
     Give full weight and full measure
     and do not defraud the people of their things
     and do not cause mischief in the land
     after it has been set right.
     That is better for you if you are believers.

86. Do not lurk on every path,
     threatening and barring from God's path
     those who believe in Him,
     seeking to make it crooked.
     And remember when you were few
     and He made you numerous;
     and see how was the consequence for those who did mischief.

87. And if there is a party of you who believe in what I have been sent with,
     and there is a party who do not believe,
     be patient till God judges between us.
     He is the best of those who judge.'

88. The notables of his people, who were haughty, said,
     'We shall drive you out, O Shu'ayb,
     and those who believe with you,
     from our settlement,
     or else you will return to our religion.'
     He said, 'Even if we are unwilling?

89. We would be inventing lies against God
     if we return to your religion
     after God has saved us from it.
     It is not for us to return to it
     unless God, our Lord, wishes.
     God embraces all things in [His] knowledge.
     We put our trust in God.
     Our Lord, decide with truth between us and our people.
     You are the best of those who decide.'

90. The notables of his people, who were unbelievers, said,
     'If you follow Shu'ayb, you will then be of the losers.'

91. So the earthquake seized them,
     and in the morning they were prostrate in their dwelling place.

92. Those who denied Shu'ayb

---

[6] Thought to be the people of Midian, but this is not certain.

– [it was] as if they had never dwelt there;
those who denied Shu'ayb
– they were the losers.

93. So he turned from them and said, 'O my people,
I conveyed to you the messages of my Lord
and I gave you good advice.
How can I grieve for a people who are unbelievers?'

94. We have not sent any prophet to a settlement
without seizing its people with misery and adversity
so that they might become humble.

95. Then We have substituted good in place of evil
till they forgot and said,
'Both affliction and happiness touched our forefathers.'
So We have seized them suddenly, when they were unaware.

96. Had the people of the settlements believed and been god-fearing,
We would have opened to them
blessings from the sky and the earth;
but they gave the lie,
and so We seized them for what they had been amassing.

97. Do the people of the settlements feel secure
that Our might will not come upon them at night
while they are sleeping?

98. Or do the people of the settlements feel secure
that Our might will not come upon them in the forenoon
while they play?

99. Do they feel secure against God's devising?
Only people who are losers feel secure against God's devising.

100. Is it not a guidance
for those who inherit the land after [those] people
that if We wish, We can smite them for their sins
and put a seal on their hearts
so that they do not hear?

101. These are the settlements,
the tidings of which We recount to you^s.
Their messengers had come to them with the clear proofs
but they would not believe what they had previously denied.
Thus God sets a seal on the hearts of the unbelievers.

102. We found no covenant with most of them.
We found most of them reprobates.

103. Then after them We sent Moses to Pharaoh and his nobles with Our signs,
but they acted wrongfully towards them.
See how was the consequence for those who wrought mischief.

104. Moses said,
     'O Pharaoh, I am a messenger from the Lord of created beings,
105. Competent only to tell the truth about God.
     I have brought you a clear proof from your Lord.
     Send the children of Israel with me.'
106. He said, 'If you bring a sign, produce it,
     if you are one of those who speak the truth.'
107. So he flung down his staff,
     and there it was, a serpent for all to see.
108. And he drew forth his hand,
     and it was white to those who looked.[7]
109. The notables of Pharaoh's people said,
     'This is a knowing sorcerer,
110. Who wishes to expel you from your land.
     What do you command?'
111. They said, 'Put him and his brother off for a while,
     and send musterers into the cities,
112. And they will bring to you every knowing sorcerer.'
113. The sorcerers came to Pharaoh saying,
     'We shall indeed have a wage,
     if we are the victors.'
114. He said, 'Yes, and you will be among those stationed near [me].'
115. They said, 'O Moses, either you cast or we cast.'
116. He said, 'Cast!'
     And when they cast,
     they put a spell on the people's eyes
     and sought to terrify them
     and produced mighty magic.
117. And We inspired Moses, saying, 'Throw your staff.'
     And lo, it swallowed what they were lyingly inventing.
118. Thus the truth came to pass,
     and what they were doing was in vain.
119. They were overcome there and made off, humbled,
120. And the sorcerers were flung down in prostration,
121. Saying, 'We believe in the Lord of created beings,
122. The Lord of Moses and Aaron.'
123. Pharaoh said, 'You have believed in Him
     before I give you permission.

---

[7] The vignette also occurs in 26:33, but 20:22, 27:13 and 28:22 have 'white, without harm'. There are Midrashic parallels. This is quite different from Exodus 4:6–7, where the hand is pulled out twice, the first time leprous and white, the second time normal.

This is a plot you have hatched in the city
to expel its people from it.
You shall know.

124. I shall cut off your hands and feet on alternate sides.
Then I shall crucify you all.'

125. They said, 'We are moving to our Lord.

126. You^s are taking vengeance on us
only because We have believed in the signs of our Lord
when they came to us.
Our Lord, pour out patience on us,
and take us as ones who have surrendered.'

127. The notables of Pharaoh's people said,
'Will you leave Moses and his people
to make mischief in the land
and to forsake you and your gods?'

127a. He said, 'We shall put their children to death
and spare their women;
We shall exert our might over them.'

128. Moses said to his people,
'Seek God's help and be patient.
The earth belongs to God.
He gives it as inheritance
to those of His servants whom He wishes.
The final issue will be in favour of those who are god-fearing.'

129. They said, 'We have suffered hurt before you came to us
and since you came to us.'
He said, 'Perhaps your Lord will destroy your enemy
and make you successors in the land and see how you act.'

130. We seized the house of Pharaoh with years [of failure]
and with a dearth of fruits,
so that they might be reminded.

131. But when good came to them they said, 'These things are our [doing];'
and if some evil befell them
they drew bad omens from Moses and those who were with him.
Truly, their drawing of ill omens should have been from God,
but most of them did not know.

132. They said, 'Whatever sign you^s bring us,
to cast a spell on us,
we shall not put our faith in you.'

133. So We sent against them the flood,
the locusts, the lice,
the frogs and the blood,

distinct signs;
but they were haughty and were a sinful people.

134. When the abomination fell on them, they said,
'O Moses, call to your Lord for us
because He has a covenant with you.
If you remove the abomination from us,
we shall have faith in you
and we shall send you forth with the Children of Israel.'

135. But when We removed the abomination from them
to a term that they would come to,
there they were, breaking their oath.

136. So We took vengeance on them
and drowned them in the sea
because they deemed Our signs false
and were heedless of them;

137. And We caused the people who had been thought weak to inherit
the eastern and western parts of the land,
on which We had bestowed blessing.
And the fairest word of your Lord was fulfilled for the Children of Israel
in return for their patience,
and We destroyed what Pharaoh and his people had been making
and what they had been building.

138. We brought the Children of Israel across the sea,
and they came to a people
who were devoted to some idols that they had.
They said, 'O Moses, make for us a god,
as they have gods.'
He said, 'You are a people who are ignorant.

139. These – all that they are concerned with will be destroyed,
and what they have been doing will be futile.'

140. He said, 'Shall I seek for you a god other than God,
when He has preferred you over all created beings?'

141. And [recall] when We rescued you from the folk of Pharaoh,
who were afflicting you with evil torment,
putting your sons to death and sparing your women.
In that there was a severe trial from your Lord.

142. And when We made an appointment of thirty nights for Moses
and rounded them off with ten [more];
and the full period of his Lord was forty nights.
And Moses said to his brother Aaron,
'Be my deputy among the people.
Set matters right,

and do not follow the way of those who do mischief.'

143. And when Moses came to Our appointed time
and his Lord had spoken to him, he said,
'My Lord, show me and I shall look at you.'
HE said, 'You will not see me;
but look at the mountain:
if it stays still in its place, you will see me.'
And when his Lord revealed Himself to the mountain,
He turned it into a flattened surface,
and Moses fell down thunderstruck
When he recovered, he said, 'Glory be to you.
I turn to you in repentance.
I am the first of the believers.'

144. HE said, 'O Moses, I have chosen you above all men
with My messages and by My speaking [to you].
Take what I have given you
and be among the thankful.'

145. And We wrote down for him on the tablets
an admonition drawn from everything
and an exposition for everything:
'So take it with power,
and order your people to take the fairest of it.
I shall show you the abode of the reprobates.

146. I shall turn away from My signs those who are unjustly haughty in the land.
If they see each sign,
they do not believe in it;
if they see the way of righteousness,
they do not choose it;
if they see the way of error,
they choose it as a way.
That is because they denied the truth of Our signs
and were heedless of them.

147. Those who deny the truth of Our signs and the meeting in the world to come
– their works are useless.
Will they be recompensed,
except for what they used to do?

148. The people of Moses,[8]
after [he had left them],
took a calf from their ornaments,
a body that could make a lowing sound.

---

[8] On the following passage see 20:80–98. See also Exodus 32.

Did they not see that it did not speak to them
and did not guide on any way?
They chose it and became wrong-doers.

149. When they fell on their hands
and they saw that they had gone astray,
they said, 'If our Lord does not have mercy on us
and does not forgive us,
we shall be the losers.'

150. When Moses returned to his people, angry and grieved,
he said, 'Evil is the way you acted as my successors after [I had left you].
Have you hastened the command of your Lord?
He threw down the tablets
and took hold of his brother's head,
dragging him towards himself.
He[9] said, 'Son of my mother,
the people thought me weak and almost killed me.
Do not allow my enemies to gloat over my misfortune,
and do not put me with the people who do wrong.'

151. He[10] said, 'My Lord, forgive me and my brother
and admit us to Your mercy.
You are the most merciful of the merciful.'

152. Those who took the calf
– anger and abasement from their Lord
will reach them in the life of this world.
Thus We requite those who invent lies.

153. But those who do evil deeds
and then repent after them and believe
– your Lord is Forgiving and Merciful
after [they have done] them.

154. When the anger abated in Moses,
he took the tablets,
and there was guidance and mercy
for those who fear their Lord
in what was inscribed on them.

155. And Moses chose his people, seventy men, for Our tryst;[11]
and when the earthquake seized them, he said,
'My Lord, had You wished,
You could have destroyed them and me before.

---

[9] Aaron.
[10] Moses.
[11] *Cf.* Numbers 11:16ff.

162

Will you destroy us for that done by the foolish amongst us?
It is only Your trial,
by which You send astray those whom You wish
and guide those whom You wish.
You are our protector.
Forgive us and have mercy on us.
You are the best of those who forgive.

156. Prescribe good for us in this world and in the next.
We have turned to You.'
HE said, 'My punishment
– I smite with it those whom I wish,
but My mercy embraces everything.
I shall ordain it for those who are god-fearing
and who pay the *zakāt* and who believe in Our signs;

157. Those who follow the messenger, the prophet of his community,
whom they will find mentioned in the *Torah* and the *Gospel* in their possession.
He will order them to do what is recognized as right
and forbid them to do what is disapproved of.
He will make the good things lawful for them
and make the bad things unlawful for them.
He will relieve them of their burden
and of the fetters that have been upon them.
Those who believe him and support him
and help him and follow the light that was sent down with him
– they are the ones who will prosper.'

158. Say, 'O people, I am the messenger of God to you all
– of Him to whom belongs the sovereignty of heaven and earth.
There is no God but Him.
He gives life and causes death.
Believe in God and His messenger,
the prophet of his community,
who believes in God and His words,
and follow him so that you may be guided aright.

159. Among the people of Moses
there is a community who guide by the truth
and act with justice through it.

160. We divided them into twelve tribes, communities;
and We inspired Moses
when his people asked him for water, saying,
'Strike the rock with your staff';
and twelve springs gushed forth from it
– each tribe knew its drinking place –

and We caused the cloud to cast shade over them;
and We sent down manna and quails, [saying],
'Eat of the good things which We have provided for your sustenance.'
They did not wrong Us, but they wronged themselves.

161. [Recall] when they were told, 'Dwell in this settlement,
and eat of it wherever you will
and say, "Unburdening";
and enter the gate in prostration,
and We shall forgive you your sins.
We shall give more to those who do good.'

162. But those of them who did wrong
substituted a different saying for that which they had been told,
and We sent upon them abomination from the sky
because of the wrong they were doing.

163. Ask[s] them about the settlement that was by the sea,
when [its people] transgressed over the Sabbath,
when their fish came to them on the day of their Sabbath,
moving from the deep water,
and did not come to them on the day when they did not keep the Sabbath.
In this way We were trying them because they were profligates.

164. [Recall] when a community of them said,
'Why do you admonish a people
whom God will destroy or punish severely?'
They said, 'As an excuse to your Lord,
and so that they will be god-fearing.'

165. When they forgot that about which they had been reminded,
We rescued those who forbade evil,
and We seized those who did wrong with a distressing punishment
because they were reprobates.

166. When they acted with disdain
concerning that which they had been forbidden,
We said to them, 'Be baboons, slinking away.'

167. And [recall] when your Lord proclaimed
He would send against them till the Day of Resurrection
those who would afflict them with an evil torment.
Your Lord is swift to punish;
yet He is Forgiving and Compassionate.

168. We cut them up into communities in the land.
Some of them righteous
and some of them short of that.
We have tested them with good things and with evil,
so that they might return.

169. They were succeeded by successors after them,
who inherited the Scripture;
but they take the chance offerings of this lowest [world]
and say, 'We shall be forgiven';
and if a similar chance offering comes to them, they will take it.
Was not the covenant of the Scripture taken concerning them,
that they should speak only the truth about God?
And have they not studied what is in it?
The world to come is better for those who are god-fearing.
Do you not understand?

170. Those who take firm hold of the Scripture and perform prayer
– We do not neglect the wages of those who put [things] right.

171. [Recall] when We shook the mountain above them
as if it were a canopy,
and they thought that it was going to fall on them;
[We said], 'Hold fast to what We have given you
and remember what is in it,
so that you may protect yourselves.'

172. And when your Lord took from the Children of Adam,
from their loins, their seed,
and made them testify concerning themselves,
[saying] 'Am I not your Lord?'
They said, 'Of course. We testify'
– lest you say on the Day of Resurrection,
'We were unaware of this.'

173. Or lest you say,
'Our forefathers associated others with God previously,
and we were [their] seed after them.
Will You destroy us because of what was done by those who wrought vanity?'

174. Thus We set out in detail the signs,
so that they will return.

175. Recite[s] to them the tidings of the one to whom We gave Our signs,
but he slipped away from them,
and Satan followed him
and he became one of those who went astray.

176. Had We wished, We would have raised him up through them,[12]
but he clung to the earth and followed his desires.
The parallel to him is that of a dog:
if you attack it, it pants,
and if you leave it alone, it pants.

---

[12] The signs.

That is the case with the people who do not believe in Our signs.
Recount to them the story,
so that they may reflect.

177. Evil as an example are those who have denied the truth of Our signs
and who used to wrong themselves.

178. Those whom God guides are rightly guided.
Those whom He leads astray
– they are the losers.

179. We have created many *Jinn* and men for Jahannam.
They have hearts, with which they do not understand;
they have eyes, with which they do not see;
they have ears, with which they do not hear.
These are like animals – no, they are further astray.
These are the heedless.

180. To God belong the most beautiful names.
Call Him by them
and have nothing to do with those who do wrong concerning His names.
They will be requited for what they have been doing.

181. Of those whom We have created
are a nation who guide by the truth
and act justly by it.

182. Those who deny the truth of Our signs
– We shall lead them on from whence they do not know.

183. I shall bear with them;
My guile is strong.

184. Have they not reflected?
Their comrade is not possessed.
He is simply a plain warner.

185. Have they not considered the kingdom of the heavens and the earth
and the things that God has created
and that it may be that their term has drawn near?
In what discourse will they believe after it?

186. Those whom God sends astray have no one to guide them.
He leaves them wandering blindly in their insolence.

187. They ask you^s about the Hour:
'When is the time of its anchoring?'
Say, 'Knowledge of it is only with my Lord.
Only He will reveal it at its proper time.
It is heavy in the heavens and the earth
– [but] it will only come to you^p suddenly.'
They ask you^s as if you were well-informed about it.
Say, 'Knowledge of it is only with God,

but most of the people do not know.'

188. Say, 'I myself have no power over benefit or harm,
save as God wills.
Had I knowledge of the Invisible,
I would have acquired much good,
and evil would not have touched me.
I am simply a warner and a bearer of good tidings
for a people who believe.

189. [It is] He who created you[P] from a single soul,
from whom He made his spouse,
that he might dwell with her.
Then when he covered her,
she bore a light burden and passed by with it;
but when it became heavy,
the two of them cried out to God, their Lord, saying,
'If you give us a righteous [son],
we shall be grateful.'

190. But after He had given them a righteous [son],
they associated others with Him
concerning that which He had given them.
God is exalted high above anything that they might associate with Him.

191. Do they associate with Him things that create nothing
and have themselves been created

192. And cannot help them
nor help themselves?

193. If you[P] call them to guidance,
they will not follow you.
It is the same for you whether you call them or are silent.

194. Those to whom you[P] call,
to the exclusion of God,
are slaves like you.
Call[P] on them [now] and let them answer you,
if you are truthful.

195. Have they feet with which they walk
or hands with which they grip
or eyes with which they see
or ears with which they hear?
Say, 'Call[P] on those whom you associate with God;
then contrive against me and give me no respite.

196. My protector is God
who has sent down the Scripture.
He gives protection to the righteous.

197. Those on whom you call apart from Him
cannot help you nor do they help themselves.'
198. If you^P call them to the guidance, they do not hear.
You^s see them looking at you and not seeing.
199. Take to forgiveness,[13] and enjoin kindness
and turn from those who are ignorant.
200. If you^s are provoked by provocation from Satan,
seek refuge with God.
He is Hearing and Knowing.
201. Those who protect themselves
when a phantom from Satan touches them,
remind themselves and, lo, they see [clearly],
202. When their brothers would lead them further into error and not stop short.
203. When you^s do not bring them a sign,
they say, 'Why have you^s not chosen one?'
Say, 'I only follow what is revealed to me from my Lord.
This is clear proof from your Lord
and a guidance and a mercy for a people who believe.'
204. When the Recitation is recited,
listen^P to it and be silent,
so that you may receive mercy.
205. Remember^s your Lord in your soul,
humbly and in fear,
without raising your voice publicly,
in the mornings and the evenings,
and do not be heedless.
206. Those who are with your^s Lord are not too proud to serve Him.
They glorify Him and prostrate themselves to Him.

---

[13] The thrust of the text here is very uncertain.

Sūra 8

This Medinan *sūra* contains a number of verses that deal loosely with the Battle of Badr; but the rhetorical nature of the piece means that most of the detail is imprecise. Nor is there any validity, other than that of Tradition, in the argument that a specific verse (verse *n* to give it a general term) fits the events as we know them from historical sources, as the accounts in the historical sources may have grown out of verse *n* and others like it. On the other hand, one should not entirely dismiss the background in those sources: there are textual variants in verse 42, for example, that may well indicate that there were real (though differing) residual folk memories of an actual situation. As was mentioned in the Introductory Note to *Sūra* 3, these problems are not uncommon in the Medinan *sūra*s, but here they seem particularly marked. This is, I believe, because the rhetoric is fast-moving and therefore loose.

The rhetorical impulse starts in the first verse, where the initial question about spoils gets some answer in the phrase 'Spoils belong to God and to the messenger', though this proves not to be the whole answer, as we find in verse 41. However, mention of God and the messenger triggers the rest of verse 1, and that in turn triggers 2–4. The *sūra* then moves abruptly into narrative about recent events (5–12). Even the narrative becomes highly charged in 11–12 and in 13 gives way to a mixture of polemic, injunction and encouragement that takes the *sūra* through to its end. Narrative verses intervene (see verses 17, 26, 30, 32, 42–44, 48–49), but most of these have a rhetorical colouring.

Bell's survey of the *sūra* allows for none of this and shows his method of analysis at its extreme. He starts correctly by saying, 'This *surah*, though usually regarded as having been composed shortly after Badr, cannot be a unity': there can be little doubt that a piece of this length would not have been originally produced as a single entity. However, his division of the *sūra* into 30 short sections has no viable basis, and he fails to see that there is linkage in the variations in assonance (11–16, 25, 47–48, 50–52): 25, 48 and 52 all pick up the assonance in 13. (See Bell, *Translation*, pp. 159–161).

The Spoils

In the name of the Merciful and Compassionate God

1. They ask you^s about the spoils of war.
    Say, 'Spoils belong to God and to the messenger.
    Be^p God-fearing and put right what is between you,[1]
    and obey God and His messenger,
    if you are believers.'

2. The true believers are
    those whose hearts are afraid when God is mentioned;
    those whose faith is increased when His signs are recited to them
    and who put their trust in their Lord;

3. Those who perform prayer
    and who spend from that which We have provided for them.

4. Those are in truth the believers.
    They have degrees [of honour] with their Lord
    and forgiveness and generous provision –

5. Just as your^s Lord caused you^s to go forth from your house with the truth,
    and a part of the believers were averse,

6. Disputing with you^s about the truth
    after it had been made clear,
    as though they were being driven to death,
    as they looked on.

7. [Recall] when God promised
    that one of the two parties[2] should be yours^p
    and you^p were longing that the one without armed protection[3] would be yours;
    but God wished to verify the truth by His words
    and to cut the last remnant of the unbelievers

8. – To verify the truth and falsify the false,
    though the sinners were averse,

9. When you^p sought your Lord's help
    and he responded to you,
    'I shall reinforce you^p with a thousand angels riding behind you.'

10. God did this only as good tidings
    and for your hearts to be reassured by it.
    Help comes only from God.
    God is Mighty and Wise.

11. When He made slumber cover you^p,

---

[1] 'Act rightly among yourselves' or 'make fair division among yourselves'.
[2] The Meccan caravan and the army sent to protect it.
[3] The Meccan caravan.

[providing you with] a security from Him
and sent down on you water from the sky
with which to purify you
and to remove from you the abomination of Satan
and to fortify your hearts
and with which to make firm your feet.

12. – When your^s Lord inspired the angels, saying,
'I am with you^p.
Make those who believe stand firm.
I shall cast terror into the hearts of those who disbelieve.
Smite upon the necks and smite every finger from them.'

13. That is because they broke with God and His messenger.
Those who break with God and His messenger
– God is severe in punishment.

14. That is for you^p;
so taste it,
and [know] that for the unbelievers there is the torment of the Fire.

15. O you who believe,
when you meet those who disbelieve marching into battle,
do not turn your backs to them.

16. Those who turn their backs to them on that day
– unless turning away to fight
or withdrawing to [join another] company –
are burdened with anger from God.
Their abode will be Jahannam
– an evil journey's end.

17. You^p did not kill them.
God killed them;
and you^s did not throw when you threw⁴
– God threw.
[That was] to test the believers by a fair test from Him.
God is Hearing and Knowing.

18. That is for you;
and [know] that God weakens the plotting of the unbelievers.

19. If you^p seek judgement,
judgement has come to you.⁵
If you cease, it will be better for you.
If you return, We shall return,
and your host will be of no avail to you,

---

⁴ Tradition tells us that Muḥammad threw a handful of pebbles at the Meccans.
⁵ The verse refers to the Meccans. There is considerable doubt about the meaning of the first sentence.

even if it is numerous.
[Know] that God is with the believers.

20. O you who believe,
obey God and His messenger,
and do not turn away from him whilst you are listening.

21. Do not be like those who say, 'We hear',
when they do not hear.

22. The worst of beasts in God's view
are the deaf and dumb who do not understand.

23. Had God known any good in them,
He would have made them hear;
yet had He made them hear,
they would [still] have turned away, averse.

24. O you who believe,
respond to God and to the messenger
when He calls you to that which will give you life;
and know that God can come between a man and his own heart
and that you will be rounded up to Him.

25. Protect yourselves against a trial
which will not smite in particular those of you who have done wrong,
and know that God is severe in punishment.

26. And recall when you were few and were thought weak in the land
and [when] you feared that the people would snatch you,
and He gave you refuge and supported you with His help
and provided you with good things,
so that you might be thankful.

27. O you who believe,
do not betray God and the messenger.
Do not betray your trusts knowingly.

28. Know that your possessions and your children are a trial,
and that there is a great wage with God.

29. O you who believe,
if you fear God,
He will assign a salvation to you
and will absolve you of your evil deeds
and will forgive you.
God is Possessed of great bounty.

30. [Recall] when those who do not believe were plotting against you[s],[6]
to bring you[s] to a halt or to kill you or to expel you.
They plot, but God plots,

---

[6] Verses 30–33 refer to the Meccan period, and verses 34 *ff.* to the Medinan period.

and God is the best of plotters.

31. When Our signs are recited to them,
    they say, 'We have heard.
    Were we to wish, we could say something like this.
    These are merely the fables of the ancients.'

32. [Recall] when they said,
    'O God, if this is the truth from You,
    rain stones from the sky upon us
    or bring a painful torment on us.'

33. But God would not punish them when you^s were amongst them.
    Nor would He punish them if they seek forgiveness.

34. Why should not God punish them,⁶
    when they bar [people] from the Sacred Mosque,
    and are not its proper protectors?
    Its proper protectors are those who fear God;
    but most of them do not know.

35. Their prayer at the House is nothing but whistling and clapping of hands:
    'So taste the torment because you have been unbelievers.'

36. Those who do not believe spend their wealth to bar [people] from God's way.
    They will spend it,
    and then it will become a grief for them,
    and then they will be overcome;
    and those who disbelieve will be rounded up into Jahannam,

37. That God may distinguish the bad from the good
    and place the bad on one another
    and heap them all together and put them in Jahannam.
    Those are the losers.

38. Tell^s those who do not believe
    if they cease [their unbelief],
    forgiveness will be granted to them for what is past.
    But if they return [to their unbelief],
    the practice of the ancients has passed away.

39. And fight^p them till there is no mischief
    and all religion is God's.
    If they cease, God is observer of what they do.

40. If they turn away,
    know^p that God is your protector.
    How excellent a protector, how excellent a helper!

41. And know^p that a fifth of whatever you take as spoils
    belongs to God and to the messenger
    and the [near] kinsmen and the orphans
    and the destitute and the traveller,

if you believe in God
and in that which We sent down to Our servant on the day of salvation,
the day the two hosts met each other.
God has power over everything.

42. When you[P] were on the nearer side of the valley
and they were on the further,[7]
and the caravan was below you.
Had you[P] made a meeting together,
you would have failed to keep it,
but [it was arranged]
so that God might conclude a matter that was to be done
so that those who perished might perish by a clear proof
and that those who lived might live by a clear proof
– God is Hearing and Knowing –

43. When God showed you[P] them in your dream as few in number;
had He shown you[P] them as many,
you would have faltered and quarrelled with each other.
But God granted you safety;
He knows the thoughts in men's breasts.

44. When He showed you[P] them in your eyes, when you met them, as few,
and made you few in their eyes,
so that God might conclude a matter that was to be done.
[All] affairs are returned to God.

45. O you who believe,
when you meet a party [of the enemy],
stand firm, and call God frequently to mind,
so that you may prosper.

46. And obey God and His messenger
and do not quarrel
lest you falter and your strength depart.
Be patient.
God is with the patient.

47. Do not be like those who went from their dwellings boastfully
to get themselves seen by the people,
and to bar [others] from God's way.
God comprehends what they do.

48. [Recall] when Satan made their actions seem fair to them and said,
'No one will overcome you to-day,
for I shall be your neighbour.'

48a. But when the two parties faced one another,

---

[7] Instead of 'nearer' and 'further' Ibn Mas'ūd read 'upper' and 'lower'.

he turned on his heels, saying,
'I am quit of you^s.
I see what you^p do not see.
I fear God – and God is severe in punishment.'

49. [And recall] when the hypocrites and those in whose hearts is sickness said,
'These people have been deluded by their religion.'
But those who put their trust in God
– God is Mighty and Wise.

50. If you^s could see when the angels take those who do not believe,
striking their faces and their backs and [saying],
'Taste the torment of the Burning.

51. This is for what your hands have sent forward,
and because God is not unjust to His servants.'

52. As was the way with Pharaoh's family and those who were before them,
– they did not believe in their Lord's signs,
and so God seized them because of their sins.
God is Strong and Severe in punishment.

53. That is because God does not change any blessing that he has bestowed on a people
until they have changed what is within themselves
and because God is Hearing and Knowing.

54. As was the way with Pharaoh's family and those who were before him
– they denied the truth of their Lord's signs,
and so We destroyed them for their sins
and drowned the family of Pharaoh.
All were wrong-doers.

55. The worst of beasts in God's view are the ungrateful ones who do not believe;

56. Those of them with whom you^s have made a covenant
and then they break their covenant every time,
and do not protect themselves.

57. If you^s come upon them in war,
drive them into those behind them and scatter them all,
so that they may be reminded.

58. If you^s fear treachery from any people
cast [your covenant] back to them equally.
God does not love those who are treacherous.

59. Let those who do not believe not suppose
[that] they have outstripped [you].
They cannot frustrate [you].

60. Make^p ready for them whatever armed force and cavalry you can,
by which you can terrify God's enemy
and your enemy and others apart from them,
whom you do not know but whom God knows.

Whatever you spend in God's way will be repaid to you in full
and you will not be wronged.

61. If they incline to peace,
you^P should incline to it and trust in God.
He is the Hearer and the Knower.

62. If they wish to deceive you^s,
God is sufficient for you^s.
He is the one who supported you^s
with His help and with the believers,

63. And has brought their hearts together
– had you^s spent all that is on earth
you^s would not have brought their hearts together,
but God brought them together.
He is the Mighty and the Wise.

64. O prophet,
God is sufficient for you and those believers who follow you.

65. O prophet,
urge on the believers to fight.
If there are twenty steadfast men among you,
they will overcome two hundred;
and if there are a hundred steadfast men among you,
they will overcome a thousand of those who do not believe,
because they are a people who do not understand.

66. Now God has lightened your^P burden
– He knows that there is weakness in you^P.
If there is a steadfast hundred
they will overcome two hundred;
and if there is a thousand of you
they will overcome two thousand,
by God's permission.
God is with the steadfast.

67. It is not for any prophet to have captives
until he bears heavily on the land.
You^P desire the chance gain of this world,
when God desires the Next World for you.
God is Mighty and Wise.

68. Had it not been for a decree[8] from God that has gone before,
a mighty torment would have touched you^P
for what you have taken.

69. Consume what you^P have taken as booty,

---

[8] It is not clear what is meant here by the Arabic *kitāb*.

    [if it is] lawful and good;
    and fear God.
    God is Forgiving and Compassionate.

70.   O prophet,
    say to the captives who are in your hands,
    'If God knows of any good in your hearts,
    He will give you better than what has been taken from you,
    and He will forgive you.
    God is Forgiving and Compassionate.'

71.   And if they wish to betray you[s],
    they have betrayed God before,
    and so He has granted [you] power over them.
    God is Knowing and Wise.

72.   Those who have believed and have migrated
    and striven with their possessions and their persons in God's way,
    and those who have given them shelter and helped them
    – those are friends of one another.

72a.   Those who have believed but have not migrated
    – you[p] have no duty of friendship towards them until they migrate;

72b.   But if they seek your[p] help concerning religion,
    it is your[p] duty to help them,
    except against a people where there is a compact between you[p] and them.
    God is Observer of what you do.

73.   Those who disbelieve are friends of one another.

73a.   If you[p] do not do this,
    there will be mischief and great corruption in the land.

74.   Those who have believed and have emigrated and striven in God's way
    and those who have given them shelter and helped them
    – these are the believers in truth.
    They will have forgiveness and a bountiful provision.

75.   Those who have believed afterwards and migrated and striven with you[p],
    they are of you;
    and those who are blood relations are nearer to one another in God's decree.
    God is Aware of everything.

Sūra 9

The *sūra* is another amalgam of passages from different times in the Medinan period, the majority of which are quite late. The reference to the battle of Ḥunayn in verse 25 must postdate that event (8 AH/ February 630 AD); and equally the reference in verse 7 to 'those with whom you have made a covenant at the Sacred Mosque' must postdate the conquest of Mecca in January of that year. For much of the *sūra*, however, the dating comes largely from the biographies of Muḥammad and depends on the extent to which the traditional accounts are accepted. Clearly, specific events are being referred to, but the rhetoric of many passages is such that the identification of verses with the events is irrelevant.

The differences of view about the context of the first part of the *sūra* are particularly marked. Here Pickthall distils the traditional view by saying that 'verses 1–12, forming the proclamation of immunity towards the idolaters were revealed after the pilgrims had started for Mecca in the ninth year of the Hijrah and sent by special messenger to Abū Bakr, leader of the pilgrimage, to be read out by 'Alī [in March 631 AD] to the multitudes at Mecca'. No doubt there was a proclamation on that pilgrimage, but the historical detail is highly suspect. Bell has a quite different view of the length of the passage involved: 1–28; but he then goes on to argue that the passage is composed of two proclamations that were originally quite separate but are now haphazardly fused into one. This view seems to stem from trying to impose a strict logic on the rhetorical parallelism of verses 1–2 and 3–3a. Therein lies the weakness of Bell's interesting article 'Muhammad's Pilgrimage Proclamation' (*Journal of the Royal Asiatic Society*, 1937, pp. 233–44).

It would seem that verses 1–2 and 3–3a provide the *sūra* with an exordium of sorts, from which a complex series of polemical passages unfold. The first of these takes up verses 3b–16. Here the polemic is against old Arabia – not only any lingering pockets of polytheists (*mushrikūn*) around Mecca but in the whole of the Hijaz and further afield. 3b sets out the basic intent; 4 makes an exception; and then 5 gives the main thrust: the polytheists are to be dealt with in a manner which the Khārijites would later appropriate for themselves. It is because of the perception of the polytheists in very general terms that the sacred months are involved. Though they are not listed, they are clearly the traditional sacred months of the general population. As is commonly the case with stern injunctions, there is some alleviation (end of 5, 6, 7). Verse 8 takes us back to the arrangements made after the conquest of Mecca, with the end of 8 showing disenchantment, and polemic follows in 9–10. Verse 11 takes us back to the end of 5, but with 12 the polemic intensifies and continues to the end of 16. Verses 17–28 form a further passage of polemic, somewhat different in thrust and tone to what has preceded, but still aimed at the polytheists. At verse 29 the attack switches to the

Prophet's enemies amongst those who are not polytheists but who do not accept his message, *i.e.* the Jews and the Christians. The attack, which lasts to verse 35, is disdainfully vague about the Jews and Christians, but unforgiving. Verses 36–37 then switch abruptly to the prohibition of intercalation, *i.e.* back to the polytheists. Verse 38 then turns to the theme that occupies most of the rest of the *sūra*: the enemy within or attached to the community. Those who do not follow the approved path, be they backsliders, hypocrites (*munāfiqūn*), unsupportive *bedu,* or builders of or worshippers at an unauthorized mosque, are all condemned. This long passage is not a unity – it is in any case occasionally broken up by verses that stress other themes – but the overall effect is unrelenting. At verse 111 the focus turns to encouragement and exhortation of the believers, but at verse 119 it moves back to the laggards and unbelievers.

There is a distinct possibility that the *sūra* was still being added to when Muhammad died. That might explain traditions that verses 128–9 were attached to the end of the *sūra* by the redactor Zayd b. Thābit when the 'Uthmanic recension was being compiled. In style, though not in subject, it has considerable affinity with *Sūra 5*.

The standard text omits the *basmala* at the beginning, making it the only *sūra* not to begin with this formula. However, we know that 'Abdallāh ibn Mas'ūd did use the *basmala* here. Unfortunately, there is no satisfactory explanation either for his inclusion of it or for its omission by others.

Repentance

1.   Immunity from God and His messenger
   towards those of the polytheists
   with whom you^P have made a covenant:
2.   Travel^P freely in the land for four months,[1]
   but know^P that you cannot frustrate God
   and that God will shame the unbelievers.
3.   And a proclamation from God and His messenger
   to the people on the day of the Great Pilgrimage[2]
   that God and His messenger are quit of the polytheists.
3a.   If you^P turn in repentance, it will be better for you;
   but if you turn your backs,
   know that you cannot frustrate God.
3b.   Give^s to those who do not believe the tidings of a painful punishment,
4.   Though that will not be the case with those polytheists
   with whom you^P have made a covenant

---

[1] The months are Rajab, Dhū l-Qa'da, Dhū l-Hijja and Muharram.
[2] The 10th of Dhū l-Hijja.

and who have then not failed you in anything
and have not supported anyone against you.
Fulfil their covenant to them [to the end of its] term.
God loves those who protect themselves.

5. Then, when the sacred months have passed,
kill[p] the polytheists wherever you find them
and take them and confine them
and lie in wait for them at every place of ambush.
If they repent and perform prayer and give the *zakāt*,
release them.
God is Forgiving and Compassionate.

6. If any of the polytheists seeks your[s] protection,
grant[s] him protection until he can hear the words of God
and then convey him to his place of safety.
That is because they are a people who do not know.

7. How can the polytheists have a treaty with God and His messenger
– except those with whom you[p] have made a covenant at the Sacred Mosque?
As long as they go straight with you[p],
act[p] straight with them.
God loves those who protect themselves.

8. How?
If they get the better of you,
they will not observe any pact or treaty concerning you.
They satisfy you with their mouths,
but their hearts refuse.
Most of them are reprobates.

9. They have bought little gain at the cost of God's signs,
and they have barred [men] from His way.
How evil is that which they have been doing.

10. They do not observe any pact or treaty concerning a believer.
These are the transgressors.

11. If they repent and perform prayer and give the *zakāt*,
[they can become] your[p] brothers in religion.
We make the signs for a people who know.

12. But if they break their oaths after they have pledged them
and make thrusts against your[p] religion,
fight[p] the leaders of unbelief
– they have no binding oaths –
so that they desist.

13. Will you[p] not fight a people who broke their oaths
and intended to drive out the messenger,
and took the initiative against you first?

Do you fear them?
God is more deserving of your fear,
if you are believers.

14. Fight them and God will punish them by your hands
and will shame them and help you against them
and heal the breasts of a people who believe;

15. And He will remove the anger in their hearts.
God relents towards those whom He wishes.
God is Knowing and Wise.

16. Or did you reckon that you would be left alone,
when God does not yet know those of you who strive
and who do not take any intimate friend
apart from God and His messenger and the believers.
God is informed of what you do.

17. It is not for the polytheists to visit God's places of worship,
witnessing against themselves that they are unbelievers.
Those – their works are in vain,
and they will remain in the Fire for ever.

18. The only ones to visit God's places of worship
will be those who believe in God and the Last Day
and perform prayer and give the *zakāt* and fear only God.
It may be that those will be among those who are guided aright.

19. Do you[p] reckon giving water to the pilgrim and visiting the Sacred Mosque
to be the same as those who believe in God and the Last Day
and strive in God's way.
They are not equal in God's view.
God does not guide the people who do wrong.

20. Those who believe and who have migrated
and striven in God's way with their possessions and their persons
are greater in rank in God's view.
Those are the triumphant.

21. Their Lord gives them the good tidings of mercy and approval from Him,
and gardens where they will have lasting bliss,

22. Remaining in them for ever.
With God is a mighty wage.

23. O you who believe,
do not take your fathers and your brothers as friends
if they prefer unbelief to belief.
Those of you who take them for friends
– those are the wrong-doers.

24. Say, 'If your fathers, your sons, your brothers,
your wives and your tribe,

and wealth you have acquired,
and commerce you fear will slacken,
and dwellings you approve of
are dearer to you than God and His messenger and striving in His way,
wait till God brings His command.
God does not guide the people who are reprobates.'

25. God has helped you on many fields and at the battle of Ḥunayn,[3]
when your multitude pleased you
but it availed you nothing.
The land, wide as it was, was too narrow for you,
and you turned your backs in retreat.

26. Then God sent His reassurance down
to His messenger and to the believers
and sent down hosts whom you could not see
and punished those who did not believe.
That is the recompense of the unbelievers.

27. Then, after that, God relents towards those whom He will.
God is Forgiving and Compassionate.

28. O you who believe,
the polytheists are unclean.
Let them not approach the Sacred Mosque after this year of theirs.
If you fear poverty,
God will give you sufficiency from His bounty, if He wishes.
God is Knowing and Wise.

29. Fight from among the people who have been given the Scripture

30. those who do not believe in God and the Last Day

31. and who do not forbid that which God and His messenger have forbidden
and who do not follow the religion of truth,
until they pay the tribute readily, having been humbled.

30. The Jews say, ''Uzayr[4] is the son of God';
and the Christians say, 'al-Masīḥ is the son of God.'
That is what they say with their mouths,
conforming to what was said by those who disbelieved before them.
God confound them.
How they are embroiled in lies!

31. They have taken their rabbis and monks
as lords apart from God

---

[3] Ḥunayn, not far from al-Ṭāʾif, is where the Muslims fought the Hawāzin tribal confederation, probably at the beginning of February 630 AD. At first the Hawāzin got the upper hand, but they were eventually defeated.

[4] Ezra.

as well as *al-Masīḥ*, the son of Mary
– yet they were commanded to serve only One God.
There is no god but Him.
May He be glorified high above what they associate with Him.

32. They wish to extinguish God's light with their mouths,
but God refuses [to do] anything other than to perfect His light,
even though the unbelievers dislike that.

33. [It is] He who has sent His messenger with the guidance and the religion of truth,
to cause it to prevail over all [other] religion,
even though the polytheists dislike that.

34. O you who believe,
many of the rabbis and monks consume people's possessions in vanity
and bar [people] from God's way.
Those who hoard gold and silver
and do not spend it in God's way
– give them the tidings of a painful torment,

35. On the day when [the gold and silver] will be heated up in the fire of Jahannam
and their foreheads, sides and backs will be branded with them:
'This is what you hoarded for yourselves.
Taste what you have been hoarding.'

36. The number of the months with God is twelve,
[laid down] in God's decree
on the day that He created the heavens and the earth.
Four of them are sacred.[5]
That is the right religion.
Do not wrong yourselves in them.
But fight the polytheists in all of them,
as they fight you in all of them.
And know that God is with those who protect themselves.

37. Intercalation[6] is a further unbelief
by which those whose who disbelieve are led astray.
They allow it one year and forbid it another year
to level up the number of what God has made sacred
and to allow what God has forbidden.
The evil of their actions has been made to seem good to them.
God does not guide the people who disbelieve.

38. O you who believe,
what is the matter with you?
When you are told, 'Go out in God's way',

---

[5] See verse 2, note 1.
[6] Literally 'postponement'.

you sink heavily to the ground.
Are you content with the life of this world
rather than the world to come?
The enjoyment of the life of this world is a little thing,
compared with the world to come.

39.   If you do not come out, He will punish you severely
and will substitute another people for you.
You will not injure him in anything.
God has power over everything.

40.   If you do not help him,[7] God has already helped him,
when those who disbelieved expelled him,
the second of two:
when the two of them[8] were in the cave
and he said to his companion, 'Do not grieve. God is with us.'
And God sent His reassurance upon him
and helped him with hosts whom you did not see,
and made the word of those who disbelieved the lowest,
while the word of God is the highest.
God is Mighty and Wise.

41.   Go out, light and heavy,[9]
and strive with your persons and your possessions in God's way.
That is better for you, if you have knowledge.

42.   Had there been chance gain nearby and an easy journey,
they would have followed you[s],
but the distance was too great for them.
But they will swear by God,
'If we had been able, we would have gone out with you.'
They destroy their souls.
God knows that they are lying.

43.   May God pardon you[s].
Why did you[s] give them permission,
until it became clear to you who told the truth
and until you knew the liars?

44.   Those who believe in God and the Last Day do not ask your[s] permission
to strive with their persons and their possessions.
God is well aware of those who protect themselves.

45.   The only ones to ask permission
are those who do not believe in God and the Last Day,

---

[7] Muḥammad.

[8] Muḥammad's companion is traditionally taken to be Abū Bakr.

[9] *i.e.* on foot or mounted.

and whose hearts feel doubt
– they waver in their doubt.
46. Had they wished to go out, they would have made some preparation for it;
but God did not want them to be sent out,
and so He held them back,
and it was said, 'Sit around with those who sit around.'
47. Had they gone forth among you,
they would have added nothing but trouble for you
and would have moved hither and thither among you,
seeking to cause mischief for you
– and there are some of you would have listened to them.
God is Aware of those who do wrong.
48. Previously they sought to cause mischief and turned things upside down for you[s]
until the truth came and God's command was made manifest,
though they were unwilling.
49. There are those among them who say,
'Give[s] me leave and do not tempt me.'
Truly they have fallen into temptation
– and Jahannam encompasses the unbelievers.
50. If good befalls you[s], they are vexed by it;
if misfortune befalls you, they say,
'We took hold of our affair beforehand,'
and they turn away, rejoicing.
51. Say, 'Only that which God has ordained for us will befall us.
He is our Protector.
Let the believers put their trust in God.'
52. Say, 'Are you waiting for anything but one of the two fairest things[10] to befall us?
In your case we are waiting
for God to afflict you with a torment from Him
or at our hands.
So wait – we shall be waiting with you.'
53. Say, 'Spend, willingly or unwillingly
– it will not be accepted from you.
You were a people who were reprobates.'
54. Nothing prevents their expenditure being accepted from them
– except that they have not believed in God and in His messenger
and come to prayer only lazily
and spend only unwillingly.
55. Let neither their possessions nor their children
win your admiration.

---

[10] Traditionally understood to be martyrdom and victory.

God wishes to punish them through those in the life of this world
and for their souls to pass away while they are unbelievers.

56. They swear by God that they are of you.
But they are not of you.
They are a people who are afraid.

57. Were they to find a place of refuge or caves
or a place to enter,
they would turn away to it in haste.

58. There are some of them who find fault with you[s] in the matter of alms.
If they are given some, they are content,
but if they are not given some, they are angry.

59. If only they were content with what God and His messenger have given them
and were to say, 'God is enough for us.
God will give us some of His bounty,
as will His messenger.
We turn to God.'

60. The alms are for the poor and the destitute,
for those who work to collect them
and those whose hearts are to be reconciled,
to free slaves and debtors,
in God's way and for the traveller
– a duty imposed by God,
and God is Knowing and Wise.

61. There are some of them who vex the prophet, saying,
'He is an ear.'
Say, 'An ear of good for you,
who believes in God and believes the believers
and is a mercy for those of you who believe.'
Those of you who vex the messenger of God will have a painful torment.

62. They swear to you[p] by God to please you,
but God and His messenger have a better right to be pleased by them,
if they are believers.

63. Do they not know that those who oppose God and His messenger
will have the Fire of Jahannam,
in which they will remain for ever?
That is the great humiliation.

64. The hypocrites are afraid lest a *sūra* should be sent down against them,
telling them what is in their hearts.
Say, 'Mock. God will bring out what you fear.'

65. If you ask them, they will say,

'We were only plunging[11] and playing.'

Say, 'Were you mocking God and His messenger and His signs?

66. Do not make any excuse.
You have disbelieved after having believed.
If We forgive one party of you,
We shall punish another party,
because they have been sinners.'

67. The hypocrites, male and female, are of a kind.
They enjoin what is recognized as disreputable
and they forbid what is recognized as reputable,
and they keep their hands shut.
They have forgotten God,
and so He has forgotten them.
The hypocrites are the transgressors.

68. God has promised the hypocrites, male and female, and the unbelievers
the Fire of Jahannam,
in which they will remain for ever.
That is enough for them.
God has cursed them,
and they will have a lasting punishment,

69. Like those before you[P] who had greater strength than you
and who had more possessions and children
and who sought enjoyment of their share
– you have sought enjoyment of your share
as did those before you,
and you have plunged[11]
like those who plunged [before you].
Their works have failed in this world and the next.
Those are the losers.

70. Have they not heard the tidings of those before them:
the people of Noah, 'Ād, Thamūd,
the people of Abraham, the men of Madyan,
and the overwhelmed settlements?[12]
Their messengers brought them clear proofs.
God would not wrong them,
but they wronged themselves.

71. The believers, male and female, are friends to one another.
They enjoin what is recognised as reputable

---

[11] See the note on 6:68.

[12] The overwhelmed settlements are also referred to in 55:53 and 69:9. They are traditionally taken to be Sodom and Gomorrah, but an Arabian location is quite possible.

and forbid what is recognized as disreputable.
They perform prayer and pay the *zakāt*
and obey God and His messenger.
These – God will have mercy on them.
God is Mighty and Wise.

72. God has promised the believers, male and female,
    gardens through which rivers flow,
    in which they will remain for ever,
    and good dwellings in the Gardens of Eden;
    and God's approval is greater.
    That is the great triumph.

73. O prophet, strive against the unbelievers and the hypocrites.
    Be harsh with them.
    Their abode is Jahannam – an evil journey's end.

74. They swear by God that they did not say it;
    but they did say the word of unbelief,
    and disbelieved after they had surrendered.
    They had in mind what they did not attain,
    and took revenge only that they might be enriched by God and His messenger
        through His bounty.
    If they repent, it will be better for them;
    if they turn away, God will inflict a painful torment
    on them in this world and in the next,
    and they will have no protector or helper in the land.

75. Among them there are those who made a covenant with God:
    'If He gives us some of His bounty,
    we shall make offerings and be among the righteous.'

76. Yet when He gave them some of His bounty,
    they were stingy with it,
    and turned away, averse.

77. In consequence He has put hypocrisy in their hearts
    until the day when they meet Him
    because they broke their promise to God
    and because they were liars.

78. Do they not know that God knows their secret and their private conversation
    and that God is the Knower of invisible things?

79. Those who find fault with those of the believers who volunteer alms
    and with those who find nothing [to give] but their endeavours
    and deride them – God derides them,
    and they will have a painful torment.

80. Ask forgiveness for them or do not ask forgiveness for them.
    [It is immaterial.]

If you ask forgiveness for them seventy times,
God will not forgive them.
That is because they disbelieve in God and His messenger.
God does not guide the people who are reprobates.

81. Those who were left behind[13]
rejoiced at sitting still behind God's messenger,
and were averse to striving in God's way
with their possessions and their persons.
They said, 'Do not go out in the heat.'
Say, 'The fire of Jahannam is hotter,
did they but understand.'

82. Let them laugh a little and let them weep much,
in recompense for what they have amassed.

83. If God returns you^s to a party of them
and they seek your permission to go out,
say, 'You will never go forth with me.
You will never fight an enemy with me.
You were content to sit still on the first occasion.
So sit with those who stay behind.'

84. Never pray^s over any of them who has died
nor stand over his grave.
They disbelieved in God and His messenger,
and they died as reprobates.

85. Let neither their possessions nor their children
win your admiration.
God wishes to punish [such disbelievers] through them in the life of this world
and for their souls to pass away while they are unbelievers.

86. When a *sūra* is sent down,
saying, 'Believe in God and strive with His messenger,'
the men of wealth among them ask permission [to see] you
and say, 'Allow us to be among those who sit at home.'

87. They are content to be with those who stay behind,
and a seal is put on their hearts,
and so they do not understand.

88. But the messenger and those who believe with him
strive with their possessions and their persons.
Those are the ones who will have the good things.
Those are the ones who will prosper.

89. God has prepared for them gardens
through which rivers flow,

---

[13] Traditionally taken to be those who did not go on the expedition to Tabūk in 9 AH.

in which they will remain for ever.
That is the great triumph.

90. Those of the *bedu*[14] who had an excuse
came for permission to be granted to them.
Those who lied to God and His messenger sat at home.
A painful torment will befall those of them who disbelieve.

91. There is no blame on the weak, the sick
and those who can find nothing to spend
if they are sincere to God and His messenger.
There is no way against those who do good
– God is Forgiving and Compassionate –

92. Nor against those to whom you[s] said
when they came to see you
for you to give them a mount,
'I cannot find anything on which to mount you.'
They turned away, with their eyes flowing with tears,
through their grief that they could not find anything to spend.

93. The way is only against those who seek your permission [to stay behind]
when they are rich.
They are content to be with those who stay behind;
and God puts a seal on their hearts,
and so they do not know.

94. When you[p] return to them, they will make their excuses to you.
Say[s], 'Do not make excuses.
We do not believe you.
God has given us some news of you.
God and His messenger will see your work,
and then you will be returned to Him who knows the Invisible and the Witnessed,
and He will tell you what you used to do.'

95. When you go back to them, they will swear to you by God,
[to get] you to turn aside from them.
Turn aside from them.
They are an abomination.
Their lodging will be Jahannam,
as a recompense for what they have been amassing.

96. They swear to you, that you may be content with them.
If you are content with them,
God is not content with the people who are reprobates.

97. The *bedu* are more firmly embedded in unbelief and hypocrisy
and are more likely not to know the limits of what God has revealed to His

---

[14] The *bedu*, the Arab nomadic tribes, are mentioned in this *sūra* and in *Sūra*s 33, 48 and 49.

messenger.
God is Knowing and Wise.

98. Among the *bedu* are those who take what they spend as an imposition
and wait for the turns of fortune to go against you.
The evil turn will be theirs.
God is Hearing and Knowing.

99. Among the *bedu* are those who believe in God and the Last Day
and take what they spend as offerings that bring them close to God
– and [likewise] the prayers of the messenger.
Truly they are an offering for them.
God will admit them to His mercy.
God is Forgiving and Compassionate.

100. Those who have precedence are the first of the Emigrants and of the Helpers
and those who followed them in goodness.
God is content with them and they with Him.
He has prepared for them gardens
through which rivers flow,
in which they will remain for ever.
That is the great triumph.

101. Among the *bedu* around you there are some hypocrites;
and among the people of al-Madina [are some who] have persisted in hypocrisy,
whom you do not know.
We know them.
We shall punish them twice;
then they will be returned to a severe torment.

102. And [there are] others who have confessed their sins.
They have mixed a righteous deed with an evil one.
Perhaps God will relent towards them.
God is Forgiving and Compassionate.

103. Take[s] alms from their possessions,
by which you[s] might purify them and make them clean,
and pray[s] for them.
Your[s] prayers are a comfort for them.
God is Hearing and Knowing.

104. Do they not know
that God accepts repentance from His servants and takes alms
and that God is the Relenting and the Compassionate?

105. And say, 'Work
– and God and His messenger and the believers will see your work.
You will be returned to the Knower of the Invisible and the Visible,
and He will tell you what you used to do.'

106. There are others who are deferred to God's decree,

whether He punishes them or relents towards them.
God is Knowing and Wise.

107. Those who have chosen[15] a mosque in opposition and unbelief,
and to cause dissent among the believers
and to provide a place where
those who previously fought God and His prophet
might lie in ambush
– they will swear, 'We only meant the best.'
God bears witness that they are liars.

108. Never stand[s] in it.
A mosque founded on piety from the first day
is more worthy for you to stand in.
In it there will be men who love to keep themselves pure.
God loves those who keep themselves pure.

109. Are those who founded their building on piety and approval from God better
or those who founded their building on the lip of a crumbling bank
that has tumbled with him into the Fire of Jahannam?
God does not guide the people who do wrong.

110. The building they built will continue to be a cause of doubt in their hearts,
unless their hearts are cut to pieces.
God is Knowing and Wise.

111. God has bought from the believers their persons and their possessions
for the price that the Garden will be theirs.
They will fight in God's way
and will kill and be killed:
a promise binding on God in the *Torah* and the *Gospel* and the Recitation.
Who fulfils His covenant more fully than God?
Rejoice[p] in the bargain you[p] have made with Him.
That is the great triumph.

112. Those who turn in repentance,
those who serve, those who praise,
those who travel [for God], those who bow,
those who prostrate themselves,
those who enjoin what is considered right
and who forbid what is considered wrong,
those who keep God's limits
– give good tidings to the believers.

113. It is not for the prophet and those who believe to seek pardon for the polytheists,
even if they were to be near kinsmen,
after it has become clear to them

---

[15] Or 'built'. The biographies of Muḥammad tell us of a mosque built in the Qubā' suburb of Medina.

that they are companions of the Fire.

114. Abraham's seeking of forgiveness for his father
was only because of a promise he had made to him.
When it became clear to him that his father was an enemy of God,
he would have nothing to do with him
– and Abraham was kind-hearted and prudent.

115. God would never lead a people astray after He had guided them
until He might make clear to them what they should guard against.
God is aware of all things.

116. To God belongs the sovereignty of heaven and earth.
He gives life and He brings death.
Apart from God you have no protector or helper.

117. God has turned to the Prophet
and to the Emigrants and the Helpers
who followed him in the hour of difficulty,
after the hearts of a party of them had almost swerved aside.
He turned towards them
– He is Kind and Compassionate –

118. And towards the three who were left behind.[16]
Then, when the earth in all its vastness was straitened for them,
and their souls were straitened for them,
and they thought that the only refuge from God was [to turn] to Him
– then He turned to them that they might repent.
God is the Relenting and the Compassionate.

119. O you who believe,
protect yourselves against God and be with the truthful.

120. It is not for the people of Medina and the *bedu* around them
to lag behind God's messenger
and to prefer their lives to his.
That is because they are not afflicted by thirst
nor by fatigue nor by hunger in God's way,
nor do they tread any step that enrages the unbelievers
nor do they gain anything from an enemy
without a good deed being written to their account through it.
God does not neglect the wage of those who do good.

121. Nor do they spend anything great or small
nor cross any valley without it being written to their account,
that God may recompense them for the best of what they used to do.

122. The believers should not go out [to fight] all in one body.
But why should not a party of every group of them go forth,

---

[16] Said to be three of the *Anṣār*.

that they may gain understanding in religion
and that they may warn their people when they return
so that they may be careful?

123. O you who believe,
fight those of the unbelievers who are near you,
and let them find harshness in you
and know that God is with those who protect themselves.

124. Whenever a *sūra* is sent down,
there are some of them who say,
'Which of you has been increased in faith by this?'
As for those who believe,
they have been increased in belief,
and they rejoice.

125. As for those in whose hearts is sickness,
they have abomination added to their abomination,
and they die while they are unbelievers.

126. Do they not see that they are tried once or twice every year?
Yet they do not turn [in repentance] nor are they reminded.

127. Whenever a *sūra* is sent down,
they look at one another:
'Does anyone see you[s]?'
Then they turn away.
God has turned their hearts
because they are a people who do not understand.

128. A messenger has come to you[P] from among yourselves
– what you[P] suffer is grievous to him.
[He is] anxious over you,
and kind and compassionate towards the believers.

129. If they turn away, say, 'God is sufficient for me.
There is no God but Him.
I put my trust in Him
– He is the Lord of the mighty throne.'

Sūra 10

This *sūra* is considered to come from the late Meccan period. Some authorities ascribe verses 40 and 94–95/96 to the Medinan period. The suggestion about 94–95 is plausible, though there are no definite indications; and there may be a case for arguing that the use of the term *ḥanīf* in verse 105 points in the same direction. Whatever the case, it would appear that the present form of the *sūra* dates from the Medinan period. A couple of verses on the revelation (1–2) lead into a short passage on God and His signs (3–6). Polemic starts at verse 7 and continues to verse 70, though it is broken up in various ways, thematically and by the frequent addresses to Muḥammad. Verses 71–93 are given over to narratives (Noah 71–4, Moses and the Children of Israel 75–93). Polemic returns with verse 93a and continues to the end of the *sūra*. Once again Muḥammad is frequently addressed. The *sūra* takes its name from the passing reference to Yūnus (Jonah) in verse 98.

Jonah

In the name of the Merciful and Compassionate God

1. *Alif, Lām, Rā'.*[1]
   These are the signs of the wise Scripture.
2. Is it a wonder for mankind
   that We have revealed to a man among them [the message],
   'Warn mankind
   and bring to those who believe the tidings
   that they will have a sure footing with their Lord'?
   The unbelievers say,
   'This man is a clear sorcerer.'
3. Your[p] Lord is God,
   who created the heavens and the earth in six days,
   then set Himself on the Throne,
   directing the affair.
   There is no intercessor unless He has given His permission.
   That is God, your Lord.
   So serve Him.
   Will you not be reminded?
4. To Him is the return for all of you[p]

---

[1] On the mystical letters see the note on 2:1.

– the promise of God is true.
He originates creation,
then causes it to return,
so that He may reward with equity
those who believe and do deeds of righteousness.
And those who disbelieve
– they will have a drink of boiling water and a painful punishment
in return for their unbelief.

5. It is He who made the sun an illumination and the moon a light,
and decreed for it mansions,
that you[P] might know the number of years and the reckoning [of time].
God created that only with the truth,
detailing the signs to a people who know.

6. In the alternation of night and day
and in what God created in the heavens and the earth
are signs for people who fear God.

7. Those who do not expect to meet Us
and are content with the life of this world
and are at rest in it
and those who are heedless of Our signs,

8. Those – their dwelling is the Fire,
because of what they have earned.

9. Those who believe and do righteous works,
their Lord guides them by their faith.
Rivers will flow beneath them in the gardens of bliss.

10. Their call there will be, 'Glory be to You, O God';
and their greeting there, 'Peace';
and the conclusion of their call will be,
'Praise belongs to God, Lord of created beings.'

11. If God were to hasten evil to people
with the same speed that they seek good to be hastened [to them],
their term would have been finished for them.
And so We leave those who do not expect to meet Us
wandering blindly in their insolence.

12. Whenever adversity touches man, he calls to Us,
[whether he is] on his side, or sitting, or standing;
but when We have removed his adversity from him,
he passes by, as though he had not called Us
to deal with any adversity that touched him.
Thus what the prodigal were doing
has been made to seem fair to them.

13. In the past We have destroyed generations before you[P]

when they did wrong
and their messengers came to them with the clear proofs,
but they would not believe.
Thus We recompense the people who sin.

14. Then We appointed you^P as successors in the land after them,
that We might see how you act.

15. And when Our signs are revealed to them as clear proofs,
those who do not expect to meet Us say,
'Bring a different Recitation from this,
or change it.'
Say, 'It is not for me to change it of my own accord.
I only follow what is revealed to me.
I fear the punishment of a mighty day
if I disobey my Lord.'

16. Say, 'Had God willed,
I would not have recited it to you^P,
nor would He have made it known to you.
I dwelt with you a lifetime before it.
Will you not understand?'

17. Who does greater wrong
than those who invent lies against God
or deny the truth of His signs?
Sinners do not prosper.

18. They worship,
to the exclusion of God,
what can neither hurt them nor benefit them.
They say, 'These are our intercessors with God.'
Say, 'Will you^P tell God
what He does not know in the heavens or on earth?'
Glory be to Him.
May He be exalted far above what they associate with Him.

19. The people were only one community,
but then they disagreed;
and had it not been for a word that had preceded[2] from your^s Lord,
there would have been a decision between them
concerning that about which they differed.

20. They say, 'Why has a sign not been sent down to him from his Lord?'
Say, 'The Invisible belongs only to God.
Wait^P. I shall be one of those who wait with you.'

21. When We cause the people to taste some mercy

---

[2] Postponing Judgement. The phrase occurs several times.

after some adversity has touched them,
lo, they have some plot against Our signs.
Say, 'God is swifter in plotting.
Our messengers note what you plot.'

22.   It is He who enables you to travel by land and sea;
then, when you are in the ships,
and they run with [the people in them] with a fair breeze
and they rejoice in it,
a storm-wind comes on them,
and the waves come on them from every side
and they think that they are engulfed.
They call to God, being sincere to Him in their faith,
'If You deliver us from this,
we shall be among the thankful.'

23.   Yet when He has delivered them,
lo, they act outrageously in the land without any justification.
O people, your outrageousness is only against yourselves.
[You have] enjoyment of the life in this world;
then your return is to Us,
and We shall tell you what you used to do.

24.   The life of this world is just like water
which We send down from the sky,
and the plants of the earth,
which men and animals eat, mingle with it;
then, when the earth has taken on its embellishment and adorned itself
and its people think that they have power over it,
Our command comes on it by night or in the day-time;
and We make it stubble
as if it had not flourished yesterday.
Thus We make the signs distinct
for a people who reflect.

25.   God summons to the abode of peace
and leads those whom He wishes to a straight path.

26.   Those who do good
will have the fairest [reward] and more.
Neither dust nor humiliation will come over their faces.
Those are the companions of the Garden,
in which they will remain for ever.

27.   Those who have amassed evil deeds
– the recompense of an evil deed will be the like of it.
Humiliation will come over them,
and they will have no protector from God.

It is as though their faces were covered with pieces of night,
bringing darkness [to them].
Those are the companions of the Fire,
in which they will remain for ever.

28. On the day when We round them all up,
then We shall say to those who associate [others with Us],
'Take up your places,
you and those whom you made Our associates.'
Then We shall set a space between them,
and those whom they made Our associates will say,
'It was not us you served.

29. God is a sufficient witness between you[P] and us.
We were unaware of your service.'

30. There every soul will experience what it has done previously.
They will be returned to God, their true Protector,
and what they used to invent will fail them.

31. Say, 'Who gives you[P] sustenance from the heavens and the earth?
Who brings forth the living from the dead
and brings forth the dead from the living?
Who possesses hearing and sight?
Who manages the affair?'
They will say, 'God'.
Say, 'Will you not fear God?'

32. That is God, your[P] true Lord.
After the truth what is there except error?
How are you turned about?

33. Thus the word of your[S] Lord
– that they do not believe –
is realized against the reprobates.

34. Say, 'Among those whom you[P] make associates
is there anyone who originates creation,
then causes it to return?'
Say, 'God originates creation,
then causes it to return.
How are you[P] involved in lies?'

35. Say, 'Among those whom you[P] make [God's] associates
is there anyone who guides to the truth?'
Say, 'God guides to the truth.
Is the one who guides to the truth more worthy to be followed
or the one who guides only if he is guided?
What is the matter with you[P]?
How do you judge?

36. Most of them follow only conjecture;
    and conjecture is of no avail against the truth.
    God is aware of what they do.

37. This Recitation is not such as could have been invented
    by any but God.[3]
    It is a confirmation of what was before it
    and a detailing of the Scripture,
    in which there is no doubt,
    from the Lord of created beings.

38. Or do they say, 'He has invented it'?
    Say, 'Then bring[P] a *sūra* like it;
    and call on those you can apart from God,
    if you are truthful.'

39. No! They have denied the truth of that whose knowledge they have not
        comprehended,
    and whose interpretation has not yet come to them.
    Those who were before them denied the truth in this way
    – and see how was the consequence for those who did wrong.

40. Among them are those who believe in it,
    and among them are those who do not believe in it.
    Your[s] Lord is well aware of those who wreak mischief.

41. If they say you[s] are a liar,
    say, 'To me is my work and to you[P] is your work.
    You have no responsibility for what I do
    and I have no responsibility for what you do.'

42. There are some of them who listen to you[s];
    but can you make the deaf hear
    even though they have no understanding?

43. There are some of them who look at you[s];
    but can you guide the blind
    even though they cannot see?

44. God does not wrong the people in anything,
    but the people wrong themselves.

45. On the day when He rounds them up,
    [it will seem] as though they had tarried only an hour of the day,
    mutually recognizing one another,
    lost will be those who have denied the truth of the meeting with God
    and who have not been guided.

46. Whether We show you[s] a part of what We promise them
    or We take you[s],

---

[3] Literally 'with the exclusion of God'.

their return is to Us;
and then God is witness of what they do.

47. Each community has a messenger.
When their messenger comes,
judgement is given between them in equity,
and they are not wronged.

48. They say, 'When will this promise [come to pass],
if you^p are telling the truth?'

49. Say, 'I have no power to harm or benefit myself,
except as God wills.
Every community has an appointed time.
When their time comes,
they cannot put it back or bring it forward by a single hour.'

50. Say, 'Have you^p considered?
If His punishment comes to you by night or by day,
what part of it will the sinners seek to hasten?'

51. Is it then, when it has come to pass,
that you^p will believe in it?
And now – when you have been seeking to hasten it?

52. Then it will be said to those who have done wrong,
'Taste the torment of eternity.
Are you being recompensed
except for what you used to amass?'

53. They ask you^s to inform them whether it is true.
Say, 'Yes, by my Lord, it is indeed true.
You^p will not be able to frustrate [it].'

54. If each soul that has done wrong were to possess all that is on earth,
it would seek to offer it as a ransom.
They will be full of secret regret
when they see the punishment
and judgement has been given between them in equity
and they are not wronged.

55. Truly, all that is in the heavens and the earth belongs to God.
Truly, God's promise is true.
But most of them do not know.

56. He brings life and brings death,
and to Him you^p will be returned.

57. O people, there has come to you
an admonition from your Lord
and a remedy for what is in [your] breasts
and a guidance and a mercy for the believers.

58. Say, 'In the bounty and mercy of God

– in that let them rejoice.
It is better than what they gather.'

59. Say, 'Have you^p considered the sustenance that God has sent down to you
and [how] you have made some of it unlawful and [some] lawful?'
Say, 'Has God given you permission,
or do you invent a lie against God?'

60. And on the Day of Resurrection
what will be the thoughts of those who make forgeries against God?
God is bountiful to the people,
but most of them are not grateful.

61. You^s are not engaged in any business
nor do you recite any recitation of it,
and none of you^p does any deed,
but We are witnesses over you^p when you are busy in it.
Not an atom's weight on earth or in heaven escapes your^s Lord,
nor what is smaller or greater than that,
without it being in a clear record.

62. Surely God's friends
– there will be no fear on them nor will they grieve.

63. Those who believe and fear God –

64. They have good tidings in the life of this world and in the world to come.
There is no changing the words of God.
That is the great triumph.

65. Do not let what they say grieve you^s.
Might belongs entirely to God.
He is the Hearer and the Knower.

66. Truly all those who are in the heavens and all those who are on earth belong to God.
Those who call on those they associate with God,
apart from God, follow
– They follow only a guess and are merely conjecturing.

67. It is He who made the night for you^p to rest in it
and the day to allow you to see.
In that there are signs for a people who hear.

68. They say, 'God has taken to Himself a son.'
Glory be to Him.
He is the All-sufficient.
To Him belong all that is in the heavens and on earth.
You^p have no authority for this [assertion].
Do you say about God that which you do not know?

69. Say, 'Those who forge lies against God will not prosper.'

70. [They will have] some enjoyment in this world;
then their return will be to Us;

then We shall make them taste the terrible torment,
because they used to disbelieve.

71. Recite to them the story of Noah:
when he said to his people,
'O my people, if my staying here and my reminding you of God's signs
weighs heavy on you,
I put my trust in God.
So resolve on your affair, with your associates.
Let not your affair be a worry to you,
but make a decision about me.
Do not wait.[4]

72. If you turn away,
I do not ask for any wage;
my wage lies only with God,
and I have been commanded to be one of those who surrender.'

73. They did not believe him,
and so We saved him and those who were with him in the ship;
and We made them successors;
and We drowned those who did not believe in Our signs.
See[5] how was the consequence for those who were warned.

74. Then after him We sent messengers to their people;
and they came to them with the clear proofs,
but they would not believe what they had previously denied.
Thus We set a seal on the hearts of the transgressors.

75. Then after them We sent Moses and Aaron
to Pharaoh and his notables with Our signs,
but they were haughty and were a sinful people.

76. When the truth came to them from Our presence,
they said, 'This is clear magic.'

77. Moses said, 'Do you say [this] about the truth when it has come to you?
Is this magic?
Sorcerers do not prosper.'

78. They said, 'Have you come to us to turn us
from what we found our forefathers practising?
[Have you come] to acquire greatness in the land?
We do not believe you.'

79. Pharaoh said,
'Bring every knowing sorcerer to me.'

80. When the sorcerers came, Moses said to them,
'Cast down what you [wish to] cast down.'

---

[4] Literally 'give me respite'.

81.   And when they had cast, Moses said,
    'What you have done is sorcery.
    God will render it useless.
    God does not cause the work of those who wreak mischief to prosper.

82.   God verifies the truth by His words,
    even though the sinners are averse.'

83.   None believed in Moses,
    except some offspring of his own people,
    through fear that Pharaoh and his notables would persecute them.
    Pharaoh was exalted in the land
    – he was one of the extravagant.

84.   Moses said, 'O my people,
    if you believe in God, put your trust in Him,
    if you have surrendered!'

85.   They said, 'We put our trust in God.
    Our Lord, do not make us a temptation for the people who are wrong-doers,

86.   But through Your mercy save us from the people who are unbelievers.'

87.   We revealed to Moses and his brother,
    'Make[5] some houses lodgings for your people in Egypt;
    and make[p] your houses places to turn to,
    and perform[p] prayer,
    and give[s] good tidings to the believers.'

88.   Moses said, 'Our Lord,
    you have given Pharaoh and his notables adornment and wealth in the life of
       this world,
    Our Lord, that [enables them to] lead [men] away from your way.
    Our Lord, obliterate their wealth and harden their hearts,
    so that they do not believe until they see the great torment.'

89.   He said, 'Your prayer has been answered.
    Keep to the straight path,
    and do not follow the road of those who have no knowledge.'

90.   We brought the Children of Israel across the sea;
    and Pharaoh and his hosts followed them in insolence and transgression.
    Then, when the drowning overtook him, he said,
    'I believe that there is no god
    save Him in whom the Children of Israel believe.
    I am one of those who surrender.'

91.   'Now? When previously you have rebelled
    and have been one of those who wreak mischief?

---

[5] In the Arabic the verbs in this verse follow a difficult pattern. The verb in the second line is in the dual, the verbs in the next two lines are in the plural, and the final one is in the singular.

92. To-day We shall deliver you^s with your body
that you may be a sign to those after you.
Many of the people are heedless of Our signs.'
93. We lodged the Children of Israel in a sure lodging,
and We gave them good things as sustenance.
And they did not disagree until knowledge came to them.
93a. Your^s Lord will judge between them on the Day of Resurrection
concerning that about which they used to differ.
94. If you^s are in doubt about what We send down to you,
ask those who recited the Scripture before you.
The Truth has come to you^s from your Lord.
Do^s not be one of the doubters.
95. And do^s not be one of those who deny the truth of God's signs,
lest you are one of the losers.
96. Those against whom the word of your^s Lord has become true
will not believe,
97. Although every sign comes to them,
until they see the painful torment.
98. Why was there not a settlement that believed and benefited by its belief
except the people of Jonah?
When they believed,
We removed from them the torment of shame in the life of this world
and gave them enjoyment for a time.
99. Had your^s Lord wished,
all those on earth would have believed,
all of them.
So would you^s force the people to become believers?
100. It is not for any soul to believe
save with God's permission.
He puts abomination on those who do not understand.
101. Say, 'See what is in the heavens and on earth.'
But neither signs nor warnings avail a people who do not believe.
102. Do they wait for anything but the like of the days of those who passed away
before them?
Say, 'Wait. I am with you amongst those who wait.'
103. Then We shall save Our messengers and those who believe.
Thus We save the believers, as is a duty for us.
104. Say, 'O people, if you are in any doubt about my religion,
I do not serve those whom you serve apart from God.
I serve God, who will take you.
I have been ordered to be one of the believers.'
105. and, 'Set^s your face towards the religion as a man of pure faith,

and do^s not be one of those who associate others with God.

106. And do^s not call,
to the exclusion of God,
on what can neither benefit you nor harm you.
If you do that,
you will then be one of the wrong-doers.

107. If God touches you^s with harm,
no one can remove it except Him;
and if He desires any good for you^s,
no one can turn back His bounty.
He causes it to fall on those whom He wishes among His servants.
He is the Forgiving and the Compassionate.'

108. Say, 'O people, the truth has come to you from your Lord.
Those who are guided aright are guided aright only for themselves;
and those who go astray, stray only against themselves.
I am not a guardian over you.'

109. Follow what is revealed to you^s and be patient
until God judges.
He is the best of judges.

Sūra 11

The *sūra* is one of those that basically consist of three main sections: (*a*) introductory polemic; (*b*) narratives about the prophets; and (*c*) peroration. It takes its name from the extended passage on the prophet Hūd and his tribe ʿĀd. This is one of six narratives about earlier prophets that form the heart of the *sūra*: Noah (verses 25–49), Hūd (50–60), Ṣāliḥ (61–68), Abraham and Lot (69–83), Shuʿayb (84–95), and a brief piece on Moses and Pharaoh (96–99). A brief refrain is used in 4 places (verses 44, 60, 68 and 95). The first section is markedly distinct from the third, as it is largely addressed to people in general with only three points at which Muḥammad is spoken to directly (verses 7, 12 and 17). The third section is largely addressed to Muḥammad himself, with more general references in verses 113 and 116. The *sūra* is generally thought to be late Meccan, and this seems right, though some alterations may have occurred at Medina.

Hūd

In the name of the Merciful and Compassionate God

1. *Alif, Lām, Rā'.*[1]
    A Scripture, whose signs have been established
    and then made distinct,
    coming from One [who is] Wise and Informed.
2. 'Do not serve[p] anyone but God.
    I am a warner and a bringer of good tidings to you[p] from Him.
3. And seek[p] forgiveness from your Lord,
    then turn to Him in repentance.
    [If you do so] He will give fair enjoyment until a stated term
    and give His bounty to everyone of merit.
    But if you turn your backs
    I fear for you the punishment of a great day.
4. To God is your return.
    He has power over everything.'
5. They fold their breasts to try to hide [their thoughts] from Him;
    [but] when they draw their clothes over themselves,
    He knows what they keep secret and what they proclaim.
    He knows well what is in their breasts.

---

[1] On the mystical letters see the note on 2:1.

6. There is no beast on the earth
    but its sustenance depends on God.
    He knows its lair and its habitation.
    Everything is in a clear record.

7. It is He who has created the heavens and the earth in six days
    – whilst His throne was upon the water –
    that He might test you[p]
    [to see] which of you is fairer in conduct.
    If you[s] say, 'You[p] will be raised after death',
    those who are unbelievers will say,
    'This is merely manifest magic.'

8. If We postpone the punishment from them till a fixed time,
    they will say, 'What is holding it back?'
    On the day it comes to them,
    it cannot be averted from them,
    and they will be engulfed by what they mocked.

9. If We cause man to taste some mercy from Us
    and then withdraw it from him,
    he is despairing and ungrateful;

10. And if We cause him to taste some blessing
    after some misfortune that had touched him,
    he will say, 'The evils have gone from me',
    and he is joyful and boastful

11. – Though that will not be the case with those who are patient and do righteous deeds:
    they will have forgiveness and a great reward.

12. Perhaps you[s] are forsaking part of what is revealed to you
    and your breast is straitened by it,
    because they say,
    'Why has a treasure not been sent down to him
    or an angel come with him?'
    You are only a warner.
    God is trustee of everything.

13. Or [because] they say,
    'He has invented it.'
    Say, 'Then bring[p] ten *sūra*s like it, invented,
    and call on everyone you can,
    to the exclusion of God,
    if you are truthful.'

14. If they do not respond to you[p],
    [you may] know[p] that it is sent down with God's knowledge
    and that there is no God but Him.
    Will you [all] submit?

15. Those who desire the present life and its adornment,
    We shall pay them in full for their deeds in it,
    and they will not be defrauded in it.
16. Those are the ones for whom there is nothing in the world to come but the Fire.
    There their deeds will be fruitless and their works in vain.
17. And those who take their stand on a clear proof from their Lord
    when a witness from Him recites it
    (and before it [there was] the Scripture of Moses as an example and a mercy)
    – those believe in it.
    But those of the parties who disbelieve it,
    the Fire is their appointed place.
    So do not be in any doubt about it.
    It is the truth from your^s Lord,
    but most people do not believe.
18. Who does greater wrong than those who invent a lie against God?
    Those will be brought before their Lord,
    and witnesses will say,
    'These are those who lied against their Lord.'
    Truly, the curse of God is on the wrong-doers,
19. Who turn [men] aside from the way of God
    and wish it to be crooked
    and who disbelieve in the world to come.
20. Those have not been able to cause frustration in the land
    and they have no friends, apart from God.
    For them the punishment will be doubled.
    They could not hear, nor could they see.
21. Those are the ones that have lost their souls
    and what they have invented has failed them.
22. There is no doubt that they will be the greatest losers in the world to come.
23. Those who believe and do righteous deeds
    and humble themselves before their Lord
    – those are the inmates of the Garden.
    They will stay there for ever.
24. The parallel between the two parties is that of the deaf-blind person
    and the one who can see and hear.
    Are they equal in likeness?
    Will you^p not be reminded?
25. We sent Noah to his people,
    'I am a clear warner for you,
26. That you should serve only God.
    I fear for you the punishment of a painful day.'
27. The notables of his people,

who disbelieved, said,
'We do not see you to be anything other than a human being like us.
We do not see that you are followed by any other than the vilest of us,
without consideration.
We do not see that you have any superiority over us.
On the contrary, we think you liars.'

28. He said, 'O my people, have you considered:
if I stand on a clear proof from my Lord
and [if] He has given me mercy from Him
and it has been obscured from your sight,
can we compel you to accept it,
when you are averse?

29. My people,
I am not asking you for any money for this.
My reward is only with God.
I shall not drive away those who believe.
They will meet their Lord.
But I see that you are an ignorant people.

30. My people,
who would help me against God if I drive them away?
Will you not be reminded?

31. I do not say to you
that the treasuries of God are with me
nor that I have knowledge of the Invisible;
nor do I say that I am an angel;
nor do I say to those whom your eyes scorn
that God will not give them good
(God knows best what is in their hearts).
If I were to do that,
I should be one of the wrong-doers.'

32. They said, 'O Noah, you have disputed with us
– and disputed much with us.
Bring to us what you promise us,
if you are truthful.'

33. He said, 'Only God can bring it to you if He wishes,
and you will not be able to frustrate [it].

34. My advice would not benefit you,
[even] if I want to give you good advice,
if God wishes to lead you astray.
He is your Lord and to Him you will be returned.'

35. Or do they say, 'He has invented it'?
Say, 'If I invent it, my sin is upon me,

but I am free of the sins that you commit.'

36. It was suggested to Noah,
'None of your people will believe,
unless they are already believers.
Do not be distressed at what they have been doing.

37. Make the ship under Our eyes and at Our inspiration.
Do not address me concerning those who do wrong.
They will be drowned.'

38. He [went about] making the ship,
and every time that some notables from his people passed by him,
they mocked him.
He said, 'If you mock us, we shall mock you even as you mock.

39. You will know to whom comes a punishment that will shame him
and on whom descends a lasting punishment.'

40. Then, when Our command came and the oven boiled[2],
We said, 'Load into it two of every kind and your family
– except for those against whom the word has already gone forth –
and those who believe.'
And there were only a few who had believed with him.

41. He said, 'Embark in it.
In God's name will be its course and its anchorage.
My Lord is Forgiving and Merciful.'

42. It sailed with them among waves like mountains,
and Noah called to his son,
who was in an isolated place,
'My son, embark with us and do not be with the unbelievers.'

43. He[3] said, 'I shall go and seek refuge on a mountain
which will protect me from the water.'
He[4] said, 'To-day there is no protector from God's command,
except for the one on whom He has mercy.'
And the waves came between the two of them,
and he was among those drowned.

44. [Then] it was said, 'O earth, swallow your water; O sky, abate.'
The water subsided, and the affair was accomplished.
[The ship] settled on al-Jūdī,[5]

---

[2] The phrase appears to echo a post-Biblical Jewish idea that the waters of the flood were hot. See also 23:27.

[3] The son.

[4] Noah.

[5] Jewish and later Muslim tradition places al-Jūdī in present day Kurdistan, but initially Arab hearers would have identified it with a mountain in northern central Arabia.

and it was said, 'Away with the wrong-doers.'

45. Noah cried out to his Lord, saying,
'My Lord, my son is one of my family.
Your promise is the truth;
You are the wisest of those who judge.'

46. He said, 'O Noah, he is not one of your family.
It would be an unrighteous deed.
Do not ask me for that of which you have no knowledge.
I admonish you not to be one of the ignorant.'

47. He said, 'My Lord, I seek refuge in You from asking You
for that of which I have no knowledge.
If You do not forgive me and do not have mercy on me
I shall be one of the losers.'

48. It was said, 'O Noah, descend with peace from Us
and with blessings on you
and on communities [that spring] from those who are with you.
And there will be [other] communities to whom We shall give enjoyment,
but then a painful punishment from Us will touch them.'

49. That is of the tidings of the Invisible,
which We impart to you.
You did not know it yourself nor did your people before this.
Have patience.
The end will be in favour of those who are god-fearing.'

50. To 'Ād [We sent] their brother Hūd.
He said, 'O my people, serve God.
You have no god except Him.
You are merely inventing.

51. My people, I am not asking you for any wage for this.
My reward is only with the One who created me.
Have you no sense?

52. My people, seek forgiveness from your Lord,
then turn to Him in repentance;
[if you do so] He will let loose the sky on you in torrents
and will add strength to your strength.
Do not turn your backs as sinners.'

53. They said, 'O Hūd, you have brought us no clear proof,
and we are not going to forsake our gods at your word,
and we shall not believe for your sake.

54. All that we can say is that one of our gods has smitten you with evil.'
He said, 'I call God as witness,
and you[p], too, bear witness
that I am free of all that you associate

55. apart from Him.
    So scheme against me all together;
    then give me no respite.
56. I have put my trust in God,
    my Lord and your Lord.
    There is no beast except He takes it by its forelock.
    My Lord is on a straight path.
57. If you turn your backs, [that is your responsibility.]
    I have proclaimed to you that with which I was sent to you.
    My Lord will make a people other than you your successors.
    You cannot injure Him in any way.
    My Lord is guardian over all things.'
58. When Our command came,
    We saved Hūd and those who believed with him through mercy from Us;
    and We saved them from a harsh punishment.
59. That was 'Ād who denied the signs of their Lord
    and rebelled against His messengers
    and followed the command of every obstinate tyrant.
60. A curse was made to follow them in this world
    and on the Day of Resurrection.
    'Ād disbelieved in their Lord.
    Away with 'Ād, the people of Hūd.
61. To Thamūd [We sent] their brother Ṣāliḥ.
    He said, 'O my people, serve God.
    You have no god except Him.
    It is He who has raised you from the earth
    and settled you in it.
    Seek His forgiveness,
    then turn to Him in repentance.
    My Lord is Near and Responsive.'
62. They said, 'O Ṣāliḥ, up to now you were the one among us
    about whom there were hopes.
    Do you forbid us to serve what our fathers served?
    We are in doubt about what you are calling us to.'
63. He said, 'O my people, have you considered:
    if I stand on a clear proof from my Lord
    and [if] He has given me mercy from Him
    Who will save me from God if I disobey Him?
    You would increase me only in loss.
64. O my people, this is the she-camel of God, a sign to you.
    Let her eat in God's land
    and do not touch her with evil,

lest you are seized by a punishment that is near.'

65. But they hamstrung her, and he said,
'Enjoy yourselves in your dwellings for three days.
That is a promise that will not be found false.'

66. When our command came,
through a mercy from Us
we saved Ṣāliḥ and those who believed with him
from the shame of that day.
Your Lord is the Strong and Mighty.

67. And the Cry seized the wrong-doers,
and in the morning they were prostrate in their abodes,

68. As if they had never flourished there.
Thamūd disbelieved in their Lord.
Away with Thamūd.

69. Our messengers came to Abraham with good news.
They said, 'Peace.'
'Peace', he replied.
Soon he came with a roasted calf.

70. When he saw that their hands were not reaching towards it,
he became suspicious of them and conceived a fear of them.
They said, 'Do not be afraid.
We have been sent to the people of Lot'.

71. His wife was standing there and she laughed.
And we gave her the good news of Isaac,
and after Isaac, Jacob.

72. She said, 'Alas for me.
Shall I bear a child when I am an old woman,
and this man, my husband, is an old man?
That is a very strange thing.'

73. They said, 'Do you wonder at God's command?
The mercy and blessings of God be on you,
O people of the house.
He is Laudable and Glorious.'

74. When the awe left Abraham and he heard the good news,
he argued with Us concerning the people of Lot.

75. Abraham was prudent, tender-hearted and penitent.

76. 'O Abraham, turn away from this.
Your Lord's command has come.
A punishment that cannot be turned back is coming upon them.'

77. And when our messengers came to Lot,
he was troubled about them and felt unable to protect them.
He said, 'This is a distressing day.'

78. His people came to him, rushing towards him
    – and before that they had been doing evil deeds.
    He said, 'Here are my daughters.
    They are purer for you.
    Fear God, and do not shame me concerning my guests.
    Is there not one right-minded man among you?'
79. They said, 'You know that we have no right to your daughters,
    and you know what we want.'
80. He said, 'Would that I had some power to deal with you
    or that I could take refuge with a strong pillar.'
81. They said, 'O Lot, we are the messengers of your Lord.
    They will not reach you.
    Travel with your family for a part of the night;
    and let none of you turn round,
    except your wife.
    That which smites them will also smite her.
    Their tryst is the morning.
    Is not the morning near?'
82. So when Our command came,
    We turned it[6] upside down and rained on it stones of baked clay,
    one after another,
83. Marked in the presence of your Lord,
    and never far from the wrong doers.
84. To Madyan [We sent] their brother Shuʿayb.
    He said, 'My people, serve God.
    You have no god apart from Him.
    Do not give short measure or short weight.
    I see that you are faring well,
    but I fear for you the punishment of an all-encompassing day.
85. My people, give full measure and full weight in justice.
    Do not defraud the people of their things,
    and do not work mischief in the land,
    causing corruption.
86. That which God leaves for you is better for you
    if you are believers.
    I am not a guardian over you.'
87. They said, 'O Shuʿayb, does your prayer tell you
    that we should abandon what our fathers used to worship
    and [abandon] doing as we wish with our property?
    You are prudent and right-minded.'

---

[6] Their settlement.

88. He said, 'O my people, have you considered
    if I stand on a clear proof from my Lord
    and [if] he provides me with a fair sustenance?
    I do not wish to go behind your backs to what I forbid you.
    I only desire to put things right as far as I can.
    My success is only with God.
    In Him I have put my trust and to Him I turn repentant.

89. O my people, let not the split with me incite you
    lest you are smitten by the like of what smote the people of Noah
    or the people of Hūd or the people of Ṣāliḥ;
    and the people of Lot are not far from you.

90. Seek your Lord's forgiveness, then turn in repentance to Him.
    My Lord is Compassionate and Loving.'

91. They said, 'O Shuʿayb, we do not understand much of what you say.
    We see that you are weak amongst us.
    But for your clan, we would have stoned you.
    You are not strong against us.'

92. He said, 'O my people, has my clan more power over you than God?
    Have you put Him behind you, neglected?
    My Lord encompasses what you do.

93. O my people, act according to your station.
    I am acting [so].
    You will know
    to whom will come a punishment that will shame him
    and who is lying.
    Keep watch. I am watching with you.'

94. When Our command came,
    We saved Shuʿayb and those who believed with him
    through mercy from Us.
    And the Cry seized the wrong-doers,
    and in the morning they were prostrate in their abodes,

95. As though they had not flourished there.
    Away with Madyan,
    just as Thamūd were removed.

96. We sent Moses with Our signs and a clear authority

97. To Pharaoh and his nobles,
    but they followed the command of Pharaoh,
    and the command of Pharaoh was not right-minded.

98. On the Day of Resurrection he will go before his people
    and will lead them to the watering-place of the Fire
    – how wretched is the watering-place to which they are led.

99. A curse was sent to follow them in this [world]

and on the Day of Resurrection.
How wretched is the offering offered to them.

100. That is some of the tidings of the settlements that we relate to you[s].
Some of them are standing and some are already reaped.

101. We did not wrong them
– they wronged themselves.
The gods on whom they called
to the exclusion of God
were of no avail to them
when the command of your[s] Lord came.
They increased them only in ruin.

102. Such is the grasp of your Lord when he grasps the settlements
that have been doing wrong.
His grasp is strong and painful.

103. In that there is a sign
for those who fear the punishment of the world to come.
That is a day on which mankind is gathered;
that is a day that will be witnessed.

104. We shall postpone it only to a term that will be counted.

105. On the day when it comes,
no soul will speak except with His permission.
Some will be wretched and others happy.

106. As for those who are wretched,
they will be in the Fire,
in which there will be sighing and sobbing for them,

107. Remaining there as long as the heavens and the earth last,
except as your Lord wishes;
your Lord carries out all that he wishes.

108. As for those who are happy,
they will be in the Garden,
remaining there as long as the heavens and the earth last,
except as your Lord wishes
– a gift unbroken.

109. So do[s] not be in doubt about what these people serve.
They serve what they serve only as did their fathers before.
We shall pay them in full their undiminished portion.

110. In the past We gave Moses the Scripture,
but there was disagreement about it;
and had it not been for a word that had preceded from your Lord,
there would have been a decision between them;
but they are in disquieting doubt about it.

111. Each one

– your^s Lord will truly pay them in full for their deeds.
He is informed of what they do.

112. So go straight, as you^s have been commanded,
together with those who repent with you.
Do not be insolent.
He is observer of what you do.

113. And do not incline^p towards those who do wrong
lest the Fire touch you
– you have no protectors apart from God –
then you will not be helped.

114. Perform^s prayer at the two ends of the day and the early parts of the night.
Good deeds drive away evil deeds.
That is a reminder for the mindful.

115. And be^s patient,
for God does not allow the wage of those who do good to be lost.

116. If only there had been,
from the generations before you^p,
men with a remnant⁷ forbidding corruption in the land,
though this was the case with a few
– those whom We saved from them.
The wrong-doers followed that in which they were pampered
and became sinners.

117. Your^s Lord was not one to destroy the settlements unjustly,
when their people were doing right.

118. Had your Lord wished,
He would have made men one community,
but they continue to differ,

119. Except those on whom your Lord has mercy.
For that He created them,
and the word of your Lord has been fulfilled:
'I shall fill Jahannam with Jinn and men, altogether.'

120. All that we tell you^s of the tidings of the messengers
is that by which We make firm your heart.
In them there has come to you the truth
and an admonition and a reminder for the believers.

121. Say to those who do not believe,
'Act according to your station.
We shall act.

122. And wait.
We are waiting.'

---

⁷ Of good sense.

123. To God belongs the Invisible in the heavens and the earth;
and to Him the whole matter is returned.
So serve Him and put your trust in Him.
Your Lord is not heedless of what you do.

Sūra 12

The *sūra* is generally considered to be from the late Meccan period, with some authorities taking the view that verses 1–3 and 7 are Medinan. It is devoted very largely to the story of Joseph, and, given the length of the narrative and its parallels with the story of Joseph in Genesis, it is of particular interest to Jews and Christians. Not all Muslims look on the narrative with favour: the Ibāḍīs take a very austere view of the description (vv. 23 *ff.*) of the attempted seduction of Joseph by 'the wife of the great one', known in later Islamic literature as Zulaykhā.

It is commonly held that this is the only *sūra* devoted to the story of a single biblical figure. Up to a point this is true of the longer *sūra*s, though *Sūra* 20, with its very long passages on Moses (9–101), is different only in that it is not wound up so quickly and that the final passage contains a version of the story of Adam and Eve (115–24). Here the last section of the *sūra*, verses 102–111, is a passage of argument that arises from the narrative, and one may view the narrative as its preamble. The *sūra* most exclusively devoted to the story of a prophet is in fact the short *Sūra* 71, which deals solely with the story of Noah.

Most western scholars have assumed that the line of the narrative, which omits large sections of the biblical account, presupposes a general knowledge of the story amongst those who first heard it. I have never been able to convince myself of this: the phrase in verse 3, the full meaning of which is, 'you were one of those not aware of the story before its revelation', is very much against it. This view also ignores Quranic narrative technique, which is at its finest in this *sūra*. The pacing of the narrative is remarkable, quickening up and slowing down as is necessary to maintain the desired impetus. The hearer, in particular, is simply carried along by a narrative whose vividness gives no time for thought about possible background material. Sketching the highlights and omitting a great deal of detail is a technique that can frequently be observed in early Arabic poetry, and no doubt it was to be found in the prose literature of the period, though too little of this survives to provide control samples.

Though the narrative's closest links are with the lengthy account in Genesis, it contains details, set out in the Commentary, that are to be found in later Jewish tradition. Though these finer details are of no great significance in themselves, they are a barrier to simple comparisons of the narratives in *Sūrat Yūsuf* and in the Bible.

Joseph

In the name of the Merciful and Compassionate God

1.   *Alif, Lam, Rā'.*[1]
     These are the signs of the clear Scripture.
2.   We have sent it down as a Recitation in Arabic,
     so that you[p] may understand.
3.   We are recounting to you[s] the finest of stories,
     for We have inspired you with this Recitation,
     and you were one of those who were not aware [of the story] before it[s
        revelation]:[2]
4.   When Joseph said to his father, 'O my father,
     I have seen eleven stars and the sun and the moon
     – I have seen them bowing down to me.'
5.   He said, 'O my son,
     do not recount your dream to your brothers
     lest they devise some piece of guile against you.
     Satan is a very clear enemy to man.
6.   In this way your Lord is choosing you;
     and He will teach you something of the interpretation of what you are told,
     and He will perfect His blessing on you
     and on the family of Jacob,
     just as he perfected it before,
     on your forefathers, Abraham and Isaac.
     Your Lord is Knowing and Wise.'
7.   In [the story of] Joseph and his brothers there are signs for those who ask questions:
8.   When they said,
     'Joseph and his brother are dearer to our father than we are,
     though there is a group of us.
     Our father is clearly in manifest error.
9.   Kill[p] Joseph or cast him out into some land,
     and your father's face will focus only on you.
     Thereafter you can be a righteous people.'
10.   One of them said, 'Do not kill Joseph.
     Just throw him into the bottom of a pit,[3]
     and some caravan will pick him out
     – if you must do something.'
11.   They said, 'Father, how is it that you do not trust us with Joseph?

---

[1] On the mystical letters see the note on 2:1.
[2] *i.e.* 'One of those who were not aware of the story before its revelation'.
[3] Or 'well'.

We really are his sincere well-wishers.

12. Send him with us tomorrow,
and he can enjoy himself and play.
We shall watch over him.'

13. He said, 'It grieves me that you should take him out.
I fear that a wolf may eat him
whilst you are paying him no attention.'

14. They said, 'If a wolf can eat him
when there is a group of us,
in that case we are losers.'

15. So when they had taken him off
and agreed to put him in the bottom of a pit;[3]
and We revealed to him,
'You[s] will tell them about this affair of theirs
when they are unaware [of who you are].'

16. And [when] they came to their father in the evening, weeping,

17. They said, 'Father, we were racing against one another,
and we left Joseph with our things;
and the wolf ate him.
But you will not believe us,
even though we are telling the truth.'

18. They brought his shirt with false blood on it.
He said, 'No!
Your souls have enticed you to do something wrong.
[May I have] fair patience.
God is the one to whom I must turn for help against what you describe.'

19. A caravan came,
and they sent their water-carrier,
and he let down his bucket.
He said, 'Good news. Here is a young man.'
They hid him away as something to sell
– but God was aware of what they were doing.

20. And they sold him for a paltry price,
some *dirham*s counted out,
[for] they were indifferent about him.

21. The Egyptian who bought him said to his wife,
'Give him good lodging.
It may be that he will be of benefit to us
or that we adopt him as a son.'
In this way we made a place for Joseph in the land.
[This was] so that We might teach him something of the interpretation of tales.
God was master of his affair,

but most of the people do not know [that].

22. When he reached his prime,
We gave him judgement and knowledge.
Thus we reward those who do good.

23. The woman in whose house he was tried to seduce him.
She shut the doors and said, 'Come on.'
He replied, 'God be my refuge.
[Your husband] is my master.
He has given me good lodging.
Those who do wrong do not prosper.'

24. She had designs on him;
and he would have had designs on her,
had he not seen the proof of his Lord.[4]
So it was,
that We might turn evil and immorality from him.
He was one of Our devoted servants.

25. The two of them raced to the door,
and she tore his shirt from behind.
They met her lord and master at the door.
She said, 'What is to be the recompense of a man
who has had evil designs against your folk,
other than that he be imprisoned or a painful punishment?'

26. He[5] said, 'She it was who tried to seduce me.'
Then one of her folk bore witness,
'If his shirt is torn from in front,
she is telling the truth, and he is a liar.

27. But if his shirt has been torn from behind,
she is lying, and he is telling the truth.'

28. When he[6] saw that his shirt was torn from behind,
he said, '[This] is one of your women's tricks.
The trickery of you women is immense.

29. Joseph, turn away from this;
and you, [my wife], seek forgiveness for your sin.
You are one of the sinners.'

30. Some women in the city said,
'The ruler's wife is trying to seduce her young man.
He has smitten her heart with love.
We think her clearly in the wrong.'

---

[4] That such action would be wrong.
[5] Joseph.
[6] The husband.

31. When she heard their sly talk,
    she invited them and prepared for them a couch
    and gave to each of them a knife.
    Then she said to Joseph,
    'Go into their presence.'
    When they saw him, they admired him,
    and they cut their hands, and said,
    'God is wonderful. This is not a mortal.
    This is nothing but a gracious angel.'
32. She said, 'This is the one about whom you blamed me.
    I did try to seduce him, but he remained chaste;
    but if he does not do what I tell him to do,
    he shall be imprisoned and shall be one of those who are humbled.'
33. He said, 'My Lord,
    I prefer prison rather than that to which these women call me;
    but if You do not turn their tricks from me,
    I shall incline to them in youthful folly
    and I shall become one of the heedless.'
34. So his Lord answered him and turned their tricks from him;
    He is the Hearer and Knower.
35. Then it seemed good to them,
    after they had seen the signs,
    to imprison him for a time.
36. Two young men entered the prison with him.
    One of them said,
    'I see myself pressing wine';
    the other said,
    'I see myself carrying on my head some bread,
    from which the birds are eating.
    Tell us its interpretation,
    for we see that you are one of those who do good.'
37. He said, 'No food from which you have your sustenance will come to you
    except I shall have told you its interpretation
    before it comes to you.
    This is from what my Lord has taught me.
    I have forsaken the religion of a people who do not believe in God
    and are unbelievers about the world to come.
38. I have followed the religion of my fathers
    Abraham and Isaac and Jacob.
    It was not for us to associate anything with God.
    That is part of God's bounty to us and to the people;
    but most of the people are ungrateful.

39. O [my] two-fellow prisoners,
    are various Lords better
    or God, the One, the Victorious?
40. Apart from Him
    you worship only names given by you and your fathers.
    God has sent down no authority for them.
    Judgement belongs only to God.
    He has ordered you to serve Him alone.
    That is the true religion;
    but most of the people do not know [that].
41. O [my] two fellow-prisoners,
    one of you will pour out wine for his master;
    the other will be crucified,
    and the birds will eat from his head.
    The matter about which you seek an opinion has been determined.'
42. He said to the one of the two he thought would be saved,
    'Mention me in the presence of your master.'
    But Satan caused him to forget to mention him to his master,
    and so he lingered in prison for several years.
43. The king said,
    'I see seven fat cows that are devoured by seven thin ones,
    and seven green ears of corn and others that are withered.
    You nobles, give me your opinions about my dream
    if you are able to interpret dreams.'
44. They replied, 'Tangled nightmares.
    We know nothing of the interpretation of dreams.'
45. The one of the two who had been saved
    [now] remembered after a time and said,
    'I shall tell you[p] its interpretation. Send me.'
46. 'Joseph, you man of truth,
    give me your opinion about seven fat cows
    that are devoured by seven thin ones
    and seven green ears of corn and others that are withered,
    so that I may return to the people,
    so that they may know.'
47. He said, 'You[p] will sow for seven years as is your custom.
    But what you harvest, leave it in the ear,
    except for a little which you may eat.
48. Then after that will come seven hard [years]
    which will devour what you have made ready for them,
    except for a little which you may store.
49. Then after that will come a year

in which the people will have rain
and in which they will press[7].'

50. The king said, 'Bring him to me.'
When the messenger came to him,
his answer was,
'Return to your master and ask him,
"What about the women who cut their hands?"
My Lord has knowledge of their tricks.'

51. He[8] said [to the women],
'What about that affair of yours
when you tried to seduce Joseph?'
They replied, 'God save him!
We know of no evil against him.'
The wife of the ruler said,
'Now the truth has come to light.
It was I who tried to seduce him.
He was truthful.'

52. 'That is so that he may know
that I did not betray him in his absence
and that God does not guide the manoeuvres of those who betray.

53. Yet I do not declare that my soul was innocent.
The soul always enjoins wrong-doing,
except so far as my Lord has mercy.
My Lord is Forgiving, Merciful.'

54. The king said, 'Bring him to me,
and I shall attach him to my person.'
And when he talked to him, he said,
'To-day you are trusted and firmly established at our side.'

55. He replied, 'Set me over the store-houses of the land.
I am a knowing guardian.'

56. Thus we gave Joseph a place in the land,
for him to settle in it wherever he wished.
We make Our mercy reach those whom We wish.
We do not let the wage of those who do good go to waste;

57. Yet the wage of the world to come is better for those who believe and are
godfearing.'

58. And Joseph's brothers came and went to see him.
He recognized them,

---

[7] The text gives no indication of what will be pressed. The common view is 'grapes', more rarely 'grapes and olives'.

[8] The king.

but they did not recognize him.

59. When he provided them with their provision, he said,
'Bring me a brother of yours from your father.
Do you not see that I give full measure?
I am the best of hosts.

60. If you do not bring him to me,
there will be no measure for you
and you will not approach me.'

61. They replied, 'We shall ask his father to send him.
We shall certainly do that.'

62. He said to his young men,
'Place their goods [back] in their baggage,
so that they may recognize them
when they go back to their people,
so that they may return.'

63. When they returned to their father, they said,
'Father, [further] measure has been denied to us;
so send our brother with us.
We shall watch over him.'

64. He replied, 'Shall I entrust him to you
in any other way than I entrusted his brother to you before?
God is better as a guardian
– He is the most merciful of the merciful.'

65. When they opened their belongings,
they discovered their goods had been returned to them.
They said, 'Father,
what more can we desire?
Here are our goods returned to us.
We can get provision for our folk
and guard our brother,
and we shall get an extra camel-load.
That is an easy measure.'

66. He said, 'I shall not send him with you
until you give me an undertaking in God's name
that you will bring him back to me
unless you are overwhelmed.'
When they gave him their undertaking, he said,
'God is the guardian of what we say.'

67. He said, 'My sons,
do not enter by one gate.
Enter by various gates.
I can avail you nothing against God.

Judgement belongs to God alone.
I put my trust in Him.
Let all the trusting put their trust in Him.'

68. And when they entered as their father had told them,
it would have availed them nothing against God.
It was simply a need in Jacob's soul
which he satisfied.
He had some knowledge
because of what We had taught him;
but most of the people do not know.

69. When they went to see Joseph,
he placed his brother at his side and said,
'I am your brother.
So do not be distressed at what they have done.'

70. When he provided them with their provision,
he put the drinking-cup into his brother's saddle-bag.
Then a crier cried, 'O caravan, you are thieves.'

71. They said as they came towards them,
'What are you missing?'

72. They replied, 'We are missing the king's goblet.
Whoever brings it will get a camel-load.
I am its guarantor.'

73. They said, 'By God,
you know that we have not come to do mischief in the land
and that we are not thieves.'

74. They replied, 'What shall be recompense for it,
if you are liars?'

75. They said, 'The recompense for it?
The person in whose saddle-bag it is found
– the recompense for it will be [with him].[9]
Thus we pay back those who do evil.'

76. Then he began with their bags,
before his brother's bag.
Then he produced it from his brother's bag.
Thus We contrived for Joseph's sake.
He was not one to take his brother under the king's law
had God not wished it.
We raise by degrees those whom We wish;
and above every man of knowledge is One who knows.

77. They said, 'If he steals,

---

[9] *i.e.* he will be seized.

there was a brother of his who stole before him.'
But Joseph kept the secret to himself
and did not reveal it to them.
He said, 'You are in an evil plight.
God is well aware of what you are describing.'

78. They said, 'O mighty one.
He has a father who is a very old man indeed.
Take one of us in his place.
We think that you are one of those who do good.'

79. He replied, 'God forbid that we should seize anyone
other than the one with whom we found our goods.
If we did that, we should be doing wrong.'

80. When they despaired of him,
they conferred together in private.
The eldest of them said,
'Do you not know that your father took from you
an undertaking in God's name?
And before that you were remiss in the matter of Joseph.
I shall not leave [this] land
until my father gives me permission
or God gives judgement in my favour.
He is the best of judges.

81. Return to your father and say,
"O father, your son stole.
We testify only to that which we know.
We could not guard against the Invisible.[10]

82. Ask the settlement in which we were
and the caravan in which we came.
We are really speaking the truth".'

83. He[11] said, 'No!
Your souls have enticed you to [do] something [wrong].
[May I have] fair patience.
It may be that God will bring them all to me.
He is the Knowing, the Wise.'

84. He turned away from them and said,
'Oh, how I grieve for Joseph.'
His eyes turned white from grief
and he was choking with emotion.

85. They said, 'By God,

---

[10] *i.e.* the unforeseeable.
[11] Jacob

229

you will never cease remembering Joseph
until you are worn out
or are one of those who perish.'

86. He said, 'I complain of my anguish and sorrow only to God.
I have some knowledge from God that you do not have.

87. My sons, go and search out news of Joseph and his brother.
Do not despair of God's comfort.
Only unbelievers despair of God's comfort.'

88. When they went to see [Joseph], they said,
'O mighty one, affliction has touched us and our folk.
We bring goods of little value.
But give us full measure and be charitable to us.
God recompenses those who are charitable.'

89. He said, 'Do you remember what you did to Joseph and his brother
when you acted with ignorance?'

90. They said, 'Are you really Joseph?'
He replied, 'I am Joseph, and this is my brother.
God has been gracious to us.
If one is god-fearing and patient,
God does not let the wage of those who do good go to waste.'

91. They said, 'By God,
God has preferred you over us.
In truth we were sinners.'

92. He said, 'To-day there will be no reproach against you.
God will forgive you.
He is the most merciful of the merciful.

93. Take this shirt of mine
and throw it over my father's face,
and he will see again.
Then bring all your family to me.'

94. When the caravan set off, their father said,
'I would say that I perceive the scent of Joseph,
but for the fact that you would think me completely wrong.'

95. They said, 'By God, you persist in your old error.'

96. When the bearer of good tidings came,
he threw it over his face
and he saw again.
He said, 'Did I not tell you that I knew something from God that you did not know?'

97. They said, 'Father,
ask forgiveness for us for our sins.
We were sinners.'

98. He said, 'I shall ask my Lord to forgive you.

He is Forgiving and Merciful.'

99.   When they came to see Joseph,
he placed his parents by his side and said,
'Enter Egypt in safety, if God wills.'

100.   He placed his parents on the throne,
and they [all] fell down before him,
prostrating themselves.
He said, 'Father,
this is the interpretation of my vision long ago.
My Lord has made it true.
He was good to me when He brought me out of prison
and then brought you from the desert,
after Satan had caused strife between me and my brothers.
My Lord is subtle in what He wills.
He is the Knowing and the Wise.

101.   My Lord, You have bestowed some power on me
and taught me something of the interpretation of tales.
O creator of the heavens and the earth,
you are my protector in this world and the next.
Take me as one who has submitted
and join me with the righteous.'

102.   That is from the tidings of the Invisible,
with which We inspire you[s].[12]
You[s] were not with them
when they agreed on their plan and were plotting.

103.   But most of the people are not believers,
even if you[s] are eager for that.

104.   You[s] do not ask them for any wage for it.
It is only a reminder to all beings.

105.   How many a sign is there
in the heavens and the earth
that they pass by and turn their faces away!

106.   And most of them do not believe in God
unless they associate others with Him.

107.   Do they feel secure
that a covering of God's punishment will not come upon them
and that the Hour will not come upon them suddenly
when they are unaware.

108.   Say, 'This is my way.
I call to God with sure knowledge, I and whoever follows me.

---

[12] The rest of the *sūra* is addressed to Muḥammad.

Glory be to God.
I am not one of those who associate others with God.'

109. We have only sent before you[s]
men whom We inspired from the people of the settlements.
Have they not travelled in the land and seen
how was the punishment of those who were before them?
The abode of the world to come is better for those who are god-fearing.
Do you[p] not understand?

110. Then, when the messengers despaired
and thought that they were deemed to be lying,
Our help came to them,
and those whom We wished were saved.
Our might cannot be turned away from the people who are sinners.

111. In their stories there is a lesson for those with understanding.
It is not a tale that is invented
but a confirmation of what [has gone] before it
and a setting forth of everything
and a guidance and a mercy
for a people who believe.

Sūra 13

The date of the *sūra* is uncertain. Its basis is almost certainly latish Meccan, but it appears to have been revised and recast during Muḥammad's early years at Medina. It is a rhetorical, allusive piece, effective as a sermon, though not straightforward reading. In his introductory note Bell is dismissive, saying that it 'seems largely to consist of scraps, which have been revised and added to at Medina'. Certainly there are some abrupt and difficult verses, with even the commentators wondering whether the text is correct (see verses 31 and 33 in particular). However, we can be reasonably sure that the terseness and rather wayward mode of expression, rhetorical in nature, were much less difficult to understand originally than they are now. Pre-Islamic poetry has many passages that are remarkably terse and/or abruptly linked but are nonetheless effective.

This abruptness affects the overall structure: there are no long sections. After the short passage on God's signs (1–4 or 1–5), there is sustained polemic over a range of rapidly changing themes.

A further feature of the *sūra* is that, although prophets are referred to, none is mentioned by name. This is unusual in a *sūra* of this length, though *Sūra* 16, a longer piece, has only two brief references to a prophet (Abraham).

Thunder

In the name of the Merciful and Compassionate God

1. *Alif, Lām, Mīm, Rā'.*[1]
   These are the signs of the Scripture.
   What has been sent down to you[s] from your Lord is the truth;
   but most of the people do not believe.
2. It is God who raised up the heavens without visible pillars;
   then He set himself on the throne
   and subjected the sun and the moon to His command,
   each running for a stated term.
   He directs the affair,[2]
   making His signs distinct,
   so that you[p] may be convinced that you will meet your Lord.
3. It is He who stretched out the earth

---

[1] On the mystical letters see the note on 2:1.
[2] Here and in verse 31 'the affair' appears to mean 'everything'.

and placed in it mountains and rivers;
and He placed in it two kinds of every fruit.
He causes the night to cover the day.
In that there are signs for a people who reflect.

4.   In the earth there are adjacent tracts
and vineyards and sown land and palms,
in clusters and not in clusters,
which are watered with one water;
and We give preference to some of them over others
in [the amount of] food they produce for eating.
In that there are signs for a people who understand.

5.   If you^s wonder, wonderful is their saying,
'When we are dust, shall we be raised in a new creation?'
Those are the ones who do not believe in their Lord.
Those are the ones who will have chains on their necks;
those are the inmates of the Fire,
in which they will dwell for ever.

6.   They ask you^s to hasten evil before good,
though examples have passed away before them.
Yet your^s Lord is forgiving to the people
despite their wrong-doing.
Your^s Lord is severe in punishment too.

7.   Those who are ungrateful say,
'Why has no sign been sent down to him from his Lord?'
You^s are simply a warner;
and for every people there is a guide.

8.   God knows what every female bears
and how wombs shrink and swell.
Everything has its measure with Him,

9.   the Knower of the Invisible and the Witnessed,
the Great, the Exalted.

10.   Alike it is for those of you who keep secret what they have to say
and those who make it public,
and those who hide themselves in the night
and those who sally forth in the day:

11.   There are angels who attend closely before and behind [each one of] them,
guarding him by God's command.
God does not change what is in a people
until they alter what is in themselves;
and when God wills ill on a people,
there is no turning it back.
Apart from Him they have no protector.

12. It is He who shows you[p] the lightning,
    for fear and for hope,
    and who produces the heavy clouds.

13. The thunder sounds loudly in praise of Him,
    and so do the angels, through fear of Him.
    He sends forth the thunderbolts
    and smites with them those whom He wishes.
    Yet they dispute concerning God.
    He is mighty in wrath.

14. The call that is true is made to Him alone.
    Those on whom they call,
    apart from Him,
    make no response to them,
    except as one who stretches out his hands to water,
    that it may reach his mouth,
    and it does not do so.
    The prayer of the unbelievers only goes astray.

15. All those who are in the heavens and the earth
    prostrate themselves to God,
    willingly or unwillingly,
    [as do] their shadows,
    in the mornings and the evenings.

16. Say, 'Who is the Lord of the heavens and the earth?'
    Say, 'God'.
    Say, 'Have you chosen protectors apart from Him
    who cannot benefit or harm [even] themselves?'
    Say, 'Are the blind and the seeing equal,
    or the darkness and the light?'

16a. Or have they assigned associates for God
    who have created as He created,
    so that [all] creation seems the same to them.
    Say, 'God is the Creator of everything.
    He is the One, the Victorious.'

17. He sends down water from the sky,
    and the *wādīs* flow according to their measure,
    and the torrent carries a scum that rises to the top;
    and there is a scum like it
    from that over which they light fire,
    seeking to [make] ornaments or [other] wares.
    Thus God coins [a parallel for] the true and the false.
    As for the scum, it disappears as rubbish;
    as for what benefits the people, it remains in the earth.

Thus God coins parallels.

18. For those who respond to their Lord is the fairest reward;
    but those who do not respond to Him
    – if they had all that is on earth and as much again,
    they would offer it as their ransom.
    Those will have the evil reckoning.
    Their abode will be Jahannam,
    an evil resting-place.

19. Are those who know
    that what has been sent down to you^s from your Lord is the truth
    like those who are blind?
    Only those possessed of understanding are reminded

20. – Those who fulfil God's covenant
    and do not violate the agreement,

21. And who join what God has commanded to be joined
    and fear their Lord and are afraid of the evil reckoning,

22. And who are patient in seeking the face of their Lord
    and perform prayer
    and spend from that which We have provided for them,
    secretly [or] in public,
    and avert evil with good
    – those will have the sequel of the abode:

23. Gardens of Eden, which they will enter,
    together with those of their forefathers and spouses and offspring who are righteous.
    The angels will go in through every gate to see them, [saying]:

24. 'Peace be upon you^p because you were patient.
    Excellent is the sequel of the abode.'

25. Those who break the covenant of God
    after [they have made] an agreement with Him
    and who sever what God has commanded to be joined
    and who make mischief in the land
    – those will have the curse;
    those will have the Evil Abode.

26. God extends provision for those whom He wishes
    and measures carefully [for those whom He wishes].
    They rejoice in the life of this world;
    but the life of this world,
    in comparison with the world to come,
    is an [ephemeral] enjoyment.

27. Those who are ungrateful say,
    'Why has a sign has not been sent down to him from his Lord?'
    Say, 'God leads astray those whom He wishes

and guides to Himself those who are penitent:

28. Those who believe
and whose hearts are at rest in the remembrance of God
– in the remembrance of God hearts are at rest –
29. Those who believe and do righteous deeds.
They will have bliss and a fair resort.'
30. Thus We have sent you^s among a community,
before which other communities have passed away,
that you may recite to them that with which We have inspired you,
when they do not believe in the Merciful.
Say, 'He is my Lord.
There is no god except Him.
In Him I put my trust and to Him is my recourse.'
31. Had [there been] a Recitation
by which the mountains were set in motion
or the earth sundered
or the dead caused to speak
– No. The affair is entirely God's.
Yet do not those who believe
despair of the [possibility] that
if God willed He would guide all the people?
And those who disbelieve will always be smitten by a smiting
for what they have done,
or it will stay near their homes until God's promise comes.
God will not fail to keep the tryst.
32. Mockery was made of messengers before you^s.
I bore with those who were ungrateful.
Then I seized them;
and how was My punishment?
33. [What of] Him who stands over every soul with what it has earned?
They associate others with God!
Say, 'Name^p them.
Or can you tell Him about the things on earth
of which He has no knowledge,
or [is what you say] a show of words?'
No. For those who do not believe
their plotting has been made to seem fair,
and they are kept from the way.
Those whom God leads astray have no guide.
34. They will have torment in the life of this world;
yet the torment of the world to come is harsher,
and they will have no one to protect them against God.

35. The picture of the Garden which is promised to those who protect themselves:
    rivers flow through it;
    its food is perpetual;
    and [so] is its shade.
    That is the sequel for those who protect themselves.
    The sequel for the ungrateful is the Fire.

36. Those to whom We have given the Scripture
    rejoice in what has been sent down to you[s].
    But there are among the parties
    those who deny some of it.
    Say, 'I am commanded to serve God
    and not to associate others with Him.
    To Him I call and to Him is my return.'

37. Thus We have revealed it as a criterion in Arabic.
    If you[s] follow their whims
    after the knowledge that has come to you,
    you will have no protector or defender against God.

38. We have sent messengers before you[s],
    and We have given them wives and offspring.
    It is not for a messenger to bring a sign
    save with God's leave.
    For every term there is a record.

39. God effaces and establishes what He wishes.
    With Him is the matrix of the Scripture.

40. Whether We show you[s] some of what We promise them
    or We take you,
    your only duty is to convey the message.
    Ours is the reckoning.

41. Have they not seen that We come to the land,
    diminishing it at its extremities?
    [When] God judges, there is none to repel His judgement.
    He is swift to the reckoning.

42. Those who were before them plotted;
    but all plotting is God's.
    He knows what each soul earns.
    Those who are ungrateful
    will know whose is the sequel of the abode.

43. Those who do not believe say,
    'You are not sent as a messenger.'
    Say, 'God is sufficient witness between me and you,
    [as are] those who possess knowledge of the Scripture.'

Sūra 14

This is traditionally thought to be a late Meccan *sūra*, with a number of Muslim authorities taking the view that verses 28–29 or 28–30 were added at Medina. Western scholars have taken different viewpoints about the *sūra*. Bell sees it as little more than a series a fragments, whilst Neuwirth argues for its homogeneity. There seems to be something in both views! One can readily divide the *sūra* into six sections (1–3; 4–17; 18–23; 24–34; 35–41; 42–52), but the material is held together by various small repetitions. The medley of themes is typical of the late Meccan period.

Abraham

In the name of the Merciful and Compassionate God

1. *Alif, Lām, Rā'.*[1]
    Scripture which We have sent down to you[s]
    that you[s] may lead the people from darkness into light,
    with the permission of their Lord,
    to the path of the Mighty and Laudable,
2. God, to Whom belongs all that is in the heavens and all that is on earth.
    Woe to those who do not believe
    because of a severe torment:
3. Those who prefer the life of this world to [that of] the next
    and turn [the people] from God's way
    and desire to make it crooked
    – they are in distant error.
4. We never sent any messenger except with the tongue of his people,
    for him to make [the message] clear to them.
    God sends astray those whom He wishes
    and guides those whom He wishes.
    He is the Mighty and the Wise.
5. We sent Moses with Our signs, saying,
    'Bring your people out of the darkness into the light;
    and remind them of God's days.
    In that there are signs for every one who is patient and thankful.
6. [Recall] when Moses said to his people,
    'Remember God's blessing to you

---

[1] On the mystical letters see the note on 2:1.

when He saved you from the folk of Pharaoh
who were afflicting you with evil torment
and slaughtering your sons and sparing your women.
In that there was a grievous trial from your Lord.'

7. And [recall] when your Lord proclaimed,
'If you are thankful,
I shall give you increase;
but if you are ungrateful,
My punishment will be severe.'

8. And Moses said, '[Even] if you and all those who are on earth are ungrateful,
God is All-sufficient and Laudable.'

9. Has there not come to you[P] the tidings of those who [came] before you?
The people of Noah and ʿĀd and Thamūd
and of those who [came] after them,
known only to God,
to whom their messengers came with clear proofs,
but they thrust their hands into their mouths and said,
'We do not believe in the message with which you[P] are sent.
We are in disquieting doubt about that to which you[P] summon us.'

10. Their messengers said, 'Is there any doubt about God,
the Creator of the heavens and the earth?
He summons you that He may forgive you your sins
and give you respite to a stated term.'
They said, 'You are only mortals like us.
You want to turn us away from what our forefathers served.
Bring us a clear authority.'

11. Their messengers said to them, 'We are only mortals like you,
but God is gracious to those of His servants whom He wishes.
It is not for us to bring you any authority,'
save with the permission of God.
Let the believers put their trust in God.

12. Why should we not put our trust in God,
when He has guided us on our ways?
We shall endure patiently under the hurt you do us.
Let the trusting put their trust in God.'

13. The ungrateful ones said to their messengers,
'We shall expel you from our land,
or you will return to our creed.'
And their Lord inspired them, saying,
'We shall destroy the wrong-doers;

14. And We shall make you dwell in the land after them.
That is for those who fear My station and fear My threat.'

15. They sought help, and every obstinate tyrant was disappointed,
16. Behind him is Jahannam, [where] he is given pus-like water to drink.
17. He sips it but can hardly swallow it
    and death comes on him from every side;
    yet he does not die
    and behind him there is a harsh torment.
18. A comparison for those who do not believe in their Lord:
    their works are like ashes which the wind scatters on a stormy day.
    They have no power over any of what they have earned.
    That is distant error.
19. Have you^s not seen that God created the heavens and the earth in truth?
    If He wishes, He can remove you^p and bring a new creation.
20. That is not a great matter for God.
21. They will all go forth to their Lord;
    and the weak will say to those who were haughty,
    'We were your followers.
    Can you avail us in any way against the punishment of God?'
    They will reply, 'Had God guided us, we would have guided you.
    It is all one for us whether we are fretful or we endure patiently.
    We have no place of refuge.'
22. And Satan will say, when the matter is decided,
    'God has made you a true promise;
    but I promised you and then I failed you.
    I had no authority over you,
    except that I called you and you answered me.
    So do not blame me, but blame yourselves.
    I cannot come to your aid, nor you to mine.
    I did not believe in that with which you associated me before.
    The wrong-doers will have a painful punishment.
23. And those who believed and did righteous deeds
    will be admitted to gardens through which rivers flow,
    dwelling in them for ever by permission of their Lord,
    their greeting there being 'Peace'.
24. Have you^s not seen how God has coined a comparison:
    a good word [is] like a good tree,
    its roots firm, its branches reaching into the sky;
25. It gives its fruit every season by permission of its Lord.
    God coins comparisons for men,
    so that they may reflect.
26. The comparison of a bad saying is [that it is] like a bad tree
    which has been uprooted from the earth and has no stability.
27. God confirms those who believe by firm speech

in the life of this world and in the world to come.
God leads astray those whom He wishes
– God does what He wishes.

28. Have you⁵ not looked at those who changed the blessing of God for ingratitude?
They caused their people to dwell in the abode of ruin

29. – Jahannam, in which they will roast:
how evil a resting-place.

30. And they have set up rivals to God,
to lead [men] astray from His way.
Say⁵, 'Enjoy yourselves.
Your journeying is to the Fire.'

31. Tell⁵ my servants who believe
[that] they should perform prayer
and spend some of that which We have provided for them,
secretly and publicly,
before there comes a day on which there will be no bargaining and no friendship.

32. It is God who has created the heavens and the earth
and has sent down water from the sky
and has brought forth with it fruits as sustenance for you,
and who subjected for you the ships
to run on the sea at His command,
and who subjected to you the rivers.

33. And He has subjected to you the sun and the moon,
constant toilers,
and He has subjected to you night and day;

34. And He has given you something of all you asked.
If you [try to] number the blessings of God,
you will never count them.
Man is a great wrong-doer and very ungrateful.

35. And [recall] when Abraham said,
'My Lord, make this territory safe
and turn me and my sons away from worshipping idols.

36. My Lord, they have led many of the people astray;
but those who follow me belong to me;
and those who oppose me
– You are forgiving and Merciful.

37. Our Lord, I have made some of my seed dwell in a valley
where there is no sown land close by Your Holy House,
our Lord, that they may perform prayer.
Cause [the] hearts of some of the people to incline to them
and give them sustenance of fruits
so that they may be thankful.

38. Our Lord, you know what we conceal and what we proclaim.
    Nothing on earth or in heavens is hidden from God.
39. Praise belongs to God,
    who has given to me, in my old age,
    Ishmael and Isaac.
    My Lord is the Hearer of prayer.
40. My Lord, make me and some of my seed perform prayer,
    and, our Lord, receive my prayer.
41. Our Lord, forgive me and my parents and the believers
    on the day when the reckoning comes to pass.'
42. Do^s not reckon that God is heedless of what the wrong-doers do.
    He is only granting them respite
    to a day on which eyes will stare,
43. As [men] hurry, raising their heads,
    their gaze not returning to them and their hearts void.
44. And warn men of the day when the torment will come to them
    and when those who have done wrong will say,
    'Our Lord, give us respite for a brief while
    and we shall answer Your call and follow the messengers.'
    'Did you^p not swear before that there would be no extinction for you?'
45. You have dwelt in the dwelling-places of those who wronged themselves,
    and it was made clear to you how We dealt with them,
    and We made examples for you.
46. They have laid their plot,
    but their plot is [known to] God,
    even though it is one by which the mountains might be moved.
47. Do^s not reckon that God will fail in His promise to His messengers.
    God is Mighty and wields vengeance.
48. On the day when the earth is changed to something else,
    and [so too] the heavens,
    and they come forth to God,
    the One, the Victorious:
49. On that day you^s will see the sinners bound together in chains,
50. Their clothing of pitch,
    their faces covered by the Fire,
51. That God may repay every soul what it has earned.
    God is swift in the reckoning.
52. This is a message for men, that they may be warned by it
    and that they may know that He is One God
    and that those who have understanding may be reminded.

Sūra 15

This is generally considered to be a middle Meccan *sūra*, though a couple of verses (24 and 87) are sometimes said to be Medinan. There are six main sections: a brief introduction (1–3); a polemical passage (4–15); a 'signs' passage (16–27); the Iblīs story, rounded off by a bridge passage on heaven and hell (28–48); punishment stories (49–84); and a peroration affirming that the Hour is coming and the message has been sent and giving encouragement to Muḥammad. The last quarter of the *sūra* has a certain number of difficulties that may be due to textual problems.

al-Ḥijr[1]

In the name of the Merciful and Compassionate God

1. *Alif, Lām, Rā'.*[2]
   These are the signs of the Scripture
   and of a clear Recitation.
2. Perhaps those who are ungrateful will wish that they were among those who have surrendered themselves.
3. Let[s] them eat and enjoy themselves
   and be diverted by hope.
   They will [come to] know.
4. We have not destroyed any settlement without it having a known decree.
5. No community outstrips its term nor postpones it.
6. They have said, 'You[s] to whom the Reminder has been sent down,
   you are possessed.[3]
7. Why do you[s] not bring us angels
   if you are one of those who speak the truth?'
8. We only send down the angels with the truth;
   and in that case they would not be given respite.
9. We have indeed sent down the Reminder,
   and We shall watch over it.
10. We sent messengers before you among the factions of the ancients,
11. And no messenger came to them but they mocked him.
12. Thus We cause it to travel into the hearts of the sinners.

---

[1] Traditionally thought to be the land of Thamūd, north of Medina.
[2] On the mystical letters see the note on 2:1.
[3] By the *Jinn.*

244

13. They do not believe in it,
    though the example of the ancients has gone before.
14. Even if We were to open to them a gate of heaven
    and they were to keep on mounting through it,
15. They would say, 'Our sight has been dazzled.
    No! We are a people who have been bewitched.'
16. We have set constellations in the sky
    and made it beautiful for those who behold it;
17. And We have guarded it from every accursed devil
18. – Except for those who listen by stealth
    – they are pursued by a clear flame.
19. And We have stretched out the earth
    and cast on to it firm mountains
    and caused to grow in it some of everything that can be weighed.
20. And We have provided livelihoods in it for you^p
    and for those for whom you make no provision.
21. There is nothing for which We do not have stores;
    and We send it down only in a known measure.
22. We send the winds to fertilize
    and We send down water from the sky
    and give it to you to drink.
    You are not the ones who store it.
23. It is We who bring life and bring death
    and We are the inheritors.
24. We know those of you who press forward
    and We know those who hang back.
25. It is your^s Lord [who] will round them up.
    He is Wise and Knowing.
26. We have created man from clay,
    from a moulded mud;
27. We created the *Jinn* before from the fire of the scorching wind.
28. And [recall] when your^s Lord said to the angels,
    'I am creating man from clay,
    from a moulded mud;
29. So when I have formed him
    and breathed into him some of My spirit,
    fall down in prostration to him.'
30. All the angels prostrated themselves, all [of them]
31. Except Iblīs.
    He refused to be amongst those who prostrated themselves.
32. HE said, 'O Iblīs, why is it
    that you are not amongst those who prostrate themselves?'

33. He said, 'I am not one to prostrate myself
    to a mortal whom You have created from clay,
    from a moulded mud.'
34. HE said, 'Leave it.[4]
    You are accursed.
35. The curse will be upon you till the Day of Judgement.'
36. He said, 'My Lord, give me respite
    till the day when they are raised.'
37. HE said, 'You are one of those given respite
38. Until the day of the known time.'
39. He said, 'My Lord,
    because You have led me astray
    I shall make things seem beautiful for them in the land
    and I shall lead them astray, all [of them]
40. Except for your devoted servants amongst them.'
41. HE said, 'This is a straight path for Me.
42. You have no authority over My servants,
    except those errant ones who follow you.'
43. Jahannam is the place promised for them all.
44. It has seven gates,
    and each gate has a portion of them assigned [to it].
45. But those who protect themselves will be among gardens and springs:
46. 'Enter them in peace and security.'
47. We have removed any rancour that may have been in their breasts.
    They will face each other on couches as brothers.
48. Fatigue will not touch them there,
    nor will they be expelled from there.
49. Tell[5] My servants that I am Forgiving and Merciful,
50. And that My torment is the painful torment.
51. And tell them of the guests of Abraham:
52. When they came to see him and said, 'Peace'.
    He said, 'We are afraid of you.'
53. They said, 'Do not be afraid.
    We bring you good tidings of a boy with knowledge.'
54. He said, 'Do you bring me good tidings,
    in spite of the fact that old age has touched me?
    What good tidings can you bring?'
55. They said, 'We bring you good tidings in truth.
    Do not be one of those who despair.'
56. He said, 'Who despairs of the mercy of His Lord,

---

[4] The Garden of Eden.

except for those who have gone astray?'

57. He said, 'What is your business, O envoys?'
58. They said, 'We have been sent to a people who are sinners,
59. Except for the family of Lot.
We shall save them[5] all,
60. Except his wife.
We have decreed that she will be among those who stay behind.'
61. When the messengers came to the family of Lot,
62. He said, 'You are an unknown folk.'
63. They said, 'No, we have brought you that about which they have doubts.
64. We have brought you the truth.
We speak truthfully.
65. Travel with your family in a part of the night.
Follow their backs;
and let none of you turn round,
but go where you are ordered.'
66. We decreed that command for him
because the last remnant of those[6] would be cut off in the morning.
67. The people of the city came rejoicing.
68. He said, 'These are my guests.
Do not disgrace me.
69. Fear God. Do not shame me.'
70. They said, 'Have we not forbidden you[s] from all created beings?'
71. He said, 'These are my daughters,
if you are going to do something.'
72. By your[7] life, they were wandering blindly in their anguish.
73. The Shout took them at sunrise.
74. We turned things upside down
and rained upon them stones of baked clay.
75. In that there are signs for those who look carefully.
76. It is indeed a road that [still] remains.
77. In that there is a sign for those who believe.
78. The men of the thicket[8] were wrong-doers.
79. So We took vengeance on them.
These two are on a clear road.
80. And the men of al-Ḥijr[9] denied the truth of those who were sent [to them].
81. We gave them Our signs,

---

[5] The family.
[6] The sinners.
[7] Addressed to Muḥammad.
[8] See also 26:176. The reference would appear to be to Madyan from the mention of Shuʿayb in 26:177.
[9] See note 1 on the title of the *sūra*.

but they turned away from them.

82. They used to hew out dwellings from the mountains,
    [in which] they [felt] secure.

83. But the Shout took them in the morning,

84. And that which they had been acquiring was of no avail to them.

85. We did not create the heavens and the earth and all that is between them
    save with the truth.
    The Hour is surely coming.
    So forgive graciously.

86. Your^s Lord is the Knowing Creator.

87. We have given you^s seven *mathānī*[10] and the great Recitation.

88. Do not stretch yours eyes
    to that which We have made some pairs of them enjoy,
    and do not grieve for them,
    and lower your wing for the believers,

89. And say, 'I am the clear warner.'

90. As We sent it down to those who have sought division,

91. Who have broken the Recitation into portions.

92. By your^s Lord, We shall question them all

93. About what they used to do.

94. So proclaim^s what you are commanded,
    and turn away from those who associate [others with God].

95. We are sufficient for you^s against those who mock,

96. Who set up [some] other god with God.
    They will [come to] know.

97. Indeed We know that your^s breast is oppressed by what they say.

98. But glorify^s your Lord with praise
    and be one of those who prostrate themselves;

99. And serve^s your Lord until the Certain[11] comes to you.

---

[10] The *mathānī* are traditionally equated with the seven verses of *Sūra* 1, but see the Commentary.

[11] Interpreted as 'death' or 'destruction'.

Sūra 16

The traditional view is that this *sūra* is mainly late Meccan, with the final section (verses 106–128) being added at Medina. It is difficult to judge what Medinan content there is in the rest of the *sūra*: more, one might guess, than is normally held to be the case, but less than was suggested by Bell, who thought that there is considerably more Medinan material than Meccan. The problem is that there is generally little difference between late Meccan and early Medinan material, unless there are pointers to a specifically Medinan context. Thus some of the verses of the final section (e.g. 106, 110, 114–116, 118 and 124) contain phrases whose context cannot be other than Medinan, and it is not unreasonable to assume that the rest of that section was at least reworked at Medina. The real difficulties lie elsewhere with verses such as 103, in which objectors to Muḥammad are normally, and probably rightly, considered to be the Meccan unbelievers. If the objectors were Medinan, the background would be startlingly different.

The *sūra* can be divided up into a dozen or so sections: a brief introductory piece on God's command (1–2) is followed by the first of a series of 'sign' passages (3–16); next comes a passage of polemic (17–47); a further sign passage (48–50); further polemic (51–65); a further sign passage (66–70); further polemic (71–77); a further sign passage (78–81); further polemic (82–89); injunctions from God (90–97); further polemic (98–105), continued in the final Medinan section (106–128). However, not too much should be made of this division, as there are various unifying threads: the refrain-like 'in this there are signs ...' (see the note on verse 11); the stress on reminder (verses 13, 17, 43, 44, 90); the theme of 'that about which they differ' that occurs in verses 39, 64, 92 and 124; and, not least, the various verses that address Muḥammad.

The Bees

In the name of the Merciful and Compassionate God

1. God's command has come;
   so do[p] not seek to hasten it.
   Glory be to Him,
   and may He be exalted away from what they associate [with Him].
2. He sends down the angels with the Spirit
   [that comes] from His command
   upon those of His servants that He wishes,
   saying, 'Give warning that there is no God but Me,
   and be pious towards Me.'

249

3. He has created the heavens and the earth in truth.
   May He be exalted away from what they associate [with Him].

4. He has created man from a drop of sperm,
   and there man is – a persuasive disputant.

5. And livestock – He has created them for you[P].
   In them are warmth and [other] benefits;
   and you may eat of them.

6. In them there is beauty for you
   when you give them rest
   and when you give them pasture.

7. They carry your loads to a settlement
   you could not reach without distress to yourselves.
   Your Lord is Kind and Compassionate.

8. [He has also created] horses and mules and donkeys
   for you to ride them,
   and as an adornment.
   He creates what you do not know.

9. It is for God to set the way
   – though some will stray from it.
   But if He had wished,
   He could have guided you all aright.

10. It is He who has sent down water for you[P] from heaven;
    from it you have drink and from it come trees
    on which you may pasture [your animals].

11. With it He causes crops,
    olives, palms, and vines and all kinds of fruit,
    to grow for you.
    In that there is a sign for people who reflect.

12. He has subjected night and day and the sun and moon to your service,
    and the stars too are held subject by His command
    – In that there are signs for a people who understand –

13. And whatever He has created for you
    in the earth in various colours;
    In that there is a sign for those who are reminded.

14. It is He who has subjected the sea,
    so that you may eat fresh fish from it
    and bring forth ornaments that you may wear.
    And you can see the ships cutting through it.
    [That is] so that you may seek some of His bounty
    and that you may be thankful.

15. He has cast on to the earth firm mountains,
    so that it does not sway with you,

and rivers and roads so that you may be guided,

16. And landmarks.
And [men] can guide themselves by the stars.

17. Is He who creates like the one who does not create?
Will you not be reminded?

18. If you [try to] reckon God's blessing,
you will not [be able to] count it.
God is Forgiving, Merciful.

19. God knows what you keep secret and what you make public.

20. Those whom they invoke,
to the exclusion of God,
create nothing,
but are themselves created.

21. They are dead [things], not living,
and they are not aware when they will be raised.

22. Your God is One God.
The hearts of those who do not believe in the world to come deny [that].
They are haughty.

23. Without doubt God knows what they keep secret and what they make public.
He has no love for the haughty.

24. When it is said to them, 'What has your Lord sent down?'
they say, 'Fables of the ancients.'

25. [That is] so they may bear their loads complete on the Day of Resurrection
and some of the burdens of those whom they lead astray
without any knowledge.
Evil is that which they will bear.

26. Those who were before them plotted;
but God attacked their building from its foundations,
and the roof fell on them from above them,
and the punishment came upon them
from a direction they did not perceive.

27. Then on the Day of Resurrection He will disgrace them,
and will say, 'Where are your associates,
for whose sake you caused disagreements?'
Those who have been given knowledge will say,
'Disgrace to-day and evil are upon the unbelievers,

28. Whom the angels take as they are still wronging themselves.'
They will try to make peace:
'We used not to do any wrong.'
That is not the case.
God is well aware of what you have been doing.

29. Enter the gates of Jahannam,

where you will stay for ever.
How wretched is the abode of the arrogant.

30. It will be said to those who are god-fearing,
'What has your Lord sent down?'
They will reply, 'Good.
For those who do good in this world there is a boon.'
But the dwelling of the hereafter is better.
How excellent is the dwelling of the god-fearing

31. – Gardens of Eden, which they will enter,
with rivers flowing through them,
where they will have what they wish.
Thus God recompenses the god-fearing,

32. Whom the angels take when they are good.
They will say, 'Peace be upon you.
Enter the garden as a recompense for what you used to do.'

33. Do they expect anything other
than that the angels will come to them
or that the command of your Lord will come?
Those who were before them did likewise.
God did not wrong them,
but they wronged themselves.

34. The evils of what they had done smote them,
and what they used to scorn encompassed them.

35. Those who associate [others with God] say, 'Had God willed,
we would not have worshipped anything to His exclusion;
neither we nor our forefathers;
nor would we have forbidden anything to His exclusion.'
Those who were before them did likewise.
And have the messengers any duty
except to deliver the message clearly?

36. We have raised in every community a messenger
to say, 'Serve God and avoid idols[1].'
Of them are some whom God guided
and some on whom error had firm hold.
So journey in the land
and see how was the punishment of those who denied [the truth].

37. Even if you[s] are eager for them to be guided,
God does not give guidance to those whom He leads astray.
They do not have any helpers.

38. They swear by God their most binding oaths

---

[1] See the note on 2:256.

that God will not raise those who die.
No! It is a promise binding on Him, a truth,
– though most of the people do not know –

39. So that He may make clear to them that about which they differ,
and so that those who disbelieve may know that they were liars.

40. All We say to a thing when We desire it
is to say to it, 'Be', and it is.

41. Those that migrated for the sake of God
after they had been oppressed,
We shall give them good lodging in this world,
and the wage of the world to come is greater
if only they knew

42. – Those who are patient and put their trust in their Lord.

43. We have sent before you[s] as messengers only men whom we inspired
– ask the people [who have] the reminder if you[p] do not know

44. – With the clear signs and the Scriptures.
And We have sent down to you[s] the reminder
for you[s] to make clear to men what has been sent down to them
and so that they may reflect.

45. Do those who devise evil deeds feel sure
that God will not cause the earth to swallow them
or that punishment will not come upon them from where they are unaware?

46. Or that He will not seize them in their going to and fro
and they will not be able to frustrate Him,

47. Or that He will not seize them little by little?
Your[s] Lord is Kind and Compassionate.

48. Have they not looked at all things God has created,
whose shadows fall to the right and to the left,
prostrating themselves to God and being lowly?

49. Every beast on earth, everything in the heavens and the angels,
[all] prostrate themselves to God.
They are not haughty.

50. They fear their Lord above them,
and they do what they are ordered.

51. God says, 'Do not adopt two gods.
There is only one God.
Show awe to Me.

52. To Him belongs all that is in the heavens and the earth.
His is [true] religion for ever.
Will you[p] fear anyone other than God?

53. Whatever blessings you[p] have are from God.
Then when affliction touches you,

you cry to Him for help.

54. Then when he removes the affliction from you,
    a group of you associate partners with their Lord,

55. To show ingratitude for what We have given them.
    So take your enjoyment.
    You will [come to] know.

56. They ascribe a share of what we have provided for them
    to something that they do not know.
    By God, you^p will be questioned about what you have been inventing.

57. And they ascribe daughters to God
    – glory be to Him –
    and to themselves what they desire.²

58. When any of them is given the good news of a daughter,
    his face stays black and he chokes on his disappointment.

59. He hides himself from the people
    because of the 'evil' of the good news he has been given.
    Shall he keep it in contempt
    or shall he bury it in the dust?
    Truly, their judgement is evil.

60. Those who do not believe in the world to come
    have a likeness of evil,
    whilst God has the highest likeness.
    He is Mighty and Wise.

61. If God were to take men to task for their wrong-doing,
    He would not leave on [earth] a single creature;
    but He is reprieving them to a stated term.
    And when their term comes,
    they will not delay it an hour
    nor advance it an hour.

62. They ascribe to God what they dislike;³
    and their tongues propound the lie
    that the fairest reward will be theirs.
    There is no doubt that theirs will be the Fire
    and that they will be hastened [into it].

63. By God, We sent messengers to nations before you^s,
    but Satan made their deeds seem fair to them.
    He is their ally to-day,
    but they will have a painful punishment.

64. We have sent down to you^s the Scripture

---

² *i.e.* sons.
³ *i.e.* daughters.

only so that you^s may explain to them that about which they differ
and as a guidance and a mercy for a people who believe.

65. It is God who has sent down water from the sky
    and through it has given life to the earth
    after it has been lifeless.
    In this there is a sign for a people who hear.

66. And there is a sign for you^p in livestock.
    We give you drink from what is in their bellies,
    pure milk, palatable to those who drink it,
    from between filth and blood.

67. And from the fruits of the palm-trees and grapes,
    from which you take intoxicants and good nourishment.
    In this there is a sign for people who understand.

68. And your^s Lord gave a message to the bees,
    'Take for yourselves houses in the mountains and the trees
    and in what men build.

69. Then eat of all the fruits
    and follow the ways of your Lord,
    which will be easy [for you].'
    There comes forth from their bellies
    a drink of various colours,
    in which is healing for men.
    In that there is a sign for a people who reflect.

70. It is God who has created you^p and then will take you.
    Among you are those who will be returned
    to the most abject [state of] life,
    so that he knows nothing after having had knowledge.
    God is Knowing and Powerful.

71. God has given preference to some of you over others in sustenance;
    but those who have been given preference
    do not hand over their sustenance to what their right hands possess,
    so that they may be equal in it.
    Do they deny the blessing of God?

72. It is God who has assigned spouses to you from [among] yourselves,
    and He has assigned to you from your spouses
    sons and grandsons,
    and He has provided you with [a share] of good things.
    Do they then believe in vanity
    and disbelieve in the blessing of God?

73. And do they serve,
    to the exclusion of God,

that which has no power to give them any provision from the heavens and
    the earth,
when they themselves are powerless?

74.   So do^P not coin any comparisons for God.
    God knows and you^P do not.

75.   God has coined a comparison:
    a slave possessed by his master,
    who has control of nothing,
    [as compared with] the one for whom We have provided
    fair provision from Ourselves
    and who spends from it secretly and openly.
    Are they equal?
    Praise belongs to God.
    But most of them have no knowledge.

76.   God has coined a comparison:
    two men,
    one of them dumb, who has control of nothing,
    a burden on his owner
    – wherever he sends him he brings back no good.
    Is he equal to one who enjoins justice and is on a straight path?

77.   To God belongs the Invisible of the heavens and the earth;
    and the matter of the Hour is like the twinkling of an eye or nearer.
    God has power over everything.

78.   It is God who brought you forth from the bellies of your mothers knowing
        nothing,
    and assigned to you hearing and sight and hearts
    so that you may be thankful.

79.   Have they not looked at the birds that are held subject in the air of heaven.
    Only God holds them [there].
    In that there are signs for a people who believe.

80.   It is God who has assigned to you^P a [place of] rest in your houses.
    He has assigned to you houses from the skins of your livestock,
    which you find light on the day that you move on
    and on the day you pitch camp,
    and from their wood and their fur and their hair
    furnishing and enjoyment for a time.

81.   It is God who has assigned to you, from that which He has created, shade;
    and from the mountains He has assigned to you places of refuge;
    and He has assigned to you coats to protect you from heat
    and coats to protect you from your own violence.
    In this way He perfects His blessing for you
    so that you will submit yourselves.

82. If they turn away, it is only your[s] duty to convey the clear message.
83. They know the blessing of God;
    then they deny it
    – most of them are unbelievers.
84. On the day when We shall raise up a witness from every community,
    no leave will be given to those who disbelieve
    and they will not be allowed to make amends.
85. – When those who do wrong see the punishment:
    it will not be lightened for them
    and they will have no respite.
86. When those who associate see their associates,
    they will say, 'God.'
    these are our partners to whom we used to call
    to Your exclusion.'
    They will fling their words back at them,
    'In truth, you are liars.'
87. On that day they will offer submission to God,
    and all that they used to invent will be lost to them.
88. Those who disbelieve and turn [people] aside from the way of God
    – for them We add punishment to punishment
    [in recompense] for the mischief they used to commit
89. – the day when We shall raise up in every community
    a witness against them from their own number.
    We have brought you[s] as a witness against these
    and have sent down to you[s] the Scripture
    as an explanation of everything
    and a guidance and a mercy and good news to those who submit.
90. God enjoins justice, doing good and giving to kinsfolk,
    whilst He forbids indecent conduct, disreputable deeds and insolence.
    He admonishes you[p] so that you may be reminded.
91. Fulfil[p] God's covenant when you have made a covenant.
    Do not break your oaths after their confirmation
    and after you have made God surety over you.
    God knows what you do.
92. Do[p] not be like the woman who breaks her thread into fibres,
    after it was strong,
    taking your oaths as a deceit amongst you,
    because there may be a community which is more numerous
    than another community.
    God is merely testing you in this.
    He will make clear to you on the Day of Resurrection
    that about which you used to differ.

93. Had God wished He could have made you one community;
but He sends astray those whom He wishes,
and He guides those whom He wishes;
and you^p will surely be questioned about what you used to do.

94. Do^p not take your oaths as a deceit amongst you,
lest a foot should slip after it has been firmly placed
and lest you should taste evil
because you have turned [people] away from the path of God
and have a severe punishment.

95. Do^p not purchase [something of] little value at the cost of God's covenant.
What is with God is better for you
if you did but know it.

96. What is with you^p fails,
but what is with God lasts.
We shall pay those who are patient their recompense
according to the best of their deeds.

97. The men and women who do righteous deeds and are believers,
We shall cause them to live a good life.
We shall pay them their recompense
according to the best of their deeds.

98. And when you^s recite the Recitation,
seek refuge in God from the accursed Satan

99. – He has no authority over those who believe
and put their trust in their Lord.

100. His power is only over those who make him an ally
and those who associate [others] with Him.

101. When We exchange one sign for another
– and God is well aware of what He sends down –
they say, 'You^s are simply inventing it.'
But most of them do not know.

102. Say, 'The Holy Spirit has brought it down from your^s Lord in truth
to give confirmation to those who believe
and as a guidance and good news for those who surrender.

103. In truth We know that they say, 'It is only a mortal who is teaching him.'
The speech of the one at whom they hint is foreign,
whereas this is clear Arabic speech.

104. Those who do not believe in God's signs
– God will not guide them,
and they will have a painful punishment.

105. It is only those who do not believe in God's signs who invent falsehood.
Those are the liars.

106. Whoever disbelieves in God after being a believer

- except in the case of those who are forced
and whose hearts are still at rest in their belief –
and those whose breasts are expanded in unbelief,
upon them will be anger from God,
and they will have a grievous punishment.

107. This is because they have preferred the life of this world to the world to come
and because God does not guide unbelieving people.

108. Those are the ones on whose hearts, hearing and sight God has set a seal.
Those are the ones who are heedless.

109. There is no doubt that they are the losers in the world to come.

110. Then your^s Lord,
in the case of those who migrated after they had been persecuted
and then strove and were steadfast
– your^s Lord is Forgiving and Merciful to them,

111. On the day when every soul will plead for itself
and every soul will be paid in full for what it has done,
and [men] will not be wronged.

112. God has coined a comparison:
a settlement that was secure, at rest,
with its provision coming to it in plenty from every place;
yet it was ungrateful for the blessings of God,
and so God let it taste the garb of hunger and fear
because of what they⁴ were doing.

113. A messenger had come to them from among their own number,
but they accused him of falsehood,
and they were smitten by punishment
while they were wrong-doers.

114. Eat^p of the good and lawful food which God has provided for you,
and be thankful for the blessing of your Lord,
if it is Him you serve.

115. He has forbidden you only carrion, blood, the flesh of the pig,
and what has been hallowed to other than God.
But whoever is forced to it,
neither wishing nor transgressing,
God is Merciful and Compassionate to him.

116. And do^p not say, because of what your tongues falsely describe,
'This is lawful, and this is forbidden',
so that you may invent falsehood against God.
Those who invent falsehood against God will not prosper.

117. A brief enjoyment

---

⁴ Its people.

– and then they will have a painful punishment.

118. To those who are Jews We have forbidden what We have told to you before.
We did not wrong them, but they wronged themselves.

119. Then your^s Lord,
in the case of those who have done evil in ignorance
and then have repented after that and made amends
– thereafter your^s Lord is Forgiving and Merciful.

120. Abraham was an example,
obedient to God, of upright faith,
who was not one of those who associate [others with God],

121. Thankful for his blessings.
He chose him and guided him to a straight path.

122. And We gave him good in this world,
and in the world to come he will be among the righteous.

123. Then We gave you^s inspiration,
'Follow^s the religion of Abraham as a man of upright faith,
who was not one of those who associate [others with God].'

124. The Sabbath was only appointed for those who disagreed about it.
Your^s Lord will surely judge between them on the Day of Resurrection,
concerning that about which they used to differ.

125. Summon^s to the way of your Lord
with wisdom and with fair admonition,
and dispute with them with what is better.
Your^s Lord is well aware of those who stray from his way,
and He is well aware of those who follow the right path.

126. If you^p punish,
punish with the like of that with which you were punished.
But if you^p endure patiently,
that is better for those who are patient.

127. Endure^s patiently
– Your^s patience comes only with the help of God.
Do^s not grieve for them,
and do not be in distress because of the plots they devise.

128. God is with those who are god-fearing and those who do good.

Sūra 17

The *sūra* is considered to be largely from the middle Meccan period, though various commentators ascribe a number of verses to the Medinan period, in particular 32–33 and 73–80/81. The reasons given for classing 32–33 as Medinan are fairly convincing, and there can be little doubt that some recasting did take place there, though it might well have started at Mecca. There is a twist at the beginning: the famous first verse, concerning the night journey, is quite detached from the rest of the *sūra*, with no connection either in content or assonance. There then follows a rhetorical section on Moses and the Children of Israel (2–8), which is picked up again in 101–106. This is followed by a piece containing a mixture of typical Meccan themes: polemic warning and 'signs' (9–21). The next section (22–39) is rather difficult to follow as it now stands. Bell rather cheaply characterizes it as 'a sort of imitation of the Decalogue', but it is more complex than that. It appears originally to have been a series of prohibitions in the singular that now appear as 22–24, 26–30 and 36–39. To this nucleus have been added some prohibitions in the plural: 25 and 31–35. Verses 40–60 bring further polemic, which gives way to the Iblīs story (61–65). A bridging 'sign' verse (66) leads back to polemic, which continues to the end of the *sūra*, interrupted only by the second narrative about the Children of Israel.

The Night Journey

In the name of the Merciful and Compassionate God

1. Glory be to Him who journeyed by night with His servant
   from the Sacred Mosque to the Furthest Mosque,[1]
   whose neighbourhood We have blessed,
   to show him some of Our signs.
   He is the Hearing and the Seeing.
2. We gave Moses the Scripture and made it a guidance for the Children of Israel,
   saying, 'Do not choose any trustee apart from Me.'
3. [They were] the seed of those whom We carried with Noah.
   He was a grateful servant.
4. And We decreed for the Children of Israel in the Scripture:
   'Twice you will cause corruption in the land,

---

[1] Muslim doctrine holds that Muḥammad was physically taken to Jerusalem. The most plausible non-Muslim view is that the verse conveys a dream or vision sequence.

and twice you will rise to a great height.'

5. When the promise of the first of these came to pass,
    We sent against you[P] servants of Ours,
    men of great might,
    who prowled through [your] dwellings,
    and it was a promise fulfilled.

6. Then once again We gave you your turn against them
    and aided you with children and wealth
    and made you greater as a company.

7. 'If you do good, you do good for your own souls;
    and if you do evil, that is also for them.'

7a. Then when the promise of the second came to pass,
    [We sent against you servants of Ours] to discountenance you[P]
    and to enter the sanctuary,
    as they entered it the first time,
    and to destroy utterly that to which they ascended.

8. Perhaps your[P] Lord will have mercy on you;
    but if you return, We shall return.
    And We have made Jahannam a prison for those who are ungrateful.

9. This Recitation guides the way to what is straightest
    and gives good tidings to the believers who do righteous deeds:
    that they will have a great reward,

10. And that for those who do not believe in the world to come
    We have prepared a painful torment.

11. But man prays for evil, as he prays for good.
    Man is ever hasty.

12. We have appointed the night and the day as two signs;
    and We have blotted out the sign of the night
    and made the sign of the day sight-giving
    that you[P] may seek bounty from your Lord
    and that you may know about the number of the years
    and about reckoning;
    and We have set everything out distinctly.

13. We have fastened the augury of every man to his neck,
    and We shall bring forth for him on the Day of Judgement
    a record that he will find wide open.

14. 'Read your record.
    To-day your soul is a sufficient reckoner against you.'

15. Those who are guided aright are so guided for themselves;
    and those who go astray stray only against themselves.
    No laden soul bears the burden of another.
    We do not punish until We have sent a messenger.

16. When We wish to destroy a settlement,
    We command its affluent people to act profligately in it,
    and the Word is realized against it,
    and We destroy it totally.
17. How many generations We have destroyed since Noah.
    And God suffices as one who is informed of and observes the sins of His servants.
18. Whoever desires [this world] that hastens away,
    We hasten for him in it whatever We wish, for whom We will;
    then We appoint for him Jahannam, in which he will roast,
    reviled and rejected.
19. Those who desire the world to come
    and strive for it as they should and are believers,
    those – their striving is gratefully accepted.
20. Each We aid, both these and those,
    from the bounty of your Lord.
    Your^s Lord's bounty is not restricted.
21. See how We prefer some of them over others;
    and the world to come is greater in degrees and greater in preferment.
22. Do^s not set up any other god with God,
    lest you^s [have to] sit down reviled and forsaken.
23. Your^s Lord has decreed that you should serve only Him
    and should show kindness to your parents.
    If one or both of them reach old age with you,
    do not say, 'fie' to them,
    and do not chide them,
    but speak to them with kindness;
24. And lower over them the wing of humility, out of mercy,
    and say, 'My Lord, have mercy on them
    in the same way that they brought me up when I was young.'
25. Your^p Lord is well aware of what is in your hearts.
    If you are righteous,
    He is ever forgiving to those who turn to Him [in repentance].
26. Give^s the kinsman his due
    and [likewise] the destitute and the traveller.
    And do^s not squander.
27. Those who squander are brethren of Satan,
    and Satan is ungrateful to his Lord.
28. If you^s turn away from them,
    seeking the mercy from your Lord that you are hoping for,
    speak to them with gentle words,
29. And do^s not keep your hand chained to your neck
    nor open it fully,

lest you[s] [have to] sit down
rebuked and denuded.

30. Your[s] Lord gives ample provision to those whom He wishes
[or] He measures it carefully.
He is informed and observing of His servants.

31. Do[p] not slay your children through fear of poverty.
We shall make provision for you and for them.
Killing them is a great sin.

32. Do[p] not come near to fornication.
It is an abomination and evil as a way.

33. Do[p] not slay the soul which God has forbidden,
unless [you have] the right [to do so].
Whoever is slain wrongfully,
We give authority to his heir [to take revenge],
but let him not go to excess in killing.
He will be helped.

34. Do[p] not approach the property of the orphan,
except with that which is better,
until he is of age;
and fulfil[p] the covenant.
The covenant will be asked about.

35. Fill[p] the measure when you measure,
and weigh with the straight balance.
That is better and fairer as a course.

36. Do[s] not follow that of which you have no knowledge.
The hearing and the sight and the heart
– of each of these there will be a questioning;

37. And do[s] not walk in the land in exultation.
You[s] will not split open the earth
nor reach the mountains in height.

38. The evil of all that has become hateful to your[s] Lord.

39. This is part of the wisdom with which your[s] Lord has inspired you.
Do[s] not set up [any] other god with God
lest you are cast into Jahannam,
rebuked and rejected.

40. Has your[p] Lord distinguished you with sons
and chosen for Himself females from the angels?
You[p] are saying something truly shocking.

41. We have turned [signs] about in this Recitation
for them to be reminded;
but it increases them only in aversion.

42. Say, 'If there were gods in addition to God,

as they say,
in that case they would have sought a way to the Possessor of the Throne.'

43. May He be glorified and exalted high above what they say.

44. The seven heavens and the earth and all that is in them glorify Him.
There is nothing that does not glorify Him by praising Him;
but you[p] do not understand their glorifying [Him].
He is Prudent and Forgiving.

45. When you[s] recite the Recitation,
We place between you and those who do not believe in the world to come
a concealed barrier,

46. And We place veils upon their hearts
so that they do not understand it
and heaviness in their ears.

46a. When you[s] mention your Lord alone in the Recitation
they turn their backs in aversion.

47. We are well aware how they listen
when they listen to you[s]
and when they conspire,
when the wrong-doers say,
'You[p] are only following a man who is bewitched.'

48. See how they coin comparisons for you[s]
and go astray and cannot find a way.

49. And they say, 'When we are bones and broken bits,
shall we be raised as a new creation?'

50. Say, 'Be stones or iron

51. Or any creation that is big in your thoughts.'
They will say, 'Who will restore us?'
Say, 'The One who created you the first time.'
They will shake their heads at you and say,
'When will it be?'
Say, 'Perhaps it is near:

52. On the day when He summons you[p]
and you respond with praise of Him
and you think that you have tarried but little.'

53. And tell[s] My servants
to speak that which is kinder.
Satan stirs up discord among them.
Satan is a clear foe for man.

54. Your[p] Lord is well aware of you.
If He wishes, He will have mercy on you;
or if He wishes, He will punish you.
We have not sent you[s] as a trustee for them,

55. For your Lord is well aware of all who are in the heavens and the earth.
    We preferred some of the prophets over others,
    and We gave psalms to David.
56. Say, 'Call upon those whom you^p have asserted [to be gods],
    to His exclusion.
    They have no power to remove harm from you
    or to cause any change.'
57. Those to whom they call will seek access to their Lord,
    whichever of them is nearer,
    and will hope for His mercy and fear His punishment.
    The punishment of your^s Lord is something to beware of.
58. There is no settlement but We shall destroy it before the Day of Resurrection
    or punish it severely.
    That is written down in the Record.
59. Nothing hinders Us from sending signs,
    except that the ancients did not think them true.
    We gave Thamūd the she-camel, a visible proof,
    but they did wrong to her.
    We send signs only to frighten.
60. And [recall] when We said to you^s, 'Your Lord encompasses mankind;'
    and We made the vision which We showed you^s only as a trial for mankind,
    and the tree cursed in the Recitation.
    We frighten them,
    but it increases them only in gross insolence.
61. And [recall] when We said to the angels,
    'Prostrate yourselves before Adam;'
    and they [all] prostrated themselves,
    apart from Iblīs.
    He said, 'Shall I prostrate myself
    to someone whom You have created from clay?'
62. He said, 'What do You think?
    This whom You have honoured above me
    – if you give me respite to the Day of Resurrection
    I shall consume his seed except a few.'
63. HE said, 'Go^s, and any of them who follows you.
    Jahannam will be your recompense,
    an ample recompense.
64. And startle^s with your voice any of them you can,
    and assemble against them your horsemen and your foot-soldiers.
    Share with them in their property and children,
    and promise them.'
    But Satan promises them only delusion.

65. My servants
    – you^s have no power over them,
    and their Lord is sufficient trustee for them,

66. Your^p Lord is the one who drives the ships for you on the sea
    for you to seek some of His bounty.
    He is indeed merciful to you.

67. When harm touches you at sea,
    all whom you invoke go astray,
    except for Him.
    Then when He has brought you safely to land,
    you turn away.
    Man is extremely ungrateful.

68. Do you feel secure that He will not cause the shore to swallow you up
    or that He will not send a sandstorm on you,
    and then you will not find a trustee for yourselves?

69. Or do you feel secure that He will not drive you back into it a second time
    and that He will not send against you a hurricane of wind
    and drown you for your ingratitude,
    and then you will not find for yourselves there
    anyone who will follow you against Us?

70. We have honoured the Children of Adam
    and carried them on land and sea
    and have provided them with good things
    and have preferred them markedly
    above many of those whom We have created.

71. On the day when We shall call all men with their record,
    whoever is given his record in his right hand
    – those will read out their record,
    and they will not be wronged one speck.

72. But those who are blind in this world
    will be blind in the world to come
    and further astray from the way.

73. They were almost able to tempt you^s from that with which We inspired you,
    to invent against Us something other than [a revelation].
    In that case they would have adopted you as a friend.

74. Had it not been the case that We had made you^s stand firm,
    you might have inclined to them a little.

75. In that case We would have caused you^s to taste double life and double death;
    then you^s would not find for yourself any helper against Us.

76. They almost scared you^s from the land,
    to drive you from it.
    In that case they would stay after you^s only briefly.

77. [That was] the custom with those of Our messengers whom We sent before you^s.
You will find no change to our custom.
78. Perform^s prayer at the setting of the sun up to the darkening of the night
and [make] the Recitation at dawn.
The Recitation at dawn is witnessed.
79. And some part of the night
– keep vigil with it as a special gift for yourself.
Perhaps your Lord will raise you to a laudable station.
80. And say, 'My Lord, cause me to enter a place that truth has entered,
and cause me to leave a place that truth has left;
and grant me authority from You to help me.'
81. And say, 'The truth has come and falsehood has vanished.
Falsehood will always vanish.'
82. We send down as part of the Recitation
that which is a healing and a mercy for the believers,
but it increases the wrong-doers only in loss.
83. When We bless Man, he turns away and moves far aside;
and when evil touches him, he despairs.
84. Say, 'Each man works according to his own manner.'
Your^s Lord is well aware of those who are best guided to a way.
85. They will ask you^s about the Spirit.
Say, 'The Spirit is part of the affair of my Lord;
and you^p have been given only little knowledge.'
86. If We wished, We could take away from you^s
that with which We inspired you.
Then you would not find for yourself
any trustee against us concerning it,
87. Except as a mercy from your Lord.
His bounty to you^s is great.
88. Say, 'If Man and Jinn were to assemble to produce the like of this Recitation,
they could not produce its like,
even though they supported one another.'
89. We have turned about for mankind in this Recitation every kind of comparison,
but most of mankind refuse anything but ingratitude;
90. And they say, 'We shall not give you^s any credence
until you cause a spring to gush forth from the earth for us,
91. Or you have a garden of palms and vines
and cause rivers to gush amongst them,
92. Or you cause the sky to fall down on us,
as you have asserted [will happen],
or bring God and the angels in front,
93. Or you have a house of ornamental work

or you ascend into the sky;
and we shall give no credence to your ascent
until you bring down for us a Scripture that we may recite.'
Say, 'Glory be to my Lord.
Am I anything but a mortal messenger?'

94. Nothing prevented mankind from believing when guidance came to them,
except that they said, 'Has God sent a mortal as His Messenger?'

95. Say, 'If there were angels on the earth walking in tranquillity,
We would have sent down to them an angel from heaven as a messenger.'

96. Say, 'God is a sufficient witness between you^p and me.
He is informed and observing of His servants.'

97. Those who are guided by God are guided aright;
and those whom He leads astray
– you^s will not find for them any protectors apart from Him.
We shall round them up on the Day of Resurrection, face down,
blind, dumb and deaf.
Their abode will be Jahannam.
Whenever it dies down,
We shall increase for them a blaze.

98. That is their recompense because they did not believe in Our signs
and said, 'When we are bones and broken bits,
shall we be raised as a new creation?'

99. Have they not seen that God,
who created the heavens and the earth,
is able to create the like of them?
He has appointed for them a term,
about which there is no doubt,
but the wrong-doers refuse anything but ingratitude.

100. Say, 'If you^p possessed the treasuries of my Lord's mercy,
[even] in that case you would hold back for fear of spending.
Man is stingy.'

101. We gave Moses nine clear signs
– Ask the Children of Israel –
when he came to them, and Pharaoh said to him,
'O Moses, I think that you are bewitched.'

102. He said, 'You^s know that none sent down these [signs] as clear proofs
except the Lord of the heavens.
O Pharaoh, I think that you are lost.'

103. He wished to scare them from the land,
but We drowned him,
and those who were with him,
altogether.

104. And after him We said to the Children of Israel,
     'Dwell in the land.
     When the promise of the next world comes to pass
     We shall bring you as a rabble.'
105. With the truth We have sent it down,
     and with the truth it has come down.
     We have sent you^s only as a warner and a bearer of good tidings.
106. And [We have sent] a Recitation,
     which We have divided
     so that you^s may recite it to mankind at intervals,
     and We have sent it down.
107. Say, 'Believe in it or do not believe.
     Those to whom knowledge has been given previously
     fall down on their chins in prostration
     when it is recited to them.
108. They say, "Glory be to God.
     The promise of our Lord is fulfilled."
109. They fall on their chins weeping,
     and it increases them in humility.'
110. Say, 'Call^P to God or call to the Merciful.
     Whichever you call to is possessed of the fairest names.
     Do not be loud in your prayer, nor hushed in it.
     Seek a way between that.'
111. And say, 'Praise belongs to God,
     who has not taken to himself a son
     and who has no partner in sovereignty
     nor any protector because He is humble.'
     Magnify^s him.

Sūra 18

This *sūra* is generally considered to be from the middle Meccan period. However, a number of Muslim authorities say that verse 28 is Medinan, and some make the same claim about 1–7/8, 83–101, and 107–110. Most of these claims are doubtful, but they are possibly a reflection of some recasting at Medina. The narratives contained in the *sūra* are striking, as some of them appear to reflect popular Near Eastern tales from a tradition quite different from that we find elsewhere in the Qur'ān. This can be seen in the story of the Seven Sleepers (verses 9–26), the beginning of the passage about Moses (60–64) and the story of Dhū l-Qarnayn (Alexander the Great) (83–99). In fact, all the stories in the Moses narrative (60–82) are different from other stories about him in the Qur'ān. The narratives have been the subject of much analysis, especially on their folkloristic aspect, but our understanding of their background is still limited.

A polemical introduction (1–8) leads to the story of the Seven Sleepers (9–26); a passage of instruction to Muḥammad (27–31) leads to a longish parable about two men and their gardens (32–44); a further comparison in 45 leads to a piece of sustained polemic (to 59). The narratives on Moses and Dhū l-Qarnayn then follow (60–99), leading into a polemical peroration (100–110).

The Cave

In the name of the Merciful and Compassionate God

1. Praise belongs to God,
    who has sent down the Scripture to his servant
    and has not set in it any crookedness
2. – Straight,
    to give warning of a stern might from Him,
    and to bring good tidings
    to the believers who do righteous deeds
    that they will have a fair reward,
3. In which they will stay for ever;
4. And to warn those who say, 'God has taken to Himself a son.'
5. They have no knowledge of it,
    nor did their forefathers.
    It is a monstrous word that comes from their mouths.
    They speak nothing but a lie.
6. If they do not believe in this discourse,
    perhaps you^s will exhaust yourself with grief,

271

following them up.

7. We have made all that is on the earth an ornament for it,
to test which of them is best in deed.

8. And We shall make what is on it barren dust.
Or do you[s] think that the Men of the Cave and of the Inscription
were a wonder among our signs?

10. When the youths betook themselves to the Cave and said,
'Our Lord, give us mercy from Your presence,
and prepare for us a way in our affair.'

11. Then We sealed up their ears in the cave
for a number of years.

12. Then We woke them that We might know
which of the two parties would calculate better
the period they had tarried.

13. We shall tell you[s] their tidings in truth.
They were youths who believed in their Lord,
and We gave them greater guidance.

14. We braced their hearts when they stood up and said,
'Our Lord is the Lord of the heavens and the earth.
We do not call to any god apart from Him.
If we were to do that, we would be speaking an outrage.

15. These people, our people, have taken to themselves gods apart from Him.
Why do they not have a clear authority for them?
And who does greater wrong than those who invent a lie against God?'

16. When you[p] have withdrawn from them and what they worship
to the exclusion of God,
take refuge in the Cave.
Your Lord will unfold for you some of His mercy
and He will prepare for you a cushion in your affair.

17. You[s] could see the sun,
when it rose,
inclining from their cave to the right;
and when it set,
going past them on the left,
while they were in a cleft in it.
That was one of God's signs.
Those whom God guides are rightly guided;
and those whom He sends astray
– you[s] will not find for them a protector who will guide them.

18. You[s] would have thought them awake though they were asleep,
and We would turn them over to the right and to the left,

with their dog stretching its paws on the threshold.
If you had looked at them closely,
you would have turned away from them in flight
and would have been filled with awe of them.

19. Thus We raised them that they might ask questions among themselves.
One of them said, 'How long have you tarried?'
They said, 'We have tarried a day or part of a day.'
They said, 'Your Lord is well aware of how long you have tarried.
Send one of you with this silver coin of yours to the city,
and let him see which of them has purest food,
and let him bring some of it to you as sustenance.
Let him be courteous and let him not make anyone aware of you.

20. If they were to become aware of you,
they would stone you
or turn you back to their creed.
Then you will never prosper.'

21. Likewise We caused [people] to stumble on them
that they might know that the promise of God is true
and that there is no doubt about the Hour.
When they were arguing among themselves over their affair,
they said, 'Build a building over them.
Their Lord is well aware about them.'
Those who prevailed over their affair said,
'Let us build a place of prayer over them.'

22. They will say, 'Three, and their dog was the fourth of them.'
They will say, 'Five, and their dog the sixth of them',
guessing at the Invisible.
They will say, 'Seven, and their dog the eighth of them.'
Say, 'My Lord is well aware of their number.
Only a few know them.'
So dispute concerning them only on a clear issue;
and do not ask any of them for an opinion about them.

23. And do not say about anything,
'I am going to do that tomorrow',

24. Save [with the proviso] that God so wills.
And mention[s] God when you forget
and say, 'Perhaps my Lord will guide me
to something nearer a correct way than this.'

25. And they tarried in the Cave three hundred years and nine more.

26. Say[s], 'God is well aware how long they tarried.
To Him belongs the Invisible in the heavens and the earth.
How well He sees and hears.

They have no protector apart from Him,
and He has no associates in His rule.'

27. Recite^s what has been revealed to you of the Scripture of your Lord.
No one can change His words.
You^s will find no refuge apart from Him.

28. Content yourself with those who call to their Lord morning and evening,
desiring His countenance,
and let not your eyes turn from them,
desiring the ornament of the life of this world;
and do not obey those whose hearts We have made heedless of Our remembrance
and who follow their desires and whose affairs are excess.

29. Say^s, 'The truth is from your^p Lord.
Let whoever wishes believe
and whoever wishes be ungrateful.
We have prepared for the wrong-doers a fire,
whose pavilion encloses them.
If they ask for showers of rain,
they will receive showers of water like molten copper
which will roast their faces.
How evil a drink; how evil a resting-place.

30. Those who believe and do righteous deeds
– We shall not neglect the reward of those who do good.

31. Those will have the gardens of Eden,
through which rivers flow.
There they will be adorned with bracelets of gold,
and will wear green garments made of silk and brocade,
reclining there on couches.
How good a reward; how fine a resting-place.

32. Coin^s for them a parable:
two men,
to one of whom We assigned two vineyards
and surrounded them with palm-trees
and set cultivated land between them;

33. Both the gardens produced their fruit and did not go wrong in any way;
and We caused a river to gush between them;

34. And [the owner] had fruit.
He said to his comrade, when he spoke to him,
'I have more wealth than you
and I am stronger in my family.'

35. He entered his garden, wronging himself.
He said, 'I do not think that this will ever perish.

36. I do not think that the Hour is coming;

and if I am returned to my Lord,
I shall find a better resort than this.'

37. When he spoke to him, his comrade said,
'Are you^s ungrateful to Him who created you from dust
and then from seed and then formed you as a man?

38. But He is God, my Lord,
and I associate no one with my Lord.

39. When you^s went into your garden,
why did you not say, "As God wills"?
There is no power except through God.
If you think that I am inferior to you in wealth and children,

40. Perhaps my Lord will give me [something] better than your garden
and [perhaps] He will send on it a thunderbolt from heaven,
and it will become smooth soil.

41. Or in the morning its water will be lost in the ground,
and you will not be able to seek it out.'

42. His fruit was encompassed,[1]
and in the morning he was wringing his hands
over what he had spent on it,
for it had collapsed on its trellises,
and he was saying, 'Would that I had not associated anyone with my Lord.'

43. He had no group to help him apart from God,
and he was helpless.

44. Protection there belongs only to God, the True.
He is better for reward and better for consequence.

45. Coin for them the comparison of the life of this world:
[it is] like water that We send down from the sky,
and the vegetation of the earth mingles with it,
then [one] morning it becomes chaff that the winds scatter.
God is omnipotent over everything.

46. Wealth and children are the ornament of the life of this world;
but the abiding things, the works of righteousness,
are better with your^s Lord for reward and better for hope.

47. On the day We cause the mountains to move
and you^s see the earth coming forward
and We round them up and leave none of them behind,

48. And they are paraded before your^p Lord in ranks:
'You^p have come to us as We first created you.
Yet you^p asserted that We would not make a tryst for you.'

49. The Record will be put in position,

---

[1] *i.e.* destroyed.

and you^s will see the sinners fearful of what is in it,
and saying, 'Alas for us.
What is there about this Record?
It leaves behind nothing small or great,
but it has counted it.'
They will find all that they have done present,
and your^s Lord will wrong no one.

50. And [recall] when We said to the angels,
'Prostrate yourself to Adam.'
So they prostrated themselves, save Iblīs.
He was one of the *Jinn*,
and he committed ungodliness against the command of his Lord.
Will you^p take him and his seed to be your protectors,
to My exclusion,
when they are an enemy to you?
That is an evil exchange for the wrong-doers.

51. I did not make them witness the creation of the heavens and the earth
nor the creation of themselves.
Nor did I take those who lead astray as a support.

52. And on the day He says,
'Call^p on My associates whom you have alleged [I have].'
And they call on them,
but they do not answer them,
for We have set a gulf between them.

53. The sinners will see the Fire
and think that they are about to fall into it
– and they will not find any way of turning from it.

54. We have turned about for man in this Recitation some of every [kind of] comparison.
Man is the most contumacious of things.

55. Nothing prevented men from believing
when guidance came to them,
or from seeking their Lord's forgiveness
except for [their idea] that the custom of the ancients will come to them
or that the torment will come to them face to face.

56. We send the messengers only as givers of good tidings and as warners;
but those who disbelieve dispute, using falsehood,
that they may rebut the truth with it.
They have taken in mockery My signs and what they have been warned of.

57. Who does greater wrong
than those who have been reminded of the signs of their Lord,
but who turn away from them
and forget what their hands have sent forward?

We have placed coverings on their hearts
so that they do not understand it,
and in their ears deafness.
And if you^s call them to the guidance,
they will never be guided aright.

58. But your^s Lord is the All-Forgiving, the One full of mercy.
If He were to take them to task for what they have earned,
He would hasten the torment for them.
But they will have a tryst
on this side of which they will find no escape.

59. Those settlements!
We destroyed them when they did wrong,
and We appointed a fixed time for their destruction.

60. Recall when Moses said to his servant,
'I shall continue until I reach the confluence of the two seas,
or else I shall go on for ages.'

61. When the two of them reached their confluence,
they forgot their fish
and it made its way into the sea, moving freely.

62. When they had passed on, he said to his servant,
'Bring us our breakfast.
We have found fatigue in this journey of ours.'

63. He² said, 'Did you^s see
that when we took refuge on the rock
I forgot the fish
– and only Satan caused me to forget to mention it –
and it made its way into the sea – a wonder?'

64. He³ said, 'This is what we are seeking.'
So they went back on their tracks,
retracing them.

65. Then they found one of Our servants,⁴
to whom We had given a mercy from Us
and taught him knowledge from Us.

66. Moses said to him, 'May I follow you
on condition that you teach me,
from that which you have been taught,
a right way?'

67. He³ said, 'You will not be able to bear with me.

---

² The servant.
³ Moses.
⁴ The traditional sources give his name as Khiḍr.

68. How can you bear patiently
    that which you have not encompassed in [your] experience?'
69. He^2 said, 'If God wills, you will find me steadfast.
    I shall not go against you in anything.'
70. He^3 said, 'If you follow me,
    do not ask me about anything
    until I make the first mention of it to you.'
71. The two of them went off;
    then, when they were sailing in the ship,
    he^3 holed it.
    He^2 said, 'Have you holed it
    to drown the people in it?
    You have done a dreadful thing.'
72. He^3 said, 'Didn't I tell you that you could not bear with me?'
73. He^2 said, 'Do not take me to task because I forgot.
    Do not impose difficulty on me because of my affair.'
74. Then two of them went off;
    then, when they met a youth and he^3 slew him,
    he^2 said, 'Have you killed an innocent soul,
    not [responsible for the slaying of another] soul?
    You have done an abominable thing.'
75. He^3 said, 'Didn't I tell you that you could not bear with me?'
76. He^2 said, 'If I ask you about anything after this,
    do not allow me to remain in your company.
    You have received excuse from me for not doing so.'
77. The two of them went off;
    then, when they came to the people of a settlement,
    they asked its people for food.
    They refused to give them hospitality,
    but [when] the two of them found a wall there on the point of falling down,
    he^3 set it straight.'
    He^2 said, 'Had you wished,
    you could have taken payment for it.'
78. He^3 said, 'This is the parting between you and me.
    I shall tell you the interpretation of that
    which you could not bear patiently.
79. As for the ship,
    it belonged to some poor people working at sea.
    I wished to make it unsound,
    for there was a king beyond them
    who was seizing every ship by force.
80. As for the youth,

his parents were believers,
and we feared that he might impose on them insolence and unbelief.

81. We wanted their Lord to give them in exchange
[one] better than him in purity and nearer in tenderness.

82. As for the wall,
it belonged to two orphan boys in the town;
and there was beneath it a treasure belonging to them;
their father had been a righteous man,
and your Lord wished them to reach maturity
and [then] bring forth their treasure as a mercy from your Lord.
I did not do it of my own bidding.
That is the interpretation of what you could not tolerate.'

83. They will ask you^s about Dhū l-Qarnayn.
Say, 'I shall recite to you^p a mention of him.

84. We gave him position in the land
and gave him a way through everything.

85. He followed a way;

86. Then, when he reached the place where the sun sets,
he found it setting in a muddy spring,
and he found a people round it.
We said, 'O Dhū l-Qarnayn,
either punish them
or take a way of kindness concerning them.'

87. He said, 'As for those who do wrong,
we shall punish them.
Then they will be returned to their Lord.
He will punish them with an abominable punishment.

88. As for those who believe and act righteously,
they will have the fairest reward as a recompense,
and We shall give them ease in Our bidding.'

89. Then he followed a way;

90. Then, when he reached the place where the sun rises,
he found it rising on a people
for whom We had made no shelter from it.

91. So [it was];
and We encompassed in [Our] experience
what was [there] with him.

92. Then he followed a road;

93. Then, when he reached the place between the two barriers,
he found on this side of them
a people who could scarcely understand any speech.

94. They said, 'O Dhū l-Qarnayn,

Yājūj and Mājūj are wreaking mischief in the land.
May we pay you tribute
on condition that you put a barrier between us and them?'

95.　He said, 'The power my Lord has given me is better;
but help me with [all the] strength [you can],
and I shall set up a rampart between you and them.

96.　Bring me pieces of iron.'
Then, when he had levelled up the gap between the two cliffs,
he said, 'Blow'.
Then, when he had made it a fire, he said,
'Bring me copper
and I shall pour it over [when it is] molten.'

97.　They were unable to scale it or to pierce it.

98.　He said, 'This is a mercy from my Lord.
But when the promise of my Lord comes to pass,
He will make it a flattened surface.
The promise of my Lord is true.'

99.　On that day We shall leave them surging into one another,
and there will be a blast on the trumpet.
Then We shall gather them together.

100.　On that day We shall present Jahannam to the unbelievers,

101.　Whose eyes were covered against My reminder
and who were unable to hear.

102.　Do those who disbelieve reckon
that they can take My servants as protectors apart from me?
We have prepared Jahannam as hospitality for the unbelievers.

103.　Say, 'Shall we inform you who will be the greatest losers in their works?

104.　[They are] those whose efforts go astray in the life of this world,
when they think they are doing good deeds.

105.　Those are the ones who do not believe in the signs of their Lord
or in [their] encounter with Him.
Their works are in vain,
and We shall not assign any weight to them on the Day of Resurrection.

106.　That is their reward:
Jahannam in return for their having disbelieved
and having taken My signs and My messengers in mockery.

107.　[But] those who believe and do righteous deeds,
the gardens of paradise are theirs for hospitality,

108.　In which they will stay for ever,
not desiring removal from there.'

109.　Say, 'If the sea were ink for the words of my Lord,
the sea would be exhausted

before the Words of my Lord are exhausted,
even if We were to bring its like as a [further] supply.'
110. Say, 'I am only a mortal like you[p].
It is revealed to me that your God is One God.
Let those who hope to meet their Lord
do righteous work and not associate anyone with the service of his Lord.'

Sūra 19

Sūrat Maryam is important in the development of the Qur'ān, as it appears to be the earliest *sūra* to relate Christian stories at length (2–15: Zachariah and the birth of John the Baptist; 16–33: Mary and the birth of Jesus). Muslim sources treat the whole *sūra* as early and offer as evidence traditions that they believe to be anchored in the first few years of Muḥammad's mission; but even if the traditions are authentic – and that is doubtful – and do indicate an early date, they do not necessarily show that the whole *sūra* is early Meccan. Nevertheless, there can be little doubt that the *sūra* is essentially Meccan, but latish rather than early. The first part of the *sūra* echoes the first chapter of St. Luke's Gospel, but certain parallels with the apocryphal Gospels, in particular with *The Infancy Gospel of James*, Chapter 11, are also to be discerned.

The *sūra* comprises four sections that are complementary to each other: 2–33, mainly narrative with the assonance in *-iyyā*; 33–40, a piece of argument, with assonance in *-īn/ ūn/ īm*, that provides a change of mood; 41–74, short narratives about prophets, ending with polemic, again with the assonance of *-iyyā*; and finally a peroration, 75–98, with assonance in *-dā/zā*. The assonance in *-iyyā*, which occurs only in this *sūra*, is striking. It is also technically difficult, and a number of the rhyme words occur once or twice in this *sūra* and nowhere else, sometimes raising problems about their meaning. Overall, however, the *sūra* comes across as a coherent and cogent whole, even though one can be certain that it was originally not one entity.

Mary

In the name of the Merciful and Compassionate God

1. *Kāf, Hā', Yā', 'Ayn, Ṣād.*[1]
2. Mention of the mercy of your[s] Lord to His servant Zachariah,
3. When he called out to his Lord in secret.
4. He said, 'My Lord,
    my bones have become very weak,
    and my head is aflame with hoariness.
    I have never been unfortunate in my supplications to You.
5. [I am making supplication now, for] I fear [that I shall have no] heirs after me,
    because my wife is barren.
    So give me, from Yourself, a successor
6. Who will inherit from me and from the family of Jacob,

---

[1] On the mystical letters see the note on 2:1. The combination found here is unique.

and make him, my Lord, well-pleasing.'

7. 'O Zachariah, We give you very good tidings of a son
whose name will be John,
a name We have never given to anyone before.'

8. He said, 'My Lord, how can I have a son
when my wife is barren,
and I have become infirm through old age?'

9. He said, '[It will be] so. Your Lord says,
"It is easy for me,
for I created you before
when you were nothing".'

10. He said, 'My Lord, make a sign for me.'
He said, 'Your sign will be that
you cannot speak to people for three days, though there is nothing wrong with you.'

11. So he left the sanctuary and went to see his people,
and he made a sign to them,
'Glorify your Lord morning and evening.'

12. 'O John, take the Scripture with power';
and We gave him discretion whilst he was still a child

13. And kindness from Us and purity;
and he was pious

14. And dutiful to his parents,
and he was not overweening or rebellious.

15. Peace on him the day he was born,
the day he dies,
and the day he is raised up alive.

16. Mention Mary in the Scripture,
when she withdrew from her folk to a place in the east.

17. And she put between them and herself a barrier.
And We sent to her Our Spirit
[who] appeared to her as a perfect man.

18. She said, 'I seek refuge from you with the Merciful,
if you are God-fearing.'

19. He said, 'I am only the messenger of your Lord,
that I may give you a pure son.'

20. She said, 'How can I have a son,
when no man has touched me
and I have not been unchaste?'

21. He said, '[It will be] so.
Your Lord says, "It is easy for me.
[We have done this] so that We may make him a sign for men
and a mercy from Us.

It is a thing decreed".'

22. So she conceived him,
and she withdrew with him to a distant place.

23. The birth-pangs drove her to the trunk of a palm-tree.
She said, 'Would that I had died before this
and become someone totally forgotten.'

24. Then he cried out to her from beneath her,
'Do not grieve.
Your Lord has placed a stream beneath you.

25. Shake the trunk of the palm-tree towards you,
and you will cause fresh, ripe dates to fall down to you.

26. Eat, drink and be consoled.
And if you meet any mortal,
say, "I have vowed a fast to the Merciful,
and I shall not speak to any person to-day".'

27. Then she brought him to her own folk, carrying him.
They said, 'O Mary, you have done an unbelievable thing.

28. O sister of Aaron,[2]
your father was not a wicked man,
nor was your mother unchaste.'

29. She pointed to him.
They said, 'How can we speak to one who is a child in the cradle?'

30. He said, 'I am the servant of God.
He has given me the Scripture, and He has made me a prophet.

31. And He has made me blessed wherever I am,
and He has charged me to pray and give alms
as long as I remain alive,

32. And [He has made me] dutiful to my mother,
and He has not made me overweening and wretched.

33. Peace be on me the day I was born,
the day I die,
and the day I shall be raised alive.'

34. That is Jesus, the son of Mary:
a statement of truth about which you[p] have doubts.

35. God is not one to take to Himself any son.
Glory be to Him. When He decides on something,
He says to it only, 'Be', and it is.

36. God is truly my Lord and your Lord.
So serve him.

---

[2] On the link between Mary and the family of 'Imrān see 3:33 and 44 *ff*. See also the notes in the Commentary.

That is a straight path.
37. But the parties have disagreed among themselves.
[There will be] woe to those who do not believe through the witnessing of an
    awesome day.
38. How well will they hear, how well will they see
on the day they come to Us.
But the wrong-doers to-day are in manifest error.
39. Warn[s] them of the day of anguish
when the matter will have been decided
while they are still in a state of heedlessness
and are unbelieving.
40. We shall inherit the earth and all who are on it,
and to Us they will be returned.
41. Mention Abraham in the Scripture.
He was a true friend of God, a prophet,
42. When he said to his father, 'O my father,
why do you worship something
that cannot see nor hear
nor be of avail to you in anything?
43. O my father, some knowledge has come to me that has not come to you.
Follow me and I shall guide you along a level path.
44. O my father, do not serve Satan.
Satan is a rebel against the Merciful.
45. O my father, I fear that some punishment from the Merciful will touch you,
and that you will become an ally of Satan.'
46. He said, 'O Abraham, are you turning away from my gods?
If you do not desist, I shall surely stone you.
Leave me for a while.'
47. He said, 'Peace be on you.
I shall ask my Lord to forgive you.
He has always shown kindness to me.
48. I shall withdraw from you[P] and from what you[P] call on to the exclusion of God.
I shall pray to my Lord.
Perhaps I shall not be unfortunate in my prayer.'
49. When he withdrew from them and from that which they were worshipping
to the exclusion of God,
We gave him Isaac and Jacob,
and each We made a prophet.
50. And we bestowed on them some of our mercy
and gave them a tongue of truth, high [in renown].
51. Mention Moses in the Scripture.
He was devoted [to God] and a messenger and a prophet.

52. We called to him from the right side of the mountain
    and brought him near in communion.
53. And We gave him, from Our Mercy, his brother Aaron as a prophet.
54. Mention Ishmael in the Scripture.
    He was true to his promise and was a messenger and prophet.
55. He used to tell his people to pray and give alms,
    and he was pleasing to his Lord.
56. Mention Idrīs[3] in the Scripture.
    He was a true friend of God, a prophet.
57. We raised him to a high position.
58. These are those whom God blessed
    among the prophets of the seed of Adam
    and of those whom we carried with Noah
    and of the seed of Abraham and Israel
    and of those whom We guided and chose.
    When the signs of the Merciful are recited to them,
    they fall down, prostrating themselves and weeping.
59. However, they have been followed by a posterity
    who have neglected prayer and have followed their own desires;
    and those will meet error.
60. This will not be the case with those who repent and believe and act righteously.
    These will enter paradise and will not be wronged in anything
61. – Gardens of Eden,
    which the Merciful has promised to His slaves in the Invisible.
    His promise is [always] fulfilled.
62. They will hear no idle chatter there, but [only] Peace';
    and they will have there their sustenance morning and evening.
63. That is the Garden which We shall give as inheritance
    to those of Our servants who are god-fearing.
64. We[4] come down only by command of your[s] Lord.
    To Him belongs all that is before us,
    all that is behind us,
    and all between the two.
    Your Lord is not forgetful
65. – Lord of the heavens and the earth and what is between them.
    So serve[s] Him and be steadfast in your worship of Him.
    Do you know any that may be named with Him?
66. Man says,
    'When I am dead, shall I be brought forth alive?'

---

[3] The identification of Idrīs is uncertain. See the Commentary.

[4] *i.e.* the angels.

67. Does Man not remember
    that We created him before,
    when he was nothing?
68. By your[s] Lord, We shall round them up and the devils [too],
    and then We shall bring them, crouching, round Hell.
69. Then We shall pluck out from every party
    whichever of them has been most stubborn against the Merciful.
70. Then We are fully aware of those of them who most deserve to roast there.
71. There is none of you who will not go down to it.
    That is a fixed decree for your Lord.
72. Then We shall rescue those who are god-fearing;
    and We shall leave the wrong-doers crouching there.
73. When Our signs are recited to them as clear evidence,
    those who disbelieve say to those who believe,
    'Which of the two parties is better in position
    and better as an assembly?'
74. But how many a generation have We destroyed before them,
    which was better off in property and appearance?
75. Say, 'Whoever is in error,
    let the Merciful extend his term for him;
    then when they see what they are promised,
    either punishment or the Hour,
    then they will know who is in worse position
    and weaker as a host.'
76. God gives further guidance to those who are guided aright;
    and the things that endure, the deeds of righteousness,
    are better with your[s] Lord for reward
    and better for return.
77. Have you[s] thought about
    the one who disbelieves in Our signs and says,
    'I shall certainly be given possessions and children'?
78. Has he cognizance of the Invisible,
    or has he acquired a covenant with the Merciful?
79. No indeed! We shall record what he says
    and We shall give him an extension of punishment.
80. We shall inherit from him what he says,
    and he will come to Us alone.
81. They have taken to themselves gods to the exclusion of God
    that they might be a power for them.
82. No indeed! They will deny their worship of them
    and become opponents of them.
83. Have you[s] not thought

how We have sent the devils against the unbelievers
to drive them to delusion?

84. So do^s not make haste against them.
We shall do a count for them.

85. On the day that we gather together the god-fearing
to the Merciful in an assembly,

86. And We drive the sinners to Hell as a herd,

87. They will have no power of intercession,
except those who have acquired a covenant with the Merciful.

88. They say, 'The Merciful has taken to himself a son[5].'

89. You^p have done a monstrous thing,

90. At which the heavens are almost torn apart
and the earth split asunder
and the mountains fall in ruins,

91. Because they have ascribed a son to the Merciful.

92. It is not fitting for the Merciful
to take to himself a son.

93. There is none in the heavens and the earth
who will not come to the Merciful as a slave.

94. He has counted them and numbered them [exactly];

95. And each of them will come to Him on the Day of Resurrection,
alone.

96. Those who believe and do good deeds,
the Merciful will assign them love.

97. We have made [this Recitation] easy through your^s tongue,
so that you may give good tidings thereby to the god-fearing
and that you may warn stubborn people.

98. How many a generation We have destroyed before them.
Can you^s perceive a single one of them?
Do you hear from them the slightest whisper?

---

[5] It is sometimes argued that the Arabic *walad* means 'offspring' in verses 88 and 92, but verse 35, where *walad* clearly means 'son', is against that.

Sūra 20

The *sūra* is generally considered to have originated in the middle Meccan period. Some authorities think that verses 130–31 are Medinan, and it may well be that the *sūra* was revised there. After a brief introduction (1–8), the core of the *sūra* comprises a series of stories about Moses (9–99/101). This is followed by a piece of polemic (100/102–114) and then by the story of Adam and Eve (115–124). Finally there is a peroration, addressed in part to Muḥammad (125–135). The first part of the *sūra* is similar in style and thrust, but not in content, to *Sūra* 12.

Ṭā' Hā'

In the name of the Merciful and Compassionate God

1. *Ṭā', Hā'*.[1]
2. We have not sent the Recitation down to you[s]
   for you to be wretched,
3. But as a reminder to those who fear,
4. A revelation from Him who created the earth and the high heavens
5. – The Merciful [who] settled himself on the throne.
6. To Him belongs all that is in the heavens and on earth
   and all that is between them and that is under the soil.
7. If you[s] speak aloud,
   He still knows the secret and [what is] more hidden.
8. God – there is no god but Him.
   His are the fairest names.
9. Have you[s] heard of the story of Moses?
10. When he saw a fire and said to his family,
    'Wait. I have spotted a fire.
    Perhaps I can bring you[p] a brand from it
    or find guidance at the fire.'
11. When he reached it, a voice called out, 'Moses,
12. I am your Lord.
    Take off your shoes.
    You are in the holy valley, Ṭuwā.
13. I have chosen you;
    so listen to what is revealed.

---

[1] On the mystical letters see the note on 2:1.

289

14. I am God.
    There is no god except Me.
    So serve Me and perform prayer for My remembrance.
15. The Hour is surely coming.
    I keep it almost hidden,
    that every soul may be rewarded for its strivings.
16. So let him who does not believe in it
    but who follows his own desires
    not turn you^s aside from it, lest you perish.
17. What is that in your right hand, Moses?'
18. He said, 'It is my staff,
    on which I lean
    and with which I beat down leaves for my sheep,
    and for which I have other uses.'
19. HE said, 'Cast it down, Moses.'
20. So he cast it down,
    and, lo, it [turned into] a serpent moving over the ground.
21. HE said, 'Grasp it and fear not.
    We shall restore it to its former state.
22. And put your hand into your arm-pit,
    and it will come forth white, without harm
    – another sign,
23. That We may show you^s some of our greatest signs.
24. Go to Pharaoh.
    He has been insolent.'
25. He said, 'My Lord, open my breast for me,
26. And ease my task for me.
27. Loose a knot from my tongue,
28. And they will understand what I say.
29. Appoint for me a minister from my family,
30. Aaron, my brother.
31. Confirm my strength with him
32. And associate him with me in my task,
33. That we may glorify You much
34. and remember You much.
35. You surely observe us.'
36. HE said, 'You are granted your request, Moses.
37. We showed you favour on another occasion,
38. When We revealed what was revealed to your mother,
39. Saying, "Cast him into the casket and cast it² into the sea,

---

² Or 'him'.

and the sea will throw it up on the shore.
An enemy of Mine and of his will take him."
And I bestowed on you love from Me,
and [it was] so that you might be formed under My eye,

40. When your sister went and said,
"Shall I show you someone who will take charge of him?"
and We restored you to your mother
that she might be comforted and not be sad;

40a. And you killed a living soul,
and We delivered you from stress
and We tested you in various ways.

40b. And you remained for some years among the people of Madyan.
Then you came [here] according to a decree, Moses,

41. And I have chosen you for Myself.

42. So go, you and your brother, with My signs,
and do not be weak in your remembrance of Me.

43. Both of you go to Pharaoh.
He has been insolent.

44. Speak to him gently so that he might be reminded or be afraid.'

45. The two of them said, 'Our Lord, we fear that
he may act excessively against us or be insolent.'

46. HE said, 'Fear not.
I am with you, hearing and seeing.

47. Both of you go to him and say, "We are two messengers from your Lord.
Let the Children of Israel go with us,
and do not torment them.
We have brought you a sign from your Lord.
Peace be on those who follow guidance.

48. It has been revealed to us that there will be torment
for those who deny the truth and turn their backs".'

49. He³ said, 'Who is the Lord of the two of you, Moses?'

50. He said, 'Our Lord is the One who gave everything its creation
and then gave guidance.'

51. He² said, 'What about previous generations?'

52. He said, 'Knowledge of them is with my Lord,
in a Scripture.
My Lord does not err or forget.

53. He has made the earth a cradle for youᴾ
and has threaded roads for you in it
and has sent down water from the sky';

---

³ Pharaoh.

and We brought forth with it various kinds of plants.

54. 'Eat^p, and pasture your livestock.
In that there are signs for men of reason.

55. From [the earth] We created you^p
and We shall return you into it
and from it We shall bring you forth a second time.'

56. We showed him all Our signs, but he denied them and refused.

57. He said, 'Moses, have you come to drive us from our land by your sorcery?

58. We shall surely bring you sorcery like it.
So fix a tryst between you^s and us,
that neither you nor we shall fail to keep,
a convenient place.'

59. He^4 said, 'Your tryst will be the gala day,
and the people will be assembled in the forenoon.'

60. So Pharaoh turned away and arranged his plan and then came.

61. Moses said to them, 'Woe to you^p.
Do not forge lies against God
lest He destroy you with a torment.
Those who forge lies are lost.'

62. They disputed their affair between themselves
and held secret conference.

63. They said, 'These two men are sorcerers
who wish to drive you^p from your land by sorcery
and to destroy your exemplary way.

64. So arrange your plan; then come in a row.
Those who gain the upper hand will prosper to-day.'

65. They said, 'Moses, either you can throw
or we shall be the first to throw.'

66. He said, 'No. You throw.'
Through their sorcery their ropes and staffs seemed to him to be slithering.

67. And Moses conceived a fear in his mind.

68. We said, 'Do not fear. You^s are uppermost.

69. Throw what is in your right hand,
and it will swallow what they have made;
for what they have made is the trickery of a sorcerer,
and the sorcerer never prospers wherever he comes.'

70. The sorcerers were all flung down prostrate.
They said, 'We believe in the Lord of Aaron and Moses.'

71. He said, 'Have you put your credence in Him before I give you permission?
He is your chief, the one who taught you sorcery.

---

^4 Moses.

I shall cut off your hands and feet alternately,
and I shall crucify you on the trunks of palm-trees;
and you will know which of us is more severe and more enduring in punishment.'

72. They said, 'We shall not prefer you^s above the clear signs that have come to us
nor above Him who has created us.
Decide what you^s will decide.
You can only decide our life in this world.

73. We believe in our Lord,
that He may forgive us our sins and the sorcery you forced us to perform.
God is better and more enduring.'

74. Those who come to their Lord as sinners,
for them Hell [waits],
where they will neither live nor die.

75. But those who come to Him as believers,
having done righteous deeds,
those will have the highest ranks:

76. Gardens of Eden,
through which flow rivers,
where they will dwell for ever.
That is the reward of those who make themselves pure.

77. We inspired Moses, saying,
'Lead away My servants by night
and strike for them a dry path in the sea,
not fearing that you^s will be overtaken
nor being afraid.'

78. Pharaoh followed them with his armies,
but part of the sea overwhelmed them.

79. And Pharaoh led his people astray and did not guide them.

80. Children of Israel, We delivered you from your enemy
and We made a covenant with you on the right side of the mountain
and caused manna and quails to come down to you.

81. Eat of the good things of what We have provided for your sustenance,
but do not go to excess in that,
lest My anger descend on you.
Those on whom My anger descends will be hurled down.

82. Yet I am forgiving to those who repent and believe
and act righteously and then are guided.

83. 'What has made you hasten from your people, Moses?'

84. He said, 'They are on my tracks,
and I have hastened to You, my Lord,
that You might be pleased.'

85. HE said, 'We have tempted your people after you left them,

and al-Sāmirī⁵ has led them astray.'

86.   So Moses returned to his people, angry and sorry.
He said, 'My people,
did your Lord not make you a fair promise?
Did the period of the covenant last too long for you,
or did you want anger from your Lord to descend on you
and so you failed [to keep] your tryst with me?'

87.   They said, 'We did not fail [to keep] our tryst with you of our own free will,
but we were loaded with burdens of the ornaments of the people,
and so we threw them into the fire,
as al-Sāmirī did.'

88.   Then he produced for them a calf,
a body that could make a lowing sound.
They said, 'This is your^p god and the god of Moses,
but he has forgotten.'

89.   Do they not see that it returns no speech to them
and has no power to hurt or profit them?

90.   But Aaron had already said to them,
'My people, you have been tempted by it.
Your Lord is surely the Merciful;
so follow me and obey my order.'

91.   They said, 'We shall continue to cleave to it
until Moses returns to us.'

92.   He said, 'Aaron,
what held you back when you saw that they had gone astray,

93.   So that you did not follow me?
Did you disobey my command?'

94.   He said, 'Son of my mother,
do not take hold of my beard or my head.
I was afraid that you would say,
"You have caused division among the Children of Israel
and you have not observed my words".'

95.   He said, 'What have you to say, O Sāmirī?'

96.   He said, 'I saw what they did not see;
so I seized a handful [of dust] from the tracks of the messenger,
and I threw it in.
My soul has enticed me thus.'

97.   He⁴ said, 'Go^s.
It will be your [lot] in this life to say,
"No contact."'

---

⁵ Thought to mean the Samaritan, but this is not certain.

And you will have a tryst that you will not fail to keep.
Look at your god to whom you continued to cleave.
We shall burn it and scatter it in the sea as dust.

98. Your[p] god is God,
apart from whom there is no other god.
He embraces everything in His knowledge.'

99. Thus We tell you[s] some of the tidings of what has gone before;
and We have given you a reminder from Us.

100. Those who turn away from [the reminder] will bear a burden on the Day of
Resurrection,

101. With which they will remain for ever
– an evil burden on the Day of Resurrection.

102. On the day when there is a blast on the trumpet
and on that day We round up the sinners white-eyed,[6]

103. Murmuring among themselves,
'You have lingered only ten [days].'

104. We are well aware of what they will say
when the most exemplary of them in conduct says,
'You have lingered only a day.'

105. They will question you[s] about the mountains.
Say, 'My Lord will scatter them as ashes,

106. And leave them as an empty plain,

107. In which you[s] will see no crookedness nor distortion.'

108. On that day they will follow the Summoner,
in whom there is no crookedness;
and voices will be hushed to the Merciful,
and you[s] will hear only a murmur.

109. On that day intercession will profit only those
to whom the Merciful has given leave
and of whose speech He approves.

110. He knows what is before them and what is behind them,
but they do not comprehend Him in knowledge.

111. Faces will be humbled to the Living, the Eternal.
Those who carry a burden of wrong-doing will be lost,

112. But those who do some deeds of righteousness and are believers
will fear neither wrong nor oppression.

113. Thus We have sent it down as a Recitation in Arabic,
and We have turned about in it some threats,
so that they may fear God
or that it may create for them a reminder.

---

[6] Or 'blind'. The Arabic is *zurq* 'blue'.

114. May God, the true king, be exalted.
    And do^s not hasten with the Recitation
    before its revelation to you is completed.
    Say, 'My Lord, increase me in knowledge.'
115. Formerly We made a covenant with Adam,
    but he forgot and We found in him no constancy.
116. [Recall] when We said to the angels,
    'Prostrate yourselves before Adam.'
    They all did so except Iblīs, who refused.
117. And We said, 'Adam, this is indeed an enemy
    to you and to your wife.
    Let him not drive the two of you from the garden
    so that you become wretched.
118. It [has been granted] to you that you will not go hungry in it nor go naked,
119. Nor will you thirst in it nor be exposed to the heat of the sun.'
120. But Satan whispered to him and said,
    'Adam, shall I show you the tree of eternity
    and a kingdom that does not decay?'
121. The two of them ate from it,
    and their bare bodies appeared to them
    and they began to cover themselves with some of the leaves of the garden,
    and Adam disobeyed his Lord and went astray.
122. Then his Lord chose him
    and he turned to Him [in repentance]
    and He guided [him].
123. HE said, 'Leave it, both of you together,
    each an enemy of the other.
    But if guidance comes to you from Me,
    those who follow My guidance
    will not go astray nor become wretched.
124. But those who turn away from My remembrance
    will have a life of narrowness,
    and We shall round them up blind on the Day of Resurrection.'
125. [Such people] will say, 'My Lord, why have you rounded me up blind,
    when I used to see?'
126. He will say, 'So it is.
    Our signs came to you^s, but you forgot them.
    In this way you^s are forgotten to-day.'
127. Thus We recompense those who are prodigal
    and do not believe in the signs of their Lord.
    The torment of the world to come is more severe and more lasting.
128. Have they not been guided by how many generations We destroyed before them,

among whose dwellings they walk?
In that there are signs for men of reason.

129. But for a word that had gone before from your^s Lord
and a stated term,
it would be following closely.

130. So endure^s patiently against what they say,
and glorify the Lord with praise
before the rising of the sun
and before its going down,
and glorify in the watches of the night
and at the two ends of the day
so that you^s may be pleasing.

131. And do^s not strain your eyes towards what We have given pairs of them to enjoy,
the flower of the life of this world,
that We may test them thereby.
The provision of your Lord is better and more enduring.

132. Order^s your people to pray and be steadfast in [prayer].
We do not ask you^s for any provision,
but We make provision for you.
And the issue is one of piety.

133. And they say, 'Why does he not bring us a sign from his Lord?'
Has not the clear proof of what is in the former Scriptures come to them?

134. Had We destroyed them with a punishment beforehand,
they would have said, 'Our Lord,
why did You not send us a messenger
so that we might have followed Your signs
before we were humbled and shamed?'

135. Say, 'Everyone is watching and waiting.
So watch^s and wait.
You will come to know who are the ones on the level path
and who are guided aright.'

Sūra 21

This is generally agreed to be a middle Meccan *sūra*. One can divide it into three main sections: polemic (1–47); legends (48–96); and further polemic (97–112). Each section comprises a number of smaller passages, with the only sustained piece being the story of Abraham (51–72). There is some evidence of modification at Medina, the most obvious being in verse 73.

The Prophets

In the name of the Merciful and Compassionate God

1. Reckoning has drawn close to the people,
   whilst they are turning away in heedlessness.
2. They play while they listen to any new reminder that comes to them from their Lord,
3. With their hearts diverted.
   Those who do wrong talk together in secret:
   'Is this anything other than a mortal like you?
   Will you take to sorcery, with your eyes open?'
4. He says, 'My Lord knows what is said in heaven and on earth.
   He is the Hearer and the Knower.'
5. No! They say, 'Tangled nightmares.
   No! He has invented it.
   No! He is a poet.
   Let him bring us a sign,
   just as the ones of old were sent [with signs].'
6. No settlement that We destroyed before them believed.
   Will they then believe?
7. We only sent as messengers before you^s men whom We inspired.
   Ask^p the people of the reminder,
   if you^p do not know.
8. We did not fashion them as bodies that did not eat food;
   nor were they immortal.
9. Then We made true the promise [we had given them]:
   We saved them and those whom We wished,
   and We destroyed the profligates.
10. We have sent down to you^p a Scripture
    in which is your reminder.
    Do you not understand?

11. How many a settlement that did wrong have We shattered,
    and raised up after it another people!
12. And when they perceived Our might,
    you could see them running from it!
13. 'Do[P] not run.
    Return[P] to that in which you were pampered
    and to your dwellings
    so that you may be questioned.'
14. They said, 'Woe upon us. We were wrong-doers.'
15. These calls of theirs continued
    till We made them a reaped harvest, extinct.
16. We were not playing when We created heaven and earth and all that is between them.
17. Had We wished to choose a diversion,
    We could have chosen it from within Us
    – had We done [anything].
18. No! We hurl the true against the false,
    and it prevails over it,
    and [the false] vanishes.
    And woe to you for what you describe.
19. To Him belong all those who are in the heavens and the earth.
    Those who are with Him are not too proud to serve Him,
    nor do they grow weary.
20. They glorify [Him] night and day,
    and they do not falter.
21. Or have they taken gods from the earth who raise the dead?
22. If there were gods in both [the heavens and the earth],
    apart from God,
    the two would go to ruin.
    Glory be to God,
    the Lord of the Throne,
    high above all that they describe.
23. He will not be questioned about what He does
    – but they will be questioned.
24. Or have they taken gods apart from Him?
    Say, 'Bring your proof!
    This is the reminder for those who are with me
    and for those who were before me.'
    But most of them do not know the truth,
    and so they are averse.
25. We never sent a messenger before you without inspiring him,
    saying, 'There is no god but Me; so serve Me.'
26. And they say, 'The Merciful has taken to himself a son.'

Glory be to Him.
No! [They are only] honoured servants.[1]

27. They do not speak till He has spoken,
and they act by His command.

28. He knows what is before them and what is behind them.
They can only intercede for those with whom He is pleased,
and they tremble in fear of Him.

29. Whoever of them says, 'I am a god, apart from Him'
– such a one We recompense with Jahannam.
Thus We recompense the wrong-doers.

30. Have those who do not believe seen
that the heavens and the earth were closed up together,
and We split them apart,
and We made every living thing of water?
Will they not believe?

31. We have placed in the earth firm mountains,
so that it does not sway with them,
and put there ravines as roads
so that they might be guided aright.

32. And We have made the heaven a well-preserved roof
– but they turn away from its signs.

33. [It is] He who created the night and the day,
and the sun and the moon,
each swimming in an orbit.

34. We have not assigned immortality to any mortal before you.
If you are to die, are they to live for ever?

35. Every soul will taste death.
We try you with good and evil as a test.
You will be returned to Us.

36. When those who do not believe see you,
they take you only as someone to be mocked:
'Is this the one who mentions your gods?'
They have no belief in the remembrance of the Merciful.

37. Man was created of haste.
I shall show you My signs,
but do not ask Me to make haste.

38. And they say, 'When is this promise to be,
if you tell the truth?'

39. If those who disbelieve only knew the time
when they cannot keep the Fire off their faces and their backs

---

[1] The angels.

and when they will not be helped.

40. No! It will come on them suddenly, surprising them.
They will be unable to ward it off,
nor will they be given a respite.

41. There was mockery of messengers before you[s],
but that which they mocked encompassed those of them who mocked.

42. Say, 'Who will guard you night and day from the Merciful?'
No! They turn away from mention of their Lord.

43. Or have they gods who protect them apart from Us?
They cannot help themselves,
nor can they be protected from Us.

44. No! We gave these and their fathers enjoyment until life grew long for them.
Do they not see that We come to the land,
diminishing it at its extremities?
Are they the conquerors?

45. Say, 'It is only through inspiration that I warn you
– but the deaf do not hear the call when they are warned.

46. If a breath of your Lord's torment were to touch them,
they would say, 'Woe on us.
We were wrong-doers.'

47. We shall set up the just balances for the Day of Resurrection,
and no soul will be wronged in any way.
If it is the weight of a grain of mustard-seed,
We shall bring it.
We suffice as reckoners.

48. In the past We gave to Moses and Aaron the salvation[2]
and illumination and a reminder for those who protect themselves,

49. Those who fear their Lord in the Invisible,
and who are afraid of the Hour.

50. This is a blessed reminder that We have sent down.
Will you deny it?

51. In the past We gave Abraham his right course
– for We knew him –

52. When he said to his father and to his people,
'What are these images to which you cleave?'

53. They said, 'We found our fathers serving them.'

54. He said, 'You and your fathers were indeed in manifest error.'

55. They said, 'Do you bring us the truth,
or are you one of those that play?'

56. He said, 'No, your Lord who created them

---

[2] Or 'Criterion'.

is the Lord of the heavens and the earth.

I am one of those who testify to that for you.

57. By God, I shall outwit your idols after you turn your backs and depart.'

58. Then he turned them into fragments,

except for a big one[3] they had,

so that they might return to it.

59. They said, 'Who has done this to our gods?

He is one of the wrong-doers.'

60. They said, 'We heard a youth named Abraham mention them.'

61. They said, 'Bring him before the eyes of the people,

that they may testify.'

62. They said, 'Are you the one who has done this to our gods, O Abraham?'

63. He said, 'No, this chief one they have did it.

Ask them, if they can speak.'

64. They turned to one another, and said,

'You are wrong-doers.'

65. They were confounded, and said,

'You know[s] that they cannot speak.'

66. He said, 'Do you serve,

to the exclusion of God,

what does not profit you or harm you in any way.

67. Fie on you and on that which you serve,

to the exclusion of God.

Do you not understand?'

68. They said, 'Burn[p] him and help your gods,

if you are going to act.'

69. We said, 'O fire, be a coolness and a peace for Abraham.'

70. They desired to plot against him,

but We made them the great losers,

71. And We delivered him and Lot

to the land that We had blessed for all created beings;

72. And We gave to him Isaac and Jacob as a special gift.

Each one [of them] We made righteous;

73. And We made them leaders, guiding by Our command,

and We inspired them with the doing of good deeds

and the performance of prayer and the giving of *zakāt*,

and they served Us.

74. And Lot

– We gave him judgement and knowledge

and We saved him from the settlement that was committing evil deeds

---

[3] Normally understood as 'the biggest idol'.

– they were an evil people, reprobates –

75. And We admitted Him to Our mercy.
He was one of the righteous.

76. And Noah,
when he called out before that,
and We responded to him,
and saved him and his family from the great disaster,

77. And We helped him against the people who denied the truth of Our signs.
They were an evil people, and so We drowned them all.

78. And David and Solomon,
when they gave judgement concerning the tilled land,
when the people's sheep had browsed in it by night,
and We bore witness to their judgements.

79. We made Solomon understand it;
and to each [of them] We gave judgement and knowledge.
Along with David, We subjected the mountains and the birds to give praise;
and We were active.

80. We taught him how to make garments
to protect you against your might.
And are you grateful?

81. To Solomon [We subjected] the wind as it blew strongly,
running at his command to the land that We had blessed.
We were aware of everything.

82. There were some of the devils who dived for him
and did other work,
and We watched over them.

83. And Job
– when he called out to his Lord, saying,
'Harm has touched me,
and You are the most merciful of the merciful.'

84. We responded to him and removed the harm that was upon him,
and We gave him his household and their like with them,
as a mercy from Us and a reminder to those who serve.

85. And Ishmael and Idrīs and Dhū l-Kifl.
Each one was of the steadfast.

86. We admitted them to Our mercy.
They were among the righteous.

87. And Dhū l-Nūn
– when he departed in anger
and thought that We had no power over him;
but he cried out in the darkness,
'There is no god but You.

Glory be to You.
I have been one of the wrong-doers.'

88. So We responded to him and delivered him from his grief.
Thus We deliver the believers.

89. And Zachariah
– when he called out to his Lord,
'O my Lord, do not leave me alone,
though You are the best of inheritors.'

90. We responded to him and gave him John
and made his wife right for him.
They used to vie in doing good deeds
and used to call to Us in longing and in fear,
and they used to humble themselves to Us.

91. And she who guarded her private parts,[4]
and then We breathed some of Our Spirit into her
and made her and her son a sign to all created beings:

92. 'This is your^P community, one community.
I am your^P Lord. Serve^P Me.'

93. But they cut up their affair between them;
yet everyone will return to Us.

94. Those who do some righteous deeds and are believers
– there will be no ingratitude for their efforts.
We record it for them.

95. There is a ban on any settlement that We have destroyed:
that they will not return;

96. And then, when Yājūj and Mājūj are let loose,
and they slip out from every slope,

97. And the true promise draws near,
you will see the eyes of those who disbelieve staring:
'Woe on us. We have been heedless of this.
No. We were wrong-doers.'

98. You and that which you serve
to the exclusion of God
are the fuel of Jahannam.
You will come down to it.

99. Had these been gods,
they would not come down to it,
but they will all remain in it forever.

100. In it there is a sighing for them;
in it they cannot hear.

---

[4] Mary.

101. Those for whom the fairest reward has gone forth from us
    – those will be removed far from it.
102. They will not hear the slightest sound from it,
    and they will remain for ever in what their souls desire.
103. The supreme terror will not grieve them,
    and the angels will receive them:
    'This is your day which you were promised.'
104. The day We roll up the heavens
    as a recorder rolls up records.
    As We began the first creation,
    We shall bring it back again
    – a promise binding on us.
    We shall act.
105. We have written in the Psalms after the Reminder:
    'The earth will be inherited by My righteous servants.'[5]
106. In this there is a message to be delivered to a people who serve.
107. We have sent you[s] only as a mercy to all created beings.
108. Say, 'It is revealed to me that your God is One God.
    Are you going to surrender?'
109. And if they turn their backs, say,
    'I have proclaimed to you all alike,
    although I do not know whether what you are promised is near or far.
110. He knows what is said openly,
    and He knows what you conceal.
111. I do not know.
    Perhaps it is a trial for you,
    with enjoyment for a time.'
112. He says, 'My Lord, judge with truth.
    Our Lord is the Merciful,
    Whose help can be sought against what you describe.'

---

[5] *Cf.* Psalm 37:29: The righteous shall inherit the land, And dwell therein for ever.

Sūra 22

There is considerable dispute among the commentators about the dating of this *sūra*. Some take it to be largely Meccan; others believe that it is largely Medinan. It certainly has a sizeable Medinan core (verses 26–41), and it would appear that any Meccan material was recast there. It has three main sections: a passage of polemic which appears to be largely of Meccan provenance – it ends, as is sometimes the case with polemical pieces, with sketches of hell and paradise (1–24); a bridge verse then leads into a Medinan piece on the Pilgrimage (26–38); and then there is a further piece of polemic and exhortation, addressed in part to Muḥammad himself (verses 39–78).

The Pilgrimage

In the name of the Merciful and Compassionate God

1. O people, fear your Lord.
   The earthquake of the Hour is a tremendous thing.
2. On the day you[p] see it,
   every nursing mother will neglect the child she is suckling,
   and every pregnant woman will deliver her burden,
   and you[s] will think the people drunk,
   though they are not drunk
   – but God's torment is severe.
3. Among the people is he who disputes[1] about God without knowledge
   and who follows every rebellious devil.
4. Against him it has been prescribed
   that whoever takes him as a friend
   will be misled by him and guided by him
   to the torment of the blaze.
5. O people, if you are in doubt about the Raising
   – We have created you from dust,
   then from a drop, then from a clot,
   then from a lump, formed or unformed,
   that We may make [things] clear to you.
5a. We settle what We wish in the wombs to a stated term,
   then We bring you forth as infants.

---

[1] Verses 3–4 and 8–15 have singular phraseology following the subject *man* 'he who', but a plural 'those who' is intended.

Then [We nurture you] that you may reach maturity.

5b.   Among you are those who die [young],
and among you are some who are returned to the most abject state of life,
so that he knows nothing after having had knowledge.[2]

5c.   And youˢ see the earth barren,
but when We send down water on it,
it stirs and swells
and puts forth some of every joyful kind [of plant].

6.   That is because God is the Truth
and because He quickens the dead
and because He has power over everything.

7.   And because the Hour is coming
– there is no doubt about it –
and because God will raise those in the graves.

8.   Among the people is he who disputes[1] about God
without knowledge or guidance or an illuminating Scripture,

9.   Turning his side that he may lead [men] away from God's way.
In this world he will have shame,
and on the Day of Resurrection We shall make him taste the doom of burning.

10.   'That is for what your hands have sent on before,
and because God does not wrong His servants.'

11.   Among the people is he who worships God on an edge.[3]
If good comes to him,
he is content with it;
but if a trial comes to him,
he turns on to his face.
He loses both this world and the next.
That is the clearest loss.

12.   He invokes,
to the exclusion of God,
what does not harm him and what does not help him.
That is the far-reaching error.

13.   He calls on him who is more likely to injure than to help
– an evil patron and an evil friend.

14.   God admits those who believe and do righteous deeds
into gardens, through which rivers flow.
God does what He wants.

15.   He who thinks that God will not help him in this world and the next,
let him stretch a rope to heaven

---

[2] Through senility.
[3] *i.e.* on the fence.

and then let him cut it,
and then let him see whether his manoeuvre will remove what is enraging them.

16. Thus We have sent it down as clear signs,
and because God guides those whom He wishes.

17. Those who believe and those who are Jews and the Ṣābi'ūn[4]
and the Christians and the Magians
and those who associate others with God
– God will distinguish between them on the Day of Resurrection.
God is Witness over everything.

18. Have you[s] not seen that prostration to God
is performed by all who are in the heavens and on earth,
the sun, the moon, the stars, the mountains,
the trees, the beasts and many of the people?
But there are many people for whom torment is due.
Those whom God abases,
there is no one to honour them.
God does what He wishes.

19. These two[5] are opponents who contend about their Lord.
Those who disbelieve
– garments of fire are cut for them,
and boiling water will be poured over their heads,

20. By which their skins and what is in their bellies will be melted;

21. And for them are hooked iron rods.

22. Whenever, in their anguish, they want to come out of it,
they are returned to it:
'And taste the torment of the burning.'

23. God admits those who believe and do righteous deeds
into Gardens, through which rivers flow;
they will be adorned there with bracelets of gold and with pearls;
and their clothes there will be silk.

24. They have been guided to fair speech and to the path of the Laudable.

25. Those who do not believe and bar [people]
from the way of God and from the Sacred Mosque
which We have assigned to the people,
equally for those who stay close to it and for the *bedu*
– Whoever wrongfully wishes to pervert its use,
We shall cause him to taste a painful torment.

26. [Recall] when We found lodging for Abraham at the place of the House,

---

[4] It is not clear precisely which group the Ṣābi'ūn were. See the note on 2:62.
[5] Often thought to refer to the subjects of verses 3 and 8, but it might just refer to believers and unbelievers.

saying, 'Do not associate anything with Me,
and purify My house for those who go round it and those who stand
and those who bow and those who prostrate themselves.

27. Proclaim^s the Pilgrimage to the people.
Let them come to you^s on foot and on every lean camel,
which will come from every deep ravine,

28. To witness things of benefit for them,
and to mention the name of God on recognized days
over the livestock that We have provided for them.
Then eat^p of them and feed the desperately poor.

29. Then let them end their unkempt state
and fulfil their vows
and go round the Ancient House.

30. That;
and those who venerate the sacred things of God
– it will be better for them with God.
Permitted to you^p are livestock,
except what is recited to you.
Avoid the abomination of idols,
and avoid the speaking of falsehood,

31. Being of pure faith towards God,
not associating anything with Him.
Whoever associates anything with God,
it is as if he has fallen from the sky
and the birds snatch him
or the wind sweeps him down to a remote place.

32. That;
and those who magnify the waymarks of God
– that is from the piety of their hearts.

33. In them there are benefits for you^p to a stated term;
then their place for sacrifice is near the Ancient House.

34. For every community We have appointed a rite,
for them to mention God's name over livestock that We have
    provided for them.
Your god is One God;
so surrender yourselves to Him
and give good tidings to the humble,

35. Whose hearts are filled with awe when God is mentioned,
and to those who are patient in enduring whatever befalls them,
and to those who perform prayer
and who spend from that which We have provided for them.

36. The camels

— We have appointed them for you^p among the waymarks of God.

In them there is good for you.

So mention God's name over them, standing in rows;

and when their flanks fall, eat from them

and feed the beggar and the suppliant.

Thus We have subjected them to you,

so that you may be grateful.

37. Their flesh and their blood will not reach God,

but the piety from you reaches Him.

Thus We have subjected them to you,

that you may magnify God for the guidance He has given you.

And give good tidings to those who do good.

38. God will defend those who believe.

God does not love any ungrateful traitor.

39. Permission is granted to those who fight because they have been wronged

— for God is able to help them —

40. Those who have been unjustly expelled from their homes

merely because they say, 'Our Lord is God.'

Had it not been for God's warding off of some men by means of others,

cloisters, churches, oratories and mosques,

in which God's name is much mentioned,

would have been destroyed.

God helps those who help Him.

God is Strong and Mighty;

41. Those who,

if We give them position in the land,

perform prayer and pay the *zakāt*

and enjoin what is recognized as right

and forbid what is recognized as wrong.

To God belongs the outcome of events.

42. If they deny the truth of your^s message,

so too did the people of Noah and ʿĀd and Thamūd before them,

43. And the people of Abraham and the people of Lot,

44. And the men of Madyan.

And Moses was denied

— and I gave a respite to the unbelievers;

then I seized them, and how was My disapproval!

45. How many a settlement We have destroyed

because it did wrong,

and it is collapsed on its supports,

and how many a deserted well and well-built tower.

46. Have they not travelled in the land,

so that they have hearts with which they can understand
and ears with which they can hear?
It is not the eyes that go blind,
but the hearts, which are in their breasts.

47. They will ask you^s to hasten the punishment.
God will not fail to keep His promise.
A day with your^s Lord is like a thousand years of your counting.

48. To how many a settlement did I give respite when it did wrong.
Then I seized it.
To Me is the journeying.

49. Say, 'O people, I am simply a plain warner to you.'

50. Those who believe and do righteous deeds
– they will have forgiveness and a generous provision.

51. And those who strive to frustrate Our signs
– they are the companions of the Fire.

52. Whenever We sent a messenger or a prophet before you^s,
and he had the desire [to recite],
Satan tampered with his desire.
But God annuls Satan's tamperings,
and then God confirms His signs.
God is Knowing and Wise.

53. [This is] so that He may make Satan's promptings a trial
for those in whose hearts is sickness
and those whose hearts are hardened
– the wrong-doers are in distant schism –

54. And that those who have been given knowledge may know
that it is the truth from your Lord
and believe in Him
so that their hearts are submissive to Him.
God is the one who guides those who believe to a straight path.

55. Those who do not believe will continue to be in doubt about it
until the Hour comes to them suddenly,
or the torment of a barren day comes to them.

56. Sovereignty on that day belongs to God.
He will judge between them.
Those who believe and do righteous deeds
will be in Gardens of Bliss,

57. And those who do not believe and deny the truth of Our signs
– they will have a humiliating torment.

58. Those who migrated in God's way and then were killed or died,
God will provide them with a fair sustenance.
He is the best of providers.

59.   He will admit them through an entry they will approve of.
      God is the Knowing and the Prudent.
60.   That;
      and those who inflict the same hurt that was inflicted on them
      and then are oppressed [again],
      God will help them.
      God is Pardoning and Forgiving.
61.   That is because God makes the night pass into the day
      and the day pass into the night
      and because God is Hearing and Observing.
62.   That is because God is the truth
      and because what they invoke,
      to His exclusion,
      is false,
      and because God is the High and the Great.
63.   Have you⁵ not seen that God has sent down water from the sky,
      and in the morning the earth is green.
      God is Gentle and Informed.
64.   To Him belongs all that is in the heavens and on earth.
      God is the All-sufficient and the Laudable.
65.   Have you⁵ not seen that God has subjected to you all that is on the earth
      and the ship that runs on the sea at His command
      and that He holds back the heaven from falling on to the earth,
      except by His permission?
      God is Kind to the people and Compassionate.
66.   It is He who gave you life and then will cause you to die
      and then will give you life [again].
      Man is truly ungrateful.
67.   To each community We have appointed a rite for them to perform.
      Let them not dispute with you⁵ about the matter
      but call⁵ to your Lord.
      You are on straight guidance.
68.   If they argue with you⁵,
      say, 'God is Well Aware of what you are doing.
69.   God will judge between you on the Day of Resurrection
      concerning that about which you used to differ.'
70.   Do you not know that God knows all that is heaven and earth?
      It is in a Record.
      That is easy for God.
71.   And they serve,
      to the exclusion of God,
      that for which He has sent down no authority

and that of which they have no knowledge.
There is no helper for the wrong-doers.

72. When Our signs are recited to them as clear evidence,
you^s recognize denial in the faces of those who disbelieve.
They almost attack those who recite Our signs to them.
Say, 'Shall I inform you of worse than that?
The Fire, which God has promised to those who do not believe.
How evil is the journey's end.'

73. O men, a comparison has been coined.
Listen to it.
Those on whom you call,
to the exclusion of God,
will never create a fly,
though they combine to do it.
And if a fly robs them of anything,
they will not rescue that from it.
Weak are both the seeker and the sought.

74. They do not measure God with His true measure.
He is the Strong and the Mighty.

75. God chooses messengers from the angels and from the people.
God is Hearing and Observing.

76. He knows all that is before them and all that is behind them,
and all matters are returned to God.

77. O you who believe,
bow down and prostrate yourselves
and serve your Lord and do good,
so that you may prosper,

78. And strive for God with the truest endeavour.
He has chosen you and has not laid upon you
any difficulty in your religion,
the faith of your forefather Abraham.
He has named you 'those who surrender'
both previously and in this [Recitation],
that the messenger may be a witness against you
and that you may be witness against the people.
Perform prayer and pay the *zakāt* and hold fast to God.
He is your Protector:
how excellent a Protector;
how excellent a Helper.

Sūra 23

Most traditional authorities treat this *sūra* as being entirely from the middle Meccan period. A few take the view that 64–77 are Medinan, but it is hard to see the basis for this, and verse 70 is typically Meccan. However, there are other verses, such as 91, that do appear to be Medinan; and it seems likely that the whole *sūra* was revised during that period. An introductory piece (1–11) deals briefly with the virtues of the believers and their rewards in paradise. Next comes a 'sign' passage (12–22), followed by a narrative drawing on various legends: Noah (23–30); unspecified, but apparently ʿĀd (31–41); unspecified, but possibly with a reference to Thamūd (42–44); Moses and Aaron (45–49); Jesus (50). A bridge passage (51–54) leads into polemic (55–77). There is then a 'sign' interlude (78–80) and further polemic (81–115). The *sūra* is rounded off by a brief peroration (116–118).

The Believers

In the name of the Merciful and Compassionate God

1. Prosperous are the believers,
2. Who are humble in their prayers,
3. And who shun idle talk,
4. And who are active in giving *zakāt*,
5. And who guard their private parts,
6. Save from their wives or what their right hands possess.
   Then they are not blameworthy
7. – But those who seek beyond that, those are transgressors.
8. Those who observe their trust and covenant,
9. And who pay heed to their prayers
10. – Those are the inheritors
11. Who will inherit paradise,
    in which they will remain for ever.
12. We created man from an extract of clay;
13. Then We placed him, as a drop, in a safe lodging;
14. Then We created from the drop a clot,
    and from the clot a lump,
    and from the lump bones;
    then We clothed the bones with flesh,
    and then produced another creature.
    Blessed be God, the fairest of creators.

15. Then after that you[P] will die,
16. Then on the Day of Resurrection you will be raised [again].
17. We created above you[P] seven paths,
    and We were not heedless of creation;
18. And We sent down from the sky water in measure
    and lodged it in the earth
    – and We can bring it out.
19. With it We have produced for you[P]
    gardens of palms and vines,
    In which there is much fruit
    and from which you can eat,
20. And a tree that grows on Mount Sinai,
    producing oil and a flavouring for those who eat.
21. In livestock there is a lesson for you[P].
    We provide you[P] with drink
    from what is in their bellies,
    and you have many benefits in them,
    and you eat of them.
22. On them, and on ships, you are carried.
23. In the past We sent Noah to his people.
    He said, 'O my people, serve God.
    You have no god but Him.
    Will you not protect yourselves?
24. The notables of his people, who disbelieved, said,
    'This is only a mortal like you[P],
    who wishes to gain pre-eminence over you.
    Had God wished, He would have sent down angels.
    We never heard of this among our forefathers of old.
25. He is only a man possessed.
    Wait and see what happens to him for a time.'
26. He said, 'My Lord, help me,
    because they believe I am lying.'
27. Then We revealed to him, 'Make the ship
    under Our eyes and Our inspiration.
    And when Our command comes and the oven boils[1],
    put two of every kind and your family into it,
    except those of them against whom the word has already preceded.
    Do not address Me concerning those who have done wrong.
    They will be drowned.
28. When you and those with you are seated in the ship,

---

[1] See the note on 11:40.

say "Praise be to God who has delivered us from the people who do wrong",

29. And say, "My Lord, cause me to land at a blessed landing place.
You are the best of those who bring people to land".'

30. In that there are signs.
We put [men] to the test.

31. Then, after them, We produced another generation,

32. And We sent among them a messenger from themselves,
saying, 'Serve God. You have no other god but Him.
Will you not protect yourselves?

33. And the notables of his people,
who were unbelievers and denied that they would encounter the world to come,
although We had given them comfort in the life of this world,
said, 'This is only a mortal like you^P,
who eats what you eat and drinks what you drink.

34. If you obey a mortal like yourselves, then you will be losers.

35. Does he promise you that
when you are dead and have become dust and bones
you will be brought forth?

36. Away, away with what you are promised.

37. There is only our life in this world.
We die and we live.
We shall not be raised again.

38. He is only a man who has invented a lie against God.
We have no faith in him.'

39. He said, 'My Lord, help me,
because they deny the truth of what I say.'

40. He said, 'One morning soon they will be repentant.'

41. So the Shout seized them justly,
and We made them wreckage.
Away with the people who do wrong.

42. Then, after them, we produced other generations.

43. No community outstrips its term or postpones it.

44. Then We sent Our messengers in succession.
Whenever its messenger came to a community,
they denied the truth of his message.
So We caused them to follow each other
and made them stories.
Away with a people who do not believe.

45. Then We sent Moses and his brother Aaron with our signs and a clear authority

46. to Pharaoh and his nobles,
but they were proud and were exalted people.

47. They said, 'Shall we believe in two mortals like us,

when their people are our servants?'

48. So they denied the truth of their message,
and were of those who were destroyed.

49. And We gave Moses the Scripture,
so that they might be guided aright;

50. And We made the son of Mary and his mother a sign
and lodged them on a height,
where there was security and a spring.

51. 'O messengers, eat of the good things and act righteously.
I am aware of what you do.

52. This is your community, one community;
and I am your Lord.
Fear me!'

53. But they have broken up their affair among them into pieces,
each party rejoicing in what is with them.

54. So leave^s them in their heedlessness till a time.

55. Do they reckon that in the possessions and the children with which We aid them

56. We vie for good things on their behalf.
But No! They are not aware.

57. Those who go in awe through fear of God,

58. And those who believe in their Lord's signs,

59. And those who do not associate any with their Lord,

60. And those who give what they give,
their hearts filled with awe,
because they are returning to their Lord,

61. These vie for good things,
and they will be first to them.

62. We do not charge any soul beyond its capacity;
and with Us is a Writing that speaks the truth,
and they will not be wronged.

63. No, their hearts are in heedlessness of this,
and they have other deeds, short of that, which they are doing.

64. And then, when We seize their affluent ones with the torment,
they cry for help.

65. 'Do not cry for help to-day.
You will not be helped from Us.

66. My signs were recited to you,
but you turned back on your heels,

67. Acting proudly towards it,[2]
shunning one who held discourse in the night.'

---

[2] The Recitation.

68. Have they not pondered what was said,
    or has something come to them
    which did not come to their forefathers of old?
69. Or did they not recognize their messenger and so rejected him?
70. Or did they say, 'He is possessed.'
    No! He has brought them the truth,
    but most of them dislike the truth.
71. Had the truth followed their whims,
    the heavens and the earth and all those in them would have been corrupted.
    No! We have brought them their reminder,
    but they turn away from their reminder.
72. Or do you^s ask them for some tribute?
    The tribute of your Lord is better.
    He is the best of providers.
73. You^s summon them to a straight path.
74. Those who do not believe in the world to come are deviating from the path.
75. Even if We had mercy on them and removed the harm that is afflicting them,
    they would persist in their insolence,
    wandering on blindly.
76. We have already seized them with torment,
    for they were not humble towards their Lord
    nor did they abase themselves.
77. But then, when We open to them a gate that leads to severe torment,
    they will be in despair about it.
78. It is He who has produced for you hearing and sight and hearts.
    Little gratitude you show.
79. It is He who scattered you in the earth,
    and to Him you will be rounded up.
80. It is He who gives life and brings death,
    and His is the alternation of night and day.
    Do you not understand?
81. No! They say the same as that said by the ancients.
82. They say, 'When we die and are dust and bones,
    shall we be raised again?
83. We and our forefathers were promised this previously.
    This is nothing but the fables of the ancients.'
84. Say, 'Who possesses the earth and all those who are in it,
    if you have knowledge?'
85. They will say, 'God'.
    Say, 'Will you not be reminded?'
86. Say, 'Who is the Lord of the seven heavens
    and Lord of the great throne?'

87. They will say, 'God'.
    Say, 'Will you not protect yourselves?'
88. Say, 'In whose hands is the dominion over everything?
    And who gives protection but needs none,
    if you have knowledge?'
89. They will say, 'God'.
    Say, 'How [is it that] you are bewitched?'
90. No! We have brought them the truth, and they are liars.
91. God has not taken to Himself any son,
    nor is there any god with Him.
    In that case each god would have taken away what it had created,
    and some of them would have risen against others.
    Glory be to God high above what they describe,
92. Knower of the Invisible and the Witnessed.
    May He be exalted above all that they associate with Him.
93. Say, 'If You are to show me what they are promised,
94. My Lord, do not put me among the people who do wrong.'
95. We are able to show you what We promise them.
96. Repel the evil deed with what is better.
    We are well aware of what they describe.
97. And say, 'My Lord, I seek refuge with you from the suggestions of the devils,
98. And I seek refuge with you, my Lord,
    lest they are present with me.'
99. And then, when death comes to one of them,
    he says, 'My Lord, return me;
100. Perhaps I shall act righteously concerning that which I have forsaken.'
     No indeed. It is only a word that he says.
     Behind them is a barrier until the day they are raised.
101. When there is a blast on the trumpet,
     on that day there will be no kinship between them,
     nor will they question each other.
102. Those whose balances are heavy
     – those are the successful;
103. And those whose balances are light
     – those are the ones who lose their souls,
     remaining for ever in Jahannam.
104. The Fire scorches their faces, and they are grim in it.
105. 'Were not My revelations recited to you?
     And did you not deny their truth?'
106. They will say, 'Our Lord, our wretchedness prevailed over us,
     and we were a people who strayed.
107. Our Lord, bring us out of it.

If we [then] revert, we shall be wrong-doers.'

108. He will say, 'Go away into it, and do not speak to me.

109. There was a party of My servants who said,
    "Our Lord, we believe;
    so forgive us, and have mercy on us.
    You are the best of those who show mercy."

110. But you^P took them as a laughing-stock,
    until they caused you to forget remembrance of Me,
    while you laughed at them.

111. To-day I have recompensed them for what they have endured,
    because they are triumphant.'

112. He will say, 'How long have you remained on earth,
    by number of years?'

113. They will say, 'We remained only a day or a part of a day.
    Ask those who count!'

114. He will say, 'You remained but a little,
    if you only knew.

115. Did you^P reckon that We created you for sport
    and that you would not be returned to Us?'

116. Exalted be God, the True King.
    There is no god but Him, Lord of the noble throne.

117. Whoever calls on another god along with God,
    a god of which he has no proof
    – his reckoning is with his Lord.
    The unbelievers will not prosper.

118. Say, 'My Lord, forgive and have mercy,
    for You are the best of those who have mercy.'

Sūra 24

The *sūra* is Medinan, and a large part of it deals with problems of social behaviour. Verses 11–19 are linked by the commentators with the aftermath of an incident on an expedition made by the Muslims against a recalcitrant tribe, the Banū l-Muṣṭaliq, at the beginning of 627 AD. Tradition tells us that Muḥammad's wife ʿĀ'isha got left behind on the return journey and was found and brought back by one of the men on the expedition. This led to some people accusing her of adultery. The passage clears her of the charge and takes to task those who spread the accusation against her. Verse 22 is also said to be a rebuke to her father Abū Bakr for his attitude towards one of the accusers. It is uncertain whether verses 2–9 antedate the incident or not. Linkage is provided in verse 10 by a phrase that recurs with a similar function in verse 20. (It is also found in a modified form in verses 14 and 21a.) These two sections (1–9 and 11–22) are followed by four generalizing verses (23–26), the last of which paves the way for more guidance: entering houses (27–29) and decorum (30–34, with 33a probably a later addition). Verses 35–46 provide a contrast by moving to God's power and signs and the believers and unbelievers, who are further mentioned in 47–57. Verses 58–63 return to guidance on decorum, with a final verse (64) on God's knowledge. The *sūra* gets its name from the striking simile in verses 35–35a.

Light

In the name of the Merciful and Compassionate God

1. A *sūra* which We have sent down and prescribed.
   We have sent down clear signs,
   so that you^p may be reminded.
2. The fornicator and the fornicatress,
   scourge^p each one of them a hundred lashes.
   Let not pity for them seize you concerning God's religion,
   if you believe in God and the Last Day.
   And let a party of believers witness their punishment.
3. The fornicator shall only marry a fornicatress or an idolatress;
   and none shall marry the fornicatress
   save a fornicator or an idolator.
   That is forbidden to believers.
4. Those who accuse chaste women,
   and then do not bring four witnesses,
   scourge them eighty lashes,
   and never accept their testimony [after that]
   – They are sinners –

5. Except in the case of those who repent and make amends.
God is Forgiving and Compassionate.

6. Those who accuse their wives and have no witnesses but themselves,
let the testimony of one of them be to witness by God four times
that he is one of the truthful,

7. And then the fifth that the curse of God is on him
if he is one of those who lie.

8. But it shall avert punishment from her
that she bear witness four times by God
that he is one of the liars,

9. And the fifth that the wrath of God be upon her
if he is one of the truthful.

10. Had it not been for God's bounty and mercy to you[P]
and that God is Relenting and Wise –

11. Those who have perpetrated the lie are a group among you.
Do[P] not reckon it a bad thing for you.
No, it is good for you.
Every man of them will have the sin he has amassed;
and the one of them who was responsible for the greater part of it
will have a great torment.

12. When you[P] heard it,
why did the believing men and women not think good in their own minds and say,
'This is a clear lie'?

13. Why did they not bring four witnesses concerning it?
Since they have not produced witnesses,
they are liars in God's view.

14. Had it not been for God's bounty and mercy to you[P]
in this world and the next,
a great torment would have touched you
for what you uttered,

15. When you[P] were receiving it with your tongues
and you were uttering with your mouths
that of which you had no knowledge
– and you reckoned it a light matter,
when in God's view it is grave –

16. And when you[P] heard it, why did you not say,
'It is not for us to speak about this.
Glory be to You.
This is a great calumny?'

17. God admonishes you[P] never to repeat the like of that,
if you are believers.

18. God makes the signs clear to you[P].

God is Knowing and Wise.

19. Those who love indecent slander to be spread abroad concerning those who believe
will have a painful punishment in this world and in the next.
God knows, when you^p do not know.

20. Had it not been for God's bounty and mercy to you^p
and that God is Kind and Compassionate –

21. O you who believe,
do not follow Satan's footsteps.
Those who follow Satan's footsteps
– he enjoins immoral behaviour and wrong-doing.

21a. Had it not been for God's bounty and mercy to you^p,
none of you would ever have been pure.
God purifies those whom He wishes.
God is Hearing and Knowing.

22. Let not those of you who have abundance and plenty
refuse to give to kinsmen,
the needy and those who have migrated in God's way.
Let them forgive and pardon.
Don't you want God to pardon you?
God is Forgiving and Compassionate.

23. Those who cast imputations on chaste, believing women who are careless
are accursed in this world and the next.
They will have a severe torment

24. On the day when their tongues and their hands
and their feet testify against them
for what they have been doing.

25. On that day God will pay them in full their just due,
and they will know that God is the clear truth.

26. Vile women are for vile men,
and vile men for vile women.
Good women are for good men,
and good men for good women.
These are cleared of what people say.
They will have pardon and a bountiful provision.

27. O you who believe, do not enter houses other than your own
until you have sought permission
and greeted the people of the house.
That is better for you,
so that you may be reminded.

28. If you^p find no one inside,
still do not enter them
until permission has been given to you;

and if you are told, 'return', return.
[That] is purer for you.
God is aware of what you do.

29.   It is no sin for you^P to enter uninhabited houses
in which there is something for you to enjoy.
God knows what you proclaim and what you conceal.

30.   Tell the believing men to lower their gaze
and to guard their private parts.
That is purer for them.
God is informed of what they do.

31.   Tell the believing women to lower their gaze
and to guard their private parts
and to show only those of their ornaments that normally appear
and to draw their coverings over the openings in their garments
and to reveal their ornaments only to their husbands
or their fathers or the fathers of their husbands
or their sons or their step-sons
or their brothers or the sons of their brothers or sisters
or their women or what their right hands possess
or their male attendants who have no desire
or children who have no knowledge of women's nakedness.
And let them not stamp their feet
so that the ornaments which they conceal are known.
O believers, all of you turn in repentance
so that you may prosper.

32.   Marry^P off the unmarried among you and the righteous among your male and
female slaves.
If they are poor, God will give them sufficiency from His bounty.
God is Embracing and Knowing.

33.   Let those who do not find [the means for] marriage
remain chaste until God gives them sufficiency from His bounty.

33a. Such of those whom your right hands possess
who seek the document,[1]
write^P it for them if you know some good in them;
and give them some of the wealth of God
that He has given to you.

33b. Do^P not force your young women to prostitution,
so that you may seek the chance gain of the life of this world,
if they wish to preserve their chastity.

---

[1] Traditionally taken to mean 'a manumission document'; but the context would appear to indicate that 'a marriage document' is intended.

If any one compels them, God will be Forgiving and Compassionate to them
after the compulsion laid on them.

34. We have sent down to you^p clear signs
and a parallel drawn from those who passed away before you
and an admonition for those who would protect themselves.

35. God is the light of the heavens and the earth.
His light is like a niche in which there is a lamp
– the lamp in a glass, and the glass like a brilliant star
– lit from a blessed tree, an olive-tree
neither from the East nor from the West,
whose oil almost glows,
even though no fire has touched it

35a. – Light upon light.
God guides to His light those whom He wishes;
and God coins parallels for the people.
God is aware of everything:

36. In houses which God has allowed to be raised and His name remembered in them;
in which He is glorified in the mornings and the evenings

37. By men who are not diverted by trade or commerce from remembrance of God
or from the performance of prayer or the giving of *zakāt*.
They fear a day when hearts and eyes will be turned about,

38. That God may recompense them with the fairest of what they have done
and increase their recompense from His bounty.
God provides for those whom He wishes, without reckoning.

39. Those who disbelieve
– their works are like a mirage in a desert,
which the thirsty man reckons to be water,
but when he gets to the spot he finds it to be nothing.
There he finds God,
and [God] pays his account in full.
God is swift in reckoning.

40. Or like the layers of darkness on a bottomless sea,
[where] he is covered by a wave
above which is another wave,
above which are clouds,
and darkness layer on layer.
When he puts out his hand,
he can hardly see it.
Those to whom God has not assigned light have no light.

41. Have you^s not seen that God is glorified
by all who are in the heavens and the earth,
and by the birds as they spread their wings?

Each – He knows its praying and its glorifying.
God is aware of what they do.

42. To God belongs the sovereignty of the heavens and the earth,
and to God is the journeying.

43. Have you⁵ not seen that God drives along clouds
and then brings them together
and makes them a mass?
You⁵ see the rain coming forth from the midst of them.
He sends down from the sky some mountains [of rain],
in which is hail,
and He smites with it those whom He wishes.
and He turns it away from those whom He wishes.
The flash of His lightning almost takes one's sight away.

44. God turns about the day and the night.
In that there is a lesson for those possessed of sight.

45. God has created every creature from water.
There are some of them that move on their bellies,
some that walk on two legs,
some that go on four.
God creates what He wishes.
God has power over everything.

46. We have sent down signs to make [things] clear.
God guides to a straight path those whom He wishes.

47. They say, 'We believe in God and the Messenger and we obey.'
After that a party of them turn away.
These are not the believers.

48. When they are called to God and His messenger
that he may judge between them,
lo, a party of them turn away.

49. If they are in the right,
they come to him submissively.

50. Is there a disease in their hearts,
or do they have doubts,
or do they fear that God and His messenger may be unjust to them?
No! They are the wrong-doers.

51. When the believers are called to God and His messenger
that he may judge between them,
the only thing they say is, 'We hear and obey.'
Those are the ones who prosper.

52. Those who obey God and His messenger
and fear God and protect themselves against Him
– those are the triumphant.

53. They swear their most solemn oaths by God
   that if you[s] order them they will go forth.
   Say, 'Do not swear;
   known obedience [is enough].
   God is informed of what you do.
54. Say, 'Obey God and obey the messenger.
   And if you turn away,
   only what is laid on him[2] rests on him[2],
   and what is laid on you rests on you.
   If you obey him[2], you will be guided.
   The messenger's only duty is to convey the message clearly.
55. God has promised those of you who believe and do righteous deeds
   that He will make them successors in the land
   in the same way that He made those who were before them successors,
   and that He will establish for them their religion
   that He has approved for them,
   and that he will give them in exchange
   security after their fear:
   'They shall serve Me,
   not associating anything with Me;
   and those who disbelieve after that
   – they are the reprobates.'
56. Perform[p] prayer and pay the *zakāt* and obey the messenger,
   so that you may receive mercy.
57. Do not reckon that those who disbelieve will frustrate [God] on earth.
   Their abode is the Fire
   – an evil journey's end.
58. O you who believe,
   let those whom your right hands possess
   and those of you who have not reached puberty
   ask permission of you three times:
   before the dawn prayer;
   when you lay aside your garments in the noon heat;
   and after the evening prayer
   – three times of nakedness for you.
   It is no sin for you or them to go round to one another
   beyond [these three times].
   – Thus God makes the signs clear for you.
   God is Knowing and Wise.
59. When the children among you reach puberty,

---

[2] Muḥammad.

327

let them ask permission,
as those before them asked permission.
Thus God makes His signs clear for you.
God is Knowing and Wise.

60. The women who are past child-bearing who have no expectation of marriage,
it is no sin for them to discard their clothes
[as long as] they do not flaunt their ornaments;
but for them to abstain is better for them.
God is Seeing and Hearing.

61. There is nothing wrong for the blind,
nothing wrong for the lame,
and nothing wrong for the sick
or for you yourselves
to eat in your houses, or the houses of your fathers, or the houses of your mothers,
or the houses of your brothers, or the houses of your sisters,
or the houses of your uncles or the houses of your aunts on your father's side,
or the houses of your uncles or the houses of your aunts on your mother's side,
or those of which you hold the keys, or [the house] of your friend.
It is no sin for you to eat together or in separate groups.
When you enter houses
greet one another with a greeting from God, one that is blessed and good.
Thus God makes the signs clear for you,
so that you may understand.

62. The believers are only those who believe in God and His messenger
and who, when they are with him on some common matter,
do not leave till they have sought his permission.
Those who ask permission of you^s
– those are the ones who believe in God and His messenger;
so if they ask your^s permission for some affair of theirs,
grant^s it to those whom you wish,
and ask forgiveness for them.
God is Forgiving and Compassionate.

63. Do not make the summoning of the messenger among you
like your summoning of one another.
God knows those of you who slip away and conceal themselves.
So let those who dissent from His command beware
lest a trial or a painful punishment befall them.

64. Truly, to God belongs whatever is in the heavens and the earth.
He knows what you are about;
and [He knows] the day they are returned to Him,
and He will tell them what they did.
God is aware of everything.

Sūra 25

This *sūra* is generally thought to be from the middle Meccan period, with a number of authorities declaring verses 68–70 to be Medinan. There are some difficulties with the way that 50–52 and 60 fit, and these are probable indications of recasting. The use of the second person singular is a prominent feature of the *sūra*. All the occurrences are traditionally taken as referring to Muḥammad, and most clearly do so; but in a few verses (e.g. 10, 43, 44, 45) the addressee could be 'man' in the singular. Certain pieces stand out thematically: 1–2, 10, 61–62 referring to God (though 10 also brings in the second person singular); 35–40, on the prophets; and 45–50, 'sign' verses. The rest of the *sūra* is polemical discourse.

Salvation

In the name of the Merciful and Compassionate God

1. Blessed is He who has sent down the salvation[1] to His slave,
   for him to be a warner to all created beings,
2. He to whom belongs the sovereignty of the heavens and the earth.
   He has not taken to Himself a son;
   nor has He any partner in sovereignty.
   He has created everything and determined it precisely.
3. But they have taken for themselves gods,
   to His exclusion,
   who create nothing but are themselves created,
   and have not the power to hurt or profit themselves
   and possess neither death nor life nor rousing.
4. Those who do not believe say,
   'This is merely a lie that he has invented,
   and others have helped him with it.'
   They have produced wrong and falsehood.
5. And they say, 'Fables of the ancients that he has had written down;
   and they are dictated to him morning and evening.'
6. Say, 'He who knows the secret in the heavens and the earth sent it down.
   He is Forgiving and Compassionate.'
7. And they say, 'What is there to this messenger?
   He eats food and walks round the markets.

---

[1] Or 'the Criterion'. There is a dispute about the meaning of the Arabic *al-furqān*.

329

Why has not an angel been sent down to him
to be a warner with him?

8. Or why is not a treasure bestowed on him,
or why does he not have a garden
from which he can eat?'
And the wrong-doers say,
'You^p are merely following a man who is bewitched.'

9. See^s how they have coined examples for you^s.
They have gone astray and cannot find a road.

10. Blessed is He who, if He wishes, will assign you^s something better than that:
gardens, through which rivers flow,
and will assign you^s palaces.

11. No. They say the Hour is a lie,
and We have prepared a Blaze
for those who say the Hour is a lie.

12. When it sees them from afar,
they will hear its roaring and sighing;

13. And when they are flung, bound together, into a narrow place in it,
they will call for a destruction there.

14. 'To-day call^p not for one destruction.
Call for many destructions.'

15. Say, 'Is that better or the Garden of Eternity,
which has been promised to the god-fearing?
It is for them a recompense and a journey's end.

16. They will have what they wish in it,
remaining there for ever.
It is a promise [whose fulfilment] can be asked of your^s Lord.'

17. On the day when He rounds up them and what they serve
to the exclusion of God
and He says, 'Was it you^p who led astray these slaves of mine
or did they themselves stray from the way?'

18. They will say, 'Glory be to You.
It was not fitting for us to take friends apart from You.'
But You gave them and their forefathers enjoyment
till they forgot the reminder and became a corrupt people.

19. And so they have considered you^p liars in what you say.
You^p cannot avert or help.
Those among you who do wrong
– We shall make them taste a great torment.

20. We never sent any messengers before you^s
but they ate food and walked around the markets.
We have made some of you^p a test for others:

'Will you^p be steadfast?'
Your Lord is Observing.

21. Those who hope not to meet Us say,
'Why have the angels not been sent down to us
or why do we not see our Lord?'
They are haughty concerning themselves
and are proud and disdainful.

22. On the day when they see the angels
– there will be no good news on that day for the sinners.
They will say, 'A forbidden ban.'[2]

23. We shall advance to the works they did
and make them scattered dust.

24. The companions of the Garden on that day
will be better in the place they stay
and the place they rest at mid-day.

25. On the day when the heaven is split asunder by clouds
and the angels are sent down –

26. On that day true sovereignty will belong to the Merciful,
and it will be a hard day for the unbelievers.

27. On the day when the wrong-doer bites his hands, saying,
'Would that I had chosen a way with the messenger.

28. Alas for me.
Would that I had not taken so-and-so as a friend.
He led me astray from the Reminder after it had reached me.

29. Satan is a forsaker of man.'

30. And the messenger says, 'My Lord,
my people have taken this Recitation as something to be shunned.'

31. Thus We have appointed an enemy from among the sinners for every prophet,
but your^s Lord suffices as a guide and a helper.

32. Those who disbelieve say,
'Why has the Recitation not been sent down to him all at once?'
[We have sent it down] thus that We may strengthen your^s heart by it,
and We have sent it down distinctly.

33. They will not bring you^s any parallel,
but We bring you^s the Truth
– better as an explanation [than the parallel].

34. Those who are rounded up on their faces [to go] into Jahannam
– those are worse in station
and further astray from a way.

---

[2] The phrase also occurs in v. 53. In both cases it seems to mean that there is a barrier that cannot be crossed.

35. In the past We gave Moses the Scripture
    and made his brother Aaron as minister with him.
36. We said, 'Go to the people who do not believe the truth of Our signs.'
    Then We destroyed them completely.
37. And the people of Noah
    – when they had denied the truth of the messengers,
    We drowned them and made them a sign for the people.
    We have prepared a painful torment for the wrong-doers.
38. And 'Ād and Thamūd and the companions of al-Rass
    and many generations between that,
39. For each of them We have coined examples,
    and each we destroyed completely.
40. And they have come by the settlement
    on which a rain of evil was sent.
    Have they not seen it?
    No. They hope [that there will be] no Raising.
41. When they see you^s, they only take you as an object of scorn:
    'Is this the one whom God has sent as a messenger?
42. He would have led us far from our gods,
    had we not been steadfast towards them.'
    They will know when they see the torment,
    who is further away from the road.
43. Have you^s seen the one who chooses his own whim as his god?
    Would you^s be guardian over him?
44. Or do you^s reckon that most of them hear or understand?
    They are only like beasts
    – No! They are further from the way.
45. Have you^s not considered your Lord
    – how He has spread the shade?
    Had He wished, He would have made it motionless
    – and then We made the sun a guide for it,
46. Then We took it to us gently.
47. It is He who has appointed the night as a garment for you^p
    and sleep as a rest
    and appointed the day for rising.
48. It is He who has loosed the winds as good tidings before His mercy;
    and We have sent down pure water from the sky,
49. That We might revive dead land with it
    and give it to drink to many men and beasts from Our creation.
50. We have turned it about among them that they might be reminded.
    But most of the people refuse anything but ingratitude.
51. If We wished, We would have raised up a warner in every settlement.

52. Do^s not obey the unbelievers
    and strive mightily with it³ against them.
53. It is He who has released the two seas,
    this one sweet and palatable,
    the other salty and bitter,
    and has put between them a barrier and a forbidden ban.⁴
54. It is He who has created man from water
    and made him related by kin and marriage,
    for your^s Lord is Powerful.
55. Yet they serve,
    to the exclusion of God,
    what can neither benefit them nor harm them.
    The unbeliever is [always] a partisan against his Lord.
56. We have sent you^s only as a bearer of good tidings and as a warner.
57. Say, 'I do not ask you^p for any wage for this,
    except that those who wish may choose a way to their Lord,'
58. And trust in the Living One, who does not die,
    and glorify Him by praising Him.
    He suffices as the One Informed of the sins of His servants,
59. Who created the heavens and the earth and what is between them in six days.
    Then He mounted the throne
    – the Merciful:
    ask any informed of Him.
60. When they are told, 'Prostrate yourselves to the Merciful',
    they say, 'What is the Merciful?
    Are we to prostrate ourselves to what you^s bid us?'
    And [this] increases their aversion.
61. Blessed is He who has set constellations in the sky
    and has placed among them a lamp
    – a moon that gives light.
62. It is He who has made the night and the day follow in succession
    for those who wish to be reminded or wish to be thankful.
63. The servants of the Merciful are those who walk on the earth in humility
    and who say 'Peace' when the ignorant address them,
64. And spend the night standing or prostrating themselves to their Lord,
65. And who say, 'Our Lord, deflect the torment of Jahannam from us.
    Its torment is an affliction.
66. It is evil as an abode and a place to stay',
67. And who, when they spend, are neither prodigal nor grudging

---

³ The Qur'ān.
⁴ See the note on v. 22.

– there is a balance between the two –

68. And who do not call to any other god together with God
and who do not kill the soul that God has forbidden,
except with justification,
and who do not fornicate
– whoever does that will meet the price of sin:

69. The torment will be multiplied for him on the Day of Resurrection,
and he will remain humiliated in it for ever,

70. Save those who repent and believe and act righteously
– God will change their evil deeds into good deeds.
God is Forgiving and Compassionate;

71. Those who repent and act righteously
turn to God in repentance;

72. And those who will not bear false witness and who,
when they pass by idle talk,
pass by with dignity;

73. And those who,
when they are reminded of their Lord's signs,
do not fall over them, deaf and blind;

74. And those who say, 'Our Lord, grant us comfort
from our wives and our offspring
and make us an example to the god-fearing.'

75. Those will be recompensed with the upper room[5] for what they endured,
and they will meet in it a greeting: peace,

76. Remaining in it for ever.
It is excellent as an abode and a place to stay.

77. Say, 'My Lord would not care about you[P] but for your calling [to Him in prayer],
for you have denied the truth,
and [that] will be something that sticks to you.'

---

[5] *i.e.* Paradise.

Sūra 26

Sūra 26 takes its name from its final passage (verses 221*ff.*), in which poets are denounced. However, its most striking feature is a succession of narratives (verses 10–191) that take up the greater part of the *sūra*. The stories begin with long passages on the major figures of Moses and Abraham (10–68 and 69–104); these are then followed by the stories of Noah (105–122), Hūd (123–140), Ṣāliḥ (141–159), Lot (160–175) and Shuʿayb (176–191). This latter sequence (105–191) has close affinity with one in *Sūra* 7 (59–102) and to a slightly lesser extent with one in *Sūra* 11 (25–95, though that includes a piece about Abraham).

The *sūra* is generally thought to be from middle Meccan period, though with some Medinan material at the end. However, Bell is surely right in arguing that there are distinct traces of Medinan revision. In fact, it would be remarkable with a piece of this length if no revision had taken place in both Mecca and Medina. There was probably some evolution in the content of the stories of both Moses and Abraham as we now find them here. In the other narratives in the *sūra* it may be the structure that evolved rather than the detail. There is much repetition of what is somewhat more than a refrain, and these passages mesh into a structural framework that takes up roughly a fifth of the *sūra*. It is also the case that the *sūra* has more assonance than one might expect – this is why, by the standard reckoning, it has so many verses.

The Poets

In the name of the Merciful and Compassionate God

1. *Ṭāʾ, Sīn, Mīm.*[1]
2. These are the signs of the clear Scripture.
3. Perhaps you[s] are tormenting yourself
   because they do not believe.
4. If We wish, We can send down a sign from the sky to them,
   and their necks will remain submissive before it
5. – But no new reminder comes to them from the Merciful
   without them turning away from it.
6. They have denied [the truth];
   but news of that which they used to mock is coming to them.
7. Have they not looked at the earth?
   How many excellent species We have caused to grow in it.

---

[1] On the mystical letters see the note on 2:1.

8. In this there is a sign
    – but most of them are not believers.
9. Your^s Lord is truly the Mighty and the Compassionate.
10. [Remember] when your^s Lord called out to Moses,
    'Go to the people who do wrong,
11. The people of Pharaoh.
    Will they not protect themselves?'
12. He said, 'My Lord,
    I fear that they will say that I lie.
13. My breast is straitened and my tongue will not move.
    So send for Aaron.
14. They hold a sin against me.^2
    I fear that they will kill me.'
15. HE said, 'Not at all.
    Both of you go with Our signs
    – We shall be with you, Hearing –
16. And come to Pharaoh and say,
    "We convey a message from the Lord of all beings.
17. Let the Children of Israel go with us".'
18. He^3 said, 'Did we not rear you^s amongst us as a child?
    Have you not remained among us for many years of your life?
19. And did you not do the deed that you did,
    being one of the ungrateful?'
20. He^4 said, 'I did it at that time,
    when I was one of those who were astray.
21. And I fled from you^s when I became afraid of you.
    Then my Lord gave me judgement
    and made me one of those sent [by Him].
22. Is that a favour about which you now reproach me,
    although you have enslaved the Children of Israel?'
23. Pharaoh said, 'What is the Lord of all beings?'
24. He^4 said, 'The Lord of the heavens and the earth and what is between them,
    if you^p are sure [in your belief].'
25. He^3 said to those around him, 'Do you not hear?'
26. He^4 said, 'Your^p Lord and the Lord of your forefathers, the ancients.'
27. He^3 said, 'Your^p messenger, who has been sent to you,
    is indeed possessed.'
28. He^4 said, 'The Lord of the east and the west and all that is between them,

---

^2 For the fullest account of Moses killing an Egyptian see 28:15–21.
^3 Pharaoh.
^4 Moses.

if you^p understand.'

29. He^3 said, 'If you^s choose a god other than me,
I shall put you amongst those who are in prison.'
30. He^4 said, 'Even if I were to bring you something convincing?'
31. He^3 said, 'Bring it, if you are truthful.'
32. At this he^4 threw down his staff,
and, behold, it turned into a serpent for all to see.
33. And he pulled out his hand,
and, behold, it was white to those who looked.
34. He^3 said to the notables around him,
'This is a learned sorcerer,
35. Who wishes to drive you from your land with his magic.
What do you command?'
36. They said, 'Put him and his brother off for a time
and send musterers into the cities,
37. And they will bring your every learned sorcerer.'
38. So the sorcerers were gathered together
for the appointed time of a fixed day;
39. And it was said to the people,
'Will you assemble?'
40. [They said], 'Perhaps we shall follow the sorcerers,
if they are the victors.'
41. When the sorcerers came, they said to Pharaoh,
'Shall we have a reward, if we are the victors?'
42. He said, 'Yes.
In that case you will be among those brought near [to me in honour].'
43. Moses said to them,
'Throw down whatever you [want to] throw down.'
44. They threw down their ropes and their sticks and said,
'By the might of Pharaoh, we shall be the victors.'
45. Then Moses threw down his staff,
and, behold, it swallowed what they were faking;
46. And the sorcerers were flung down in prostration.
47. They said, 'We believe in the Lord of all beings,
48. The Lord of Moses and Aaron.'
49. He^3 said, 'Do you^p believe in Him before I give permission?
He is your chief, who has taught you sorcery.
Now you will know.
49a. I shall cut off your hands and feet alternately,
and I shall crucify you all.'
50. They said, 'There will be no harm.
We are going off to our Lord.

51. We are eager for our Lord to forgive us our sins,
    because we are the first of the believers.'
52. We suggested to Moses,
    'Travel by night with my servants,
    for you^p will be followed.'
53. Pharaoh sent musterers into the cities [to say],
54. 'These are a small troop;
55. They are enraging us,
56. But we are a host who are on our guard.'
57. [In this way] We brought them out of gardens and springs
58. And treasures and a noble station.
59. Thus it was;
    and We caused the Children of Israel to inherit them.
60. And they followed them at sunrise.
61. When the two hosts saw each other,
    the companions of Moses said,
    'We are being overtaken.'
62. He said, 'No! My Lord is with me.
    He will guide me.'
63. We suggested to Moses,
    'Strike the sea with your staff.'
    It parted, and each part was like a vast mountain.
64. Then We brought the rest near to that.
65. And We saved Moses and all those who were with him.
66. Then We drowned the rest.
67. In that there is a sign,
    but most of them have not become believers.
68. Your Lord is Mighty and the Compassionate.
69. Recite to them the story of Abraham:
70. When he said to his father and his people,
    'What do you worship?'
71. They said, 'We worship idols,
    and we shall continue to cleave to them.'
72. He said, 'Do they hear you when you call?
73. Or do they benefit you or harm you?'
74. They said, 'But we found our fathers acting thus.'
75. He said, 'Have you considered what you have been worshipping,
76. You and your forefathers?
77. They are an enemy to me,
    except for the Lord of all beings,
78. Who created me and guides me,
79. And Who gives me food and drink,

80. And Who heals me when I am sick,
81. And Who makes me die and then gives me life again,
82. And Whom I desire to forgive me my sins on the Day of Judgement.
83. My Lord, grant me judgement
    and join me with the righteous;
84. And give me a reputation for truth among those who come later;
85. And place me among those who inherit the garden of bliss.
86. Forgive my father.
    He is one of those who have gone astray.
87. And do not shame me on the day when [men] are raised,
88. The day when neither wealth nor children are of any benefit,
89. Except for those who come to God with a sound heart.'
90. And the garden will be brought near for those who are god-fearing;
91. And the fire will be brought forward for those who have gone astray.
92. It will be said to them,
    'Where is that which you have been worshipping
93. to the exclusion of God?
    Can they help you or themselves?'
94. Then they will be pitched into it,
    they and those who have gone astray,
95. And the hosts of Iblīs, all of them.
96. They will say,
    when they are quarrelling with each other in it,
97. 'By God, we were in manifest error,
98. When we made you^p equal with the Lord of all beings.
99. It was only the sinners who led us astray.
100. Now we have no intercessors,
101. Nor any loyal friend.
102. If only we had another turn
    so that we might be among the believers.'
103. In that there is a sign,
    but most of them have not become believers.
104. Your^s Lord is the Mighty and the Compassionate.
105. The people of Noah denied the truth of those who were sent,
106. When their brother Noah said to them,
    'Will you not protect yourselves?
107. I am a faithful messenger for you.
108. Fear God and obey me.
109. I am not asking you for any wage for this.
    My reward is only with the Lord of all beings.
110. Fear God and obey me.'
111. They said, 'Shall we believe you,

when the vilest are your followers?'

112. He said, 'What knowledge have I about what they have been doing?

113. Their account rests only with my Lord,
if you^P did but know it.

114. I am not going to drive away the believers.

115. I am only a clear warner.'

116. They said, 'If you do not desist, O Noah,
you will be amongst those who are stoned.'

117. He said, 'My people have disbelieved me.

118. Make an opening between me and them;
and save me and those of the believers who are with me.'

119. So We saved him and those who were with him in the laden ship.

120. Then, afterwards, We drowned the rest.

121. In that there is a sign,
but most of them have not become believers.

122. Your Lord is the Mighty and the Compassionate.

123. ʿĀd denied the truth of those who were sent,

124. When their brother Hūd said to them,
'Will you not protect yourselves?

125. I am a faithful messenger for you.

126. Fear God and obey me.

127. I am not asking you for any wage for this.
My reward is only with the Lord of all beings.

128. Do you build on every eminence a sign to amuse yourselves?

129. And do you acquire towers
so that you may dwell there for ever?

130. And when you make an assault,
do you make your assault as overweening people?

131. Fear God and obey me.

132. Fear Him who has helped you with the things you know,

133. Who has helped you with livestock and sons,

134. And gardens and springs.

135. I fear for you the punishment of an awesome day.'

136. They said, 'It is the same to us
whether you^s preach or are not a preacher.

137. This is merely the creation of the ancients.

138. We shall not be punished.'

139. And they disbelieved him;
and so we destroyed them.

139a. In that there is a sign,
but most of them have not become believers.

140. Your Lord is the Mighty and the Compassionate.

141. Thamūd denied the truth of those who were sent,
142. When their brother Ṣāliḥ said to them,
     'Will you not protect yourselves?
143. I am a faithful messenger for you.
144. Fear God and obey me.
145. I am not asking you for any wage for this.
     My reward is only with the Lord of all beings.
146. Will you be left secure in what is here,
147. Among gardens and springs
148. And sown lands and palm-trees with slender spathes?
149. And will you skilfully hew out houses from the mountains?
150. Fear God and obey me.
151. Do not obey the command of the prodigal,
152. Who cause corruption in the land
     and do not put things right.'
153. They said, 'You⁵ are just like one of the bewitched.
154. You are merely a mortal like us.
     Bring a sign if you speak the truth.'
155. He said, 'This is a she-camel.
     She has a right to drink
     and you have a right to drink on an appointed day.
156. Do not touch her with evil
     lest the punishment of an awesome day seize you.'
157. But they hamstrung her
     – and then they were repentant.
158. So punishment overtook them.
159. In that there is a sign,
     but most of them have not become believers.
159a. Your Lord is the Mighty and the Compassionate.
160. The people of Lot denied the truth of those who were sent.
161. When their brother Lot said to them,
     'Will you not protect yourselves?
162. I am a faithful messenger for you.
163. Fear God and obey me.
164. I am not asking you for any wage for this.
     My reward is only with the Lord of all beings.
165. Do you come to the males of created beings,
166. And leave alone the wives that your Lord has created for you?
     No! You are a people who transgress!'
167. They said, 'If you do not desist, O Lot,
     you will be one of those cast out.'
168. He said, 'I am one of those who hate what you do.

341

169. My Lord, save me and my family from what they do.'
170. So We saved him and his family, all of them,
171. Except an old woman among those who tarried.
172. Then we destroyed the others.
173. We caused a rain to fall on them;
and evil is the rain of those who have been warned.
174. In that there is a sign,
but most of them have not become believers.
175. Your Lord is the Mighty and the Compassionate.
176. The men of the thicket denied the truth of those who were sent:
177. When their brother Shuʿayb said to them,
'Will you not protect yourselves?
178. I am a faithful messenger for you.
179. Fear God and obey me.
180. I am not asking you for any wage for this.
My reward is only with the Lord of all beings.
181. Give full measure and do not be people who cause loss.
182. Weigh with the straight balance,
183. Do not defraud the people of their things,
and do not work mischief in the land, causing corruption.
184. Fear Him who created you and the masses of former times.'
185. They said, 'You^s are just like one of the bewitched.
186. You are merely a mortal like us.
We think that you are a liar.
187. Make fragments fall on us from the sky,
if you are truthful.'
188. He said, 'My Lord is well aware of what you are doing.'
189. But they denied him,
and they were seized by the punishment of the day of shadows.
It was the punishment of an awesome day.
190. In that there is a sign,
but most of them have not become believers.
191. Your^s Lord is the Mighty and the Compassionate.
192. It is the message sent down by the Lord of all beings,
193. Which the faithful spirit has brought down
194. Upon your^s heart, that you may be one of the warners,
195. In a clear Arabic tongue.
196. It is in the scrolls[5] of the ancients.
197. Is it not a sign for them
that the learned of the Children of Israel know it?

---

[5] Or 'psalms'.

198. If We had sent it down to one of the foreigners,
199. And had he recited it to them,
     they would not have believed in it.
200. Thus We have made a way for it into the hearts of the sinners.
201. They will not believe in it
     until they see the painful punishment,
202. So that it will come to them suddenly
     when they are not aware,
203. And they will say,
     'Are we to be reprieved?'
204. Do they seek to hasten Our punishment?
205. Have you^s considered:
     if We give them enjoyment for years
206. And then they are visited by what they have been promised,
207. What they have been allowed to enjoy
     will avail them nothing.
208. We have not destroyed any settlement
     without it having had warners
209. For a reminder.
     We have not been wrong-doers.
210. The satans did not bring it down.
211. That is not for them to do,
     nor can they do so.
212. They are removed far from hearing.
213. Do^s not call on another god with God,
     lest you become one of those who are punished.
214. And warn^s your tribe, your near relations,
215. And lower your wing to those believers who follow you.
216. If they disobey you^s, say,
     'I am not responsible for what you do.'
217. Rely^s on the Mighty and the Compassionate,
218. Who sees you when you stand,
219. And [sees] your turning about among those who prostrate themselves.
220. He is the Hearer and the Knower.
221. Shall I tell you^p of those on whom the satans descend?
222. They descend on every sinful liar.
223. They listen,
     but most of them are liars.
224. And there are the poets,
     who are followed by those who go astray.
225. Have you^s not seen [how] they wander in every valley,
226. And [how] they say what they do not do?

227. That is not the case with those who believe and do righteous deeds
and remember God often and help themselves
after they have been wronged.
Those who do wrong will surely know by what overturning
they will be overturned.

Sūra 27

This is classed as a middle Meccan *sūra*. It falls into three main sections: a brief introduction that ends with an affirmation that Muḥammad is receiving his Recitation from God (1–6); a series of narratives: Moses (7–14), David, Solomon and the Queen of Sheba (15–44), Thamūd (45–53), Lot (54–58); and a longish passage, partly polemic but mainly on God's attributes, Muḥammad from time to time being addressed directly (59–93). The account of Solomon and Sheba (17–44) recalls a Jewish Aramaic account found in the *Second Targum on Esther* rather than the biblical account in *1 Kings* 10 (repeated in *2 Chronicles* 9).

The Ants

In the name of the Merciful and Compassionate God

1. *Ṭā', Sīn.*[1]
   These are the revelations of the Recitation and a clear Scripture,
2. A guidance and good tidings for the believers
3. Who perform prayer and pay the *zakāt*
   and are sure about the world to come.
4. For those who do not believe in the world to come,
   We have made their works seem fair to them,
   and so they wander blindly.
5. Those are the ones who will have an evil torment.
   They will be the greatest losers in the world to come.
6. You[s] are receiving the Recitation
   from One who is Wise and Knowing.
7. Recall when Moses said to his folk,
   'I have spotted a fire.
   I shall bring you news of it
   or bring you a flame, a brand,
   so that you may warm yourselves.'
8. But when he reached it, there was a call to him,
   'Blessed is whoever[2] is in the fire and whoever[2] is about it.
   Glory be to God, Lord of created beings.
9. Moses, it is I, God, the Mighty and the Wise.

---

[1] On the mystical letters see the note on 2:1.

[2] There are several interpretations of the two 'whoever's: God and God; God and Moses; Moses and the angels, etc.

10. Throw down your staff.'
    When he saw it quivering
    as though it were a demon[3],
    he turned to flee and did not look back.
    'O Moses, do not be afraid;
    messengers are not afraid in my presence,

11. Except for those who have done wrong
    and have then turned to good after evil.
    I am Forgiving and Merciful.

12. Put your hand into folds of your clothes
    and it will come forth white, without hurt.
    [This will be] among nine signs to Pharaoh and his people.
    They are a profligate people.'

13. Yet when Our signs came to them, plain to see,
    they said, 'This is clear magic.'

14. And they denied them,
    through pride and wrong-doing,
    even though their souls acknowledged them.
    Look how was the end of those who wrought mischief.

15. We gave knowledge to David and Solomon.
    They said, 'Praise belongs to God,
    who has preferred us over many of His believing servants.'

16. Solomon was David's heir.
    He said, 'O mankind,
    we have been taught the speech of birds,
    and we have been given [some] of everything.
    This is clear preference.'

17. The hosts of Solomon were rounded up for him:
    Jinn, men and birds;
    and they were urged on.

18. Then where they came to the valley of ants,
    an ant said, 'O ants,
    enter your dwellings
    and Solomon and his hosts will not crush you
    when they do not see [you].'

19. He smiled, laughing at its speech, and said,
    'My Lord, press me to be thankful for Your blessings,
    which you bestowed on me and on my parents
    and [press me] to do a righteous thing that you approve of,
    and admit me, by Your mercy, among Your righteous servants.'

---

[3] Or a 'large snake'. The phrase is also found in 28:31.

20. He reviewed the birds, and then he said,
    'Why is it that I do not see the hoopoe?
    Is it amongst those who are absent?

21. I shall punish it severely or I shall slaughter it,
    or else it must bring me clear authority.'

22. [The hoopoe] was not long in coming and said,
    'I have picked up news that you have not picked up,
    and I have brought you sure tidings from Saba'.

23. I found a woman ruling them.
    She has been given [some] of everything,
    and she has a mighty throne.

24. I found her and her people prostrating themselves to the sun and not to God.
    Satan has made their deeds seem fair to them
    and has turned them from the way;
    and so they are not guided aright,

25. So that they do not prostrate themselves to God,
    who brings forth what is hidden in the heavens and on earth.
    He knows what you conceal and what you make public.

26. God,
    there is no god except Him,
    the Lord of the mighty throne.'

27. He[4] said, 'We shall see whether you have spoken the truth
    or are one of the liars.

28. Take this letter of mine and drop it before them.
    Then turn away and see what they return.'

29. She[5] said, 'O notables,
    a noble letter has been dropped before me.

30. It is from Solomon
    and it is in the name of the Merciful, the Compassionate,

31. Saying, "Do not exalt yourselves against me,
    but come to me in surrender".'

32. She[5] said, 'O notables,
    give me your opinion in my affair.
    I do not decide a matter until you give me witness.'

33. They said, 'We are possessed of strength and mighty prowess,
    but the matter rests with you.
    So consider what you will order.'

34. She said, 'When kings enter a settlement,
    they wreak havoc on it and humiliate its mighty.

---

[4] Solomon.
[5] The Queen of Sheba.

Thus they will do.

35. I am going to send a present to them
and see what the messengers bring back.'

36. When he came to Solomon,
He[4] said, 'Are you[P] offering me riches?
What God has given me is better than what He has given you[P].
No, you[P] are taking pleasure in [making] your gift.

37. Return to them.
We shall come to them with hosts
that they will be unable to resist;
and we shall eject them from there,
humiliated and abased.'

38. He[4] said, 'O notables,
which one of you will bring me her throne
before they come to me in surrender?'

39. An *'Ifrīt*[6] of the *Jinn* said, 'I shall bring it to you
before you can rise from your place.
I have strength [to do it] and I am trustworthy.'

40. One who had some knowledge of the Scripture said,
'I shall bring it before your[s] glance returns to you.'
When he saw it set before him,
He[4] said, 'This is part of My Lord's bounty
to test me whether I am grateful or ungrateful.
Those who give thanks do so only for their own souls' good;
and those who are ungrateful
– my Lord is All-sufficient [but] Generous.'

41. He said, 'Disguise her throne for her,
and we shall observe
whether she is guided aright
or is of those who are not guided aright.'

42. When she came, she was asked,
'Is your throne like this?'
She said, 'It looks like that.'
We had been given knowledge before [she came],
and we had surrendered ourselves.

43. What she served,
to the exclusion of God,
was a barrier to her.
She was from a people who were ungrateful.

44. It was said to her, 'Enter the hall.'

---

[6] A kind of *Jinn*.

When she saw it, she thought it was a pool
and she bared her legs.
He said, 'It is a polished hall, made of glass.'
She said, 'My Lord, I have wronged myself.
Together with Solomon, I surrender myself to God,
Lord of created beings.'

45. We sent to Thamūd their brother Ṣāliḥ,
saying, 'Serve God.'
But, lo, they were two parties disputing with one another.

46. He said, 'O my people, why do you seek to hasten evil before good?
Why do you not seek forgiveness from God,
so that you will be treated mercifully?'

47. They said, 'We regard you[s] and those who are with you as ill-omened.'
He said, 'Your[p] augury is with God.
No. You are a people who are being tested.'

48. There were in the city nine people
who made mischief in the land and did not put things right.'

49. They said, 'Swear to one another by God,
"We shall attack him and his family by night;
then we shall tell his protector,
'We did not witness the destruction of his family.'
We are people who tell the truth".'

50. They plotted a plot;
but We plotted a plot,
while they were not aware.

51. See how was the consequence of their plotting.
We destroyed them and their people, all [of them].

52. Those are their houses, ruined for the wrong they did.
In that there is a sign for a people who know.

53. But We saved those who believed and were god-fearing.

54. And [We sent] Lot, when he said to his people,
'Will you commit abomination,
when you can see [what you are doing]?

55. Do you approach men in lust rather than women?
No, you are people who are ignorant.'

56. The only answer of his people was to say,
'Expel the family of Lot from your settlement.
They are people who seek to be pure.'

57. We saved him and his family,
except for his wife.
We decreed that she should be among those who tarried.

58. We caused rain to fall on them,

and evil is the rain of those who have been warned.

59. Say, 'Praise belongs to God,
and peace be on His servants whom He has chosen.'
Is God better or that which they associate [with him]?

60. Is He not the one who has created the heavens and the earth
and sent down for you^p water from the sky,
through which We have caused to grow gardens full of beauty
whose trees you could not grow?
Is there a god in addition to God?
No, they are a people who deviate [from the truth].

61. Is He not the one who made the earth a firm place
and set rivers amid it
and placed on it firm mountains
and placed a partition between the two seas?
Is there a god in addition to God?
No. Most of them have no knowledge.

62. Is He not the one who answers the harassed person
when he calls to Him
and removes evil and makes you viceroys of the earth?
Is there any god in addition to God?
Little are you^p reminded.

63. Is He not the one who guides you^p in the darkness of the land and the sea;
who looses the winds as harbingers of His mercy?
Is there any god in addition to God?
May God be exalted high above what they associate with Him.

64. Is He not the one who originates creation,
then causes it to happen again;
who gives you^p sustenance from the heaven and the earth?
Is there any god in addition to God?
Say, 'Bring your^p proof, if you are truthful.'

65. Say, 'None of those who are in the heavens and the earth
knows the Invisible, except God,
nor do they know when they will be raised.

66. No, their knowledge fails concerning the world to come.
No, they are in doubt about it.
No, they are blind to it.'

67. Those who do not believe say,
'When we and our forefathers have become dust,
shall we be brought forth?

68. We and our forefathers have been promised this before.
These are only the fables of the ancients.'

69. Say, 'Travel in the land

and see how was the end of the sinners.'

70. Do not grieve for them,
and do not be distressed because of their plotting.

71. They say, 'When is this threat [coming],
if you^p speak the truth?'

72. Say, 'Perhaps some of that which you^p seek to hasten is already close behind you.'

73. Your^s Lord is full of bounty for mankind,
but most of them are not grateful.

74. Your^s Lord knows all that your breasts conceal
and all that they make public.

75. There is no hidden thing in heaven or the earth
but it is in a clear record.

76. This Recitation recounts to the Children of Israel
most of that about which they differ.

77. It is truly a guidance and a mercy for the believers.

78. Your^s Lord will decide between them through His judgement.
He is the Mighty, the Knowing.

79. Put^s your trust in God.
You^s stand on the clear truth.

80. You^s cannot make the dead hear,
nor can you make the deaf hear the call
when they turn their backs and move away.

81. You^s cannot guide the blind from their error.
You^s cannot make [anyone] hear
except those who believe in Our signs
and surrender themselves.

82. When the Word falls on them,
We shall bring forth from the earth
a beast that will address them,
'Mankind was not convinced by Our signs.'

83. And [recall] the day when We shall round up
from every community
a troop of those who denied the truth of Our signs,
and they will be urged on;

84. Then when they come, He will say,
'Did you^p deny the truth of My signs,
when you had no comprehension of them?
And what else have you been doing?'

85. And the Word will fall on them for the wrong that they have done,
and they will not speak.

86. Have they not considered that We made the night for them to rest in
and the day to allow them to see?

In that there are signs for a people who believe,

87. On the day when there is a blast on the trumpet
and all those who are in the heavens and on earth are terrified,
save those whom God wishes,
and everyone will come to Him abject,

88. And you^s will see the mountains that you supposed to be firm
passing by like clouds
– the work of God, who has perfected everything.
He is informed of what you^P do.

89. Those who come with a good deed will have better than it:
they will be safe from terror on that day.

90. Those who come with evil will be cast face first into the Fire:
'Are you^P being recompensed but for what you have been doing?'

91. I⁷ have only been commanded to serve the Lord of this territory
who made it sacred.
Everything belongs to Him.
And I have been commanded to be one of those who surrender themselves,

92. And to recite the Recitation.
Those who are guided aright
are guided only for themselves;
and those who stray
– say, 'I am only a warner.'

93. And say, 'Praise belongs to God.
He will show you^P His signs
and you^P will recognize them.
Your^s Lord is not heedless of what you^P do.'

---

⁷ Muḥammad.

Sūra 28

This is normally considered to be a late Meccan *sūra*, with verses 52–55 being ascribed to the Medinan period. Verse 85 is sometimes said to have been revealed during Muḥammad's *hijra* to Medina, but this view seems to arise from the content of the verse. The first part of the *sūra* (1–42) is similar in many ways to the main part of *Sūra* 20, with a brief introduction leading into a complex story, here that of Moses, Pharaoh and Madyan. The next passage (43–56) leads to polemic through an address to Muḥammad, telling him how he has received knowledge of Moses and earlier events through God's mercy. The polemic continues (57–75) until the story of Qārūn, Korah of the Old Testament, is introduced (76–82). The story is rounded off by two verses on the world to come (83–84), and these are followed by a further address to Muḥammad.

The Story

In the name of the Merciful and Compassionate God

1. *Ṭā', Sīn, Mīm.*[1]
2. These are the signs of the Scripture that makes things clear.
3. We shall relate to you[s] some of the story of Moses and Pharaoh in truth,
   for a people who believe.
4. Pharaoh became exalted in the land
   and divided its people into factions,
   seeking to weaken a party among them
   by slaying their sons and sparing their women.
   He was one of those who wreak mischief.
5. We wished to show favour to those who had been treated as weaklings in the land
   and to make them examples
   and to make them the inheritors,
6. And to give them a place in the land,
   and to show Pharaoh and Hāmān[2] and their hosts
   what they feared from them.
7. We inspired the mother of Moses, 'Suckle him,
   but when you fear for him throw him into the sea,
   neither fearing nor grieving.

---

[1] On the mystical letters see the note on 2:1.
[2] Pharaoh's chief minister.

We shall return him to you
and make him one of our messengers.'

8. The family of Pharaoh picked him out [of the sea],
    for him to become an enemy and a sorrow for them.
    Pharaoh and Hāmān and their hosts were sinners.

9. The wife of Pharaoh said,
    'He will be a consolation for me and you.
    Do not kill him.
    Perhaps he will profit us
    or we shall adopt him as a son.'
    They were not aware.

10. Next morning the heart of the mother of Moses [was like a] void.
    She almost revealed [the truth] about him,
    but for the fact that We fortified her heart
    that she might be one of the believers.

11. And she said to his sister, 'Trace him.'
    She³ saw him from afar,
    while they were not aware.

12. Beforehand We had forbidden foster-mothers for him;
    so she said, 'Shall I show youᴾ a household
    who will take charge of him for you
    and will be good counsellors for him?'

13. And We returned him to his mother,
    that she might be comforted and not grieve
    and that she might know that the promise of God is true,
    but most of them do not know.

14. When he reached maturity and perfection,
    We gave him judgement and knowledge.
    Thus We reward those who do good.

15. He entered the city at a time when its people were off their guard;
    and he found two men fighting there,
    one from his own faction and the other from his enemies.
    The one who was from his faction
    sought his help against the one who was from his enemies;
    so Moses struck him and finished him off.
    He said, 'This is of Satan's doing.
    He is an enemy who clearly leads astray.'

16. He said, 'My Lord, I have wronged himself.
    Forgive me.'
    So He forgave him.

---

³ The sister.

He is the Forgiving, the Merciful.

17.   He said, 'My Lord, as You have been kind to me,
I shall never be a partisan of the sinners.'

18.   In the morning he was in the city,
afraid and vigilant;
and there was the man who had sought help from him the day before,
shouting out to him.
Moses said to him, 'You are clearly misguided.'

19.   When he wanted to assault the man who was an enemy to the two of them,
[the man] said, 'O Moses, do you want to kill me
as you killed a soul yesterday?
You only want to be tyrannical in the land.
You do not want to be one of those who put things right.'

20.   Then a man came running from the furthest part of the city.
He said, 'O Moses, the notables are conspiring against you,
to kill you.
Go. I am one of those who give you good advice.'

21.   So he left the city, fearful and vigilant.
He said, 'My Lord, deliver me from the wrong-doing people.'

22.   When he turned towards Madyan,
he said, 'Perhaps my Lord will guide me to the level path.'

23.   When he came to the water of Madyan,
he found a community of people taking water.
He found, apart from them, two women holding back [their animals].
He said, 'What is the matter?'
They said, 'We cannot water [our flocks]
until the shepherds bring [their animals] back [from the water],
for our father is a very old man.'

24.   So he watered [their animals] for them.
Then he turned away into the shade,
and he said, 'My Lord,
I am in need of whatever good You may send down to me.'

25.   One of the two women came to him, walking modestly.
She said, 'My father summons you^{s}
to recompense you with payment for drawing water for us.'
When he came to him and told him the story,
he said, 'Do not fear;
you have escaped from the people who do wrong.'

26.   One of the two of them said, 'O my father, hire him.
The best man you can hire is the one who is strong and trustworthy.'

27.   He said, 'I wish to marry you to one of these two daughters of mine
on condition that you hire yourself to me for eight years.

If you make it a full ten,
that will be of your own accord.
I do not wish press you hard.
If God wishes, you will find me to be one of the righteous.'

28. He said, 'That is [what will be] between you and me.
Whichever of the two terms I fulfil,
it will be no injustice to me.
God is guarantor of what we say.'

29. When Moses had completed the term and departed with his household,
he observed a fire on the side of mountain.
He said to his household, 'Stay [here].
I have seen a fire.
Perhaps I shall bring you news from it or a brand of fire,
so that you may warm yourselves.

30. When he reached it,
he was called to from the right hand bank of the *wadi*
in the blessed spot, from the tree,
'O Moses, I am God, Lord of created beings.

31. Throw down your staff.'
When he saw it quivering
as though it were a demon,
he turned to flee and did not look back;
'O Moses, advance and do not be afraid.
You are one of those who are secure.

32. Put your hand into folds of your clothes
and it will come forth white, without hurt.
And draw back your side from fear.
These are two proofs from your Lord
to Pharaoh and his notables.
They are a profligate folk.'

33. He said, 'My Lord, I killed a soul among them,
and I fear that they will kill me.

34. My brother Aaron is more eloquent than me.
Send him with me as a helper
to confirm that I speak the truth.
I fear that they will say that I lie.'

35. He said, 'We shall strengthen your arm through your brother,
and We shall give to the two of you an authority.
They will not reach the two of you because of Our signs.
You two and those who follow you will be the victors.'

36. When Moses came to them with Our signs as clear proofs,
they said, 'This is merely invented magic.

We never heard of this among our forefathers, the ancients.'

37. Moses said, 'My Lord is well aware of
who has brought guidance from His presence
and who will have the sequel of the abode.
The wrong-doers will not prosper.'

38. Pharaoh said, 'O nobles,
I do not know that you have any god but me.
O Hāmān, light a fire on the clay,
and make for me a high building
so that I may climb up to see the god of Moses.
I think that he is one of the liars.'

39. He and his hosts were haughty in the land without right,
and thought that they would not be returned to Us.

40. And so We seized Him and his hosts
and cast them into the sea.
See how was the end of those who did wrong.

41. We made them leaders who summon [men] to the Fire
and they will not be helped on the Day of Resurrection.

42. We made a curse follow them in this world,
and they will be among the abhorred on the Day of Resurrection.

43. We gave the Scripture to Moses
after We had destroyed the former generations,
clear proof for mankind
and a guidance and a mercy
so that they might be reminded.

44. You⁵ were not on the western side⁴
when We decreed the commandment to Moses
and you were not among those present.

45. But We raised up generations, whose lives were long.
Nor were you⁵ a dweller among the people of Madyan,
reciting Our revelations to them,
but We kept sending messengers.

46. You⁵ were not on the side of the mountain
when We called out,
but [knowledge of it comes] as a mercy from your Lord
that you may warn a people
to whom no warner had come before you
so that they may be reminded.

47. Had it not been the case that a misfortune might befall them
for what their hands have sent forward

---

⁴ Of Mt. Sinai.

and that they might say, 'O our Lord,
why did You not send us a messenger
so that we might have followed Your signs
and be among the believers?'...[5]

48.   But when the truth has come to them from Us,
they have said,
'Why has he not been given
the like of what was given to Moses?'
Yet did they not disbelieve
in what was previously given to Moses?
They say, 'Two pieces of magic that support each other;'
and they say, 'We do not believe in either.'

49.   Say, 'Then bring a Scripture from God
that gives you better guidance than the two of them,
and I shall follow it,
if you are telling the truth.'

50.   And if they do not answer you[s],
know[s] that they are only following their whims.
And who is further astray than him who follows his whim
without guidance from God?
God does not guide the people who are wrong-doers.

51.   We have caused the Word to reach them
so that they may be reminded.

52.   Those to whom We previously gave the Scripture
– they believe in it.

53.   When it is recited to them, they say,
'We believe in it.
It is the truth from our Lord.
We had surrendered before it [came].'

54.   These will be given their reward twice over
because they have been patient
and repel evil by good
and spend from what We have provided for them.

55.   And when they hear idle talk, they turn away from it and say,
'We have our works and you[p] have yours.
Peace be on you[p].
We do not seek the ignorant.'

56.   You[s] do not guide those whom you love,
but God guides those whom He wishes.

---

[5] The verse ends in an incomplete sentence, with verse 48 taking the argument off in a different direction.

He is well aware of those who are guided.

57. They say, 'If we follow the guidance with you^s,
we shall be snatched from our land.'
Have We not established for them a secure sanctuary,
to which the fruits of everything are brought,
a provision from Us?
But most of them do not know.

58. How many settlements have We destroyed
that acted insolently in their way of life!
There are their dwellings
which have not been inhabited after them
except for a little.
We were the inheritors.

59. But your^s Lord did not destroy the settlements
until He sent to their mother[-town]
a messenger who would recite to them Our signs.
And We destroyed the settlements
only when their folk were wrong-doers.

60. Whatever you have been given is a [temporary] enjoyment
and ornament of the life of this world.
What is with God is better and more lasting.
Will you not understand?

61. Are those to whom We have made a fair promise and who receive it
like those to whom We have granted the enjoyment of the life of this world
but who will be among those brought forward on the Day of Resurrection?

62. On the day when He will call to them and say,
'Where are those whom you asserted to be "My associates"?'

63. Those against whom the Word is realized will say,
'Our Lord, these are those whom we led astray.
We led them astray,
just as we had gone astray ourselves.
We declare our innocence to You.
They never served us.'

64. And it will be said, 'Call to your associates',
and they will call to them,
but they will give no answer to them,
and they will see the torment.
If only they had been guided.

65. On the day when He will call to them and say,
'What answer did you give to the messengers?'

66. – On that day the tidings will be obscure for them,
nor will they [be able to] ask each other.

67. As for those who repent and believe and do right,
    they may be among those who prosper.
68. Your Lord creates what He wills and chooses.
    They have no choice.
    Glory be to God.
    May He be exalted above what they associate with Him.
69. And your Lord knows what their breasts conceal and what they make public.
70. And He is God.
    There is no god except Him.
    Praise belongs to Him in the first world and the next.
    His is the judgement,
    and to Him you will be returned.
71. Say, 'Have you considered?
    If God makes night continuous for you until the Day of Resurrection,
    which god other than God will bring you light?
    Will you not hear?'
72. Say, 'Have you considered?
    If God makes the day-time continuous for you until the Day of Resurrection,
    which god other than God will bring you night
    in which you can rest?
    Will you not see?
73. Of His mercy He has made for you night and day
    that you may rest therein
    and that you may seek some of His bounty
    and that you may be thankful.'
74. On the day when He will call to them and say,
    'Where are those whom you asserted to be my associates?'
75. And We shall draw out a witness from every community
    and say, 'Bring your proof.'
    And they will know that the truth belongs to God
    and that what they have been inventing will fail them.
76. Qārūn was of the people of Moses.
    He oppressed them.
    We had given him so much treasure
    that its keys would have weighed down
    a company of men endowed with strength.
    When his people said to him, 'Do not exult.
    God does not love those who exult.
77. But seek the Abode that is to follow,
    among that which God has given you;
    and do not forget your portion in this world.
    Be kind in the way that God has been kind to you.

Do not seek mischief in the land.
God does not love those work mischief.'

78. He said, 'It has been given to me
only because of knowledge that I have.'
Did he not know that God had destroyed
From the generations that were before him
men who had greater strength than him
and had amassed more.
The sinners are not questioned about their sins.

79. He went out to meet his people in his finery.
Those who desired the life of this world said,
'Would that we had the like of what has been given to Qārūn.
He is endowed with great good fortune.'

80. But those who had been given knowledge said,
'Woe upon you.
The reward of God is better
for those who believe and act righteously.
Only the steadfast will attain it.'

81. So We caused the earth to swallow him and his dwellings.
He had no host to help him,
apart from God,
and he was not one of those who could help themselves.

82. Next morning those who had longed to have his place the previous day were saying,
'Woe. God extends provision for those of His servants whom He wishes
or measures it carefully.
If it were not the case that God had been gracious to us,
He would have caused us to be swallowed up.
Woe. The ungrateful will not prosper.'

83. That abode [is] the world to come
– We assign it to those who do not want elevation or mischief in the land.
The outcome is for those who protect themselves.

84. Those who bring good deeds will have better than them;
those who bring evil
– those who do evil deeds
will only be recompensed for what they used to do.

85. He who has laid the Recitation on you^s
will restore you to a place of return.

85a. Say, 'My Lord is well aware who brings guidance
and who is in manifest error.'

86. You^s did not hope that the Scripture would be cast to you,
except as a mercy from your Lord.
So do not be a supporter of the unbelievers.

87. And let them not turn you^s from the signs of God
    after they have been sent down to you.
    Call^s [mankind] to your Lord,
    and do not be one of those who associate [others with God].

88. And do^s not call on another god together with God.
    There is no god except Him.
    Everything will perish except His face.
    To Him belongs the Judgement
    and you will be returned to Him.

Sūra 29

This is normally considered to be a late Meccan *sūra*, though many Muslim scholars add the rider that verses 1–11 are Medinan. However, it seems unlikely that this passage was added *in toto*. It is more probable that it has a Meccan core that was expanded at Medina by the addition of verses 10–13. The *sūra* has a comparatively simple structure: a passage of polemic (2–13); a longish series of punishment stories (14–44); and a passage of instructions to Muḥammad and further polemic (45–69).

The Spider

In the name of the Merciful and Compassionate God

1. *Alif, Lām, Mīm.*[1]
2. Do men think
   that they will be left to say, 'We believe'
   without being tested?
3. We tested those who were before them.
   Truly God knows those who are truthful.
   Truly He knows those who lie.
4. Or do those who do evil deeds think
   that they can outstrip Us?
   Evil is their judgement.
5. Those who hope to meet God
   – God's term is coming.
   He is the Hearer and the Knower.
6. Those who strive,
   strive only for themselves.
   God has no need of created beings.
7. Those who believe and do good works
   – We shall redeem them of their evil deeds
   and We shall recompense them
   with the best of what they have been doing.
8. We have enjoined man to treat his parents well;
   but if the two of them strive to make you[s] associate with Me
   that of which you have no knowledge,
   do not obey them.

---

[1] On the mystical letters see the note on 2:1.

To Me is your^p return,
and I shall tell you^p what you used to do.

9.   Those who believe and do good works,
We shall admit them among the righteous.

10.   Amongst men there are those who say, 'We believe in God',
but if they are hurt for the sake of God,
they take the persecution of men as God's punishment;
but if victory comes from your^s Lord,
they say, 'We were with you^p.'
Is not God well aware of what is in the bosoms of created beings?

11.   Truly God knows those who believe;
and truly He knows the hypocrites.

12.   Those who disbelieve say to those who believe,
'Follow our way, and let us carry your sins.'
They cannot carry any of their sins.
They are indeed liars.

13.   They will surely carry their own burdens
and [other] burdens with their own;
and they will be questioned on the Day of Resurrection
about that which they used to invent.

14.   We sent Noah to his people,
and he tarried amongst them for a thousand years
all but fifty years;
and the flood engulfed them,
for they were wrong-doers.

15.   We rescued him and those [with him in] the ship,
which We made a sign for created beings.

16.   And [We sent] Abraham:
when he said to his people,
'Serve God and fear Him.
That is better for you if you did but know.

17.   You serve only idols,
to the exclusion of God,
and you create a lie.
Those whom you serve
to the exclusion of God
have no sustenance for you.
So seek provision with God
and serve Him and be grateful to Him.
To Him you will be returned.

18.   But if you deny the truth,
communities have denied before you.

It is only for the messenger to convey the message clearly.'

19.   Have they not seen how God originates creation
and then brings it back again.
That is easy for God.

20.   Say, 'Journey[p] in the land and see how He originated creation.
Then God will cause the later growth to grow.
God has power over everything.

21.   He punishes those whom He wishes
and He has mercy on those whom he wishes.
To Him you[p] will be turned.

22.   You cannot frustrate [Him] on earth or in heaven;
nor have you any protector or helper apart from Him.'

23.   Those who disbelieve in God's signs and in the meeting with Him
– those have despaired of My mercy;
those will have a painful torment.

24.   The only answer of his folk was to say,
'Kill him or burn him.'
Then God delivered him from the Fire.
In that there are signs for people who believe.

25.   He said, 'You have chosen idols
to the exclusion of God
only because of the affection between you in the life of this world.
Then on the Day of Resurrection
you will deny one another and curse one another.
Your abode will be the Fire,
and you will have no helpers.

26.   And Lot believed him, and said,
'I am going to migrate to my Lord.
He is the Mighty and the Wise.'

27.   And We gave him Isaac and Jacob
and placed prophecy and the Scripture among his progeny.
We gave him his reward in this world,
and he will be among the righteous in the world to come.

28.   And [recall] Lot: when he said to his people,
'You commit indecency
such as no created being has ever done before.

29.   Do you really approach men
and bar the way and commit what is disreputable in your assembly?'
The only answer of his folk was to say,
'Bring God's torment to us, if you are telling the truth.'

30.   He said, 'My Lord, help me against the people who wreak mischief.'

31.   When Our messengers brought Abraham the good news,

they said, 'We are going to destroy the people of this settlement.
Its people have been wrong-doers.'

32. He said, 'Lot is in [the settlement].'
They said, 'We are well aware of who is there.
We shall save him and his family,
except for his wife,
who will be one of those who tarry.'

33. When Our messengers came to Lot,
he was troubled about them[2]
for he had no power to protect them;[2]
but they said, 'Do not fear or grieve.
We shall rescue you and your family,
except for your wife,
who will be one of those who tarry.

34. We are going to bring down
on the people of this settlement abomination from heaven
because they have been profligates.'

35. We have left a clear sign of that for a people who understand.

36. To Madyan [We sent] their brother Shuʿayb.
He said, 'My people, serve God
and look for the Last Day
and do not make mischief in the land, causing corruption.'

37. But they declared him a liar,
and so the earthquake took them
and in the morning they were prostrate in their dwelling.

38. And [recall] ʿĀd and Thamūd,
for it is clear to you from their dwelling-places.
Satan made their deeds seem fair to them,
and turned them from the way,
though they thought they saw clearly

39. – And Qārūn and Pharaoh and Hāmān.[3]
Moses brought them clear proofs,
but they were haughty in the land.
Yet they did not outstrip [Us].

40. We took each one for his sin.
Among them were those on whom We sent a sandstorm,
and among them were those who were taken by the shout,
and among them were those whom We caused the earth to swallow
and among them were those whom We drowned.

---

[2] *i.e.* the messengers.
[3] See 28:76 *ff.*

God would not wrong them,
but they wronged themselves.

41. Those who take for themselves patrons
to the exclusion of God
are like the spider that takes for itself a house.
The frailest of [all] houses is that of the spider,
if they did but know.

42. God knows what they call on to the exclusion of Him.
He is the Mighty and the Wise.

43. These comparisons are coined by Us for mankind,
but only those with knowledge will understand them.

44. God created the heavens and the earth in truth.
In that there is a sign for the believers.

45. Recite^s what has been revealed to you of the Scripture and perform prayer.
Prayer prohibits indecency and what is disreputable.
Remembrance of God is greater,
and God knows what you do.

46. Do not dispute with the people of the Scripture
except with what is better,
unless [it is] with those of them that have done wrong.

46a. Say^p, 'We believe in that which has been revealed to us
and what has been revealed to you.
Our God and your God are one.
We surrender to Him.'

47. Thus We have sent down the Scripture to you^s.
Those to whom We have given the Scripture believe in it;
and among those people[4] are some who believe in it.
Only the unbelievers deny Our signs.

48. You did not recite any Scripture before this
nor did you write it with your right hand.
In that case those who follow falsehood would have doubted.

49. No. It[5] is clear signs in the breasts of those who have been given knowledge.
Only the wrong-doers deny Our revelations.

50. They say, 'Why have signs not been sent down to him from his Lord?'
Say, 'The signs are only with God.
I am simply a clear warner.'

51. Is it not sufficient for them
that We have sent down to you^s
the Scripture to be recited to them.

---

[4] *i.e.* the Meccans.
[5] *i.e.* the Recitation.

In that there is a mercy and a reminder to a people who believe.

52. Say, 'God is sufficient witness between you and me.
He knows what is in the heavens and the earth;
and those who believe in vanity and do not believe in God
– they are the losers.'

53. They ask you to hasten the torment.
But for a stated term,
the torment would have come to them.
It will indeed come upon them suddenly,
when they are not aware.

54. They ask you^s to hasten the torment.
Jahannam will encompass the unbelievers,

55. On the day when the torment will cover them
from above them and from below their feet,
and He will say, 'Taste what you used to do.'

56. O my servants who believe, My land is wide.
Serve Me alone.

57. Every soul will taste death.
Then you will be returned to Us.

58. Those who believe and do righteous deeds
– We shall lodge them in lofty rooms in the garden,
through which rivers flow.
They will remain there for ever.
Excellent is the reward of those who labour,

59. Who are patient and put their trust in their Lord.

60. How many a beast is there that does not bear its own provision;
but God provides sustenance for it and for you^p.
He is the Hearer and the Knower.

61. If you^s ask them, 'Who created the heavens and the earth
and subjected the sun and the moon?'
they say, 'God.'
How then are they involved in lies?

62. God makes generous provision for those of His servants whom He wishes
or measures carefully for them.
God is aware of everything.

63. If you^s ask them, 'Who has sent water down from the sky
and revived with it the earth after it had died off?'
they will say, 'God'.
Say, 'Praise belongs to God.'
Yet most of them do not understand.

64. The life of this world is merely a game and a pastime.
The home that is to come

– that is Life, did they but know it.

65.   When they embark in ships, they call on God,
     being sincere to Him in their belief;
     but when He brings them safely to land,
     they associate [others] with Him,

66.   Let them be ungrateful for what We have given them
     and let them enjoy themselves.
     But they will [come to] know.

67.   Have they not seen that We have made a secure sanctuary,
     while all around them the people are being snatched away?
     Do they believe in vanity
     and do they not believe in the blessing of God?

68.   Who does greater wrong
     than those who invent lies against God
     or deny the truth when it has come to them?
     Is there not a lodging for the unbelievers in Jahannam?

69.   Those who strive for Our sake
     – We shall indeed guide them to Our ways.
     God is with those who do good.

Sūra 30

This *sūra* is generally considered to be late Meccan, though some Muslim sources think that verse 17 is Medinan. On the other hand, some western scholars would date verses 1–4 as quite late, though their arguments are not convincing. However, some recasting at Medina seems quite likely. The *sūra* falls into five sections: the unusual opening passage on the Greeks (Byzantines), who are not mentioned elsewhere in the Qur'ān (1–4a); a polemical passage (4b–18); a piece on 'signs' (19–29); two parallel exhortations (30–42 and 43–51) and a peroration addressed both to Muḥammad and to the people (52–60).

The Greeks

In the name of the Merciful and Compassionate God

1. *Alif, Lām, Mīm.*[1]
2. The Greeks have been defeated
3. In the nearest part of the land;
   but after their being vanquished
   they will be victorious,
4. In a few years;
   the matter belongs to God before and after
   – and on that day the believers will rejoice
5. In God's help.
   He helps those whom He wishes.
   He is the Mighty and the Merciful.
6. The promise of God
   – God does not break His promise, but most men do not know.
7. They know an outward appearance of the life of this world,
   and they are heedless of the world to come.
8. Have they not reflected about themselves?
   God did not create the heavens and the earth and what is between them,
   save with the truth and a stated term.
   Yet most men do not believe in [their] meeting with the Lord.
9. Have they not travelled in the land and seen
   how was the end of those before them?
   They were stronger than themselves

---

[1] On the mystical letters see the note on 2:1.

and they tilled the earth and cultivated it
more than they have cultivated it.
Their messengers came to them with the clear proofs.
God would not wrong them,
but they used to wrong themselves.

10. Evil was the end of those who did evil,
because they denied the truth of God's signs and mocked them.

11. God originates creation, then causes it to return.
Then you will be returned to Him.

12. On the day when the Hour comes,
the sinners will be in despair.

13. They will have no intercessors amongst those they associate with God
and they will not believe in them.

14. On the day when the Hour comes,
on that day they will be separated.

15. As for those who have believed and done righteous deeds,
they will be made happy in a meadow.

16. As for those who have disbelieved
and denied the truth of Our signs and the meeting of the Hereafter,
those will be brought into the torment.

17. Glory be to God in your^p evening times and your morning times;

18. To Him belongs the praise in the heavens and on earth
– and when the sun goes down and at your noon times.

19. He brings forth the living from the dead;
and he brings forth the dead from the living.
He revives the earth after it has died off.
In that way you^p will be brought forth.

20. And of His signs is that He has created you from dust.
Then, behold, you are mortals spreading abroad.

21. And of His signs is that He has created, from yourselves,
spouses that you may dwell with them,
and He has put love and mercy amongst you.
In that there are signs for a people who reflect.

22. And of His signs is the creation of the heavens and the earth
and the variety of your tongues and colours.
In that there are signs for those who know.

23. And of His signs is your slumbering by night and day
and your seeking some of His bounty.
In that there are signs for a people who hear.

24. And of His signs He shows you lightning,
for fear and for hope,
and sends down water from the sky

371

and revives the earth with it
after it has died off.
In that there are signs for a people who understand.

25. And of His signs is that heaven and earth stand firm by His command;
then when He summons you[p] from the earth,
behold you will come forth.

26. To Him belong all those who are in the heavens and the earth.
All are obedient to Him.

27. It is He who originates creation,
then causes it to return
– it is very easy for Him.
His is the highest likeness in the heaven and the earth.
He is the Mighty and the Wise.

28. He has coined a parallel from [among] yourselves:
do you have,
from among those whom your right hands possess,
any associates in what We have provided for you
so that you are equal in it
and you fear them as you fear each other?
Thus We make distinct the signs for a people who understand.

29. No. Those who do wrong follow their whims without any knowledge.
Who can guide those whom God has led astray?
They have no helpers.

30. Set[s] your face towards the religion as a man of pure faith,
God's original creation,
upon which He created mankind.
There is no changing God's creation.
That is the right religion,
but most people do not know

31. – turning to Him in penitence.
Fear[p] Him and perform prayer
and do not be among those who associate others with God,

32. Among those who have divided up their religion and become parties,
each party rejoicing in what they have.

33. When harm touches the people they invoke their Lord,
turning to Him in penitence.
Then when He gives them a taste of His mercy,
lo, a party of them associate others with their Lord,

34. To be ungrateful for what We have given them.
[They will be told,] 'Enjoy yourselves:
you will come to know.'

35. Or have We sent down on them any authority,

and does it speak of that with which they have been associating Him?

36. When We give the people a taste of mercy, they rejoice in it;
    but if a piece of evil befalls them
    because of what their hands have sent forward,
    lo, they despair.

37. Have they not seen that God makes generous provision for those whom He wishes
    and measures closely [for those whom He wishes].
    In that there are signs for a people who believe.

38. Give the kinsman his due,
    and the destitute and the traveller.
    That is better for those who seek God's face
    – those are the ones who will prosper.

39. What you^p give in usury² that it may give increase among the wealth of the people
    will have no increase with God;
    but what you give as alms, seeking God's face
    – those are the ones who receive increase many times over.

40. [It is] God who has created you^p and then given you sustenance.
    Then He will cause you to die;
    then He will give you life.
    Is there any of those you associate with God who can do any of that?
    Glory be to him.
    May He be exalted far above that which they associate with Him.

41. Corruption has appeared in the land and in the sea
    because of what the hands of the people have gained,
    that He may make them taste some part of what they have done,
    so that they may return.

42. Say, 'Travel in the land
    and see how was the end of those who were before.
    Most of them associated [others] with God.'

43. Set your^s face towards the true religion
    before a day which cannot be averted comes from God.
    On that day they will be sundered.

44. Those who are ungrateful bear the consequences of their ingratitude;
    whilst those who act righteously make provision for themselves,

45. That He may reward from His bounty
    those who believe and do righteous deeds.
    He does not love the ungrateful.

46. And of His signs is that He sends the winds as bearers of good tidings
    and to give you a taste of His mercy,
    and that ships may run at His command,

---

² This appears to be the earliest verse to refer to usury. See, in particular, 2:275 *ff.*

and that you may seek some of His bounty,
and that you may be grateful.

47. Before you[s] We sent messengers to their people.
They brought the clear proofs to them;
and We took revenge on those who sinned.
It was a duty to Us to help the believers.

48. [It is] God who sends the winds;
and they stir up clouds;
and He spreads them in the sky as He wishes
and breaks them into pieces.
Then you[s] see the rain coming from within them.
When He makes it fall on those of His servants that He wishes,
lo, they rejoice,

49. Though before that they were in despair
– before it was sent down on them.

50. So look at the marks of God's mercy:
how he revives the earth after it has died off.
He is truly the quickener of the dead.
He is able to do all things.

51. If We send a wind and they see it[3] growing yellow,
they remain ungrateful after that.

52. You[s] cannot make the dead hear,
nor can you make the deaf hear the call
when they turn their backs and avert themselves.

53. Nor can you[s] lead the blind from their error.
The only ones you[s] can make hear
are those who believe in Our signs,
for they surrender themselves.

54. [It is] God who has created you[p] out of weakness;
then He has appointed strength after weakness;
then after strength He has appointed weakness and grey hair.
He creates what He wishes.
He is the Knowing and the Mighty.

55. And on the day when the Hour rises
the sinners will swear that they tarried only an hour.
Thus are they involved in lies.

56. But those who have been given knowledge and faith say,
'You[p] have tarried in God's record until the Day of the Raising.
This is the Day of the Raising;
but you have had no knowledge.'

---

[3] The vegetation produced by the rain.

57. On that day those who have done wrong will not profit from their excuses,
nor will they be allowed to make amends.
58. In this Recitation We have coined for mankind every kind of parallel;
and if you^p bring them a sign
those who are ungrateful say,
'You are simply workers of vanity.'
59. Thus God sets a seal on the hearts of those who do not know.
60. So have patience.
God's promise is true.
[Do] not let those who have no certainty make you^s unsteady.

Sūra 31

The *sūra* is generally considered to be late Meccan, though some Muslim commentators hold the view that verses 26–28 are Medinan. This is not impossible, and may point to a stage in the evolution of the *sūra*. The *sūra* divides into five sections: the 'signs' and those who accept them (1–5); polemic and 'sign' material (6–11); Luqmān's address to his son (12–19); further polemic and 'sign' material (20–32); peroration.

Luqmān

In the name of the Merciful and Compassionate God

1. *Alif, Lām, Mīm.*[1]
2. These are the signs of the wise Scripture,
3. As a guidance and a mercy for those who do good,
4. Who perform prayer and pay the *zakāt*
   and are sure about the world to come.
5. These have guidance from their Lord;
   these are the ones who prosper.
6. Among the people are those who buy diverting tales
   to lead [people] away from the path of God without any knowledge
   and to take it in mockery.
   Those will have a humiliating punishment.
7. When Our signs are recited to them,
   they turn away in pride
   as though they had not heard
   – as if there were heaviness in their ears.
   Give them good tidings of a painful punishment.
8. Those who believe and do righteous deeds
   will have the gardens of bliss,
9. In which they will stay for ever,
   God's promise in truth.
   He is the Mighty and the Wise.
10. He has created the heavens without supporting pillars that you[p] can see;
    and He has cast firm mountains on to the earth
    so that it does not shake with you[p];

---

[1] On the mystical letters see the note on 2:1.

and He has spread abroad in it some of every [species of] beast;
and We have sent down water from the sky
and caused to grow in [the earth] some of every generous kind [of plant].

11. This is God's creation;
so show me what has been created by those apart from Him.
No. The wrong-doers are in clear error.

12. We gave Luqmān wisdom, saying, 'Give thanks to God.
Those who give thanks
do so only for the good of their own souls.'
Those who are ungrateful
– God is All-sufficient and Laudable.

13. And [recall] when Luqmān said to his son,
admonishing him,
'O my son, do not associate any partner with God.
Associating partners with God is a grievous wrong.'

14. We have charged man concerning his parents
– his mother bore him in weakness upon weakness,
and his weaning was in two years
– saying, 'Show thanks to Me and to your parents.
The journeying is to Me.'

15. But if the two of them strive with you
to make you associate with Me
that about which you have no knowledge,
do not obey them.
Keep them kindly company in this world,
but follow the way of those who turn to Me.
Then your return will be to Me,
and I shall tell you what you used to do.'

16. 'O my son, if it is the weight of a grain of mustard
and if it is in rock
or in the heavens or on earth,
God will bring it forth.
God is Kind and Informed.

17. O my son, perform prayer,
enjoin what is reputable
and forbid what is disreputable,
and endure patiently what befalls you.
That comes from determination in affairs.

18. Do not turn your cheek from men in disdain,
and do not walk in the land in exultation.
God does not love anyone who is conceited and boastful.

19. Be modest in your walk and keep your voice low.

The most disagreeable voice is that of the ass.'

20. Have you^p not seen that God has subjected to you
all that is in the heavens and on earth,
and has lavished on you His blessings,
outward and inward?
But there are among men those who dispute about God
without knowledge or guidance or a Scripture that gives light.

21. If they are told,
'Follow that which God has sent down',
they say, 'No. We follow that which we found our forefathers doing.'
Would [that be so] if Satan were calling them
to the torment of the blaze?

22. Whoever surrenders his face to God and does good
has grasped the firmest handle.
With God is the outcome of affairs.

23. Those who disbelieve
– let not their unbelief sadden you^s.
Their return is to Us;
and We shall tell them what they did.
God is aware of [the thoughts in men's] breasts.

24. We give them a little comfort,
then We compel them to a rough torment.

25. If you^s ask them, 'Who created the heavens and the earth?'
they will say, 'God'.
Say, 'Praise belongs to God.'
But most of them do not know.

26. All that is in the heavens and on earth belongs to God.
God is the All-sufficient and Laudable.

27. If all the trees on earth were pens and the sea [ink],
with seven seas after it to replenish it,
the words of God would not be used up.
God is Mighty and Wise.

28. The creation and raising of you all is only like that of single soul.
God is Hearing and Observing.

29. Have you^s not seen that God merges the night with the day
and the day with the night
and subjects the sun and the moon,
each running to a stated term,
and that God is informed of what you do?

30. That is because God is the Truth
and what they invoke apart from Him is the False
and that God is the Exalted and the Great.

31. Have you^s not seen that the ships run on the sea through the blessing of God

   that He may show you some of his signs?

   In that there are signs

   for everyone who is steadfast and grateful.

32. When waves cover them like shadows,

   they call on God,

   devoting their religion solely to Him.

   But when He brings them safely to land,

   there are some of them who are lukewarm.

   Our signs are denied only by those who are treacherous and ungrateful.

33. O man, fear your Lord,

   and be afraid of a day when no father will give satisfaction for his child

   and no child will give satisfaction for his father in anything.

   God's promise is true.

   So do not be deluded by the life of this world

   and do not be deluded by the Deluder concerning God.

34. God – He has knowledge of the Hour;

   He sends down the rain;

   He knows what is in the wombs.

   No soul knows what it will earn tomorrow,

   and no soul knows in what land it will die.

   But God is Knowing and Informed.

Sūra 32

The *sūra* is generally held to be late Meccan. However, many Muslim authorities think that verses 16–20, or at least 18–20, are Medinan, though the reasons for their view are not cogent. Verses 1–3 form a brief introduction, which is followed by a 'sign' passage (4–9). Verses 10–28 form a piece of polemic, recast, it would appear, from shorter pieces, Muḥammad being addressed in 11, 23 and 25. He is also addressed in the little peroration (29–30).

Prostration

In the name of the Merciful and Compassionate God

1. *Alif, Lām, Mīm.*[1]
2. The sending down of the Scripture,
   in which there is no doubt,
   from the Lord of created beings.
3. Or do they say, 'He has invented it.'
   No. It is the truth from your[s] Lord,
   that you[s] may warn a people
   to whom no warner has come before you[s],
   so that they may be guided aright.
4. [It is] God who created the heavens and the earth
   and what is between them in six days.
   Then He mounted the Throne.
   You[p] have no protector or intercessor
   apart from Him.
   Will you[p] not be reminded?
5. He directs the affair from heaven to earth;
   then it goes up to Him in a day,
   the measure of which is a thousand years of your[p] counting.
6. That is the Knower of the Invisible and the Witnessed,
   the Mighty, the Merciful,
7. Who has made well everything that He has created.
   He began the creation of man from clay;
8. Then He made his seed from an extract of base fluid;
9. Then He fashioned him and breathed some of His spirit into him;

---

[1] On the mystical letters see the note on 2:1.

and He made for you^P hearing and sight and hearts.
How little gratitude you^P show!

10. And they say, 'When we have become lost in the earth,
shall we be in a new creation?'
No. They do not believe in the meeting with their Lord.

11. Say^s, 'The angel of death, who has been given charge of you^P,
will gather you, and then you will be returned to your Lord.'

12. If only you^s could see when the sinners hang their heads before their Lord
[and say], 'Our Lord, We have seen and heard;
so return us and we shall act righteously.
We are convinced.'

13. Had We wished, We could have given every soul its guidance;
but the declaration from Me is [to be] realized:
'I shall fill Jahannam with *Jinn* and men altogether.

14. So taste^P!
Because you^P have forgotten the meeting of this day of yours,
We have forgotten you.
Taste the torment of eternity in recompense for what you used to do.'

15. Our signs are believed in only by those who,
when they are reminded of them,
fall down in prostration
and glorify their Lord with praise
and are not haughty;

16. Their sides draw away from their couches
as they call out to their Lord in fear and desire,
and they spend from that which We have provided for them.

17. No soul knows what comfort is hidden away for them
as a reward for what they have been doing.

18. Are those who are believers like those who are profligates?
[No.] They are not equal.

19. As for those who believe and do righteous deeds
they will have the gardens of the refuge,
as hospitality for what they used to do.

20. As for those who are profligates,
their refuge will be the Fire.
Whenever they desire to leave it
they will be returned into it,
and they will be told,
'Taste the torment of the fire which you used to deny.'

21. We shall indeed let them taste the least torment before the greatest,
so that they may return.

22. Who does greater wrong

than those who are reminded of the signs of their Lord
but then turn away from them?
We shall take vengeance on the sinners.

23. We gave Moses the Scripture –
Do[s] not be in doubt concerning the meeting with Him –
and We made it a guidance for the Children of Israel.

24. And We appointed leaders from amongst them,
guiding by Our command,
when they were patient and were certain about Our signs.

25. Your[s] Lord will distinguish between them on the Day of Resurrection
concerning that about which they used to differ.

26. Have they not been guided by how many generations We have destroyed before
them,
among whose dwelling places they walk?
In that there are signs.
Will they not hear?

27. Have they not seen that We drive water to the land that has no vegetation
and bring forth crops through it,
from which both they and their livestock eat?
Will they not see?

28. And they say, 'When will this victory [occur],
if you[p] are telling the truth?'

29. Say[s], 'On the day of victory
those who do not believe will find no profit in their faith,
nor will they have a respite.'

30. So turn[s] away from them and wait.
They are [also] waiting.

Sūra 33

This is a Medinan *sūra*. From the events that it refers to (the Siege of Medina, the despatching of the Banū Qurayẓa, Muḥammad's marriage to Zaynab bint Jaḥsh), most of it dates from the latter part of 627 AD, though perhaps some verses (e.g. 41–44) may be the reworking of earlier material. As with most Medinan *sūra*s, the relationship of the various thematic passages is complex, with internal cross-references and bridging pieces helping to provide linkage. After a brief introduction addressed to Muḥammad (1–3), there is an important piece that stresses the importance of blood relationships and abolishes adoptive and similar rights (4–6). A bridge passage (7–8) then leads into a lengthy piece on the siege of Medina and the affair of the Banū Qurayẓa (9–27). There is then an abrupt transition to a series of pieces (28–34, 37–40, 50–59) devoted to the regulation of behaviour within the Muslim community and in particular to Muḥammad's wives. At two natural breaks more general passages have been added (35–36, then 41–44 plus 45–48 and a bridging verse 49). Verses 60–73 form a peroration that is built up by some reference back to earlier parts of the *sūra* but even more by the use of typical polemical themes. The name of the *sūra* comes from *al-aḥzāb* 'the parties', the term used to describe the joint force of Meccans and *bedu* who laid siege to Medina.

The Parties

In the name of the Merciful and Compassionate God

1. O prophet, fear God
    and do not obey the unbelievers and the hypocrites.
    God is Knowing and Wise.
2. And follow what is revealed to you[p] from your Lord.
    God is informed of what you do,
3. And put[s] your trust in God.
    God is sufficient as a trustee.
4. God has not put two hearts inside any man,
    nor has He made your wives
    whom you declare to be as your mothers' backs[1]
    your [real] mothers;
    nor has He made your adopted sons your [real] sons.
    That is what you say with your mouths,
    but God speaks the truth
    and guides to the [right] way.

---

[1] A traditional pre-Islamic divorce formula.

5.   Call[P] them after their fathers.
That is fairer with God.
If you do not know their fathers,
they are your brothers in religion and your clients.
There is no sin for you in any mistakes you have made
but there is in what your hearts have intended.
God is Forgiving and Compassionate.

6.   The prophet is closer to the believers than they are themselves,
and his wives are their mothers;
but blood relations are nearer to one another in God's decree
than the believers and the emigrants,
though you should act in a way recognized as proper towards your friends.
That is written in the decree.

7.   [Recall] when We took a covenant from the prophets
– from you and from Noah and Abraham
and Moses and Jesus, the son of Mary.
We took a binding covenant from them,

8.   That He might ask the truthful about their truthfulness.
And He has prepared a painful torment for the unbelievers.

9.   O you who believe, remember God's blessing to you
when hosts came [against] you,
and We sent against them a wind
and hosts that you[P] did not see,
though God is observer of what you do.

10.   When they came [against] you from above you and from below you,
and when [your] eyes swerved and [your] hearts reached [your] throats,
and you were supposing things about God,

11.   There the believers were tried and shaken greatly;

12.   And when the hypocrites and those in whose hearts is sickness were saying,
'God and His messenger have promised us nothing but illusion.'

13.   And when a party of them said,
'O people of Yathrib, there is no place for you to stand;
so return.'
And a group of them sought permission to leave from the prophet, saying,
'Our houses are exposed,'
though they were not exposed.
They merely wished to flee.

14.   If an entry had been made against them through the area of those houses
and they had been asked to [join in] the mischief,
they would have done so,
and they would have hesitated only a little about it.

15.   Yet previously they had made a covenant with God

that they would not turn their backs.
Fulfilment will be asked of covenants with God.

16. Say, 'Flight will not benefit you,
   if you flee from death and killing.
   In that case you will only be given little enjoyment.'

17. Say, 'Who is the one who can preserve you from God,
   if He wishes evil on you or wishes mercy on you.
   They will not find that they have any protector or helper
   apart from God.'

18. God is well aware of those of you who cause hindrance
   and those who say to their brothers, 'Come to us',
   and who come to the fray but little,

19. Being niggardly towards you^P.
   When fear comes,
   You^s see them looking at you with rolling eyes
   like the one who faints from death;
   and when fear goes, they flay you with sharp tongues,
   being niggardly of good things.
   Those have not believed
   and God makes their deeds fail.
   That is easy for God.

20. They reckon that the parties have not gone away.
   If the parties come [again],
   they would wish they were nomads among the *bedu*,
   asking for news of you^P;^2
   and if they were among you,
   they would fight only a little.

21. In the messenger of God you^P have a good example
   for those who hope for God and the Last Day
   and remember God often.

22. When the believers saw the parties, they said,
   'This is what God and His messenger promised us.
   God and His messenger have told the truth.'
   And it increased them only in faith and surrender.

23. Among the believers there are some men who have been true to the covenant
   they made with God.
   There are some of them who have fulfilled their vow [by death];
   and there are some of them who are still waiting,
   not having altered at all,

24. That God may recompense those who have been true for their truth

---

^2 From the safety of the desert.

and punish the hypocrites if He wishes,
or may relent towards them.
For God is Forgiving and Compassionate.

25. God drove those who have disbelieved back in their rage.
    They gained no good.
    God averted fighting from the believers.
    God is strong and Mighty.

26. He brought those of the people of the Scripture who backed them[3]
    down from their strongholds,
    and cast terror into their hearts.
    Some you have killed;
    some you have taken prisoner.

27. And He caused you to inherit their land and their dwellings
    and their possessions and a land you have not trodden.
    God has power over everything.

28. O prophet, say to your wives,
    'If you want the life of this world and its ornament, come.
    I shall make provision for you and release you fairly.

29. But if you want God and His messenger and the World to Come,
    God has prepared a great wage for those of you who do good.'

30. O wives of the prophet,
    whoever of you acts with clear impropriety,
    the punishment for her will be doubled.
    That is easy for God.

31. Whoever of you submits to God and His messenger and acts righteously
    – We shall give her
    her wage twice over.
    We have prepared for her a generous provision.

32. O wives of the prophet,
    you are not like any other women.
    If you fear God,
    do not be submissive in your speech,
    lest someone in whose heart is sickness be filled with desire,
    but speak in a way that is recognized as proper;

33. And stay in your apartments.
    Do not adorn yourselves with the adornment of the age of ignorance of old.
    Perform prayer and pay the *zakāt*
    and obey God and His messenger.
    God wants to remove abomination from you,
    O people of the household,

---

[3] Understood to be the Banū Qurayẓa.

and to cleanse you.

34. Remember those of the signs of God and of wisdom
that are recited to you in your apartments.
God is Gentle and Informed.

35. The men and women who surrender,
the men and women who believe,
the men and women who are obedient,
the men and women who are truthful,
the men and women who endure,
the men and women who are humble,
the men and women who give alms,
the men and women who fast,
the men and women who guard their private parts,
the men and women who remember God often
– for them God has prepared forgiveness and a great wage.

36. When God and His messenger have decided a matter,
it is not for any believing man or woman to have any choice in the affair.
Whoever disobeys God and His messenger
has gone astray in manifest error.

37. [Recall] when you⁵ said to the one on whom God and you yourself have
bestowed favour,[4]
'Keep your wife to yourself and fear God',
and you hid within yourself what God would reveal,
and you feared the people
when God had better right to be feared by you.
When Zayd had finished with her,
We gave her to you in marriage,
so that there should be no difficulty for the believers
concerning the wives of their adopted sons,
when they have finished with them.
God's command was fulfilled.

38. There is no difficulty for the prophet in that which God has ordained for him:
God's practice concerning those who passed away previously
– God's command is a fixed decree –

39. Who conveyed God's messages and feared Him and no one else apart from God.
God is sufficient as a reckoner.

40. Muḥammad is not the father of any of your men,
but the messenger of God and the seal of the prophets.
God is aware of everything.

41. O you who believe, remember God often,

---

[4] Zayd ibn Ḥāritha, Muḥammad's adopted son.

42. And glorify Him morning and evening.
43. It is He who blesses you, [as do] His angels,
    to bring you out of the darkness into the light.
    He is Merciful to the believers.
44. Their greeting on the day they meet Him will be, 'Peace'.
    He has prepared for them a generous wage.
45. O prophet, We have sent you as a witness
    and a bringer of good tidings and a warner,
46. And as a summoner to God,
    by His permission,
    and as an illuminating lamp.
47. And give^s the believers the good tidings
    that they will have a great bounty from God.
48. Do not obey the unbelievers and the hypocrites.
    Ignore their vexation and put your trust in God.
    God is sufficient as trustee.
49. O you who believe, If you marry believing women
    and divorce them before you touch them
    you have no period to count against them.
    Make provision for them and release them fairly.
50. O prophet, We have made lawful for you
    your wives to whom you have given their wages,
    and those possessed by your right hand from what God has given you as booty,
    the daughters of your paternal uncles and aunts,
    the daughters of your maternal uncles and aunts,
    who have migrated with you,
    and any believing woman if she gives herself to the prophet,
    (and the prophet wishes to take her in marriage)
    devoting herself solely to you^s,
    to the exclusion of the believers
    – We know what we have ordained for them
    concerning their wives and those whom your right hands possess
    – that there may be no difficulty for you.
    God is Forgiving and Compassionate.
51. You^s may put off those of them whom you wish
    and take to you those you wish;
    and [you may take again] those that you desire of the ones you have set aside
    – it is no sin for you.
    That is more appropriate as a way for them to be comforted
    and not to grieve
    and for all of them to be content with what you give them.
    God knows what is in your hearts.

God is Knowing and Prudent.

52. Henceforth other women are not lawful for you[s],
    nor are you to take other wives in exchange,
    even though their beauty wins your admiration,
    except for those possessed by your right hand.
    God is Watcher over everything.

53. O you who believe,
    do not enter the apartments of the prophet
    unless invited for a meal
    without waiting for the proper time.
    When you are invited, enter;
    and when you have fed, disperse,
    without lingering for conversation.
    That would vex the prophet,
    but he is ashamed to [ask] you [to leave];
    but God is not ashamed of the truth.

53a. When you[p] ask them[5] for anything,
    ask them from behind a curtain.
    That is purer for your hearts and for theirs.
    It is not for you to vex God's messenger,
    nor to marry his wives after him, ever.
    That is important with God.

54. Whether you reveal something or keep it hidden,
    God is Aware of everything.

55. There is no sin for them
    concerning their fathers, their sons,
    their brothers, the sons of their brothers,
    the sons of their sisters or their women
    or those possessed by their right hands.
    [O wives,] fear God.
    God is witness of everything.

56. God and His angels bless the prophet.
    O you who believe, bless him and salute him.

57. Those who vex God and His messenger
    – God has cursed them in this world and the next,
    and has prepared for them a humiliating torment.

58. Those who vex believing men and women
    without them having earned [that]
    have laid upon themselves slander and manifest sin.

59. O prophet, tell your wives and daughters and women-folk of the believers

---

[5] The wives of Muḥammad.

to draw their robes close to them.
That is more appropriate as a way for them to be recognized and not vexed.
God is Forgiving and Compassionate.

60. If the hypocrites and those in whose hearts is sickness
and the alarmists in the city do not desist,
We shall urge you[s] against them.
Then they will be your neighbours there only for a little while,

61. Accursed, and they will be seized wherever they are found
and will be slaughtered

62. – God's practice among those who passed away previously.
You[s] will not find any change in God's practice.

63. The people ask you[s] about the Hour.
Say, 'Knowledge of it is only with God.
What will give you knowledge?
Perhaps the Hour is nigh.'

64. God has cursed the unbelievers and prepared a Blaze for them.

65. They will remain in it for ever;
and they will find no protector or helper.

66. On the day when their faces are turned over in the Fire,
they will say, 'Would that we had obeyed God
and obeyed His messenger!'

67. And they will say, 'Our Lord,
we obeyed chiefs and our great men,
and they led us astray from the way.

68. Our Lord, give them double torment and curse them with a great curse.'

69. O you who believe,
do not be like those who vexed Moses,
and then God declared him innocent of what they said,
and he was eminent with God.

70. O you who believe,
fear God and speak straight speech,

71. And He will set right your deeds for you
and forgive you your sins.
Those who obey God and His messenger gain a great triumph.

72. We offered the trust to the heavens and the earth and the mountains,
but they refused to carry it and were afraid of it.
And man carried it,
and he has become a great wrong-doer and very foolish.

73. [This is] so that God may punish the men and women of hypocrisy
and the men and women who associate others [with God],
but [also] so that God might relent towards the men and women who believe.
God is Forgiving and Compassionate.

Sūra 34

This *sūra* is generally considered to be late Meccan. Some Muslim authorities think that verse 6 is Medinan, and their view may indicate some echo of a revision at Medina. The *sūra* falls into four unequal sections: a couple of verses are the prelude to some polemic (3–9); there are then three briefly told stories (David 10–11; Solomon 12–14; Saba' [Sheba] 15–20); a bridging verse leads to further polemic that continues to the end of the *sūra*, much of it in the form of instructions to Muḥammad.

Saba'

In the name of the Merciful and Compassionate God

1. Praise be to God,
    to whom belongs all that is in the heavens and all that is on earth.
    To Him also belongs praise in the world to come.
    He is the Wise and the Informed,
2. Who knows what penetrates into the earth
    and what comes out of it
    and what descends from heaven
    and what ascends into it.
    He is the Merciful and Forgiving.
3. Those who are ungrateful say,
    'The Hour will never come to us.'
    Say, 'Yes, it will.
    By my Lord, Knower of the Invisible,
    it will certainly come to you.
    Not an atom's weight either in heaven or on earth escapes Him.
    Everything, [whether] smaller or bigger than that, is in a clear record,
4. That He may recompense those who believe and do righteous deeds.
    They will have a pardon and a rich provision.
5. But those who strive against Our signs,
    trying to make them ineffective,
    theirs will be a painful torment of abomination.
6. Those who have been given knowledge
    see that what has been sent down to you from your Lord is the truth
    [which] guides to the path of the Mighty and Praiseworthy.'
7. Those who are ungrateful say,
    'Shall we show you[p] a man who will tell you[p]

391

[that] when you^p have been totally torn to pieces
you^p will be in a new creation?

8. Has he invented a lie against God or is he possessed?'
No.
Those who disbelieve in the world to come are in torment and distant error.

9. Have they not looked at the heaven and earth
that is before them and that is behind them?
If We wish, We can cause the earth to swallow them
or cause the heavens to fall on them in pieces.
In that there is a sign for every repentant servant.

10. In the past We gave David a bounty from Us,
[saying], 'O mountains, echo [God's praises] with him,
and you birds also.'
And We softened iron for him,

11. Saying, 'Make⁵ long coats of mail and measure carefully in sewing them together.'
Do right, [all of you].
I can see what you do.

12. And [We gave] to Solomon the wind:
its morning course was a month's journey,
and its afternoon course was a month's journey.
And We caused a spring of copper to flow for him.
And of the *Jinn* there were those who worked before him,
by permission of his Lord;
and those of them who deviated from Our command
– We shall cause them to taste the torment of the blaze.

13. They made for him what he wished:
sanctuaries, statues,
basins like cisterns, and cooking-pots fixed firmly into the ground.
'Work, O family of David, in thankfulness.
Few among My servants are the thankful.'

14. And when We decreed that he should die,
nothing showed them that he was dead
but the creature of the earth eating away his staff;
and when he fell, the *Jinn* saw clearly
that if they had known the Invisible
they would not have remained in humiliating toil.

15. There was a sign for Saba' in their dwelling-place
– two gardens,
[one] on the right and [one] on the left:
'Eat of the sustenance of your Lord and be grateful to Him.
A good land and a forgiving Lord.'

392

16. But they turned away and so we loosed on them the flood of ʿArim,[1]
and in exchange for their two gardens
we gave them two gardens which produced bitter fruit
and tamarisks and a few *sidr*-trees.[2]

17. This We gave them as recompense for their ingratitude.
And do We requite [any] but the truly ungrateful?

18. We put between them and the settlements We have blessed
[other] settlements that were clearly visible,
and We measured the journeying between them,
[saying], 'Journey safely between them by night and by day.'

19. They said, 'Our Lord, make the stages of our journey longer.'
They wronged themselves;
and so We made them bywords
and tore them completely to pieces.
In that there are signs for every one who is truly steadfast and grateful.

20. Iblīs found his opinion of them true,
and they followed him,
save for a group of believers,

21. Though he had no authority over them,
except for Us to recognize
those who believe in the world to come
from those who are in doubt about it;
for your Lord is guardian over everything.

22. Say, 'Call on those you have asserted [to be gods],
to the exclusion of God.
They do not possess an atom's weight in the heavens or on earth.
They have no partnership in either of them;
nor has He any supporter among them.'

23. Intercession is of no benefit with Him
except for those to whom He grants permission.
Then when their hearts are empty,
they say, 'What did your Lord say?'
and they reply, 'The Truth;
He is the Exalted and the Great.'

24. Say, 'Who gives you sustenance from the heavens and the earth?'
Say, 'God.
Either we or you are following guidance
or are in manifest error.'

25. Say, 'You will not be asked about the sins we have committed,

---

[1] The bursting of the dam of Ma'rib in Yemen.
[2] Thought to be the species *Zizyphus Spina Christi*. See also 53:14 and 16 and 56:28.

nor shall we be asked about what you are doing.'

26. Say, 'Our Lord will bring us together,
and then He will bring us together in truth.
He is the Judge and the Knowing.'

27. Say, 'Show me those whom you have joined as partners with Him.
No, you cannot.
He is God, the Mighty and the Wise.'

28. We sent you[s] only as a bringer of good tidings and as a warner to all mankind,
but most people have no knowledge.

29. And they say, 'When is this threat [going to happen],
if you are telling the truth?'

30. Say, 'You will have an appointment on a day
that you can neither postpone nor bring forward.'

31. Those who are ungrateful say, 'We shall not believe in this Recitation
nor in that which was before it.'
But if only you[s] could see,
when the wrong-doers are forced to stand before their Lord,
[how] they rebut each other.
Those who were thought weak say to those who were thought strong,
'But for you, we would have been believers.'

32. Those who were thought strong will say to those who were thought weak,
Was it us who turned you away from guidance after it had come to you?
No. You were sinners.'

33. Those who were thought weak will say to those who were thought strong,
'No. [It was the] scheming by night and day [on your part],
when you ordered us to disbelieve in God
and to set up peers to Him.'
They will be full of secret regret when they have seen the torment.
We shall place fetters on the necks of those who disbelieve.
Will they be recompensed for anything other than what they used to do?

34. We did not send any warner into a township,
but its affluent ones declared,
'We do not believe in the message with which you[p] are sent.'

35. And they have said, 'We have more wealth and children.
We shall not be punished.'

36. Say, 'My Lord makes generous provision for those whom He wishes
or measures it closely;
but most people have no knowledge.'

37. Neither your wealth nor your children are what brings you close to Us.
It is only those who believe and do good [who will draw near].
These will have a double reward for what they did,
and they will be secure in high rooms.

38. Those who busy themselves with Our signs,
    seeking to frustrate them
    – they will be brought into the torment.

39. Say, 'My Lord makes generous provision for those of His servants whom He wishes
    [or] measures it closely for them.
    Whatever you expend, He will replace.
    He is the best of providers.'

40. On the day that He musters them all
    – then He will say to the angels,
    'Is it these who used to worship you?'

41. They will say, 'Glory be to You.
    You are our protector,
    to the exclusion of them.
    No, they used to serve the *Jinn*.
    Most of them believe in them;'

42. On that day none of you will have any benefit or harm for any other.
    We shall say to those who have done wrong,
    'Taste the torment of the Fire which you used to deny.'

43. When Our signs are recited to them as clear proofs,
    they say, 'This is only a man who wishes to turn you away
    from what your forefathers used to serve;'
    and they say, 'This is nothing but an invented lie;'
    and those who disbelieve say of the truth when it comes to them,
    'This is simply persuasive magic.'

44. But We have given them no Scriptures to study,
    nor have We sent to them any warner before you.

45. Those who were before them denied the truth,
    and [these] have not attained a tenth of what we bestowed on them.
    They denied my messengers,
    and how was My disapproval!

46. Say, 'I exhort you only to one thing:
    that you rise for God in twos or singly
    and then reflect.
    Nothing possesses your comrade.
    He is simply a warner for you before a severe torment.'

47. Say, 'Whatever reward I have asked you for is for you.
    My reward rests only with God.
    He is Witness over everything.'

48. Say, 'My Lord hurls forth the truth.
    [He is] the Knower of unseen things.'

49. Say, 'The truth has come.
    The false neither originates nor restores.'

50. Say, 'If I stray, I stray only to my own disadvantage;
    and if I am guided aright,
    it is because of that with which my Lord inspires me.
    He is Hearing and Near.'
51. If only you^s could see
    when they are terrified
    and there is no escape
    and they are seized from a nearby place;
52. And they say, 'We believe in it.'
    How can they reach [faith] from a distant place,
53. When they disbelieved in it before?
    They conjecture at the Invisible from a distant place.
54. A barrier has been put between them and what they desire,
    as was done with the likes of them before.
    They were in disquieting doubt.

Sūra 35

This is generally agreed to be a late Meccan *sūra*, though there seems to be evidence of some recasting in Medina. It begins with a brief piece of praise to God (1–2), which is followed by a passage of warning (3–8) and one on 'signs' (9–14). These are followed by further warning and 'sign' passages, in which Muḥammad is addressed and which end with references to the scripture (15–26; 27–32). A brief piece on heaven and hell develops from verse 32 (33–37). Finally there is a peroration of polemic and warning (38–45).

The Angels

In the name of the Merciful and Compassionate God

1. Praise belongs to God,
   the Creator of the heavens and the earth,
   who has appointed as messengers the angels
   with wings, two, three or four each,
   and who gives increase to whatever He wishes in creation.
   God has power over everything.
2. The mercy that God opens up for mankind, none can withhold;
   and that which He withholds none can loose after Him.
   He is the Mighty and the Wise.
3. O mankind, remember God's blessing to you.
   Is there any creator,
   other than God,
   who brings you sustenance from the sky and the earth?
   There is no god but Him.
   How are you caused to lie?
4. If they deny the truth of [what] you[s] [say],
   messengers before you were considered liars.
   But all matters are brought back to God.
5. O mankind, the promise of God is true.
   So let not the life of this world deceive you.
   Let not the deceiver deceive you about God.
6. Satan is an enemy for you[p];
   so treat him as an enemy.
   He only summons his party
   to be among the companions of the blaze.

7. Those who are ungrateful will have a severe punishment,
   while those who believe and do righteous deeds
   will have forgiveness and a great reward.

8. [What about] those the evil of whose deeds seems so fair to them
   that they think it good?
   God leads astray those whom He wishes
   and guides those whom He wishes.
   So let not your^s soul depart in regret for them.
   God is aware of what they do.

9. It is God who sends the winds,
   which then stir up cloud.
   We drive it to a land that is dead,
   and through it revive the earth after it has died off.
   Thus is the Rising.

10. Those who desire glory
    – glory belongs entirely to God.
    Good words ascend to Him;
    and He raises the righteous deed.
    But those who plot evil deeds will have a severe punishment.
    The plotting of such men will come to nothing.

11. [It is] God [who] created you from dust,
    then from fluid;
    then He made you pairs¹.
    No female conceives or brings forth,
    save with His knowledge.
    No one is given a long life or has his life cut short,
    but it is in a record.
    That is easy for God.

12. The two seas are not alike.
    This is sweet and fresh and good to drink;
    and that is salty and bitter.
    Yet from each you^p eat fresh meat and bring forth ornaments to wear.
    And you see the ships cleaving through them
    so that you may seek some of His bounty
    and so that you may be thankful.

13. He makes the night enter into the day,
    and the day into the night,
    and He has subjected the sun and the moon to [your] service,
    each of them running for a stated term.
    That is God, your^p Lord.

---

¹ Or 'species'.

His is the Kingdom,
and those you invoke,
to His exclusion,
do not own even the skin of a date-stone.

14. If you[p] call to them, they cannot hear your call;
and if they could hear, they would not answer you.
On the Day of Resurrection they will disown your[p]
associating them with God.
No one informs you[s] like One who is informed.

15. O men, you are the ones who are in need of God.
God is the All-sufficient and the Laudable.

16. If He wishes, He can remove you and bring a new creation.

17. That is not a great matter for God.

18. No laden soul bears the burden of another;
and if one that is heavily burdened calls for its load to be carried,
none of it will be carried,
even though [the one called to] is of close kin.
You[s] warn only those who fear their Lord in the Invisible
and who perform prayer.
Those who purify themselves
do so only for themselves.
To God is the journeying.

19. The blind and the seeing are not equal,

20. Nor are the darkness and the night,

21. Nor the shade and burning heat;

22. Nor are the living and the dead equal.
God causes to hear those whom He wishes.
You[s] cannot make those who are in the graves hear.

23. You are merely a warner.

24. We have sent you with the truth,
as a bearer of good tidings and a warner.
There is no community but a warner has passed away among them.

25. If they treat you[s] as a liar,
those before them also denied the truth.
Their messengers came to them with the clear proofs
and with the Psalms and with the illuminating Scripture.

26. Then I seized those who were ungrateful;
and how was My disapproval!

27. Have you[s] not seen that God sends down water from the sky?
With it We bring forth fruits of different colours.
And in the mountains [too] there are streaks of various colours:
white, red and pitch-black.

28. And in men and wild creatures and livestock there are likewise different colours.
    Only those of God's servants who have some knowledge fear Him.
    God is Mighty and Forgiving.
29. Those who recite God's Scripture and perform prayer and spend,
    secretly or openly,
    from that which We have given them as sustenance
    can hope for a trade that does not come to nothing,
30. So that He may pay them their wages in full and increase them in His bounty.
    He is Forgiving and Grateful.
31. That Scripture which We have inspired in you[s] is the truth,
    confirming what was before it.
    God is informed and observing of His servants.
32. Then We gave the Scripture as inheritance
    to those whom We chose of our servants.
    Among them are some who wrong themselves
    and some who are sparing
    and some who are foremost in good works,
    by the leave of God.
    That is the great favour.
33. Gardens of Eden:
    they will enter them and will be adorned there
    with bracelets of gold and with pearls;
    and their clothing there will be silk.
34. They say, 'Praise belongs to God,
    who has removed grief from Us.
    Our Lord is Forgiving and Grateful,
35. Who, of His bounty, has allowed us to settle in the Abode,
    where no weariness or fatigue touches us.'
36. Those who are ungrateful will have the fire of Jahannam.
    They will not be done with and die,
    and there will be no alleviation for them of its punishment.
    Thus We recompense every ungrateful one.
37. There they shout, 'Our Lord, take us out.
    We shall do right, not what we used to do.'
    'Did We not give you life long enough
    for those who would receive a reminder to be reminded,
    when a warner had come to you?
    So taste.
    The wrong-doers will have no helper.'
38. God knows the Unseen of the heavens and the earth.
    He is aware of the thoughts in men's breasts.
39. It is He who has made you[p] successors in the land.

Whoever is ungrateful has his ingratitude [marked up] against him.
This ingratitude only makes the ungrateful more hateful to their Lord.
This ingratitude only increases the ungrateful in loss.

40. Say, 'Have you considered your associates on whom you call,
to the exclusion of God?
Show me what part of the earth they have created.
Or have they any partnership in the heavens?'
Or have We given them a Scripture,
so that they have a clear proof from it?
No. The wrong-doers promise one another nothing but delusion.

41. God holds the heavens and the earth firm,
so that they do not move away.
If they move away,
no one will hold them firm after Him.
He is Prudent and Forgiving.

42. They swore by God their most binding oaths
that if a warner were to come to them
they would be more ready to accept guidance
than any of the communities.
But when the warner came to them,
it increased them only in aversion,

43. Being haughty in the land and plotting evil.
But evil plots encompass only those who plot.
Can they expect anything but the custom of the ancients?[2]
You will find no way of changing God's custom.
You will find no way of altering God's custom.

44. Have they not travelled in the land
and seen how was the end of those who were before them,
who were mightier than them?
God is not one to be frustrated by anything in the heavens or on earth.
He is Knowing and Powerful.

45. If God were to take men to task for what they have amassed,
He would not leave on the surface of [the earth] any creature that moves.
But He is deferring them to a stated term.
When their term comes, God is observer of His servants.

---

[2] *i.e.* what happened to earlier peoples.

Sūra 36

The *sūra* is traditionally thought to be middle Meccan, though some Muslim authorities take verses 12, 45 and possibly 47 to be Medinan. The situation appears to be somewhat more complex than that, with the *sūra* having grown over a period. As it now stands, it divides into five main sections: a warning passage (1–12); a punishment parable, similar to that in 68:17–34, about an overweening and unjust people (13–29); a piece on God's signs (33–44); an eschatological passage (48–68); and a mixed peroration (69–83) about Muḥammad and to Muḥammad and also including 'sign' passages that might originally have formed part of the third section. The *sūra* contains two brief bridge-passages (30–32 and 45–47) that have been found troublesome by the commentators.

Yā' Sīn

In the name of the Merciful and Compassionate God

1. *Yā', Sīn.*[1]
2. By the decisive Recitation,
3. You[s] are one of those who have been sent
4. On a straight path,
5. The revelation of the Mighty and Merciful,
6. For you to warn a people whose forefathers were not warned,
    and who are heedless.
7. The word has proved true for most of them;
    yet they do not believe.
8. We have put fetters on their necks,
    reaching up to their chins,
    so that [their heads] are raised.
9. We have put a barrier before them and a barrier behind them;
    and We have covered them so that they cannot see.
10. It is all one to them whether you[s] have warned them or not
    – they do not believe.
11. You[s] warn only those who follow the reminder and fear the Merciful in the Invisible.
    So give them the good news of forgiveness and a generous reward.
12. It is We who bring the dead to life
    and We record what they have forwarded and their tracks,
    and We have counted everything in a clear record.
13. Coin[s] for them a comparison:

---

[1] On the mystical letters see the note on 2:1.

the inhabitants of the settlement,
when those who were sent came to them;

14. When We sent two men to them, but they called them liars;
so We reinforced them with a third.
The [three] said, 'We have been sent to you.'

15. They said, 'You are only mortals like us.
The Merciful has not sent down anything.
You are simply telling lies.'

16. The [three] said, 'Our Lord knows we are sent to you.

17. Our duty is only to convey the message clearly.'

18. They said, 'We regard you as ill-omened.
If you do not desist, we shall stone you,
and a painful punishment from us will touch you.'

19. The [three] said, 'Your omen is with you.
If you are warned, ...
But you are a prodigal people.'

20. A man came running from the furthest part of the city.
He said, 'My people,
follow those who have been sent.

21. Follow those who do not ask you for any reward
and who are rightly guided.

22. Why should I not serve Him who has created me
and to whom you[p] will be returned?

23. Am I to adopt
to the exclusion of Him
gods whose intercession will be of no avail to me
if the Merciful desires harm for me
and who will not save me?

24. In that case I should be in manifest error.

25. I believe in your[p] Lord. So listen to me!'

26. He was told, 'Enter the garden.'
He said, 'Would that my people knew

27. How my Lord has forgiven me and made me one of the honoured.'

28. We did not send any army down from heaven on his people after him.
We do not send down.

29. There was only one shout,
and they were extinct.

30. Alas for the servants!
Whenever a messenger comes to them,
they mock him.

31. Have they not seen how many generations We have destroyed before them
[and] that they do not return to them?

32. Every one will be brought before Us in a body.
33. A sign for them is the dead earth
    which We have revived
    and brought forth from it grain,
    so that they may eat it.
34. And We have placed in it gardens of palm-trees and vines
    and We have caused springs to gush there,
35. So that they may eat its fruits
    and what their right hands have laboured on.
    Are they not thankful?
36. Glory be to Him who created all the pairs[2]
    of what the earth causes to grow
    and of themselves
    and of what they do not know.
37. A sign for them is the night:
    We strip it of the day and they are in darkness;
38. And the sun:
    it moves to a resting-place fixed for it
    – that is the decree of the Mighty and Knowing;
39. And the moon:
    We have decreed for it stations,
    until it returns like an old palm-bough.
40. It is not right for the sun to overtake the moon,
    nor should the night outstrip the day.
    Each swims in an orbit.
41. A sign for them is that We carried their seed in the laden ship,
42. And that We have created for them the like of it,
    in which they can sail.
43. And if We wish, We drown them;
    they make no cry nor are they saved,
44. Except through a mercy from Us and for enjoyment for a time.
45. When it is said to them, 'Fear what is before you and what is behind you
    so that you may find mercy'
46. – But none of the signs of their Lord comes to them
    without them turning away from it.
47. When they are told,
    'Spend some of that which God has given you as sustenance',
    the unbelievers say to the believers,
    'Are we to feed someone whom God could feed if He wished?
    You are in nothing but manifest error.'

---

[2] Or 'species'.

48. They say, 'When is this promise,
    if you are telling the truth?'
49. They are waiting only for one shout,
    which will take them whilst they are disputing.
50. They can make no bequest,
    nor can they return to their own folk.
51. There will be a blast on the trumpet,
    and they will slip from their graves to their Lord.
52. They say, 'Woe on us.
    Who has raised us from our resting-place?
    This is what the Merciful promised.
    Those who were sent spoke the truth.'
53. There is only one shout;
    then they are brought before us in a body.
54. To-day no soul will be wronged in anything,
    nor will you^p be recompensed
    except for what you have been doing.
55. The people of the garden to-day are happy in what occupies them,
56. They and their spouses reclining in shade on couches.
57. There they have fruit;
    they have whatever they call for;
58. 'Peace', a greeting from a compassionate Lord.
59. 'Separate yourselves to-day, you sinners.
60. Did I not enjoin you, you sons of Adam,
    that you should not serve Satan
    – he is a clear enemy to you –
61. And that you should serve Me?
    This is a straight path.
62. But he has led astray a great multitude of you.
    Did you not understand?
63. This is Jahannam, which you were promised.
64. Roast in it to-day for your unbelief.'
65. To-day We seal their mouths,
    and their hands address us
    and their feet bear witness to what they have been amassing.
66. And were We to wish, We could obliterate their eyes,
    and they would still try to be first to the path.
    But how could they see?
67. And were We to wish, We could transform them where they were,
    and they would not be able to go forward nor could they return.
68. Those to whom We give long life,
    we reverse them in their constitution.

Do they not understand?

69. We have not taught him poetry.
That is not proper for him.
This is only a reminder and a recitation that is clear,

70. That he might warn those who are alive
and that the word may be proved true against the unbelievers.

71. Have they not seen that We created for them
from Our handiwork livestock, which they may own?

72. And have made the livestock submissive to them,
some to ride on, others to eat.

73. In them they have drinks and [other] benefits.
Will they not be thankful?

74. But they have adopted gods,
to the exclusion of God
so that they might be helped.

75. They cannot help them,
even if they are a host made ready.

76. So let their words not grieve you[s].
We know what they conceal and what they proclaim.

77. Has not man seen that We created him from a drop?
Yet he is an open opponent.

78. He has coined for Us a likeness[3]
and forgotten his creation.
He says, 'Who will give life to bones
when they are decayed?'

79. Say, 'He who caused them to grow on the first occasion
will give them life.
He knows all creation,

80. Who has made for you fire out of the green trees.
– From them you can produce flame.'

81. Is not the One who created the heavens and the earth
able to create the like of them?
Of course he can.
He is the Creator and the Knower.

82. His command,
when He wishes something
is simply to say to it, 'Be', and it is.

83. Glory be to Him,
in whose hand is dominion over everything,
and to whom you are returned.

---

[3] *Cf.* 43:17.

Sūra 37

Most of the *sūra* seems to be from relatively early in the Meccan period, though a few verses appear to be later. As one might expect with a piece of over 180 verses, the structure is complex: a massed entity containing material of different dates and occasionally somewhat heterogeneous ideas. Nevertheless, it holds together, particularly in recitation, and attempts to re-order some of the material, *e.g.* the repositioning by Bell and Blachère of verses 82 and 83, are ill-conceived.

The first section of the *sūra* is brief: three verses of *kāhin*-type oaths, followed by the strong asseveration in verse 4, 'Your God is One'. Verse 5 is an expansion of this; and it appears that its mention of 'the heavens' provides the link with verses 6–10, which sketch in an allusive way the evil role of the devils and the torment inflicted on them. Verse 11, which has the same minimal assonance as 4–10, is a bridging verse addressed to Muḥammad, who is also addressed in verse 12. There, however, the use of the word *bal* at the beginning of the verse together with a change of assonance show that a new section has started. As far as verse 17 the theme is the scoffing of the unbelievers. Muḥammad is again addressed in verse 18, in which he is told to warn the unbelievers. Without further ado, the first of the main sections of the *sūra* begins at verse 19 and continues to verse 68. It divides up as follows: 19–33: Judgement; 34–39: admonition; 40–49: Paradise; 50–61: Hell as seen from Paradise; 62–68: Hell itself. This is followed by another bridging passage, the Hell of verse 68 being linked to a piece on erring peoples, which leads naturally to the second main section on earlier messengers (75–148). Apart from that dealing with Abraham, the sketches are brief, with some of them embellished by verses that are a kind of refrain. Those mentioned are Noah (75–82); Abraham (83–101; 102–111; also 112–113 with Isaac); Moses and Aaron (114–122); Elijah (123–132); Lot (133–138); and Jonah (139–148). Verse 149 takes us abruptly back to the present messenger, reminding us in passing of verses 11 and 12, and then into a passage of argumentation about God's relationships with others: the angels are not God's daughters (149–157); and the *Jinn* are subservient and not related (158). Verses 159 and 160 link back to 149 and also pave the way for the peroration (161–182). This is kaleidoscopic, the dominant themes being God's glory and the inevitability of punishment for those who do not heed His message.

Those who draw up ranks

In the name of the Merciful and Compassionate God

1.   By those who draw up ranks,[1]
2.   And by those who drive,
3.   And by those who recite a reminder,
4.   Truly your[p] God is One,
5.   Lord of the heavens and of the earth and of what is between them
     and Lord of the sun's rising-places.
6.   We[2] have adorned the nearest heaven with the adornment of the stars,
7.   And [We have placed them] as a protection against every rebellious devil.
8.   They cannot listen to the highest host,
     for they are pelted from every side,
9.   Rejected – and theirs is a lasting punishment –
10. Except for the one who snatches a fragment,
     and [any such] is pursued by a piercing flame.
11. So ask[s] them for their view.
     Are they stronger as a creation,
     or those whom We created?
     We created them of clinging clay.
12. Yet you[s] marvel when they mock
13. And are not mindful when they are reminded.
14. When they see a sign, they seek to mock,
15. And they say, 'This is simply manifest sorcery.
16. When we are dead and have become dust and bones,
     shall we be raised
17. Together with our forefathers, the ancients?'
18. Say, 'Yes, and you will be abject.'
19. There will simply be one drive;
     and there they will be, watching;
20. And they will say, 'Woe upon us,
     this is the Day of Judgement.
21. This is the Day of Separation,
     which you used to say was a lie.'
22. 'Round up[3] those who have sinned
     together with their wives and what they used to worship
23. To the exclusion of God,
     and guide them along the path to Hell;

---

[1] Verses 1–3 are traditionally thought to refer to angels.

[2] 'We' refers to God.

[3] The command is to unspecified angels.

24. And stop them
    – they are to be questioned,
25. "Why do you not help one another"?'
26. No! On that day they will seek to submit.
27. They will draw near to one another, asking each other questions.
28. [Some] say, 'You used to come to us from the right hand.'[4]
29. [Others] say, 'But you were not believers.
30. We had no authority over you.
    No, you were an impious folk.
31. [Now] the word of our Lord has been realized against us.
    We are tasting.
32. We caused you to go astray
    – we had gone astray ourselves.'
33. That day they will all share in the punishment.
34. Thus we deal with the sinners.
35. When it was said to them,
    'There is no god but God',
    they were disdainful,
36. And would say,
    'Are we to abandon our gods for the sake of a poet,
    a man possessed?'
37. No,
    he has brought the truth and confirmed those sent before.
38. You will indeed taste the painful punishment,
39. Nor will you be recompensed for anything other than what you did.
40. This will not be the case with the sincere servants of God
41. – They will have a known provision:
42. Fruits; and they will be honoured
43. In the gardens of bliss,
44. On couches, facing one another.
45. And a cup from a spring will be passed round among them,
46. Clear and sparkling,
    a delight to those who drink,
47. In which there is no headache,
    nor do they become intoxicated from it.
48. And with them are women of modest glances,
    with lustrous eyes,
49. As if they were hidden eggs.
50. They will draw near to one another, asking each other questions.
51. One of them says, 'I had a comrade,

---

[4] *i.e.* 'we trusted you'.

52. Who would say,
    "Are you[s] one of those who believe [the message]?
53. When we are dead and become dust and bones,
    shall we be judged"?'
54. [Another] says, 'Will you[p] look down?'
55. He looks down and sees him in the midst of Hell.
56. He says, 'By God, you[s] almost destroyed me.
57. But for the blessing of my Lord
    I would have been one of those brought [into Hell].
58. Do we really not die,
59. Except for our first death,
    and shall we not be punished?
60. This is truly the mighty triumph.
61. For the like of this let the workers work.'
62. Is this better as hospitality or the tree of *al-Zaqqūm*?[5]
63. We have appointed it as a trial for the wrong-doers.
64. It is a tree that comes out of the root of Hell.
65. Its spathes are like the heads of devils.
66. They eat of it and fill their bellies from it.
67. Then on top of it they will have a brew of scalding water.
68. Then their return will be to Hell.
69. They found their fathers had gone astray,
70. But they hasten to follow them.
71. Most of the men of old went astray before them,
72. And We sent among them warners.
73. See then how was the consequence for those who were warned,
74. Except for the sincere servants of God.
75. Noah called out to Us, and how excellent was the Answerer.
76. We delivered him and his household from the great distress,
77. And made his seed the survivors,
78. And left for him among posterity [the greeting],
79. 'Peace be on Noah among all beings.'
80. Thus we truly recompense those who do good.
81. He was one of our believing servants.
82. Then We drowned the rest.
83. Abraham was of his party,
84. When he came to his Lord with a sound heart;
85. When he said to his father and his people,
    'What are you worshipping?
86. Is it a lie, gods other than God, that you desire?

---

[5] See also 44:43 and 56:52.

87. What do you think of the Lord of all beings?'
88. He cast a glance at the stars,
89. And he said, 'I feel ill'.
90. They shunned him, turning their backs.
91. He turned aside to their gods and said,
'Will you not eat?
92. Why do you not speak?'
93. And he turned upon them,
striking [them] down[6] with his right hand.
94. People came rushing to him.
95. He said,
'Do you worship what you carve from stone,
96. When God created you and that which you make?'
97. They said,
'Build a building for him,
and throw him into blaze'.
98. They desired to plot against him,
but We made them come worse off.
99. He said,
'I am going to my Lord.
He will guide me.
100. O my Lord, give me one of the righteous.'
101. So We gave him the good news of a prudent son.
102. When [the boy] was old enough to run at his side,
he said, 'O my son, I have seen in my dreams
that I shall sacrifice you.
Look, what do you think?'
He said, 'O my father, do what you are commanded.
You will find me, if God wills,
to be one of the steadfast.'
103. When they had surrendered themselves,[7]
and he had flung him on to his forehead,
104. We called out to him, 'O Abraham,
105. You have made [your] vision come true.
Thus We recompense those who do good.
106. That was truly the great test.'
107. And We ransomed [the boy] with a mighty sacrifice.
108. And We left for him among posterity [the greeting],

---

[6] Literally 'a blow'.
[7] This appears to be the earliest passage to use the verb *aslama* 'to submit oneself', from which *al-islām* 'submission [to God]' and *muslim* 'one who submits [to God]' also come.

109. 'Peace be on Abraham'.
110. Thus We truly recompense those who do good.
111. He was one of our believing servants.
112. And We gave him the good news of Isaac as a prophet from among the righteous,
113. And We blessed him and Isaac.
    Of their seed there are those who do good and those who manifestly wrong
        themselves.
114. We were gracious to Moses and Aaron,
115. We delivered the two of them and their people from the great distress.
116. We aided them, and they became the victors.
117. We gave them the Scripture that seeks to make clear,
118. And We guided them on the straight path.
119. And We left for them among posterity [the greeting],
120. 'Peace be on Moses and Aaron.'
121. Thus we truly recompense those who do good.
122. They were two of our believing servants.
123. Ilyas,[8] too, was one of those sent:
124. When he said to his people,
    'Will you not fear God?
125. Do you call out to Baal
    and forsake the best of creators?
126. God, your Lord and the Lord of your forefathers?'
127. But they disbelieved him,
    and they will be arraigned,
128. Except for the sincere servants of God.
129. And we left for him among posterity [the greeting],
130 'Peace be on Il Yāsīn.'[7]
131. Thus We truly recompense those who do good.
132. He was one of our believing servants.
133. Lot, too, was one of those who were sent.
134. When we saved him and his family – all
135. Except an old woman amongst those who lingered.
136. Then We destroyed the rest.
137. You[p] pass close to them in the morning
138. And at night.
    Will you not understand?
139. Jonah, too, was one of those who were sent:
140. When he fled to the laden ship,
141. And drew lots and was of the rejected.
142. And the fish swallowed him,

---

[8] Elijah.

while he was blameworthy.

143. Had he not been one of those who glorify God,
144. He would have lingered in its belly
    till the day when [men] will be raised.
145. Then We cast him up on to a desert, and he was sick;
146. And We caused a tree of gourds to grow over him.
147. We sent him as a messenger to a hundred thousand or more,
148. And they believed.
    So We gave them enjoyment for a time.
149. Ask them for their view:
    'Does your[9] Lord have daughters and they[10] sons?
150. Or did We create the angels females,
    while they looked on?'
151. It is indeed of their own lying [that] they say,
152. 'God has fathered offspring.'
    They are indeed liars.
153. Has He chosen daughters rather than sons?
154. How do you[P] come to such a judgement?
155. And will you not be reminded?
156. Or do you have some clear authority?
157. Produce your Scripture,
    if you speak the truth.
158. They have set up a relationship between Him and the *Jinn*;
    but the *Jinn* know that they will be arraigned
159. – God be glorified far above what they describe –
160. Except for the sincere servants of God.
161. You[P] and that which you worship
162. – You cannot stir up [anyone] against Him,
163. Except those who will roast in Hell.
164. There is not one of us but has a known place.
165. We are those who draw up ranks,
166. We are those who glorify.
167. Indeed they used to say,
168. 'If only we had a reminder from the ancients,
169. We would be sincere servants of God.'
170. But they have disbelieved in it
    – but they shall know.
171. Our word has already gone before to Our servants who were sent with the message:
172. They are the ones who will be helped.

---

[9] *i.e.* Muḥammad.
[10] *i.e.* the Meccan unbelievers.

173. And Our hosts
  – they are the victors.
174. So withdraw^s from them for a time,
175. And watch them
  – they will see.
176. Is it to Our punishment that they seek to hasten?
177. When it descends into their courtyard,
  how terrible will be the morning of those who have been warned.
178. So withdraw^s from them for a time.
179. And watch
  – they will see.
180. May your^s Lord, the Lord of might,
  be glorified far above what they describe.
181. Peace be on those sent with the message,
182. And praise is to God, Lord of all beings.

Sūra 38

The *sūra* is traditionally considered to be of the middle Meccan period. It starts abruptly, with the initial oath giving way in verse 3 to a passage of polemic (3–11). This is then followed by a long narrative passage on various prophets (12–49), which gives way to a piece on heaven and hell. The final section is a mixed passage (65–88), partly addressed to Muḥammad but largely given over the story of Iblīs (71–85).

Ṣād

In the name of the Merciful and Compassionate God

1. *Ṣād.*[1]
   By the Recitation which contains a reminder.
2. No. Those who are ungrateful are in pride and schism.
3. How many generations have We destroyed before them,
   and they cried out,
   but there was no time to escape.
4. They are astonished that a warner has come to them from their own number.
   The ungrateful ones[2] say, 'This is a lying sorcerer.
5. Has he made the gods One God?
   That is an astounding thing.'
6. The notables among them go off, saying,
   'Go[P] and be steadfast to your gods.
   That is a thing to be desired.
7. We have not heard of this in the last religion.[3]
   This is something that has been invented.
8. Has the reminder been sent down to him from among us [all]?'
   No. They are in doubt about My reminder.
   No. They have not yet tasted My punishment.
9. Or have they the treasuries of the mercy of your[s] Lord,
   the Mighty and the Munificent,
10. Or have they the kingdom of the heavens and the earth and what is between them?
    Let them ascend the ropes.[4]

---

[1] On the mystical letters see the note on 2:1.
[2] Or 'the unbelievers'.
[3] Possibly a reference to Christianity, though this is very doubtful.
[4] *Cf.* 40:36–37.

11.   A host of parties is there, routed.

12.   Before them the people of Noah denied,
        [as did] ʿĀd and Pharaoh,
        the man with the pegs,[5]

13.   And Thamūd and the people of Lot
        and the men of the thicket
        – they were the parties.

14.   Every one of them denied the truth of the messengers,
        and My punishment was justified.

15.   These wait only for one Shout
        from which there is no respite.

16.   They say, 'Our Lord,
        hasten for us our share before the Day of Reckoning.'

17.   Bear[s] patiently with what they say,
        and remember Our servant David,
        the man of might.
        He was a penitent.

18.   With him We subdued the mountains
        to give glory at evening and sunrise;

19.   And the birds were rounded up, all turning to him.

20.   We strengthened his kingdom,
        and We gave him wisdom and decisive speech.

21.   Have you[s] heard of the tidings of the dispute
        when they walled the sanctuary,

22.   When they went in to see David,
        and he took fright at them?
        They said, 'Do not be afraid.
        [We are] two disputants,
        one of whom has wronged the other.
        So judge between us with truth,
        and do not transgress;
        and guide us to the level path.'

23.   'This is my brother.
        He has ninety-nine ewes,
        and I have one ewe.
        He said, "Entrust it to me",
        and he overcame me in talking to me.'

24.   He said, 'He has wronged you
        in asking you to add your ewe to his.
        Many partners wrong each other,

---

[5] A man of wealth and power.

except those who believe and do good works,
and they are few.'
David guessed that We had tested him,
and he sought forgiveness from his Lord,
and he fell in prostration and repented.

25. So we forgave Him that.
He had nearness to Us and a fair resort.

26. 'O David, We have made you a viceroy in the land.
Judge between the people in truth.
Do not follow caprice,
lest it lead you away from the way of God.
Those who stray from the way of God will have a severe punishment
for having forgotten about the Day of Reckoning.'

27. We did not create in vain the heavens and the earth and what is between them.
That is the guess of those who are ungrateful.
Woe to the ungrateful because of the Fire.

28. Shall We treat those who believe and do righteous deeds
like those who do mischief in the land?
Shall We make those who protect themselves
like the profligates?

29. A Scripture which We have sent down to you, blessed,
for them to ponder its signs
and for men of understanding to reflect.

30. We gave Solomon to David.
How excellent a servant!
He was penitent

31. When he was shown the standing steeds in the evening,

32. And he said, 'I have loved the love of good things
rather than the remembrance of my Lord
until it[6] has disappeared behind the veil.

33. Bring them back to me.'
And he began to stroke their legs and necks.

34. We tried Solomon and set on his throne a figure.
Then he repented.

35. He said, 'My Lord. Forgive me
and give me a kingdom that no one may have after me.
You are the Giver.'

36. So We made the wind subject to him,
running at his command, gently,
wherever he decided,

---

[6] This is usually interpreted as the sun disappearing behind the veil of darkness.

37. Likewise the satans,
    every builder and diver,
38. And others linked together in fetters:
39. 'This is Our gift.
    Bestow[s] or withhold without reckoning.'
40. He had nearness to Us and a fair resort.
41. Mention Our servant Job,
    when he called out to his Lord, saying,
    'Satan has touched me with fatigue and torment.'
42. 'Stamp your foot.
    This is a cool washing-place and a drink.'
43. We gave to him his family
    and the like of them with them,
    as a mercy from Us and as a reminder for men of understanding:
44. 'Take in your hand a bundle of grass,
    and strike with it,
    and do not break your oath.'
    We found him steadfast.
    How excellent a servant!
    He was penitent.
45. Mention Our servants Abraham and Isaac and Jacob,
    men of might and vision.
46. We distinguished them with a pure quality,
    remembrance of the Abode.
47. With Us they are of the chosen, the good.
48. Mention Ishmael and al-Yasaʿ and Dhū l-Kifl.
    Each [of them] is one of the chosen.
49. This is a reminder.
    For those who protect themselves there is a fair resort:
50. Gardens of Eden,
    the gates of which are opened to them,
51. In which they recline
    and call for abundant fruit and for drink.
52. With them are women who restrain their glances,
    companions.
53. This is what you are promised for the Day of Reckoning.
54. This is Our provision,
    which will never fail.
55. This
    – but for the transgressors there will be an evil resort:
56. Jahannam, in which they will roast.
    How evil a resting-place.

57. This
    – so let them taste it –
    and scalding water and pus,
58. And other things of the same kind, in pairs.
59. 'This is a troop rushing in with you^p.
    There is no welcome for them.
    They will roast in the Fire.'
60. They say, 'No. It is you^p for whom there is no welcome.
    You prepared this for us.
    How evil is the abode.'
61. They say, 'Our Lord, give a double torment in the Fire
    to those who prepared this for us.'
62. And they say, 'How is it that we do not see
    men whom we counted amongst the wicked?
63. Did we take them as a laughing-stock?
    Or have our eyes missed them?'
64. That is true
    – the wrangling of the people of the Fire.
65. Say, 'I am only a warner.
    There is no god but God,
    the One, the Victorious,
66. Lord of the heavens and the earth and what is between them,
    the Mighty, the Forgiving.'
67. Say, 'It is a mighty tiding.
68. From which you^p turn away.
69. I had no knowledge of the highest host when they disputed.
70. All that is revealed to me is that I am a clear warner.'
71. When your^s Lord said to the angels,
    'I shall create mankind from clay.
72. When I have formed him
    and breathed some of my Spirit into him,
    fall down, prostrating yourself to him.'
73. All the angels prostrated themselves,
    every one,
74. Save Iblīs.
    He was haughty and one of those who were ungrateful.
75. He said, 'O Iblīs, what has prevented you from prostrating yourself
    to that which I have created with my hands?
    Are you haughty or are you one of the lofty ones?'
76. He said, 'I am better than him.
    You created me from fire
    and You created him from clay.'

77. HE said, 'Leave [this place].
    You are accursed.
78. My curse is upon you to the Day of Judgement.'
79. He said, 'My Lord, give me a respite
    till the day they are raised.'
80. HE said, 'You are amongst those reprieved
81. Until the day of the known time.'
82. He said, 'By Your might,
    I shall lead them all astray,
83. Except for the devoted servants amongst them.'
84. HE said, '[This is] the truth.
    I speak the truth,
85. I shall fill Jahannam with you
    and those of them who follow you, every one.'
86. Say, 'I do not ask you for a fee for this,
    and I am not one of those who take things upon themselves.
87. It is nothing but a reminder for all beings.
88. You will certainly know its tidings after a while.'

Sūra 39

This is generally considered to be a late Meccan *sūra*, though some commentators hold the view that verses 53–55 are Medinan. The reasons for this Medinan ascription are not convincing, nor are Bell's for suggesting that much of the *sūra* is Medinan. Yet it is reasonable to suggest that its contents have a fair number of links with *Sūras* 2 and 3, which are Medinan, and with *Sūras* 6 and 7, which are largely late Meccan. This seems to indicate a core of late Meccan material, recast and expanded at Medina. As it stands, the structure is loose. There is a brief introduction on the Scripture (1–2), which is taken up again in various other verses (23, 27–28, 41, 65), but the main part of the *sūra* contains typical polemical material, interspersed with some 'sign' material and the like (4–66). The most prominent theme is the Day of Resurrection (15, 24, 31, 47, 60), and this is taken up in the peroration (67–75). The second person singular occurs with some frequency. On most occasions Muḥammad is addressed; but this is not so in verse 59 and may not be so in such verses as 60 and 21.

The Troops

In the name of the Merciful and Compassionate God

1. The sending down of the Scripture from God, the Mighty, the Wise.
2. We have sent down to you^s the Scripture with the truth.
   So serve^s God, devoting [your] religion solely to him.
3. Truly, pure religion belongs to God.
   Those who take protectors to His exclusion,
   [saying], 'We serve them only that they might bring us near to God,'
   – God will judge between them about that in which they differ.
   God does not guide those who are lying and ungrateful.
4. Had God wished to take for Himself a son,
   He would have chosen whatever He wished
   from that which He has created.
   Glory be to Him.
   He is the One, the Victorious.
5. He has created the heavens and the earth with the truth,
   wrapping night around day and day around night,
   and He has subjected the sun and the moon to service,
   each one running for a stated term.
   Is not He the Mighty, the Forgiving?
6. He created you^p from a single soul;

then He made its mate from it;
and He has sent down to you eight beasts, paired together.
He created you in the bellies of your mothers,
creation after creation,
in triple darkness.
That is God, your Lord.
To Him belongs the Kingdom.
There is no god but Him.
How is it that you^p are turned?

7. If you^p are ungrateful, God is independent of you;
but He is not pleased with ingratitude on the part of His servants.
Yet if you^p are thankful,
He is pleased by it for you.
No laden [soul] bears the burden of another.
It is to your^p Lord that you will return,
and He will inform you of what you have been doing.
He knows the thoughts in men's breasts.

8. When some harm touches man,
he calls on his Lord,
turning to Him in penitence;
but when He grants him a blessing from Himself,
he forgets what he was calling out to Him before,
and he sets up rivals [to God]
to lead [men] from His way.
Say, 'Enjoy your^s ingratitude for a little.
You are one of the companions of the Fire.'

9. [But what about] those who are obedient in the watches of the night,
prostrating themselves and standing [in prayer],
being careful about the world to come
and hoping for the mercy of their Lord?
Say, 'Are those who know and those who do not know equal?'
Only those possessed of understanding are reminded.

10. Say, 'O my servants who believe,
be god-fearing towards your Lord.
Those who do good in this world will receive good.
God's earth is spacious.
The steadfast will be paid their wages in full,
without reckoning.'

11. Say, 'I have been commanded to serve God,
devoting my religion exclusively to Him,

12. And I have been commanded to be the first of those who submit.'

13. Say, 'If I disobey my Lord,

I fear the torment of a mighty day.'

14. Say, 'God I serve, devoting my religion exclusively to Him;
15. So serve^p what you wish apart from Him.'
    Say, 'The losers will be those who lose themselves
    and their families on the Day of Resurrection.
    That will indeed be the manifest loss.
16. They will have awnings of fire above them
    and awnings [of fire] beneath them.
    That is what God uses to frighten His servants,
    "O my servants, fear Me".'
17. Those who avoid serving idols¹ and turn penitent will have good tidings.
    So give^s good tidings to My servants,
18. Who listen to the declaration and follow the best of it.
    Those are the ones whom God has guided.
    Those are men possessed of understanding.
19. [What about] those on whom the word of torment is fulfilled?
    Will you^s rescue those who are in the Fire?
20. But those who fear their Lord will have chambers,
    with chambers built over them,
    through which rivers flow
    – God's promise.
    God does not break His promise.
21. Have you^s not seen that God has sent down water from the sky
    and has caused it to pass into the earth as springs.
    With it He brings forth crops of various colours;
    then they wither, and you^s see them turning yellow;
    then He makes them chaff.
    In that there is a reminder for men of understanding.
22. [What about] those whose bosoms God has expanded for submission,
    so that they enjoy a light from their Lord?
    But woe to those whose hearts are hardened against remembrance of God.
    Those are in manifest error.
23. God has sent down the fairest discourse,
    a consistent Scripture, *mathānī*,²
    at which the skins of those who fear their Lord creep;
    but then their skins and their hearts soften to remembrance of God.
    That is God's guidance,
    by which He guides those whom He wishes;
    and those whom God leads astray have no guide.

---

¹ See the note on 2:256.
² See the note on 15:87.

24. [What about] those who protect themselves with their faces
against the evil of doom on the Day of Resurrection?
The wrong-doers will be told, 'Taste what you used to earn.'
25. Those before them denied the truth,
and so doom came to them from where they were not aware.
26. God made them taste shame in the life of this world;
and the doom of the world to come will be greater,
if they did but know it.
27. We have coined for men in this Recitation every kind of comparison
so that they may be reminded:
28. A Recitation in Arabic,
containing no crookedness,
so that they may protect themselves.
29. God has coined a likeness:
a man in whom disagreeing partners share
and a man belonging solely to one man.
Are the two equal in likeness?
Praise belongs to God.
No, most of them do not know.
30. You[s] are mortal and they are mortal;
31. Then on the Day of Resurrection you[p] will dispute before your Lord.
32. Who does greater wrong
than those who tell lies against God
and deny the truth when it comes to them?
Is there not in Jahannam a lodging for those who are ungrateful?
33. Those who come with the truth and believe it
– those are the ones who protect themselves.
34. They will have what they wish with their Lord.
That is the reward of those who do good:
35. God will remit from them the worst of what they have done
and recompense them with the best of what they have done.
36. Is not God sufficient for His servant,
though they would frighten you[s] with those apart from Him?
There is no guide for those whom God sends astray.
37. But there is no one who can lead astray those whom God guides.
Is not God mighty and able to take vengeance?
38. If you[s] ask them, 'Who created the heavens and the earth?',
they reply, 'God'.
38a. Say, 'Have you[p] considered what you call on
to the exclusion of God?
If God intends harm for me, are they able to remove His harm?
Or if He intends mercy for me,

are they able to withhold His mercy?'

38b. Say, 'God is my reckoning.
Those who trust put their trust in Him.'

39. Say, 'O my people, act according to your station.
I am going to act [accordingly].
You will know

40. On whom will come a torment that will shame him
and on whom will alight an abiding torment.'

41. We have sent down to you^s the Scripture for mankind with the truth.
Those who are guided aright,
that is to their own advantage;
and those who go astray,
that is to their disadvantage.
You are not a trustee for them.

42. God takes souls at the time of their death;
and [He takes] in their sleep those that have not died;
and He keeps those for whom He has ordained death,
and He releases the others to a stated term.
In that there are signs for people who reflect.

43. Or have they chosen intercessors to the exclusion of God?
Say, 'Even though they have no power and no understanding?'

44. Say, 'To God belongs all intercession.
His is the kingdom of the heavens and the earth.
Then you^p will be returned to Him.'

45. When God alone is mentioned,
the hearts of those who do not believe in the world to come shudder;
and when those apart from Him are mentioned, they rejoice.

46. Say, 'O God, Creator of the heavens and the earth,
Knower of the Invisible and the Witnessed,
You will judge between Your servants
concerning that about which they used to differ.'

47. If those who do wrong were to possess
all that is in the earth and as much again,
they would offer it all to ransom themselves
from the evil of the torment on the Day of Resurrection;
but that on which they had [never] reckoned
will appear to them from God.

48. And the evil of that which they have amassed will appear to them,
and they will be encompassed by that at which they used to mock.

49. When harm touches man, he calls to Us.
Then when We confer a blessing from Us,
he says, 'I obtained it only through knowledge.'

No. It is a trial, but most of them do not know [that].

50. Those who were before them said it,
but what they had been amassing was of no avail to them

51. And the evils of what they amassed smote them.
Those who do wrong from among these men
will be smitten by the evils of what they amassed,
and they will not be able to frustrate [that].

52. Do they not know that God makes generous provision for those whom He wishes
or measures carefully?
In that there are signs for a people who believe.

53. Say, 'O my servants, who have been prodigal against yourselves,
do not despair of God's mercy.
God can forgive sins altogether.
He is the Forgiving, the Compassionate.

54. Turn in penitence to your Lord
and submit to Him before the torment comes to you.
At that point you will not be helped.

55. Follow^p the best of what has been sent down to you from your Lord,
before torment comes to you suddenly,
when you are unaware.'

56. Lest a soul say, 'Alas for my neglect of God.
I was indeed one of those who scoffed;'

57. Or [lest it] say, 'If only God had guided me,
I should have been one of those who protected themselves;'

58. Or [lest it] say, when it sees the torment,
'If only I had another chance,
I would be one of those who do good.'

59. Yes indeed.
My signs have come to you^s,
but you denied their truth
and were haughty and were one of the ungrateful.

60. On the Day of Resurrection you^s will see those who lied against God.
Their faces will be blackened.
Is there not in Jahannam an abode for those who are haughty?

61. God will rescue those who protect themselves.
In their place of safety
evil will not touch them nor will they grieve.

62. God is the Creator of everything.
He is Guardian over everything.

63. He owns the keys of the heavens and the earth,
and those who disbelieve in the signs of God
– those are the losers.

64. Say, 'Do you^p command me to serve any other than God, you ignorant ones?'
65. Inspiration has come to you^s and those who were before you:
    'If you^s associate others with God,
    your work will surely fail,
    and you will be one of the losers.'
66. No. Serve^s God and be one of the thankful.
67. They have not measured God with His real measure,
    when the earth in its entirety will be His handful
    on the Day of Resurrection,
    and the heavens will be rolled up in His right hand.
    Glory be to Him.
    May He be exalted far above that which they associate [with Him].
68. There will be a blast on the trumpet,
    and all who are in the heavens
    and all who are on earth
    will swoon,
    except for those whom God wishes.
    Then there will be a second blast,
    and behold, they will be standing,
    looking and waiting;
69. And the earth will shine with the light of its Lord,
    and the Record will be set in place,
    and the prophets and witnesses will be brought,
    and judgement will be made between them with the truth,
    and they will not be wronged;
70. And each soul will be paid in full for what it has done.
    He is well aware of what they do.
71. Those who are ungrateful will be driven into Jahannam in troops;
    and then, when they reach it,
    its doors will be opened,
    and its keepers will say to them,
    'Did not messengers from among you^p come to you
    reciting to you the signs of your Lord
    and warning you of the meeting of this day of yours?'
    They will reply, 'Yes indeed.
    But the word of torment has been fulfilled against the ungrateful.'
72. It will be said, 'Enter the gates of Jahannam,
    to dwell in it for ever.
    How wretched is the abode of the haughty.'
73. But those who fear God will be driven into the Garden in troops;
    and then, when they reach it,
    its doors will be opened,

and its keepers will say to them,
'Peace upon you! You are good.
Enter it, to remain for ever.'

74. They will say, 'Praise belongs to God,
who has been true to us in His promise
and has made us inherit the land,
for us to dwell where we wish in the Garden.
How excellent is the wage of those who work.'

75. You^s will see the angels thronging round the Throne,
glorifying their Lord with their praise.
Judgement will be made among them with the truth,
and it will be said,
'Praise belongs to God, Lord of all beings.'

Sūra 40

This is usually thought to be a late Meccan *sūra*, with verses 56–57 being Medinan additions. Bell is probably right in thinking that revisions at Medina were wider than the mere addition of two verses. After a brief introduction (1–4), there is a long passage of polemic, dwelling in particular on the Day of Judgement (5–76), into which are set (*a*) a narrative about Moses and Pharaoh (23–46) and (*b*) a brief piece on prophecy (51–55), including an exhortation to Muḥammad. The second insert is taken up again at the beginning of the peroration, which offers further encouragement to Muḥammad and to the believers (77–85).

The Believer

In the name of the Merciful and Compassionate God

1. *Hā', Mīm.*[1]
2. The sending down of the Scripture from the Mighty and Knowing God,
3. The Forgiver of sins, the Accepter of penitence,
   Severe in punishment, Bountiful.
   There is no god but Him.
   To Him is the journeying.
4. The only ones to argue about the signs of God
   are those who do not believe.
   Do not be deluded by their going to and fro in the land.
5. Before them the people of Noah and the factions after them denied the truth,
   and every community had it in mind to seize their messenger
   and put forward false arguments to refute the truth.
   Then I seized them, and how was My punishment.
6. Thus is the Word of your Lord realized against those who do not believe:
   they are the companions of the Fire.
7. Those who bear the throne and those around it
   glorify their Lord with praise
   and believe in Him
   and seek forgiveness for those who believe,
   'Our Lord, You embrace everything in mercy and knowledge.
   Forgive those who repent and follow Your way.

---

[1] On the mystical letters see the note on 2:1. The combination *ḥā' mīm* is found at the beginning of *Sūra*s 40, 41, 42, 43, 44, 45 and 46. As a group these *sūra*s are known as the *ḥawāmīm*.

Protect them from the torment of Hell,

8. Our Lord,

and admit them into the Gardens of Eden,

which you have promised them,

with those of their fathers and their wives and seed who have been righteous.

Truly you are the Mighty and the Wise.

9. Protect them against evil deeds.

Those whom You protect from evil deeds on that day,

You have had mercy on them.

That is the mighty triumph.

10. Those who have not believed will be called to:

'God's hatred is greater than your hatred of yourselves,

when you were summoned to the faith and you did not believe.'

11. They will say, 'Our Lord,

you have caused us to die twice,

and You have given us life twice.

We confess our sins.

Is there any way to get out?'

12. That is because when God was invoked alone

you did not believe;

but if others were associated with him

you believed.

Judgement belongs to God, the Exalted, the Great.

13. [It is] He who shows you His signs

and sends down for you provision from the sky.

Only those who turn in penitence are reminded.

14. Call to God, devoting your religion solely to Him,

even though the unbelievers are averse

15. – Lofty in degrees,

the Lord of the Throne,

casting the spirit of His command

on those of His slaves whom He wishes,

to warn of the Day of Meeting

16. – The day when they come forth,

with nothing about them being concealed from God.

'Whose is the sovereignty to-day?'

'[It belongs] to God, the One, the Mighty.

17. To-day each soul is recompensed with what it has amassed.

There is no wrong to-day.

God is swift in reckoning.'

18. Warn them of the Day of the Imminent,

when hearts are in throats,

[and] they choke with anguish.
Those who do wrong have no friend
nor any intercessor who will be heeded.

19. He knows the treachery of the eyes
and what the breasts conceal.

20. God judges by the truth,
and those to whom they call
apart from Him
judge by nothing.
God is the Hearing and the Observing.

21. Have they not travelled in the land
and seen how was the end of those who were before them?
They were greater than these in power
and in the traces [they left] on earth.
But God seized them for their sins,
and they had no protector from God.

22. That was because their messengers used to bring them the clear proofs,
but they did not believe.
So God seized them.
He is Powerful and Severe in punishment.

23. In the past We sent Moses with Our signs and a clear authority

24. To Pharaoh and Hāmān and Qārūn.
They said, 'A lying sorcerer.'

25. When he brought the truth to them from Us,
they said, 'Kill the sons of those who believe with him,
but spare their women.'
But the guile of the unbelievers is [always] in error.

26. Pharaoh said, 'Let me kill Moses,
and let him call to his Lord.
I fear that he will alter your religion
or cause corruption to appear in the land.'

27. Moses said, 'I take refuge with my Lord and your Lord
from every haughty man who does not believe in the Day of Reckoning.'

28. A believer in Pharaoh's family,
who concealed his belief,
said, 'Are you going to kill a man because he says,
"My Lord is God",
and has brought you the clear proofs from your Lord?
If he is lying, his lies will be reckoned against him;
if he is telling the truth,
some of what he promises you will befall you.
God does not guide any one who is a lying profligate.

431

29. O my people, you have sovereignty to-day,
    being uppermost in the land.
    But who will help us against God's might,
    if it comes to us?'
    Pharaoh said, 'I show you only what I think,
    and I guide you only on the way that is right.'
30. The one who believed said, 'O my people,
    I fear for you something similar to the day of the factions,
31. Like the case of the people of Noah
    and ʿĀd and Thamūd and those after them.
    God wishes no wrong to His servants.
32. O my people, I fear for you the Day of Calling together,
33. The day when you turn your backs and retreat.
    You have no protector against God.
    Those whom God sends astray have no guide.
34. In the past Joseph brought youᵖ the clear proofs,
    but you continued to be in doubt
    about what he brought you;
    then when he perished you said,
    "God will never send a messenger after him."
    Thus God sends astray anyone who is a doubting profligate.'
35. Those who engage in disputes concerning God's sign,
    without any authority that has come to them
    – [their action] is of grievous hatefulness with God
    and with those who believe.
    Thus God sets a seal on every arrogant, contumacious heart.
36. Pharaoh said, 'O Hāmān, build me a high building
    so that I may reach the ropes,
37. The ropes of heaven,
    and look on the God of Moses,
    although I think him a liar.'
    Thus was the evil of Pharaoh's deeds made to seem good to him,
    and he was barred from the way.
    Pharaoh's guile [ended] only in ruin.
38. The one who believed said, 'O my people,
    follow me and I shall guide you to the way that is right.
39. O my people, the life of this world is a passing enjoyment.
    The world to come is the abode of stability.
40. Those who do an evil deed will only be recompensed by its like;
    whilst those who do a righteous deed,
    be they male or female,
    and are believers

– they will enter the Garden,
where they will be given sustenance without reckoning.

41. O my people, how is it that I call you to deliverance
and you call me to the Fire?

42. You call me to disbelieve in God
and to associate with Him that of which I have no knowledge,
whilst I call you to the Mighty, the Forgiver.

43. There is no doubt that what you call me to
cannot be invoked in this world,
nor in the next,
and that our return is to God
and that the profligates will be the companions of the Fire.

44. You will remember what I say to you.
I entrust my affair to God.
God is observer of his servants.'

45. And so God protected him against the evils of their plotting,
and evil punishment encompassed the family of Pharaoh –

46. The Fire,
to which they are exposed morning and evening,
and on the day when the Hour rises up:
'Cause the family of Pharaoh to enter the most awful torment.'

47. When they argue with one another in the Fire,
the weak will say to those who were proud,
'We were your followers.
Can you be of avail to us with any part of the Fire?'

48. Those who were proud say, 'We are all in it.
God has given judgement between His servants.'

49. Those in the Fire say to the keepers of Jahannam,
'Call to your Lord
and He will lighten for us one day of the torment.'

50. They will say, 'Did not your messengers bring you the clear proofs?'
They will reply, 'Yes, they did.'
They will say, 'Then you call!'
But the calling of the unbelievers is only in error.

51. Truly We help Our messengers and those who believe,
in the life of this world
and on the day when the witnesses arise,

52. The day when the wrong-doers do not profit from their excuses.
Theirs is the curse, and theirs is the evil abode.

53. In the past We gave Moses the guidance,
and We caused the Children of Israel to inherit the Scripture,

54. A guidance and a reminder for men of understanding.

55. Have^s patience. God's promise is true.
    Seek^s forgiveness for your sin,
    and glorify your Lord by praising Him in the evening and the early morning.
56. Those who engage in disputes about God's signs
    without any authority having come to them
    – there is only expectation of grandeur in their breasts,
    and they will never reach it.
    Seek^s refuge with God.
    He is the Hearing and the Observing.
57. The creation of the heavens and the earth is greater than the creation of mankind,
    but most of the people do not know [that].
58. The blind man and the one who sees are not equal;
    nor are those who believe and do righteous deeds and the wrong-doer.
    Little do you^p reflect.
59. The Hour is coming
    – there is no doubt about it;
    but most of the people do not believe.
60. Your^p Lord has said, 'Call to Me
    and I shall answer you.
    Those who are too proud to serve me will enter Jahannam in abjectness.
61. [It is] God who made the night for you to rest in it
    and the day to give sight.
    God is possessed of bounty for the people,
    but most of the people are not grateful.
62. Such for you is God, your Lord,
    the creator of everything.
    There is no God but Him.
    How are you involved in lies?
63. Thus those who deny God's signs are involved in lies.
64. [It is] God who made for you^p the earth as a dwelling place and the sky as a canopy,
    and fashioned you and fashioned you well
    and provided you with good things as sustenance.
    Such for you is God, your Lord.
    Blessed be God, Lord of created beings.
65. He is the Living.
    There is no god save Him.
    Call to Him, devoting your religion solely to Him.
    Praise belongs to God, Lord of created beings.
66. Say, 'I have been forbidden to serve those to whom you call,
    to the exclusion of God,
    since the clear proofs have come to me from My Lord,
    and I have been ordered to surrender to the Lord of created beings.

67. [It is] He who created you from dust,
    then from sperm,
    then from a clot,
    then brings you forth as infants,
    then [arranges] that you attain maturity
    and then that you become old men
    – though there are some of you who are taken before it –
    and that you reach a stated term,
    and that you may understand.
68. [It is] He who gives life and brings death.
    When He has decided a matter,
    He simply says 'Be', and it is.
69. Have you not considered those who engage in disputes about God's signs,
    how they are turned about?
70. – Those who deny the Scripture
    and that with which we have sent our messengers.
    They will know!
71. Behold the fetters and chains around their necks.
    They are dragged
72. Into the boiling water
    and then they thrust into the Fire.
73. Then it is said to them,
    'Where is that which you used to associate with God
74. Apart from God?
    They say, 'They have failed us.
    No. We previously used to call to nothing.'
    Thus God sends the unbelievers astray:
75. 'This is because you rejoiced on earth without right
    and because you were exultant.
76. Enter the gates of Jahannam,
    in which you will remain for ever.
    Evil is the lodging of those who are proud.'
77. Have^s patience.
    God's promise is true.
    Whether We show you some of what We promise them
    or We take you,
    they will be returned to Us.
78. Before you in the past We sent messengers,
    among them those of whom We have told you
    and those of whom We have not told you;
    but no messenger had the right to produce a sign
    save with God's permission.

When God's command comes,
judgement is given with truth,
and there the workers of vanity will be lost.

79.   [It is] God who has assigned livestock to you^P,
for you to ride some of them and eat some of them

80.   – You^P have many benefits from them –
and for you to reach on them a need that is in your breasts,
and you are carried on ships [just as] you are borne on them.

81.   And He shows you^P His signs
– and which of God's signs will you deny?

82.   Have they not travelled in the land
and seen how was the end of those before them?
They were greater than them in power
and in the traces [they left] on earth.
But what they used to amass was of no avail for them.

83.   And when their messengers brought them the clear proofs,
they rejoiced in the knowledge they had
– and they were encompassed by what they used to mock.

84.   And when they saw Our might, they said,
'We believe in God alone
and we reject what we used to associate with Him.'

85.   But their faith did not avail them
when they saw Our might
– the way of God that has happened in the past
concerning His servants.
There the unbelievers will be lost.

Sūra 41

The *sūra* is considered to be late Meccan. It falls into at least ten sections: revelation and the people (1–4); polemic (5–12); ʿĀd and Thamūd (13–18); judgement (19–23); Hell (24–29); paradise (30–32); further polemic (33–40); passage about scripture, present (41–44) and past (45–46); a peroration finishing with encouragement to Muḥammad (47–53). Against this, there is only one change of assonance, after verse 38.

Expounded

In the name of the Merciful and Compassionate God

1. *Ḥā', Mīm.*[1]
2. Revelation from the Merciful and Compassionate,
3. Scripture whose signs are expounded,
   as a Recitation in Arabic
   for a people who have knowledge,
4. [Through] a bearer of good tidings and a warner.
   But most of them turn away and do not hear.
5. They say, 'Our hearts are veiled from that to which you call us,
   and in our ears is heaviness,
   and between us and you there is a veil.
   Act [in your way];
   we shall be acting in Ours.'
6. Say, 'I am only a mortal like you[p].
   It has been revealed to me
   that your god is One God.
   Take the straight path to Him
   and seek His forgiveness.
   Woe to those who associate partners with God,
7. Who do not give the *zakāt*
   and who do not believe in the world to come.'
8. Those who believe and do righteous deeds
   will have an unbroken reward.
9. Say, 'Do you not believe in the One who created the earth in two days?
   Do you set up rivals to Him?

---

[1] On this group of mystical letters see the note on 40:1.

He is the Lord of created beings.

10. He placed [on the earth] firm mountains rising over it,
and He blessed it,
and measured in it its sustenance in four days,
equal for those who ask.

11. Then He moved to the sky, which was smoke,
and said to it and to the earth,
"Come willingly or unwillingly".
The two of them said, "We come willingly".

12. He finished them as seven heavens in two days,
and revealed in each heaven its command.'
We adorned the lowest heaven with lamps
and as a guard.
That is the measuring of the Mighty and the Knowing.

13. But if they turn away,
say, 'I have warned you of a thunderbolt
like the thunderbolt of 'Ād and Thamūd;

14. When the messengers came to them
from before them and from behind them,
saying, 'Serve only God.'
They said, 'Had our Lord willed,
He would have sent down angels.
We do not believe that with which you have been sent.'

15. As for 'Ād, they were haughty in the land without right,
and they said, 'Who has greater power than us?'
Did they not see that God,
who created them,
has greater power than them?
They denied our signs.

16. Therefore We sent down on them a wind,
raging in bitterly cold days,
to make them taste the torment of shame in the life of this world
– and the torment of the world to come will be more shameful,
and they will not be helped.

17. As for Thamūd, We guided them,
but they preferred blindness to guidance;
so the thunderbolt of punishment,
degradation,
took them for what they had been amassing.

18. But We delivered those who believed and were god-fearing.

19. On the day when the enemies of God are rounded up to the Fire, driven on,

20. Then, when they reach it,

their hearing and their sight and their skins
bear witness against them about what they had been doing,

21. And they say to their skins,
'Why do you testify against us?';
they say, 'We have been given speech by God,
who can give speech to everything
and who created you the first time
and to whom you will be returned.

22. You did not take cover from your hearing and your sight and your skins bearing
witness against you.
You thought that God would not know much of what you were doing.

23. That, the thought that you thought about your Lord,
has destroyed you.
You are now among the losers.'

24. If they persist,
the Fire will be a lodging for them;
and if they ask for favour,
they will not be among those to whom favour is shown.

25. We assigned them comrades,
who made what was before them
and what was behind them
seem fair to them.
The saying concerning nations,
of both *Jinn* and men,
that passed away before them,
has been realized against them.
They have been losers.

26. Those who do not believe say,
'Do[P] not listen to this Recitation,
but talk idly during it,
so that you may prevail.'

27. We shall surely make those who do not believe taste a terrible torment
and We shall give them as recompense
the worst of what they used to do.

28. That is the recompense of God's enemies:
the Fire.
They will have in it the abode of eternity,
as a recompense for the denial of Our signs.

29. Those who do not believe say,
'Our Lord, show us the two groups,
of both *Jinn* and men,
who led us astray.

We shall place them beneath our feet
that they may be among the lowest.'

30. [But] those who say, 'Our Lord is God',
and then follow the straight way,
the angels descend on them, saying,
'Do not fear. Do not grieve.
Rejoice in the Garden which you have been promised.

31. We are your friends in the life of this world and in the next.
In it you will have all that your souls desire;
in it you will have all you call for

32. – Hospitality from One [who is] Forgiving and Compassionate.'

33. Who speaks more fairly than the one who calls to God
and does what is righteous and says,
'I am one of those who surrender'?

34. Good and evil deeds are not equal.
Repel [evil] with what is fairer,
and, lo, the one with whom you are at enmity
will become like a warm friend.

35. Only those who are steadfast will meet with it.
Only the one possessed of a great fortune will meet with it.

36. If a provocation from Satan provokes you,
seek refuge in God.
He is the Hearer and the Knower.

37. Of His signs are the night, the day,
the sun and the moon.
Do not prostrate yourselves to the sun nor to the moon;
but prostrate yourselves to God,
who created them,
if you serve Him.

38. If they are proud
– those who are with your Lord glorify Him night and day
and do not grow tired.

39. Of His signs is that you see the earth humble;
and when We send down on it water,
it stirs and grows.
The One who gives it life is
the One who gives life to the dead.
He has power over everything.

40. Those who pervert Our signs are not hidden from Us.
Are those who are hurled into the Fire better
or those who come in security on the Day of Resurrection?
Do what you will.

He is observer of what you do.

41. Those who disbelieve in the Reminder when it has come to them
– truly it is a mighty Scripture.

42. Falsehood cannot come to it from before it or from behind it,
a sending down from One [who is] Wise and Praiseworthy.

43. You⁵ are told only what the messengers before you were told.
Your⁵ Lord can forgive or inflict a painful punishment.

44. If We had made it a foreign Recitation,
they would have said,
'Why are its signs not made clear?
Foreign and Arabic?'
Say, 'For those who believe it is a guidance and a healing.
Those who do not believe
– there is heaviness in their ears
and [their unbelief] is a blindness for them.
Those are called to from afar.'

45. In the past We gave Moses the Scripture,
but there was disagreement about it;
and had it not been for a word that had preceded from your Lord,
there would have been a decision between them;
but they are in disquieting doubt about it.

46. He who acts righteously does so for himself;
he who does wrong does so against himself.
Your Lord is not a wrong-doer to His servants.

47. To Him is referred knowledge of the Hour.
No fruit comes forth from its sheath
and no female becomes pregnant or gives birth
except with His knowledge.

47a. On the day when He calls out to them,
'Where are those you associated with Me?'
they will say, 'We proclaim to you,
"There is no witness among us".'

48. That which they used to call to before has strayed from them,
and they think that they will have no place of refuge.

49. Man is never tired of calling for good,
but if evil touches him
he is disheartened and desperate.

50. If We cause him to taste some mercy from Us
after some harm has touched him,
he will say, 'This is mine.
I do not think that the Hour is coming.
If I am returned to my Lord,

I shall have with Him the fairest reward.'
But We shall surely tell those who do not believe what they did.
We shall make them taste a harsh torment.

51. When We bless man, he turns away and withdraws,
but when evil touches him, wide-ranging are his prayers.

52. Say, 'Have you^p considered?
If it² is from God and you reject it
– who is further astray
than the one who is in distant schism?

53. We shall show them Our signs on the horizons and in themselves
until it becomes clear to them that it is the truth.
Is it not sufficient that your Lord
is witness over everything?

54. They are in doubt about [their] meeting with their Lord.
But truly He encompasses everything.

---

² The Recitation.

Sūra 42

This *sūra* is generally thought to be from the late Meccan period, though some Muslim commentators believe verses 23–27 and possibly 39–41 to be Medinan. The flow of the material makes it hard to divide the *sūra* into sections. The most obvious breaks are after verses 8, 23 and 48. It is largely a polemical piece, stressing God's 'signs' and might. There are none of the normal narrative stories that one might expect in a *sūra* from this period. In this respect it is similar to *Sūra* 13.

Counsel

In the name of the Merciful and Compassionate God

1. *Ḥā', Mīm.*
2. *'Ayn, Sīn, Qāf.*[1]
3. Thus God, [who is] Mighty and Wise reveals to you^s
    and to those before you.
4. To Him belongs what is in the heavens
    and what is on earth.
    He is the Exalted and the Mighty.
5. The heavens are almost split asunder from above
    when the angels glorify their Lord by praising him
    and seek forgiveness for all those on earth.
    Truly God is the Forgiving and Compassionate.
6. Those who have chosen protectors to His exclusion
    – God is watcher over them.
    You^s are not a guardian for them.
7. Thus We have revealed to you^s a Recitation in Arabic
    for you to warn the mother of settlements[2] and those around it
    and for you to warn of the Day of Gathering,
    of which there is no doubt.
    A part of them will be in the Garden
    and a part of them in the Blaze.
8. Had God willed, He could have made them one community,
    but God admits to His mercy those whom He wishes.

---

[1] On these mystical letters see the note on 40:1. This is the only *sūra* to have the additional letters *'ayn, sīn, qāf.*

[2] Mecca.

The wrong-doers have no protector and no helper,

9. Or have they chosen protectors to His exclusion?
But God is the protector.
He gives life to the dead
and He has power over everything.

10. Whatever you[p] differ about,
judgement on it belongs to God.
That is God, my Lord;
in Him I have put my trust and to Him I turn,

11. The creator of the heavens and the earth.
He has appointed for you,
from yourselves, pairs,
and also pairs from livestock,
in which He gives you increase.
There is nothing like Him.
He is the Hearing and the Observing.

12. His are the keys of the heavens and the earth.
He extends the provision for those whom He wishes
and He measures it carefully.
He is aware of everything.

13. He has instituted for you[p]
that religion which He ordained on Noah
and what We have revealed to you[s]
and what We enjoined on Abraham and Moses and Jesus,
saying, 'Establish[p] the true religion
and do not be[p] divided about it.'
That to which you[s] call those who associate others with God is hard for them.
God chooses for Himself those whom He wishes
and guides to Himself those who turn [to Him].

14. They were divided only after knowledge had come to them,
in outrage between themselves.
Had it not been for a word[3] that had already preceded from your[s] Lord for a
stated term,
judgement would have been made between them.
And those to whom the Scripture has been given as inheritance after them
are in disquieting doubt about it.

15. Therefore summon[s] [them] and follow the straight path
as you[s] have been commanded;
and do not follow their whims,
but say, 'I believe in the Scripture that God has sent down,

---

[3] See the note on 10:19. The phraseology here is more complex than usual.

and I have been commanded to be just among you.
God is our Lord and your Lord.
To us are our works, and to you are your works.
There is no argument between you and us.
God will bring us together.
To Him is the journeying.'

16. Those who argue about God after answer has been made to them,
their argument is untenable with their Lord.
Wrath will be upon them,
and they will have a severe torment.

17. [It is] God who has sent down the Scripture and the Balance with the truth.
What will give you^s knowledge?
Perhaps the Hour is something near.

18. Those who do not believe in it seek to hasten it,
whilst those who believe are in fear of it
and know that it is the truth.
Those who dispute about the Hour are truly in distant error.

19. God is kind to His servants.
He gives sustenance to those whom He wishes.
He is the Strong and the Mighty.

20. Those who wish to cultivate the world to come
– We give them increase in its cultivation.
And those who wish to cultivate this world,
We give them some of it,
but they have no share in the world to come.

21. Or do they have associates who have instituted for them in religion
things that God has not allowed.
Had it not been for the word of decision,
judgement would have been given between them.
The wrong-doers will have a painful torment.

22. You^s can see the wrong-doers in fear of what they have amassed,
which is about to befall them;
while those who believe and do righteous deeds
will be in the meadows of the Gardens,
having what they wish from their Lord.
That is the great bounty.

23. That is the good news which God gives to His servants who believe and do
righteous deeds.
Say, 'I do not ask you^p for any fee for it
but only love concerning kinsmen.
Whoever garners a good deed,
We shall give him greater good for it.

God is Forgiving and Grateful.'

24. Or they say, 'He has invented a lie against God'.
    If God wishes, He will set a seal on your[s] heart.
    By His words God can erase the false and verify the truth.
    He is aware of [the thoughts in] the breasts [of men].

25. [It is] He who accepts repentance from His servants
    and who pardons evil deeds.
    He knows what you[p] do.

26. And He answers those who believe and do righteous deeds
    and gives them an increase of His bounty;
    but the unbelievers will have a severe punishment.

27. If God were to make liberal provision for His servants,
    they would be insolent in the land;
    but He sends down in measure what He wishes.
    He is Informed and Observing of His servants.

28. It is He who sends down the rain after they have despaired,
    and He spreads His mercy.
    He is the protector who deserves praise.

29. Of His signs is the creation of the heavens and the earth
    and the beasts He has dispersed in them.
    He is able to gather them when He wishes.

30. Whatever misfortune may befall you[p] is for what your hands have amassed.
    He pardons much.

31. You[p] cannot frustrate [Him] on earth.
    You have no protector or helper apart from God.

32. Of His signs are the ships running in the sea,
    like waymarks;

33. If He wishes He calms the wind
    so that they remain motionless on its surface.
    – in that there are signs for every steadfast, grateful person –

34. Or He wrecks them[4] for what they[5] have amassed.
    But He pardons much.

35. Those who dispute concerning Our signs
    know that they have no place of shelter.

36. Whatever you[p] have been given is the enjoyment of the life of this world.
    Whatever is with God is better and more lasting
    for those who believe and put their trust in their Lord,

37. And for those who shun heinous sin and immorality
    and forgive when they are angry,

---

[4] The ships.
[5] Those on board.

38. And for those who answer their Lord and perform prayer
and whose affair is counsel between them
and who spend some of that which We have provided for them,
39. And for those who help themselves when oppressive treatment befalls them.
40. The recompense of evil is the same amount of evil.
Whoever turns away [from evil] and makes amends,
his wage is with God.
He does not love those who do wrong.
41. Those who help themselves after they have suffered wrong,
there is no way against them.
42. The way is against those who wrong the people
and act oppressively in the land without right
– for them there is a painful torment.
43. Those who are steadfast and are forgiving
– that comes from determination in affairs.
44. He whom God sends astray has no friend after Him.
You^s will see the wrong-doers,
when they have seen the torment,
say, 'Is there any way of averting [it]?'
45. You^s will see them exposed to it,
abject in humiliation,
looking with a stealthy glance;
and those who believe will say,
'The losers are those who lose themselves and their families on the Day of
Resurrection.
The wrong-doers will surely be in a lasting punishment.'
46. They will have no protectors to help them,
apart from God;
and those whom God sends astray
– for them there is no road.
47. Answer^p your Lord
before a day which cannot be averted comes from God.
You will have no refuge on that day and no denial.
48. If they turn away, We have not sent you^s to be a guardian over them.
It is only your^s duty to convey [the message].
When we let man taste some mercy from Us,
he rejoices in it;
but if some evil befalls them
because of what their hands have forwarded,
man is ungrateful.
49. God's is the sovereignty of the heavens and the earth.
He creates what he wishes.

He gives females to those whom He wishes
and males to those whom He wishes.

50. Or He pairs them, males and females,
    and makes barren those whom He wishes.
    He is Knowing and Powerful.

51. It has not been granted to any mortal to be spoken to by God
    except by revelation
    or from behind a screen;
    or He will send a messenger to reveal what He wishes
    by His permission.
    He is Lofty and Wise.

52. And thus We have inspired you^s with a Spirit of Our command.
    You did not know what the Scripture was nor the Faith,
    but We made it a light,
    by which We guide such of Our servants as We wish.
    You^s guide to a straight path,

53. The path of God,
    to whom belongs all that is in the heavens
    and all that is on earth.
    Truly all things journey to God.

Sūra 43

This is generally thought to be a middle Meccan *sūra*, though some Muslim commentators say that verse 45 is Medinan and others say the same of verse 54. There is some evidence of recasting (see, for example, the note on verse 88). The *sūra* falls into five main sections: introductory (1–4); polemic (5–25); narratives about Abraham, Moses and Jesus (26–65); a passage of polemic and eschatology (66–83); and a peroration (84–89).

The Ornaments

In the name of the Merciful and Compassionate God

1.   *Ḥā', Mīm.*[1]
2.   By the clear Scripture
3.   – We have made it a Recitation in Arabic,
     so that you[p] may understand.
4.   It is in the matrix[2] of the Scripture, with Us, lofty and wise.
5.   Shall We ignore you[p] because you have been a profligate people?
6.   How many a prophet We sent among the ancients,
7.   and not a prophet came to them but they mocked him.
8.   So We destroyed men of greater might than them,
     and the example of the ancients passed away.[3]
9.   If you[s] ask them, 'Who created the heavens and the earth?'
     they will say 'They were created
     by the Mighty and Knowing One,
10. Who has made the earth as a cradle for you[p]
     and has put roads in it for you,
     for you to find the right way,
11. Who has sent down water from heaven in measure;
     and We have revived dead land with it.
     Thus you will be brought forth.
12. Who created the species, all of them,
     and assigned to you those ships and beasts that you ride,
13. For you to settle on their backs

---

[1] On this group of mystical letters see the note on 40:1.
[2] The Arabic is *umm* 'mother'. See also 3:7 and 13:49.
[3] *i.e.* passed into history.

449

and then remember the blessing of your Lord,
when you are settled on them,
and that you may say,
"Glory be to Him, who has subjected this to us
when we were not equal to it.

14. We turn to our Lord".'

15. But they have assigned a part of His servants to Him.[4]
Man is clearly ungrateful.

16. Or has He taken to himself,
from all that He creates, daughters,
and [at the same time] favoured you with sons?

17. And when one of them is given the good tidings of what he has struck as a
likeness[5] to the Merciful,
his face remains blackened
and he is choking with rage:

18. 'One who is raised among ornaments
and not visible at the time of dispute.'

19. And they have made the angels who are the servants of God females.
Did they witness their creation.
Their testimony will be recorded
and they will be questioned.

20. They say, 'Had the Merciful wished,
we would not have served them.'
They have no knowledge of that.
They only guess.

21. Or did We bring them a Scripture before this,
to which they hold fast?

22. No. They say, 'We found our forefathers following a religion,
and we are guided over their traces.'

23. Thus We never sent any warner into a settlement
without its affluent people saying,
'We found our fathers following a religion,
and we are following on their traces.'

24. He[6] said, 'And if I were to bring you better guidance than that
on which you found your forefathers?'
They replied, 'We do not believe what you were sent with.'

25. So We took vengeance on them.
See how was the consequence for those who denied the truth.

---

[4] *i.e.* said that the pagan goddesses are God's daughters. See what follows.
[5] *i.e.* is told of the birth of a daughter.
[6] The messenger.

26. And [recall] when Abraham said to his father and his family,
    'I am quit of what you serve,
27. Except for Him who created me,
    for He will guide me.'
28. And he made it an enduring word among his posterity,
    so that they might return.
29. No. I granted enjoyment to these and their fathers
    [only] until the truth and a clear messenger came to them.
30. And when the truth came to them,
    they said, 'This is sorcery, and we reject it.'
31. They say, 'Why has this Recitation not been sent down
    to an important man from the two settlements?'[7]
32. Is it they who divide out your Lord's mercy?
    We have divided out their livelihood among them in the life of this world
    and We have raised some of them above others in rank,
    for some of them to take others in servitude.
    And the mercy of your Lord is better than what they gather.
33. Were it not for the fact that mankind would be one nation,
    We would appoint for those who do not believe in the Merciful
    roofs of silver for their houses and stairs by which to ascend
34. And doors for their houses,
    and couches on which to recline,
35. And ornaments.
    All that is but the enjoyment of the life of this world
    – the world to come with your Lord
    is for those who are god-fearing.
36. Whoever is blind to remembrance of the Merciful,
    We assign to him a satan who is his comrade.[8]
37. They will indeed turn them aside from the way,
    though they reckon that they are being guided aright;
38. Then, when he comes to Us, he will say,
    'Would that there were between you[s] and me
    the distance of the two places where the sun rises
    – an evil companion.'
39. There will be no profit for you[p] today,
    since you did wrong,
    in the fact that you will share in the torment.
40. Can you[s] make the deaf hear or guide the blind

---

[7] Traditionally understood as Mecca and al-Ṭā'if.
[8] Those referred to in the singular in v. 36 are referred to in the plural in v. 37 and then again in the singular in v. 38.

or those who are in manifest error.

41. If We take you^s away,
We shall take vengeance on them,

42. Or if We show you^s that which We have promised them,
We have power over them.

43. So hold^s fast to what has been revealed to you.
You^s are on a straight path.

44. It is indeed a reminder for you^s and your people;
and you^p will be questioned.

45. Ask^s those of Our messengers whom We sent before you
whether We appointed gods to be served,
apart from the Merciful.

46. In the past We sent Moses to Pharaoh and his nobles with Our signs.
He said, 'I am the messenger of the Lord of created beings.'

47. But when he brought them Our signs,
they laughed at them.

48. Every sign We showed them was greater that the previous one,
and We seized them with torment
so that they might return.

49. They said, 'O sorcerer, call to your Lord for us
by the covenant He has made with you,
and we shall be guided aright.'

50. But when We removed the torment from them,
they broke their promise.

51. Pharaoh proclaimed among his people, saying,
'O my people, do I not possess the kingdom of Egypt
and these rivers flowing beneath me?
Do you not see?

52. Am I [not] better than this man,
who is contemptible and scarcely makes [himself] clear?

53. Why have bracelets of gold not been cast on him
or the angels come, joined with him?'

54. He made his people unsteady, and they obeyed him.
They were a people who were reprobates.

55. When they had angered Us,
We took vengeance on them and drowned them all.

56. We made them a thing of the past and an example for those of later times.

57. When the son of Mary is cited as an example,
your people turn away from it.

58. They say, 'Are our gods better or is he?'
They cite him to you only for argument.
No! they are a contentious people.

59. He is only a servant on whom We bestowed blessing,
    and We made Him an example for the Children of Israel.
60. Had We wished, We could have appointed angels among you as successors in
    the land.
61. [The Recitation] is knowledge concerning the Hour.
    Have no doubt about it, but follow Me.
    This is a straight path.
62. Let not Satan turn you^p aside.
    He is a clear enemy for you.
63. When Jesus came with the clear proofs,
    he said, 'I have come to you with wisdom
    and to make clear to you some of that about which you differ.
    Fear God and obey me.
64. God is your Lord and my Lord.
    Serve Him.
    This is a straight path.
65. The parties among them differed.
    Woe to those who did wrong,
    because of the torment of a painful day.
66. Do they wait for anything but the Hour
    to come on them suddenly when they are unaware?
67. On that day friends will be foes to one another
    – though that will not be the case with the god-fearing.
68. 'My servants, today there is no fear on you
    nor will you grieve,
69. [You] who believed in Our signs
    and were people who surrendered,
70. Enter the Garden, you and your wives.
    You will be treated with honour.
71. Trays of gold and goblets will be brought round to them,
    and in it there is what their souls desire
    and their eyes find pleasant.
    You^p will remain in it for ever.
72. This is the Garden which you have been given as an inheritance
    in return for what you used to do.
73. In it there is abundant fruit, of which you may eat.
74. The sinners will remain for ever in the torment of Jahannam.
75. There will be no abatement for them
    and they are in despair at it.
76. We have not wronged them
    – they wronged themselves.
77. They proclaim, 'O Master,

453

let your Lord be finished with us.'
He replies, 'You[P] will linger.
78. We brought you the truth,
but most of you were averse to the truth.'
79. Or have they determined something?
We too determine.
80. Or do they reckon that We do not hear their secret and their private talk?
Of course We do, and our messengers,[9] who are with them, record.
81. Say, 'The Merciful does not have a son.
I am first among [His] servants.
82. Glory be to the Lord of the heavens and the earth,
Lord of the Throne,
far above what they describe.
83. Let them plunge[10] and play
until they meet the day they were promised.
84. It is He who is God in heaven and God on earth.
He is the Decisive and The Wise.
85. Blessings be to Him who has sovereignty of the heavens and the earth and what
is between them
and who has knowledge of the Hour
and to whom you will be returned.
86. Those to whom they call apart from Him
have no power of intercession,
except in the case of those who bear witness to the truth and who have knowledge.
87. If you ask them who created them,
they will say, 'God.'
How are they involved in lies?
88. And for his saying,[11] 'My Lord,
these are a people who do not believe,'
89. Pardon[s] them and say, 'Peace.'
They will know.

---

[9] Traditionally interpreted as 'the angels'.

[10] See the note on 6:68.

[11] There is a problem with the text here. The verse appears to begin in mid-sentence.

Sūra 44

The *sūra* is considered to be from the middle Meccan period. This seems likely, though there may have been some recasting, particularly of the first few verses. The *sūra* falls into six sections: introduction (1–8); a passage of polemic and eschatology (9–16); a narrative of the punishment of Pharaoh's people and the saving of the Children of Israel (17–33); a further passage of polemic and eschatology (34–42); culminating in a piece contrasting hell and heaven (43–57); and two final verses addressed to Muḥammad (58–59).

Smoke

In the name of the Merciful and Compassionate God

1. *Ḥā', Mīm.*[1]
2. By the Scripture that makes plain
3. – We have revealed it on a blessed night
   – We are always warning –
4. In which every wise command is made clear,
5. As a command from Us
   – We are always sending –
6. As a mercy from your[s] Lord
   – He is the Hearer and the Knower –
7. The Lord of the heavens and the earth and what is between them,
   if you[p] are certain [in your faith],
8. There is no god but Him.
   He gives life and brings death
   – your Lord and the Lord of your forefathers.
9. No! They are in doubt, playing.
10. So wait[s] for the day when the sky will bring a visible smoke
11. Which will envelop the people.
    This will be a painful torment.
12. 'Our Lord, remove this torment from us.
    Truly we are believers.'
13. How will the reminder [help] them?
    – for a clear messenger has come to them,
14. [And] then they have turned their backs on him and said,

---

[1] On this group of mystical letters see the footnote on 40:1.

455

'Someone taught, someone possessed.'

15. We remove the torment a little
    – and you^P return [to your old ways].

16. On the day when We make the mightiest assault,
    We shall take vengeance.

17. Before them We tested the people of Pharaoh,
    when a noble messenger came to them,

18. Saying, 'Deliver^P God's servants² to me.
    I am a trustworthy messenger for you^P,'

19. And, 'Do^P not rise high against God.
    I come to you^P with a clear authority.

20. I have taken refuge with my Lord and your Lord
    lest you stone me.

21. If you do not believe in me, withdraw from me.'

22. He called to his Lord, saying,
    'These are a sinful people.'

23. 'Then go^s forth with My servants by night.
    You^P will be followed.

24. Leave^s the sea motionless.
    They are a drowned host.'

25. How many gardens and springs they have left behind,

26. And crops and noble sites,

27. And pleasant things in which they took delight.

28. Thus;
    and We made them all an inheritance for other people.

29. And heaven and earth did not weep for them,
    and they were not reprieved.

30. And We delivered the Children of Israel from the humiliating torment,

31. From Pharaoh.
    He was high, one of the extravagant.

32. We chose them, through knowledge, above created beings,

33. And We gave them those of Our signs that contained a manifest trial.

34. These men say,

35. 'There is only our first death.
    We shall not be raised.

36. Bring our fathers, if you^P speak the truth.'

37. Are they better or the people of Tubba'³ and those before them,
    whom We destroyed?
    They were sinners.

---

² Here 'God's servants' refers to the Children of Israel.

³ Title of kings of the Yemen.

38. We did not create the heavens and the earth and what is between them, in play.
39. We only created them in truth,
    but most of them do not know that.
40. The day of decision is their appointed time,
    all [of them] –
41. The day when a patron will be of no avail for a client,
    and they will not be helped,
42. Except those on whom God has mercy.
    He is the Mighty and the Compassionate.
43. The tree of *al-Zaqqūm*[4]
44. Is the food of the sinner,
45. Like molten metal boiling in the bellies
46. As scalding water boils.
47. 'Take him and thrust him into the midst of Hell.
48. Then pour over his head some of the tormenting scalding water.'
49. 'Taste[s]. You are the mighty and the noble.[5]
50. This is that about which you[p] had doubts.'
51. Those who protect themselves will be in a secure station,
52. Among gardens and springs,
53. Wearing silk and brocade, facing one another.
54. Thus;
    and We shall pair them with maidens with dark, lustrous eyes.
55. There, in security, they will call for every kind of fruit.
56. There they will not taste death,
    except the first death;
    and He will protect them from the torment of Hell –
57. A bounty from your[s] Lord.
    That is the great triumph.
58. We have made it[6] easy by your[s] tongue,
    so that they may be reminded.
59. So wait.
    They are waiting.

---

[4] *Cf.* 37:62 and 56:52.
[5] The phrase is sarcastic.
[6] The Recitation.

Sūra 45

This *sūra* is generally considered to be late Meccan, though some authorities believe that verse 14 is Medinan. As with *Sūra* 42, there are none of the normal narrative stories. After a couple of verses about the message, the *sūra* has two main sections: the first (3–19) is on God's signs; the second (20–35) contains polemic. Two verses in praise of God then round the piece off. A large proportion of the *sūra* is found elsewhere in various Meccan and early Medinan *sūra*s. The Commentary lists the more important cross-references.

The Crouching

In the name of the Merciful and Compassionate God

1. *Ḥā', Mīm.*[1]
2. The sending down of the Scripture from the Mighty and Wise God.
3. In the heavens and the earth there are signs for the believers,
4. And in your[p] creation and the beasts that He spreads abroad
    there are signs for a people who are sure,
5. And in the alternation of day and night
    and the provision which God sends down from the sky,
    with which He brings life to the earth after it has died off,
    and in the turning about of the winds
    there are signs for a people who understand.
6. These are God's signs that We recite to you[s] in truth;
    and after God and His signs
    in which discourse will they believe?
7. Woe to every sinful liar,
8. Who hears God's signs recited to Him,
    and then persists in being haughty
    as though he had not heard them.
    Give[s] him the tidings of a painful torment.
9. When he knows anything of Our signs,
    he takes them in mockery.
    These people will have a humiliating torment.
10. Behind them is Jahannam,
    and that which they have amassed will avail them nothing,

---

[1] On these mystical letters see the note on 40:1.

458

nor will what they have taken as protectors
to the exclusion of God.
They will have a great torment.

11. This is a guidance
– and those who deny the truth of their Lord's signs
will have a painful torment of abomination.

12. It is God who has subjected the sea for you[p],
that the ships may run on it by His command
and that you may seek some of His bounty
and that you may be grateful,

13. And who has subjected for you all that is in the heavens and the earth,
[which is all] from Him.
In that there are signs for a people who reflect.

14. Tell those who believe
to forgive those who do not hope for the days of God,
that He may requite a people for what they have been amassing.

15. If anyone acts righteously, it is to his own advantage;
and if anyone does wrong, it is to his disadvantage.
Then you[p] will be returned to your Lord.

16. In the past We gave the Children of Israel the Scripture
and the Judgement and the Prophethood,
and We provided them with good things
and preferred them over all created beings,

17. And We gave them clear proofs of the matter.
They only differed after knowledge came to them,
through insolence amongst themselves.
Your[s] Lord will judge between them on the Day of Resurrection
concerning that about which they used to differ.

18. Then We set you[s] on a clear way [that comes] from [Our] affair.[2]
So follow it,
and do not follow the whims of those who do not know.

19. They can avail you[s] nothing against God.
The wrong-doers – truly they are friends of one another,
but God is the friend of those who protect themselves.

20. This is clear evidence for the people
and a guidance and a mercy for a people who are sure.

21. Or do those who commit evil deeds reckon
that We shall make them as those who believe and do righteous deeds,
being equal in their living and their dying?
How ill they judge!

---

[2] The meaning of the Arabic is not clear.

22. God has created the heavens and the earth in truth,
    for every soul to be requited for what is has amassed.
    And they will not be wronged.

23. Have you^s seen the one who takes his whim as his god
    and God sends him astray,
    despite some knowledge,
    and seals his hearing and his heart
    and places a covering on his sight.
    Who will guide him after God [has sent him astray]?
    Will you^p not be reminded?

24. They say, 'There is only our life in this world.
    We die and we live, and only time destroys us.'
    They have no knowledge of that.
    They only guess.

25. And when Our signs are recited to them as clear proof
    their only argument is to say, 'Produce our forefathers,
    if you^p tell the truth.'

26. Say, 'God gives you life, and then brings death to you,
    and then He will gather you to the Day of Resurrection
    of which there is no doubt,
    but most men do not know.'

27. To God belongs the sovereignty of the heavens and the earth.
    On the day when the Hour arises,
    on that day those who do vain things will be lost.

28. You^s will see each community crouching,
    each community summoned to its record:
    'To-day you^p will be requited for what you used to do.'

29. This is Our record, which speaks the truth about you.
    We have caused all that you did to be recorded.

30. As for those who believe and do righteous deeds,
    their Lord will admit them into His mercy.
    That is the clear triumph.

31. As for those who do not believe:
    'Were not My signs recited to you?
    But you were haughty and were a sinful people.

32. And when it was said, "God's promise is true,
    and there is no doubt about the Hour",
    you said, "We do not know what the Hour is.
    We think that it is only conjecture,
    and we are not sure".'

33. The evils of what they did will appear to them,
    and what they used to ridicule will encompass them.

34. It will be said, 'To-day We forget you[P],
    just as you forgot the meeting on this day of yours.
    Your abode is the Fire, and you will have no helpers.
35. This is because you took God's signs in mockery
    and [because] the life of this world beguiled you.'
    To-day they will not be brought forth from it
    nor will they be allowed to make amends.
36. Praise belongs to God,
    Lord of the Heavens and Lord of the earth,
    Lord of all created beings.
37. To Him belongs the majesty in the heavens and the earth.
    He is the Mighty and the Wise.

Sūra 46

This is generally thought to be a late Meccan *sūra*, with various authorities considering a number of verses (10, 15–18, 35) to be Medinan. The justification for these Medinan ascriptions is not clear, but once again they may tell us something about the evolution of the *sūra*. It begins with a couple of verses about the message and ends with one of encouragement to Muḥammad. Division of the rest into sections is somewhat arbitrary because of the rhetorical nature of much of the *sūra*. The most obvious breaks come after verses 14, 20, and 29.

The Sand-Dunes

In the name of the Merciful and Compassionate God

1. *Ḥā', Mīm.*[1]
2. The sending down of the Scripture from the Mighty and Wise God.
3. We created the heavens and the earth and what is between them
   only with the truth and a stated term.
   Yet those who disbelieve turn away
   from that about which they have been warned.
4. Say, 'Have you[p] considered what you call on apart from God?
   Show me what part of the earth they have created?
   Or have they a share of the heavens?
   Bring me a Scripture from before this,
   or some trace of knowledge,
   if you speak the truth.'
5. Who is further astray than those who call,
   to the exclusion of God,
   on those who will not answer them until the Day of Resurrection
   and are heedless of their calling,
6. And who will be enemies to them
   when the people are mustered
   and will deny their worship?
7. When Our signs are recited to them as clear evidence,
   those who disbelieve say of the truth,
   when it has come to them,
   'This is manifest sorcery.'

---

[1] On this group of mystical letters see the note on 40:1.

462

8. Or do they say, 'He has invented it'?
    Say, 'If I have invented it,
    you^P have nothing to help me against God.
    He is well aware of what you engage in.
    He is sufficient witness between me and you.
    He is Forgiving and Compassionate.'
9. Say, 'I am not something new among the messengers,
    and I do not know what will be done with me or with you^P.
    I only follow what is revealed to me.
    I am only a warner.'
10. Say, 'Have you^P considered?
    If it is from God and you do not believe in it,
    and a witness from the Children of Israel has testified
    to its like and has believed,
    and you are haughty
    – God does not guide the people who do wrong.'
11. Those who do not believe say of those who believe,
    'If it were something good,
    they would not have got to it before us,'
    even when they are not guided by it.
    They will say, 'This is an ancient lie.'
12. But before it was the Scripture of Moses as a model and a mercy;
    and this is a Scripture confirming [it] in Arabic speech,
    to warn those who do wrong
    and good tidings for those who do good.
13. Those who say, 'Our Lord is God'
    and then go along the straight path
    – there is no fear upon them nor will they grieve.
14. These are the companions of the Garden,
    in which they will remain for ever,
    as a recompense for what they used to do.
15. We have charged man to be kind to his parents
    — his mother has carried him in travail
    and given birth to him in travail,
    and the carrying of him and the weaning of him are thirty months;
    and then, when he attains maturity and reaches forty years,
    he says, 'My Lord, press me to give thanks for Your blessing,
    which You have bestowed on me and on my parents
    and to act with righteousness that is pleasing to You;
    and be good to me in my posterity.
    I have turned towards You in repentance,
    and I am one of those who have surrendered.'

16. These are the ones from whom We shall accept
    the best of what they have done
    and whose evil deeds We shall pass over.
    [They are] among the companions of the Garden
    – the promise of the truth,
    which they were promised.

17. But the one who says to his parents,
    'Fie on you both.
    Do you promise me that I shall be brought forth [again]
    when generations have already passed away before me?'
    while the two of them call to God for help,
    'Woe on you^s. Believe.
    God's promise is true',
    and he replies, 'These are only the fables of the ancients.'

18. Such are those on whom have come true
    the stories about communities of *Jinn* and men
    that have passed away before them.
    They are the losers.

19. For each there are grades according to what they have done.
    [That is] so that He may pay them in full for their deeds
    – and they will not be wronged.

20. On the day when those who disbelieve are exposed to the Fire,
    [it will be said], 'You squandered your good things in your life on earth
    and took your enjoyment of them.
    To-day you are recompensed with the torment of humiliation,
    because you were unjustly haughty in the land
    and because you were profligates.'

21. Mention^s the brother of ʿĀd
    when he warned his people among the sand-dunes
    – and warners have passed away [both] before and after him
    – saying, 'Serve only God.
    I fear that the torment of a mighty day will come upon you.'

22. They said, 'Have you^s come to tell lies
    to turn us from our gods?
    Bring^s us what you promise us,
    if you are one of those who speak the truth.'

23. He said, 'Knowledge is only with God.
    I convey to you^p that with which I have been sent,
    but I see that you are a people who are ignorant.'

24. Then when they saw it² as a cloud coming towards their valleys,

---

² Their destruction.

they said, 'This is a cloud that is going to give us rain.'
'No. It is what you wished to hasten:
a wind, in which is a painful torment,

25. Destroying everything by command of its Lord.'
In the morning nothing could be seen of them but their dwellings.
Thus We requite the people who are sinners.

26. And We had given them a position such as We have not given you;
and We gave them hearing and sight and hearts.
But neither their hearing nor their sight nor their hearts
availed them anything,
since they used to deny God's signs.
What they used to mock encompassed them.

27. In the past We have destroyed the settlements that are around you[p];
and We have turned about Our signs,
so that they might return.

28. Why were they not helped by those whom they had chosen as intercessors,
gods apart from God?
No, they failed them.
That was their lie and what they used to invent.

29. And [recall] when We turned to you[s]
a number of the *Jinn*,
who listened to the Recitation.
When they attended it, they said, 'Be[p] silent',
and when it was finished, they went back to their people as warners.

30. They said, 'Our people, we have heard a Scripture
that has been sent down after Moses,
confirming what was before it,
guiding to the truth and to a straight path.

31. Our people, answer God's summoner and believe in Him,
and He will forgive you some of your sins
and protect you from a painful torment.

32. Those who do not answer God's summoner will not frustrate [Him] on earth
and they have no protectors apart from Him
– those are in manifest error.'

33. Have they not seen that God,
who created the heavens and the earth
and was not wearied by creating them,
is able to give life to the dead?
Yes, He has power over everything.

34. On the day when those who disbelieve are exposed to the Fire,
[they will be asked], 'Is not this the truth?'
They will reply, 'Yes, by our Lord.'

He will say, 'Taste the torment
in return for your unbelief.'

35. Have[s] patience,
as the messengers of determination had patience.
Do not seek[s] to hasten [the doom] for them.
On the day when they see what they have been promised,
it will seem to them as if they had lingered [in the grave]
for only an hour of a single day.
A proclamation!
Will any be destroyed but the people who are profligate?

Sūra 47

The majority of this *sūra* appears to come from relatively early in the Medinan period, with some later revision and additions. The first part (verses 1–19) has as its underlying theme the contrast between the believers and the unbelievers, though this is interrupted by such verses as 4, an exhortation to fight the unbelievers, and 15, a sketch of paradise. Verses 20–31 deal firmly with the backsliders and faint-hearted 'those in who hearts is sickness'. Verse 32 picks up by contrast verses 1–2 and leads into a peroration urging belief and virtue. The *sūra* has a somewhat unusual, but effective, assonance pattern not found elsewhere in the Qur'ān.

Muḥammad

In the name of the Merciful and Compassionate God

1. Those who disbelieve and turn [men] from God's way
    – He causes their works to go astray;
2. But those who believe and do righteous deeds
    and believe in what has been sent down to Muḥammad
    – and it is the truth from their Lord –
    He redeems their evil deeds for them
    and makes good their condition.
3. That is because those who disbelieve follow what is false
    and those who believe follow the truth from their Lord.
    Thus God strikes parallels for the people.
4. When you[p] meet [in battle] those who disbelieve,
    [let there be] smiting of their necks;
    and then, when you have wrought havoc amongst them,
    make fast the bonds;
    then afterwards [let there be] grace or ransom,
    until war lays down its burdens.
4a. That is [how you should act].
    Had God wished, He would have avenged Himself upon them,
    but [this is] that He may try you through one another.
    And those who are killed in God's way
    – He will not send their works astray;
5. He will guide them and make good their states,
6. And will admit them to the Garden which He has made known to them.
7. O you who believe,
    if you help God, He will help you and make your feet firm.

8. And those who disbelieve,
   [there will be] perdition for them
   and He will send their works astray.
9. That is because they are averse to what God has sent down.
   And so He has made their works fruitless.
10. Have they not travelled in the land
    and seen how was the consequence for those who were before them?
    God destroyed them.
    For the unbelievers there will be the likes of that.
11. That is because God is the protector of those who believe
    and because the unbelievers have no protector.
12. God will admit those who believe and do righteous deeds into gardens,
    through which rivers flow;
    while those who do not believe take their enjoyment
    and eat as livestock eat
    – the Fire will be their abode.
13. How many a settlement,
    which had greater power than your[s] settlement[1] that has expelled you,
    have We destroyed,
    and [its people] had no helper.
14. Are those who rely on clear evidence from their Lord
    like those whose evil deeds have been made to seem fair to them
    and who have followed their own whims?
15. The likeness of the Garden which the god-fearing have been promised:
    in it there are rivers of water whose taste remains pure;
    and rivers of milk whose taste does not go sour;
    and rivers of wine, a pleasure for those who drink;
    and rivers of purest honey;
    in it they will have some of every kind of fruit
    and forgiveness from their Lord.
    Are they like those who remain for ever in the Fire
    and are given boiling water to drink
    that tears apart their bowels?
16. Among them are those who listen to you[s];
    then, when they leave your presence,
    they say to those to whom knowledge has been given,
    'What has he just said?'
    Those are the ones on whose hearts God has set a seal,
    and they follow their own whims.
17. And those who are guided aright

---

[1] Mecca.

– He increases them in guidance
and gives them their fear of God.

18. Do they² expect anything except the Hour
– that will come on them suddenly.
The portents for it have come.
So when it comes, how can their reminder [help] them?

19. Knowˢ that there is no god but God
and seek forgiveness for your sin
and for the believers, men and women.
God knows where youᵖ turn about and where you lodge.

20. Those who believe say,
'Why has a *sūra* not been sent down?'
Then, when a clear *sūra* is sent down
and fighting is mentioned in it,
youˢ see those in whose hearts is sickness
looking at you with the look of one who swoons in death.
More fitting for them is

21. Obedience and honourable speech.
When the matter is determined
it will be better for them
if they are true to God.

22. If youᵖ turn away,
are you likely to wreak corruption in the land
and sever the ties of kinship?

23. Those are the ones whom God has cursed
and has made them deaf and blinded their sight.

24. Will they not ponder on the Recitation,
or are there locks on their hearts?

25. Those who have turned their backs and gone away,
after the guidance has become clear to them,
– Satan has tempted them,
and [God] has given them latitude.³

26. That is because they have said to those who dislike what God has sent down,
'We shall obey youᵖ in some of the affair,'
but God knows their secrets.

27. How [will it be for them] when the angels take them,
beating their faces and their backs?

---

² The unbelievers.
³ This is my attempt at the problematical phrase *amlā lahum*. Two diametrically opposed solutions are current. The first proposes that there is a change of subject and the phrase means 'and [God] has given them respite'. The other suggestion is that *amlā lahum* means 'he has dictated to them', in which case Satan remains the subject.

28. That will be because they have followed that which angers God
and have disliked what pleases Him.
And so he has made their works fail.

29. Or do those in whose hearts in sickness
reckon that God will not bring to light their ill-will?

30. If We wished, We would show them to you[s],
and you would know them by their marks
and by the twisting of their speech.
God knows your deeds.

31. We shall try you[p] until We know
those of you who strive hard and are steadfast,
and until We test your tidings.

32. Those who do not believe and who turn [men] away from God's way
and who oppose the messenger
after guidance has been made clear to them,
will not harm God in any way,
and He will make their works fail.

33. O you who believe, obey God and obey the messenger,
and do not render your own works vain.

34. Those who do not believe and who turn [people] away from God's way
and then die when they are unbelievers,
God will not forgive them.

35. So do not weaken and call for peace,
when you have the upper hand;
for God is with you.
He will not grudge you your works.

36. The life of this world is only a sport and a diversion.
If you[p] believe and protect yourselves,
He will give you your wages
and will not ask you for your possessions.

37. If He were to ask you for them and to press you,
you would be niggardly,
and He would bring to light your ill will.

38. There you are.
You are called on to spend in God's way,
but there are some of you who are niggardly.
Those who are niggardly are only niggardly to themselves.
God is the All-sufficient, and you[p] are the needy.
If you turn away, He will replace you by another people;
and then they will not be like you.

Sūra 48

Commentators agree that the events referred to in this *sūra* are the expeditions to al-Ḥudaybiya and to Khaybar in 628 AD. That must be the case with much of the material from verse 10 onwards, but the first part of the *sūra* might well be, as Bell suggests, the reworking of a piece that originated after the battle of Badr.

The Victory

In the name of the Merciful and Compassionate God

1. We have given you^s a clear victory,
2. That God may forgive you^s your past sin
   and your sin which is to come,
   and that He may complete His blessing to you
   and guide you on a straight path,
3. And that God may help you with mighty help.
4. [It is] He who sent down the reassurance into the hearts of the believers
   that they might add faith to their faith
   – to God belong the hosts of the heavens and the earth;
   God is Knowing and Wise –
5. That He may admit the believers, men and women,
   to gardens through which rivers flow,
   in which they will remain for ever,
   and that he may redeem their evil deeds for them.
   That is a mighty triumph with God.
6. And that He may punish the hypocrites, both men and women,
   and those, both men and women, who associate others with God,
   who think evil thoughts about God.
   Against them is the evil turn of fortune.
   God is angry with them and has cursed them
   and has prepared for them Jahannam
   – an evil journey's end.
7. To God belong the hosts of the heavens and the earth.
   God is Mighty and Wise.
8. We have sent you^s as a witness
   and a bearer of good tidings and a warner,
9. That you^p may believe in God and His messenger
   and support Him and revere Him

and glorify Him morning and evening.

10. Those who swear allegiance to you[s]
are swearing allegiance to God.
The hand of God is above their hands.
Whoever breaks his oath breaks it against himself;
but whoever fulfils the covenant he has made with God,
He will give him a mighty wage.

11. The *bedu*[1] who were left behind will say to you[s],
'Our possession and households kept us busy;
so seek forgiveness for us.'
They say with their tongues
what is not in their hearts.

11a. Say, 'Who possesses anything that will avail you[p] against God,
if He desires harm for you or desires benefit for you?
No. God is informed of what you[p] do.

12. No. You[p] thought that the messenger and the believers would never return to
their households.
That was made to seem fair in your hearts.
You had evil thoughts and you were a corrupt people.'

13. Those who do not believe in God and His messenger
– We have prepared a blaze for the unbelievers.

14. To God belongs the sovereignty of the heavens and the earth.
He forgives those whom He wishes
and punishes those whom He wishes.
God is Forgiving and Compassionate.

15. Those who were left behind will say,
when you[p] set out to take spoils,
'Let us follow you',
wishing to alter God's words.
Say, 'You[p] shall not follow us.
Thus God has spoken previously.'
They will say, 'No. You[p] envy us.'
No. They understand only a little.

16. Say to the *bedu* who were left behind,
'You will be summoned against a people of great might,
whom you will fight or they will surrender.
If you obey, God will give you a fair wage;
but if you turn away as you did before,
He will punish you most painfully.'

17. There is no blame on the blind or on the lame or on the sick

---

[1] See the note on 9:90.

– those who obey God and His messenger
will be admitted by Him to gardens,
through which rivers flow;
but those who turn away
– He will punish them most painfully.

18. God was pleased with the believers
when they swore allegiance to you[s] under the tree,
and He knew what was in their hearts.
And so He sent down reassurance to them
and rewarded them with a victory near at hand,

19. And numerous spoils to take.
God is Mighty and Wise.

20. God has promised you[p] numerous spoils to take,
and has hastened these to you,
and has restrained the hands of the people from you.
[This is] so that it may be a sign to the believers
and that He may guide you on a straight path.

21. And other [spoils] that you[p] were not able to take
are encompassed by God.
God has power over everything.

22. If those who disbelieve had fought you[p],
they would have turned their backs;
and then they would find no protector or helper.

23. That is God's practice,
which has happened in the past.
You[p] will not find alteration in God's practice.

24. [It is] He who has restrained their hands from you[p]
and your hands from them in the valley of Mecca,
after He had made you victors over them.
God is observer of what you do.

25. [It is] they who disbelieved and barred you[p] from the Sacred Mosque
and [barred] the offering which was prevented from reaching its place of sacrifice.
And had it not been for the believing men and women,
whom you[p] do not know,
lest you should have trampled on them,
and guilt befallen you unwittingly because of them
– that God may admit to His mercy those whom He wishes.
Had they been clearly separated,
We would have punished the unbelievers among them most painfully.

26. When[2] those who disbelieved set fierceness in their hearts,

---

[2] This verse is an expansion on v. 25.

the fierceness of the age of ignorance,
and God sent down his reassurance to His messenger and to the believers,
and fastened on them the word 'piety',
to which they have the best right and are worthy of it.
God is aware of everything.

27. God has fulfilled in truth the vision he gave to His messenger:
you^p will enter the sacred mosque,
if God wills, in security,
your heads shaven, your hair cut short, not fearing.
He knew what you^p did not know;
and He has appointed before that a victory near at hand.

28. [It is] He who sent His messenger with the guidance and the religion of truth
to make it prevail over all religion.
God is sufficient witness.

29. Muḥammad is the messenger of God.
Those who are with him
are hard on the unbelievers,
merciful among themselves.
You see them bowing and prostrating themselves,
seeking bounty and approval from God.
Their mark is on their faces
from the effect of prostration.
That is what they are compared to in the *Torah*;[3]
in the *Gospel* they are compared to a seed
that puts forth its shoot and strengthens it,
so that it grows stout and rises firm on its stalk,
delighting the sowers[4]
– that He may enrage the unbelievers through them.
God has promised those of them who believe and do righteous deeds
forgiveness and a great wage.

---

[3] There is no exact parallel in the Old Testament. Possibly Deut. 6:8 and 11:18 are in the background.
[4] *Cf.* Mark 4:26 *ff.*

Sūra 49

This Medinan *sūra* comes from quite late in Muḥammad's life, probably 631 AD, when delegations were coming to visit him from all over the Arabian peninsula. It lays down further rules of behaviour for the faithful, with the final passage (14–18) aimed at bringing the *bedu* into line.

The Apartments

In the name of the Merciful and Compassionate God

1. O you who believe,
   do not be forward before God and His messenger.
   Fear God; God is Hearing and Knowing.
2. O you who believe,
   do not raise your voices above that of the prophet,
   and do not speak loudly to him,
   as you do to one another,
   lest your works fail whilst you are not aware.
3. Those who keep their voices down in the presence of God's messenger
   – these are they whose hearts God has tested for piety.
   They will have forgiveness and a mighty wage.
4. Those who call to you[s] from behind the apartments
   – most of them have no sense.
5. Had they the patience [to wait] until you[s] come out to them,
   it would be better for them.
   God is Forgiving and Compassionate.
6. O you who believe,
   if some reprobate brings you tidings,
   be clear about it,
   lest you smite a people in ignorance
   and next morning regret what you have done.
7. Know[p] that the messenger of God is among you.
   If he were to obey you in much of what is going on,
   you would be in distress;
   but God has endeared belief to you,
   making it seem fair in your hearts;
   and He has made unbelief and immorality
   and rebellion repugnant to you.
   Those are the rightly guided,

8. As a bounty and a grace from God.
   God is Knowing and Wise.
9. If two parties of the believers fight each other,
   make things right between them.
   If one party of them wrongs the other,
   fight the one that does wrong
   until it returns to God's command.
   If it returns, set things right between them justly and act equitably.
   God loves those who act equitably.
10. The believers are brethren.
    Set things right between your two brothers and fear God,
    so that you may receive mercy.
11. O you who believe,
    let not a people scorn another people who may be better than them;
    nor let women scorn women who may be better than them.
    Do not find fault with one another,
    nor insult each other with nicknames.
    Evil is the term 'vicious conduct', after belief.
    Those who do not turn in repentance
    – those are the wrong-doers.
12. O you who believe,
    avoid much suspicion:
    some suspicion is a sin.
    Do not spy; nor be backbiters of one another.
    Would one of you like to eat the flesh of his brother
    when he is dead?
    You would hate it.
    Fear God. God is Relenting and Compassionate.
13. O people, We have created you male and female
    and made you races and tribes
    that you may know one another.
    The noblest of you in the sight of God is the most god-fearing.
    God is Knowing and Informed.
14. The *bedu* say, 'We believe.'
    Say, 'You do not believe, but say, "We surrender",
    for Faith has not yet entered your hearts.'
    If you obey God and His messenger,
    He will not withhold from you any of your deeds.
    God is Forgiving and Compassionate.
15. The believers are those who believe in God and His messenger
    and then do not doubt,
    but strive with their possessions and their persons for God's sake.

Those are the truthful ones.

16. Say to them, 'Will you teach God about your religion,
when God knows what is in the heavens and what is on earth?
God is aware of everything.'

17. They reckon it a favour to you^s that they have surrendered.
Say, 'Do not reckon your^p surrender a favour to me.
No. God is conferring a favour on you,
because He has guided you to belief,
if you are truthful.

18. God knows the Invisible of the heavens and of the earth.
God is observer of what you do.'

Sūra 50

This *sūra* is traditionally considered to be a middle Meccan piece, though Bell would place it later. The major part of the *sūra* (verses 2–38) is made up of a dozen vignettes of typical themes: ingratitude, God's signs, the resurrection, judgement, heaven and hell. Even the punishment stories are reduced to a brief mention (12–14). The final passage (39–45) mixes exhortation to Muḥammad with a further warning about the day of judgement.

Qāf

In the name of the Merciful and Compassionate God

1. *Qāf.*[1]
   By the glorious Recitation.
2. No. They[2] marvel that a warner has come to them from among themselves.
   The ungrateful ones say, 'This is a strange thing.
3. When we are dead and have become dust, [shall we be restored]?
   That is a distant return.'
4. We know what the earth takes away from them,[3]
   and We have a document that preserves [a record].
5. No. They denied the truth when it came to them;
   and now they are in a confused state.
6. Have they not looked at the heaven above them,
   how We built it and adorned it
   and [how] it has no cracks?
7. And [how] We have extended the earth
   and cast on it firm mountains,
   and [how] We have caused every splendid species to grow in it,
8. An insight and a reminder for every penitent slave.
9. And We sent down from the sky blessed water,
   and thereby We caused to grow gardens and grain for reaping
10. And tall date-palms with compact spathes,
11. As sustenance for [Our] servants;
    and thereby we revived land that was dead.
    Thus will be the coming forth.

---

[1] On the mystical letters see the note on 2:1.

[2] The Meccan unbelievers.

[3] How the dead decay in the earth.

12. Before them the people of Noah denied the truth,
    as did the men of al-Rass and Thamūd,
13. And ʿĀd and Pharaoh and the brethren of Lot,
14. And the men of the thicket, and the people of Tubbaʿ.
    Every one [of them] denied the truth of their messengers,
    and My threat came true.
15. Were We worn out by the first creation?
    No, but they are in doubt about a new creation.
16. We created man,
    and We know what his soul whispers to him,
    for We are nearer to him than his jugular vein.
17. When the two Receivers receive him,
    one sitting on the right,
    one sitting on the left.
18. Not a word does he utter but a ready watcher is by him.
19. The agony of death comes in truth.
    That is what you^s have been avoiding.
20. There will be a blast on the trumpet.
    That is the day of the threat.
21. Each soul will come accompanied by a driver and a witness.
22. 'You were in neglect of this;
    and so We have removed your covering from you.
    To-day, therefore, your sight will be sharp.'
23. His companion will say,
    'This is what I have ready.'
24. 'You two, cast into Jahannam every rebellious man of ingratitude,
25. Hinderer of good, transgressor, doubter,
26. Who adopts another god along with God.
    Throw him into the severe punishment.'
27. His companion says, 'Our Lord,
    I did not make him insolent.
    He was in distant error.'
28. HE says, 'Do^p not dispute in My presence.
    I have already sent you the threat.
29. What has been said is not changed in My presence.
    I am not one who does wrong to [His] servants.'
30. – The day when We shall say to Jahannam,
    'Have you been filled?',
    and it will say, 'Are there still more?'
31. And the Garden is brought near for those who protect themselves
    [and is] not far away:
32. 'This is what you^p are promised for every mindful penitent

33. – the one who fears the Merciful in the Invisible
and comes with a penitent heart.
34. Enter[p] it in peace.
That is the day of eternity.'
35. They will have whatever they wish there.
And with Us there is still more.
36. How many generations have We destroyed before them
who had greater strength than they did,
and who searched [every corner of] the land
to see if there was refuge.
37. In that there is a reminder for anyone who has a heart
or will give ear and be a witness.
38. We created the heavens and the earth and what is between them in six days
and no weariness touched us.
39. So be[s] patient in the face of what they say,
and glorify your Lord by praising Him
before the rising and the setting of the sun
40. And during the night
and glorify Him at the ends of prostrations.
41. And listen for the day when the crier will proclaim from a place nearby,
42. The day when they hear the Shout in truth.
That is the day of coming forth.
43. It is We who give life and cause death,
and to Us is the journeying
44. – The day when the earth is split away from them as they hasten.
That is a rounding up that is easy for Us.
45. We are well aware of what they say.
You[s] are not one who coerces them.
Remind with the Recitation those who fear My threat.

Sūra 51

This is one of the group of *sūra*s (the others are 37, 77, 79 and 100) that begin with a fairly specialized form of *kāhin*-style material. It is normally taken to be an early Meccan *sūra*. However, as the *sūra* now stands it may be that only verses 1–9 are early. Verses 10–46 have themes that are found in early material, but they also seem to show some later development, for example the use of *muslim* in verse 36; and 47–60, most of which refer back in a fairly complex way to earlier parts of the *sūra*, are probably even later. There is, however, little to support Bell's suggestion that there was a considerable Medinan input.

Those that scatter

In the name of the Merciful and Compassionate God

1. By those that scatter,
2. By those that bear a burden,
3. By those that run with ease,
4. By those that distribute,[1]
5. That which you[p] are promised is indeed true:
6. The judgement will indeed happen.
7. By the heaven with its tracks,
8. You speak at variance;
9. Some are involved in lies about it.
10. Perish the conjecturers,
11. Heedless in overwhelming ignorance.
12. They ask, 'When is the Day of Judgement?'
13. On a day when they are tormented over the Fire:
14. 'Taste your torment.
    This is what you sought to hasten.'
15. The god-fearing will be among gardens and springs,
16. Taking that which their Lord has given them.
    Before that they used to do good.
17. Little of the night they used to slumber,
18. And in the mornings they used to seek forgiveness.
19. And among their possessions was a share for the beggar and the outcast.
20. In the earth there are signs for those with sure faith,

---

[1] The first four verses are usually taken to refer to the angels (*cf.* 37:1–3) or the winds.

21. And in yourselves.
    Do you[P] not see?
22. And in the sky is your[P] sustenance
    and what you are promised.
23. By the Lord of the heaven and earth it is true;
    [as true] as it is that you[P] speak.
24. Have you[s] heard of the honoured guests of Abraham?
25. When they came to see him and said, 'Peace.'
    He said, 'Peace, people unknown.'
26. Then he went aside to his household
    and brought a fat calf.
27. And he offered it to them,
    saying 'Will you not eat?'
28. Then he conceived a fear of them.[2]
    They said, 'Do not be afraid',
    and they gave him the good news of [the birth of] a wise son.
29. His wife came forward to him, clamouring,
    and she smote her face
    and said, 'A barren old woman.'
30. They said, 'Thus says your Lord.
    He is the Wise, the Knowing.'
31. He said, 'O messengers, what is your business?'
32. They said, 'We are sent to a sinful people,
33. To let loose on them stones of clay,
34. Marked for the prodigal in the presence of your Lord.'
35. We brought out those there who were believers,
36. But We found there only one family of those who had surrendered themselves,
37. And We left there a sign for those who fear the painful punishment.
38. [There is a sign,] too, in Moses,[3]
    when We sent him to Pharaoh with a clear authority.
39. But he turned his back, with his court,
    and said, 'A sorcerer or one possessed.'
40. So We seized him and his armies
    and flung them into the sea,
    for he was blameworthy.
41. [There is a sign] too, in ʿĀd,
    when We sent loose on them the withering wind,
42. Which spared nothing on which it came,
    but turned it into decayed matter.

---

[2] Because they did not eat.
[3] *Cf.* 7:103 *ff.*

43. [There is a sign,] too in Thamūd,
    when they were told, 'Take your enjoyment for a time.'
44. But they disdained the command of their Lord,
    and the thunderbolt took them as they watched.
45. And they could not stand up,
    nor did they find help.
46. And the people of Noah before that:
    they were a reprobate people.
47. Heaven – We built it with might.
    We are the One who made it wide.
48. And earth – We spread it out,
    and how excellent is the spreader.
49. And of everything We created two kinds
    so that you^p might be reminded.
50. So flee^p to God.
    I am a clear warner from Him to you^p.
51. And do not set up any other god along with God.
    I am a clear warner from Him to you.
52. In the same way no messenger came to those before them
    without them saying 'a sorcerer or one possessed.'
53. Have they bequeathed it to one another?
    No! they are an insolent people.
54. So withdraw^s from them
    – you^s will not be blamed –
55. But give^s a reminder.
    The reminder will profit the believers.
56. I^4 created *Jinn* and men only so that they might serve Me.
57. I^4 do not desire any sustenance from them,
    nor do I ask that they should feed Me.
58. God is the One who gives sustenance,
    the Possessor of strength, the Firm.
59. Those who do wrong will have a portion
    like the portion of their fellows.
    So let them not ask Me to hasten [it].
60. Woe to those who are unbelievers
    because of that day of theirs which they are promised.

---

^{4} Here 'I' refers to God.

Sūra 52

The *sūra* is traditionally agreed to be early Meccan, and that appears to be a correct assessment of almost all of it. After *kāhin*-style oaths (1–6), there is an eschatological passage (7–28), which is in turn followed by a polemical piece, which contains (in verses 27–34) a vivid sketch of the disdainfully dismissive views of the pagan Meccans about Muḥammad. The final two verses, which are addressed to Muḥammad (as is also the case with verses 29, 31, 40 and 45), may have been added slightly later.

The Mountain

In the name of the Merciful and Compassionate God

1. By the mountain,[1]
2. By a Scripture inscribed
3. On unrolled parchment,
4. By the frequented house,[2]
5. By the uplifted roof,[3]
6. By the sea kept full,
7. The punishment of Your[p] Lord will surely come to pass.
8. There is nothing that can ward it off.
9. On the day when heaven heaves,
10. And when the mountains are set in motion
11. – Woe on that day to those who deny [the truth],
12. Who play at plunging[4]
13. – On the day when they are thrust into the fire of Jahannam:
14. 'This is the Fire which you used to deny.
15. Is this magic or is it you who do not see?
16. Roast in it,
    bear it patiently or not
    – it is all the same for you.
    You are being recompensed for what you used to do.'
17. But the god-fearing will be in gardens and bliss,
18. Rejoicing in what their Lord has given them

---

[1] This is traditionally taken to mean Mt. Sinai.
[2] This is traditionally taken to mean the Kaʿba.
[3] The sky.
[4] See the note on 6:68.

– their Lord has protected them from the punishment of Hell.

19. 'Eat and drink [what is] wholesome,
as a recompense for what you used to do;'

20. Reclining on couches placed in rows.
And We shall pair them with maidens with dark, lustrous eyes.

21. Those who believe and whose seed follows them in belief,
We shall join their seed with them,
and We shall not deprive them of any of their work.
Every man will be pledged for what he has earned.

22. We shall provide for them fruit and meat,
as much as they desire.

23. There they will pass to one another a cup.
There there is no idle chatter nor any imputation.

24. And youths circle them, waiting on them,
as if they were hidden pearls.

25. And they go round to one another,
asking each other questions,

26. They say, 'Before [this] we always used to be fearful concerning our family,

27. But God has been gracious to us
and protected us against the punishment of the burning heat.

28. Before [this] we used to pray to Him.
He is the Kind, the Compassionate.'

29. So give^s the reminder.
By the grace of your Lord you are not a soothsayer nor one possessed.

30. Or they say, 'A poet for whom we await the ill-doings of fate.'

31. Say, 'Wait^p.
I shall be one of those waiting with you.'

32. Do their minds tell them to do this?
Or are they an insolent people?

33. Or do they say, 'He has invented it'?
No! They do not believe.

34. Let them bring a discourse like it,
if they tell the truth.

35. Or were they created out of nothing?
Or are they the creators?

36. Or did they create the heavens and the earth?
No. They have no certainties.

37. Or do they have the treasures of your^s Lord?
Or do they have charge?

38. Or do they have a ladder on which they can listen?
Let their listener bring clear authority.

39. Or does He have daughters and you^p sons?

40. Or do you^s ask them for a fee,
   so that they are weighed down with debt?
41. Or have they [knowledge of] the Invisible,
   and so can write it down?
42. Or do they desire some trickery?
   It is those who disbelieve who are tricked.
43. Or do they have any god other than God?
   Glory be to God from all that they associate with Him.
44. Even if they were to see fragments falling from heaven,
   they would say, 'Massed clouds.'
45. So leave them until they meet their day on which they will be thunderstruck
46. – A day on which their trickery will avail them nothing
   and they will not be helped.
47. For those who do wrong
   there is a punishment on this side of that,
   but most of them do not know [that].
48. So wait^s patiently for the judgement of your^s Lord,
   for you^s are before Our eyes;
   and glorify^s your^s Lord by praising Him when you^s arise
49. And during the night,
   and glorify^s Him at the setting of the stars.

Sūra 53

This *sūra* is perhaps best known as the 'temporary home' of the so-called 'satanic verses'; but much more remarkable are the two passages (verses 6–10 and 13–18) which describe visions that Muḥammad is pictured as having had. Muslim views eventually came out in favour of these being two visions of Gabriel; but some companions of the Prophet, including Ibn ʿAbbās and Anas ibn Mālik, believed that the visions were of God; and this is the simplest way of understanding what the Arabic says. Whichever view is taken, the crucial point is that the experiences are depicted as visual. The picture presented by the biographies of the Prophet, *ḥadīth* and related materials is that Muḥammad's experiences were aural rather than visual: he normally heard Gabriel.

The greater part of the *sūra* is early Meccan, but, as noted below, verse 23 is generally agreed to be Medinan, and verses 26–32 almost certainly date from the same period. The beginning of the *sūra* is echoed in 81:20–23, which is usually considered to be a later passage – though this is by no means certain.

The *sūra* falls into five sections:

(*a*) 1–18 addressed to the Meccans, deal, in a rhetorical way, with Muḥammad and his visions.

(*b*) 19–25 similarly addressed to the Meccans, show an abrupt change of theme to that of pagan deities. They are possibly a separate revelation from verses 1–18. Note, however, that verse 23 is much later: it is traditionally accepted as having been added at Medina. Thematically, verse 23 is integrated, but it has a later style, with less assonance – it is more than four times as long as the surrounding verses. It has all the appearance of a substitution that makes points that would have not been in the original text. The Commentary sets out the reasons for believing that it replaced the so-called 'satanic verses'.

(*c*) 26–32 Here the verses are considerably longer than those that have preceded them (with the exception of the added verse 23). The Meccans are no longer being addressed. Instead, Muḥammad is addressed in verses 29 and 32 and mankind in verse 32. There can be little doubt that this section is a few years later than most of the material in the *sūra*. It is not unreasonable to suppose that it was added at the same time as verse 23.

(*d*) 33–56 Short verses return. First there is an address to Muḥammad and then a sketching in of some basic beliefs. There must be some doubt whether verse 56 is integral or a bridge verse to the final section.

(*e*) 57–62 The assonance in -*ā*, used in verses 1–56, ceases. There are two verses with assonance in -*fa*, three with -*ūn*, and a final verse ending in -*ū*. This little peroration 'the hour is nigh' fits neatly on to what has preceded, but the breaking of the assonance in -*a* may well point to it originally having been a separate piece.

The Star

In the name of the Merciful and Compassionate God

1. By the star when it sets,
2. Your[p] comrade[1] has not gone astray,
    nor has he erred,
3. Nor does he speak out of caprice.
4. This[2] is simply a revelation that is being revealed,
5. Taught to him by one great in power,
6. Possessed of strength.
    He stood straight
7. On the highest horizon;
8. Then he drew near and came down,
9. [Till] he was two bows' length away or even nearer;
10. Then he inspired his servant with his inspiration.
11. His heart has not lied [about] what he saw.
12. Will you[p] dispute with him about what he sees?
13. Indeed, he saw him on another descent
14. By the *sidr*-tree[3] of the boundary,
15. Near to which is the garden of refuge,
16. When the *sidr*-tree[3] was covered by its covering.
17. His eye did not swerve nor turn astray.
18. Indeed, he saw [one] of the greatest signs of his Lord.
19. Have you[p] considered al-Lāt and al-'Uzzā
20. And Manāt,[4] the third, the other?
21. Do you have males, and He females?
22. That would then be an unjust division.
23. They are merely names
    which you[p] and your forefathers have bestowed.
    God has sent down no authority in them.

---

[1] A reference to Muḥammad, addressed to the Meccans.

[2] This recitation.

[3] On the *sidr*-tree see 34:16.

[4] The names refer to three stone idols (goddesses) worshipped by some pre-Islamic Arabs.

They follow only surmise and what their souls desire
– and that when guidance has come to them from their Lord.

24. Or will man have whatever he desires,
25. When the hereafter and the first life belong to God?
26. How many an angel is there in the heavens
whose intercession is of no avail
save after God gives permission
to whom He wills and is pleased.
27. Those who do not believe in the hereafter
give the angels the names of females.
28. They have no knowledge of that.
They only follow guesswork,
and guesswork is of no avail against the truth.
29. So turn^s away from him who turns his back on Our Remembrance,
and desires only the present life.
30. That is the sum of their knowledge.
Your^s Lord knows full well
those who have gone astray from His way,
and He knows full well
those who are guided.
31. To God belongs all that is in the heavens and on the earth,
for Him to requite those who do evil for what they have done,
and to requite those who have done good with the fairest [reward].
32. Those who avoid the heinous sins and wrongdoings,
[but commit] venial offences
– [for them] your^s Lord is embracing in His forgiveness.
He is well aware of you^p
[from the time] when He raised you from the earth
and when you were foetuses in your mothers' bellies.
Do not assert yourselves to be pure.
He is well aware of those who fear God.
33. Have you^s considered the person who turns his back
34. And gives little and is grudging?
35. Does he possess the knowledge of the Invisible,
so that he sees?
36. Or has he not been told
of what is in the scrolls of Moses
and Abraham, who paid his debt in full?
38. – That no laden soul bears the load of another,
39. And that a man will have only what he has striven for,
40. And that his striving will be seen,
41. Then he will be recompensed for it with the fullest recompense?

42. And that the final end is to your^s Lord,
43. And that it is He who makes [men] laugh and makes [them] weep,
44. And that it is He who makes [men] die and makes [them] live,
45. And that He created the two pairs, male and female,
46. From a drop of sperm when it was ejaculated,
47. And that on Him rests the second growth,
48. And that it is He who gives wealth and riches,
49. And that it is He who is the Lord of Sirius,[5]
50. And that He destroyed ʿĀd, the first,
51. And Thamūd, and He did not spare them,
52. And the people of Noah before
      – for they did grievous wrong and were vile transgressors –
53. And He also overthrew the overturned settlements,
54. So that they were covered by that which covered [them].
55. Then on which of your^s Lord's bounties do you cast doubt?
56. This is a warner, of the warners of old.
57. The Imminent is imminent.
58. None apart from God can remove it.
59. Do you^p then marvel at this discourse,
60. And do you laugh, and do you not weep,
61. While you amuse yourselves?
62. Bow down before God and serve Him.

---

[5] Sirius was associated by early Arabs with very hot weather ('dog days').

Sūra 54

This *sūra* is traditionally considered to be middle Meccan; and basically that appears to be the case, though there are one or two indications of modifications at Medina (see verses 43–45). The three sections into which the *sūra* naturally divides (1–8 warnings; 9–42 narratives; 43–55 further warnings) may originally have been three separate passages that came together because of the assonance. The second section contains three refrains which several times come together to form frameworks akin to those in *Sūra* 26. It also shares some of the story line of that *sūra*, though here the narratives (Noah 9–17; 'Ād 18–22; Thamūd 23–32 and Lot 33–40) are very brief – for example, Lot's wife is not mentioned. A reference to the family of Pharaoh (41–42) provides a bridge to the third section.

The Moon

In the name of the Merciful and Compassionate God

1. The Hour has drawn near
   – the moon has been split.
2. But if they[1] see a sign,
   they turn away and say,
   'Never-ending magic.'
3. They have denied the truth and followed their own whims.
   But everything is settled.
4. The news that has come to them contains a deterrent
5. – Eloquent wisdom.
   But warnings are of no avail.
6. Turn[s] from them.
   On the day when the Summoner gives the summons for an abominable thing,
7. They will come forth from the tombs with downcast eyes
   as if they were scattered locusts,
8. Hastening towards the Summoner.
   The unbelievers will say, 'This is a difficult day.'
9. Before them the people of Noah denied the truth;
   they denied Our servant and said, 'A man possessed',
   and he was driven away.
10. So he called to his Lord,

---

[1] The unbelievers.

491

'I am overcome. Help!'

11. So We opened the doors of heaven to water that poured down,
12. And We made the earth gush with springs;
     and the waters came together for a matter that had been decreed.
13. And We carried him in a vessel of planks and nails,
14. Which sailed before Our eyes
     as a recompense for the one who was disbelieved.
15. And We left it as a sign,
     but are there any that are reminded?
16. How then were My punishment and My warnings?
17. We have made the Recitation easy to remember
     – but are there any that are reminded?
18. 'Ād denied the truth,
     and how were My punishment and my warnings?
19. We let loose on them a tempestuous wind
     on a day of never-ending calamity,
20. Sweeping men away
     as though they were the stumps of uprooted palm-trees.
21. How then were My punishment and My warnings?
22. We have made the Recitation easy to remember
     – but are there any that are reminded?
23. Thamūd denied the truth.
24. They said, 'Are we to follow a single mortal from amongst us?
     In that case we would be in error and madness.
25. Has the remembrance been cast on him [alone] from us?
     No, he is an impudent liar.'
26. 'They will know tomorrow who is an insolent liar.
27. We shall send the she-camel as a test for them.
     Watch them and be patient.
28. Tell them that the water is to be divided between them,
     and every drink will be come to in turn.'
29. They called to their comrade
     and he took her in hand and hamstrung her.
30. How then were My punishment and My warnings?
31. We sent on them a single shout
     and they were like the stubble of the builder of a fold.
32. We have made the Recitation easy to remember
     – but are there any that are reminded?
33. The people of Lot denied the truth.
34. We sent a storm of stones on them,
     apart from the family of Lot,
     whom we saved at dawn

35. – a blessing from Us.
Thus We reward those who are thankful.

36. He had warned them of Our assault,
but they doubted the warnings.

37. They tried to tempt him concerning his guests,
so We obliterated their eyes.
Taste My punishment and My warnings.

38. A punishment that had been settled
befell them in the morning.

39. Taste My punishment and My warnings.

40. We have made the Recitation easy to remember
– but are there any that are reminded?

41. The warnings came to the family of Pharaoh.

42. They counted Our signs false, all of them;
so We seized them with the grip of One who is mighty and powerful.

43. Are the unbelievers among you better than these?
Or do you have immunity [promised to you] in the scrolls?[2]

44. Or do they say,
'We are a body that will be victorious'?

45. Their host will be routed,
and they will turn their backs.

46. No! their tryst is the Hour,
and the Hour is full of disaster and bitterness.

47. The sinners are in error and madness.

48. On the day they are dragged into the Fire on their faces
[they will be told], 'Taste the touch of Saqar[3].'

49. We have indeed created everything with a measure.

50. Our affair is but one [moment],
like a flash to the eye.

51. We have destroyed your likes,
but is there any that is reminded?

52. Everything they did is in the scrolls.[2]

53. Everything little and great is recorded.

54. Those who are god-fearing [will dwell] among gardens and a river

55. In a sure abode in the presence of a Mighty King.

---

[2] Or 'scriptures'.
[3] A name of Hell. See the note on 74:26.

Sūra 55

This *sūra* is early Meccan in origin. It is notable for the refrain that first appears in verse 13 and then recurs another 30 times. It is unlike most other refrains in the Qur'ān, as it is essentially external to the structure of the *sūra*: a viable piece remains if the refrains are ignored. There is an insistent link between man and the *Jinn*, not least in the refrain, leading to heavy use of the Arabic dual, sometimes in a rhetorical rather than a precise manner.

The Merciful

In the name of the Merciful and Compassionate God

1. The Merciful –
2. He has taught the Recitation,
3. Created man,
4. Taught him exposition.
5. The sun and moon are in a reckoning.
6. The stars[1] and the trees bow down.
7. He has raised up the Heaven, and He has set the balance,
8. That you[P] may not transgress in the balance.
9. Perform[P] weighing with justice
    and do not skimp in the balance.
10. He has put down the earth for all creatures;
11. In it there are fruit and palm-trees bearing blossoms,
12. Husked grain and fragrant herbs.
13. – Which of your Lord's bounties will you two[2] deny?
14. He created man from clay like potter's clay,
15. And He created the *Jinn* from smokeless fire.
16. – Which of your Lord's bounties will you two deny?
17. Lord of the two easts and two wests.
18. – Which of your Lord's bounties will you two deny?
19. He has released the two seas [that] meet together,
20. Between them a barrier which they do not transgress.
21. – Which of your Lord's bounties will you two deny?
22. From which come pearls and coral.

---

[1] Or 'shrubs'.

[2] Men and *Jinn*.

494

23. – Which of your Lord's bounties will you two deny?
24. To Him belong the [ships] that run, raised up in the sea like way-marks.
25. – Which of your Lord's bounties will you two deny?
26. Everyone on it³ perishes,
27. But the face of yourˢ Lord, which is full of glory and honour, endures.
28. – Which of your Lord's bounties will you two deny?
29. Those in the heavens and on earth ask him [for favours];
    every day He is engaged in some labour.
30. – Which of your Lord's bounties will you two deny?
31. We shall have leisure for you, O two weights,⁴
32. – Which of your Lord's bounties will you two deny?
33. O company of *Jinn* and men,
    if you are able to penetrate any of the regions of the heavens and the earth,
    penetrate them.
    You will not do so without authority.
34. – Which of your Lord's bounties will you two deny?
35. There will be sent on the two of you a flame of fire and molten brass
    and you will receive no help.
36. – Which of your Lord's bounties will you two deny?
37. When the heaven is split and turns crimson like red leather,
38. – Which of your Lord's bounties will you two deny?
39. On that day neither man nor *Jinn* will be questioned about his sin.
40. – Which of your Lord's bounties will you two deny?
41. The sinners will be known by their marks,
    and they will be seized by their feet and forelocks.
42. – Which of your Lord's bounties will you two deny?
43. This is Hell, which the sinners deny;
44. They will circle between it and boiling hot water.
45. – Which of your Lord's bounties will you two deny?
46. But for the one who fears the time when he will stand before his Lord
    there are two gardens,
47. – Which of your Lord's bounties will you two deny?
48. With branches,
49. – Which of your Lord's bounties will you two deny?
50. In which two springs flow,
51. – Which of your Lord's bounties will you two deny?
52. In which there are species of every fruit in pairs,
53. – Which of your Lord's bounties will you two deny?
54. Reclining on couches whose linings are of brocade;

---

³ On earth.

⁴ Or, possibly, 'O two races'.

and the freshly gathered fruit of the two gardens is near.

55. – Which of your Lord's bounties will you two deny?
56. Among them are women of modest gaze,
57. – Which of your Lord's bounties will you two deny?
58. As if they were rubies and coral.
59. – Which of your Lord's bounties will you two deny?
60. Will the reward of goodness be anything other than goodness?
61. – Which of your Lord's bounties will you two deny?
62. Nearer than these will be two [other] gardens,
63. – Which of your Lord's bounties will you two deny?
64. With dark green foliage,
65. – Which of your Lord's bounties will you two deny?
66. In which are two gushing springs,
67. – Which of your Lord's bounties will you two deny?
68. In which are fruits – palms and pomegranates
69. – Which of your Lord's bounties will you two deny?
70. In which are good and beautiful women,
71. – Which of your Lord's bounties will you two deny?
72. With lustrous eyes, restrained in tents,
73. – Which of your Lord's bounties will you two deny?
74. Untouched before by either men or *Jinn*,
75. – Which of your Lord's bounties will you two deny?
76. Who recline on green cushions and fine carpets.
77. – Which of your Lord's bounties will you two deny?
78. Blessed is the name of your[s] Lord who is endowed with glory and honour.

Sūra 56

This *sūra* is essentially early Meccan. As it now stands, it falls into three sections. The first, verses 1–56, is a complex passage or, rather, a series of passages, which, after (*a*) a *kāhin*-style beginning (verses 1–7), centres on (*b*) verses 8–10. Verses 11–26 (*c*) then expand on verse 10, (*d*) verses 27–40 on verse 8; and (*e*) verses 41–56 on verse 9. The varying assonance in sub-sections (*c*), (*d*) and (*e*) points to compound material, as do a couple of abrupt changes of thematic direction. The one really startling variation in assonance, in verse 41, is almost certainly later material, but this is crucial in linking the passage that follows it back to verse 9. The second main section, verses 57–74, deals with God's power over creation; and the third, verses 75–96, is a mixed peroration, referring first to the Qur'ān and God's power and then harking back to the beginning of the *sūra*. In this final section verses 87–88 refer back to verse 11 and thus to verse 10, verses 89–90 to verse 8, and verses 91–94 to verse 9. The last verse in the third section (verse 96) is the same as the last in the second (verse 74), an unusual but by no means unparalleled linkage.

The Event

In the name of the Merciful and Compassionate God

1. When the event occurs
2. – And there is no denying that it will occur –
3. Abasing, exalting;
4. When the earth is shaken,
5. And the mountains are flattened,
6. And become scattered dust
7. And you[p] become three kinds:
8. The companions of the right[1]
   (and what are the companions of the right?);
9. The companions of the left[2]
   (and what are the companions of the left?);
10. Those who win the race,[3]

---

[1] *i.e.* the saved.
[2] *i.e.* the damned.
[3] *i.e.* the fortunate few.

who win the race –[4]

11. They are those brought near,
12. In gardens of bliss,
13. A throng of the ancients
14. And a few from the later ones,
15. On woven couches,
16. Reclining on them, facing one another;
17. Immortal youths go round amongst them,
18. With goblets and ewers and a cup from a spring,
19. From which they do not suffer headaches nor are they intoxicated,
20. And with whatever fruit they choose,
21. And with whatever fowl they desire,
22. And maidens with dark, lustrous eyes,
23. Like hidden pearls,
24. A recompense for what they have done.
25. They hear neither idle chatter there nor imputations,
26. But only the saying, 'Peace, Peace.'
27. The companions of the right
    (what are the companions of the right?)
28. Among the thornless *sidr*-trees,[5]
29. And acacias set in rows,
30. And extended shade,
31. And outpoured water,
32. And abundant fruit,
33. Neither cut off[6] nor forbidden,
34. And raised couches.
35. We have produced them[7]
36. And made them virgins,
37. Loving, well-matched,
38. For the companions of the right,

---

[4] Verse 10 is the site of one of the most interesting Shīʿī (and thus non-canonical) variants. Ibn Masʿūd and Ubayy b. Kaʿb are alleged to have read:

> Those who are first in faith in the Prophet
> Are ʿAlī and his descendants
> Whom God has chosen from among his companions
> And made them protectors over other people.
> These are the winners who will inherit paradise.
> They will remain in it for ever.

[5] On the *sidr*-tree see 34:16 and 53:14 and 16.
[6] 'Not cut off': 'unfailing'.
[7] The pronoun is feminine plural.

498

39. A throng of the ancients,
40. And a throng of the later ones.
41. And the companions of the left
    (what are the companions of the left?)
42. Among searing wind and scalding water,
43. And shadow of black smoke,
44. Not cold nor kind.
45. Before that they were pampered,
46. And they used to persist in the great sin
47. And they used to say,
    'When we die and become dust and bones,
    shall we be raised,
48. Together with our forefathers of old?'
49. Say, 'The ancients and the later ones
50. Will be gathered together to the appointed time of a known day.
51. Then, O you who go astray and deny,
52. You will eat of trees of *Zaqqūm*,[8]
53. Filling your bellies from them,
54. And drinking scalding water on top of that,
55. Drinking as does a camel desperate with thirst.'
56. That will be their hospitality on the Day of Judgement.
57. We have created you[p].
    Why will you not believe the truth?
58. Have you[p] considered what you ejaculate?
59. Did you create, or are We the creator?
60. We decree death among you,
    – and We are not to be evaded –
61. So that we can put others like you in your place
    and raise you [again] in a form[9] you do not know.
62. You have [come to] know the first growth.
    Why are you not reminded?
63. Have you[p] considered what you till?
64. Are you the ones that sow it, or are We the Sowers?
65. Were We to wish it,
    We could make it fragments
    and you would still jest,
66. 'We are burdened by debt;
67. No! We are deprived!'
68. Have you[p] considered the water that you drink?

---

[8] On the *Zaqqūm*-tree see also 37:62 and 44:43.
[9] Or 'in conditions'.

69. Are you the ones who bring it down from the rain-clouds,
    or are We the One who bring it down?
70. Were We to wish it,
    We could make it bitter.
    Why are you not thankful?
71. Have you^p considered the fire that you light?
72. Are you the ones who made its timber grow,
    or are We the One who causes it to grow?
73. It is We who have made it a reminder and a provision for the desert-dwellers.
74. So glorify^s the name of your^s Mighty Lord.
75. No! I swear by the sites of the stars
76. – and it is a mighty oath if only you^p knew –
77. It is a noble recitation
78. In a hidden Scripture,
79. Which only the purified will touch,
80. A revelation from the Lord of all beings.
81. Do you^p hold this discourse in disdain?
82. Do you^p make it your living to deny [the truth]?
83. Why, when [the soul] reaches the throat,[10]
84. As you^p are watching –
85. Yet We are nearer to him[11] than you^p are,
    but you cannot see [Us].
86. Why, if you^p are not to have your debts settled,
87. Do you not return it,
    if you speak the truth?
88. If he is one of those brought near,
89. There will be rest and fragrance and a garden of bliss.
90. If he is one of the companions of the right,
91. There will be the greeting 'Peace is yours^s'
    from the companions of the right.
92. But if he is one of those who deny the truth and go astray,
93. [His] hospitality will be of scalding water
94. And the roasting of Hell.
95. This is indeed the certain truth.
96. So glorify^s the name of your Mighty Lord.

---

[10] *i.e.* dies.
[11] *i.e.* the dead man.

Sūra 57

The bulk of this *sūra* is traditionally classed as early Medinan, though part of verse 10, the whole of 13 and part of 27 appear to be later. Much of the *sūra* stands as a creed, though there is some exhortation and some polemical material.

Iron

In the name of the Merciful and Compassionate God

1. All that is in the heavens and the earth glorify God.
   He is the Mighty and the Wise.
2. His is the sovereignty of the heavens and the earth.
   He brings life and He brings death.
   He has power over everything.
3. He is the First and the Last,
   the Outward and the Inward.
   He has knowledge of everything.
4. [It is] He who created the heavens and the earth in six days
   and then settled on the Throne.
   He knows what penetrates into the earth
   and what comes forth from it
   and what comes down from heaven
   and what ascends to it.
   He is with you[p] wherever you are.
   God is observer of what you[p] do.
5. His is the sovereignty of the heavens and the earth.
   [All] things are brought back to God.
6. He makes the night enter into the day
   and the day into the night.
   He knows the thoughts in the breasts [of men].
7. Believe[p] in God and His messenger;
   and spend some of that to which He has made you[p] successors.
   For those of you who believe and spend
   there will be a great reward.
8. Why do you[p] not believe in God,
   when the messenger calls you to believe in your Lord,
   and when God has taken your covenant,
   if you are believers?

9.   [It is] He who sends down clear signs to His slave,
      that He may bring you^p forth from darkness into light.
      God is Gentle to you and Compassionate.

10.   Why do you^p not spend in the way of God,
      when the inheritance of the heavens and the earth belongs to God?
      Those of you who spent and fought before the victory[1]
      are not on the same level:
      Those are greater in rank than those who spent and fought afterwards.
      God has promised each the fairest reward.
      God is informed of what you^p do.

11.   Who is the one who will make God a fair loan,
      that He may multiply it for him,
      and he will have a generous reward?

12.   On the day when you^s see the believers, men and women,
      with their light running before them and on their right,
      [it will be said], 'Good news for you to-day:
      gardens through which rivers flow,
      in which you will stay forever.
      That is the great triumph.'

13.   On the day when the hypocrites, men and women,
      will say to those who believe,
      'Look at us so that we may borrow some of your light.'
      It will be said, 'Go back behind you and seek light.'
      A wall will be put between them,
      in which there is a gate,
      the inner side of which is mercy,
      and the outward has the torment against it.

14.   They will call to them, 'Were we not with you?'
      They will say, 'Yes, but you tempted yourselves
      and waited and doubted, and wishes deluded you,
      and the deluder deluded you concerning God,
      until God's command came.

15.   To-day no ransom will be taken from you^p nor
      from those who did not believe.
      Your abode is the Fire.
      That is your protector
      and evil is the journeying.'

16.   Has the time not come for the hearts of those who believe
      to be humble to the Reminder of God
      and to the truth that has been revealed

---

[1] Usually thought to mean the conquest of Mecca.

and for them not to be like those to whom the Scripture was previously given;
but the term was long for them
and their hearts became hardened
and many of them [were] reprobates.

17. Know^P that God revives the earth after it has died off.
We have made Our signs clear for you
so that you^P may understand.

18. Those who give alms, men and women,
and give God a fair loan,
will have it multiplied,
and they will have a generous reward.

19. Those who believe in God and his messengers
– they are the loyal ones and the witnesses with their Lord.
They will have their wage and their light;
but those who do not believe and deny the truth of Our signs
– they are the companions of the Fire.

20. Know^P that the life of this world is only play and idleness
and ornament and mutual boasting among you
and rivalry in wealth and children.
[It is] like rain,
the vegetation produced by which pleases the unbelievers;
then it withers,
and you^s see it turning yellow,
and then it becomes chaff.
In the world to come there is severe torment
but also forgiveness and satisfaction from God,
whilst the life of this world is only the enjoyment of delusion.

21. Race^P to forgiveness from your Lord
and to a garden whose breadth is like that of heaven and earth.
It has been prepared for those who believe in God and His messengers.
That is the bounty of God.
He gives it to those whom He wishes.
God is endowed with the great bounty.

22. No disaster strikes in the land or among yourselves
unless it is in a record,
before We bring it into being.
That is easy for God –

23. That you do not grieve for what has escaped you
or are filled with joy at what He has given you.
God does not love any of those who are proud and boastful,

24. Who are niggardly and tell the people to be niggardly.
And those who turn away

– God is the All-sufficient and the Laudable.

25. In the past We sent Our messengers with the clear proofs
and We sent down with them the Scripture and the Balance
that the people might uphold justice;
and We sent down iron,
in which there is great strength and [many] benefits for the people.
[We did this] so that God might know who helps Him and His
    messengers in the Invisible.
God is Strong and Mighty.

26. In the past We sent down Noah and Abraham,
and We placed Prophecy and the Scripture among their seed;
and [some] of them are guided aright,
but many of them are profligates.

27. Then We caused Our messengers to follow in their footsteps.
We caused Jesus, the son of Mary, to follow
and We gave him the *Gospel*;
and We placed compassion and mercy in the hearts of those who followed him.
But monasticism they invented.
We did not prescribe it for them
[but it arose] through desire for God's satisfaction;
and they did not observe it as they should have done.
So We gave those of them who believed their wage;
but many of them are profligates.

28. O you who believe,
fear God and believe in His messenger,
and He will give you a double portion of His mercy
and make for you a light,
by which you can walk;
and He will forgive you.
God is Forgiving and Merciful,

29. That the people of the Scripture may know
that they have no power over any of God's bounty
but that the bounty is in the hand of God,
to give to those whom He wishes.
God is endowed with the great bounty.

Sūra 58

This Medinan *sūra* is traditionally dated to the return of the Muslims from the expedition to al-Ḥudaybiya in 628 AD, but this is not certain. In any case it is a composite piece, with verses 11–13 possibly being the latest material it contains. Though some of the subjects touched on (divorce, private meetings, meetings with the Prophet) are mundane, the religious rhetoric of the *sūra* is powerful.

The Woman who Argued her Case

In the name of the Merciful and Compassionate God

1. God has heard the words of the woman who disputes with you[s] about her husband
   and who complains to God.
   God hears the discussion of the two of you.
   God is Hearing and Observing.
2. Those of you who make their wives like their mothers' backs
   – they are not their mothers.
   Their mothers are only those who gave birth to them.
   They speak unacceptable words and a falsehood.
   God is Pardoning and Forgiving.
3. Those who make their wives like their mothers' backs
   and then return to what they have said:
   [the penalty is] the freeing of a slave before they touch each other.
   That is what you[p] are admonished to do.
   God is informed of what you do.
4. He who does not find [the means to do that]
   must fast for two successive months
   before they touch each other;
   and he who is unable [to fast]
   must feed sixty destitute people.
   This is that you[p] may believe in God and His messenger.
   These are God's limits
   – and for the unbelievers there is a painful doom.
5. Those who oppose God and His messenger have been humbled
   as those before them were humbled.
   We have sent down clear signs
   – and for the unbelievers there is a humiliating doom,
6. On the day when God will raise them all

and will tell them what they did.
God has kept count of it,
when they have forgotten it.
God is witness over everything.

7. Have you^s not seen that God knows all that is in the heavens and on earth?
There is no private meeting of three men
but He is the fourth of them,
nor of five but He is the sixth
nor less than that nor more
but He is with them, wherever they may be.
Then on the Day of Resurrection He will tell them what they did.
God is aware of everything.

8. Have you^s not considered those who were forbidden to meet together privately
and [who now] return to that which they had been forbidden
and meet together privately in sin and in enmity
and in disobedience to the messenger?
When they come to you^s
they greet you with a greeting God has never used to you,
and they say within themselves,
'Why does God not punish us for what we say?'
Jahannam will suffice them
– they will roast in it.
Evil is the journeying.

9. O you who believe,
when you meet together privately,
do not do so in sin and enmity
and disobedience to the messenger
but in piety and fear of God.
Fear God to whom you will be rounded up.

10. Private meetings are from Satan,
that he may sadden those who believe;
but he cannot harm them at all,
save with God's permission.
Let the believers put their trust in God.

11. O you who believe,
when you are asked to make room in assemblies, make room,
God will make room for you;
and when you are asked to move up, move up
– and God will raise in rank those of you who have believed and have been
given knowledge.
God is informed of what you do.

12. O you who believe,

when you have private audience with the messenger,
offer alms before your meeting.
That is better and purer for you.
But if you do not find [the means]
God is Forgiving and Compassionate.

13. Are you^p afraid to offer alms before your meeting?
If you do not and God relents towards you,
perform prayer and give the *zakāt*
and obey God and His messenger.
God is informed of what you do.

14. Have you^s not considered those who take as friends
a people with whom God is angry?
They are neither of you^p nor of them.
They swear on falsehood, knowing [what they are doing].

15. God has prepared a severe torment for them.
What they have been doing is truly evil.

16. They take their oaths as a protection
and they turn [people] from God's way.
They will have a humiliating torment.

17. Their possessions and their children will avail them nothing against God.
These are the companions of the Fire,
in which they will dwell for ever.

18. On the day when God raises them all together,
they will swear to Him as they swear to you^p
and will reckon that they have something to stand on.
Truly, they are the ones who lie.

19. Satan has overcome them and caused them to forget remembrance of God.
These are the party of Satan.
Truly Satan's party are the ones who will lose.

20. Those who oppose God and His messenger
– those are among the most abject.

21. God has written, 'I shall conquer, along with My messengers.'
God is Strong and Mighty.

22. You^s will not find a people who believe in God and the Last Day
being loving to those who oppose God and His messenger,
although they are their fathers or their sons
or their brothers or their clan.
Those – He has inscribed faith on their hearts
and has strengthened them with a Spirit from Him;
and He will admit them into gardens,
through which rivers flow,
in which they will remain for ever.

God is pleased with them, and they with Him.
These are God's party.
Truly, God's party are those who will prosper.

Sūra 59

This Medinan *sūra* has one passage (verses 2–17) that appears to refer to the events that led up to and followed the expulsion from Medina of one of its Jewish tribes, the Banū l-Naḍīr. This can be dated to the summer of 625 AD. However, the passage is couched in the same rhetorical language that we find in the 'historical passages' in *Sūras* 3 and 8. The view that the Banū l-Naḍīr are being referred to is perhaps reinforced if it is accepted that another Jewish tribe, the Banū Qaynuqā', who were expelled from Medina some fifteen months before the Banū l-Naḍīr, are referred to in verse 15. Unfortunately, that verse is also rhetorical and vague. The later parts of the *sūra* change theme: verses 18–21 are an admonition to the believers, and 22–24 are a paean to God.

The Rounding Up

In the name of the Merciful and Compassionate God

1. All that is in the heavens and the earth glorify God.
   He is the Mighty and the Wise.
2. [It is] He who has driven those of the people of the Scripture who have disbelieved
   from their dwellings for the first rounding up.
   You[p] did not think that they would leave,
   and they thought that their strongholds would defend them against God.
   But God reached them from a place they did not reckon on
   and cast terror into their hearts,
   and they destroyed their houses
   with their own hands and the hands of the believers.
   Reflect, those of you who have eyes.
3. But for the fact that God had decreed exile for them,
   He would have punished them in this world.
   In the next world they will have the torment of the Fire.
4. That is because they opposed God and His messenger.
   Those who oppose God
   – God is severe in His punishment.
5. Whatever palm-trees you[p] cut down or left standing on their roots,
   that was by God's permission[1]
   and that He might shame the reprobates.
6. That which God has given to His messenger as booty from them
   – you[p] have not pressed any horse or camel against it;

---

[1] This is a contradiction of Deuteronomy 20:19

but God gives authority to His messengers over whomsoever He wishes.
God has power over everything.
7. That which God has given to His messenger as booty from the people of the settlements
belongs to God and His messenger,
and to near kin, orphans, destitute and travellers
that it may not become something circulating in turn
between the rich among you.
Whatever the messenger gives you[p], take[p] it.
Whatever he forbids you to have, leave it alone,
and fear God.
God is severe in His punishment.
8. [It is for] the poor emigrants who were driven from their homes and their possessions,
who seek bounty and approval from God
and who help God and His messenger.
These are the truthful.
9. And those who occupied the dwelling and the faith before them[2]
love those who have migrated to them
and do not find in their breasts any need for what they have been given
and give preference [to the emigrants] over themselves,
even though there is poverty amongst them.
Those who are saved from their own greed
– those are the ones who prosper.
10. Those who have come after them say,
'Our Lord, forgive us and our brothers
who have preceded us in the faith,
and do not put in our hearts any rancour
towards those who have believed.
Our Lord, You are Kind and Compassionate.'
11. Have you[s] not seen those who are hypocrites[3] saying,
to their brothers of the people of the Scripture who are unbelievers,
'If you[p] are forced to leave, we shall leave with you,
and we shall never obey anyone concerning you;
and if you are attacked, we shall help you.'
God bears witness that they are lying.
12. If they are forced to leave, they will not leave with them;
and if they are attacked they will not help them.
If they do help them, they will certainly turn their backs,

---

[2] The *Anṣār*.
[3] *Munāfiqūn*.

and then they will not be helped.

13. You^p cause greater fear in their breasts than God.
    That is because they are a people who do not understand.

14. They will not fight you^p in a body
    unless [they are] in fortified settlements or behind walls.
    Among themselves their might is great
    – and you reckon them a group –
    but their hearts are scattered.
    That is because they are a people who do not understand.

15. Like those who, shortly before them,
    tasted the mischief of their affair,
    They will have a painful torment.

16. Like Satan, when he said to man, 'Be ungrateful';
    then when he was ungrateful, he said,
    'I have nothing to do with you^s.
    I fear God, Lord of all beings.'

17. The consequence for both of them is that they will be in the Fire,
    in which they will remain for ever.
    That is the recompense for those who do wrong.

18. O you who believe, fear God;
    and let every soul observe what it has sent on for the morrow;
    and fear God.
    God is informed of what you do.

19. Do not be like those who forgot God,
    with the result that He caused them to forget themselves.
    Those are the reprobates.

20. The companions of the Garden and the companions of the Fire are not equal.
    The companions of the Garden are the winners.

21. Had We sent this Recitation down on a mountain,
    you^s would have seen it humbled and split asunder through fear of God.
    These parallels are coined by us for the people
    so that they may reflect.

22. He is God.
    There is no god but Him,
    Knower of the Invisible and the Witnessed.
    He is the Merciful and the Compassionate.

23. He is God.
    There is no god but Him,
    the King, the Holy, the Peace, the Faithful,
    the Watcher, the Mighty, the Compelling.
    Glory be to God, far above what they associate [with Him].

24. He is God, the Creator, the Maker, the Shaper.

To Him belong the fairest names.
All that is in the heavens and the earth glorify Him.
He is the Mighty and the Wise.

Sūra 60

The *sūra* is thought to be late Medinan, coming from the period between the treaty of al-Ḥudaybiya and the conquest of Mecca in January 630 AD. This certainly appears to be the case with verses 7–13, but Bell may be right in suggesting that verses 1–4 are the reworking of an earlier piece of which 5–6 were also a part. Verses 7–9 are of political importance, as they appear to mention in a very guarded way the possibility of a reconciliation with the Meccans; so too are 10–12, as they are thought to sanction modifications of the treaty of al-Ḥudaybiya of 628 AD.

She who is to be Examined

In the name of the Merciful and Compassionate God

1. O you who believe, do not take My enemy and your enemy as friends,
   offering them friendship
   when they have disbelieved in the truth that has come to you,
   driving out you and the messenger
   because you believe in God, your Lord.
   If you go forth to strive in My way and to seek My approval
   [and yet] secretly show them friendship
   – when I am well aware of what you hide and what you proclaim
   – those of you who do that
   stray from the straight way.
2. If they come upon you, they will be enemies to you
   and will stretch their hands and their tongues against you for evil.
   They long for you to disbelieve.
3. Neither your ties of kin nor your children will profit you on the Day of Resurrection.
   He will separate you.
   God is observer of what you do.
4. You have a good example in Abraham and those who were with him
   when they said to their people,
   'We have nothing to do with you
   nor with what you serve to the exclusion of God.
   We deny you,
   and hostility and hate have appeared between you and us for ever,
   until you believe in God alone'
   – except that Abraham said to his father,
   'I shall seek forgiveness for you,
   though I have nothing to help you against God'

513

– 'Our Lord, we place our trust in You
and we turn in repentance to You.
To You is the journeying.

5. Our Lord, do not make us a temptation for those who do not believe;
and forgive us, Our Lord,
You truly are the Mighty and the Wise.'

6. In them you[p] have a good example for those who hope for God and the Last Day.
But whoever turns away
– God is the All-sufficient and the Laudable.

7. Perhaps God may establish friendship between you
and those of them with whom you are at enmity
God is Mighty,
and God is Forgiving and Compassionate.

8. God does not forbid you to act virtuously and with justice
towards those who have not fought you over religion
and have not driven you from your dwellings.
God loves those who act justly.

9. God only forbids you to make friends
of those who have fought you over religion
and have driven you from your dwellings
and helped in your expulsion.
Those who make friends of them
– those are the wrong-doers.

10. O you who believe,
when believing women come to you as emigrants,
examine them.
God is well aware of their faith.
If you know them to be believers
do not return them to the unbelievers.
[Such women] are not lawful for them,[1]
nor are they[1] lawful for those women.
So give them[1] [back] what they have spent.[2]
It is no sin for you to marry them
when you have given them their wages.[3]
Do not hold on to the ties with unbelieving women,
but ask for what you spent[2]
– and let [the unbelievers] ask for what they have spent.[2]
That is the judgement of God.

---

[1] *i.e.* the unbelievers.

[2] *i.e.* spent on dowries.

[3] *i.e.* dowries. See 4:24.

He judges between you.
God is Knowing and Wise.

11. If any of your[p] wives slip away from you to the unbelievers
and you retaliate,
give to those whose wives have gone the same as they have spent.[2]
And fear God, in whom you are believers.

12. O prophet, when believing women come to you,
offering allegiance to you
on the basis that they will not associate anything with God
nor steal nor fornicate nor kill their children,
nor produce any lie they devise between their hands and their feet,[4]
nor disobey you in something recognized as right,
accept[s] their allegiance
and seek God's forgiveness for them.
God is Forgiving and Compassionate.

13. O you who believe, do not take as friends
a people with whom God is angry
and who have despaired of the World to Come,
as the unbelievers have despaired of those who are in the graves.

---

[4] Traditionally understood to mean 'claim legitimacy for an illegitimate child'.

Sūra 61

The *sūra* is traditionally taken to be early Medinan, with verses 2–4 being linked to the Battle of Uḥud in 625 AD. There is nothing against this link, though there is nothing but tradition to confirm it. Bell makes the point that verse 5 is distinctly less favourable to Judaism than 6 and 14 are to Christianity. This, he suggests, points to a time of worsening relations between the Muslims and the Jews of Medina. In a rough way, verses 2–9 and 10–14 are parallel passages of polemic.

The Ranks

In the name of the Merciful and Compassionate God

1. All that is in the heavens and the earth glorify God.
   He is the Mighty and the Wise.
2. O you who believe, why do you say what you do not do?
3. It is most hateful to God that you say what you do not do.
4. God loves those who fight in His way in ranks,
   as though they are a solid building.
5. [Recall] when Moses said to his people,
   'O my people, why do you harm me,
   when you know that I am God's messenger to you?'
   And when they swerved, God caused their hearts to swerve.
   God does not guide people who are reprobates.
6. And [recall] when Jesus, the son of Mary said,
   'O Children of Israel, I am God's messenger to you,
   confirming the *Torah* that was [revealed] before me,
   and giving you good tidings of a messenger
   who will come after me, whose name will be Aḥmad.'[1]
   And when he brought them the clear proofs,
   they said, 'This is clear magic.'
7. Who does greater wrong than the one who invents falsehood against God
   when he is summoned to Submission?
   God does not guide people who do wrong,
8. Who wish to extinguish God's light with their mouths,
   but God will perfect His light,
   though the unbelievers are averse.

---

[1] Traditionally understood to be Muḥammad.

9.   [It is] He who has sent His messenger with the guidance
and the religion of the truth,
that He may make it pre-eminent over all religion,
though those who associate [others with God] are averse.

10.   O you who believe, shall I show you a trade
that will deliver you from a painful torment?

11.   You should believe in God and His messenger
and strive in God's way with your possessions and your persons.
That is better for you, did you but know it.

12.   He will forgive you your sins
and admit you to gardens through which rivers flow,
and to fine dwelling-places in the Gardens of Eden
– That is the great triumph –

13.   And other things which you love:
help from God and a victory near.
Give[s] good tidings to the believers.

14.   O you who believe, be God's helpers,
just as Jesus, son of Mary, said to the Disciples,
'Who are my helpers towards God?'
The disciples said, 'We are God's helpers'.
And a party of the Children of Israel believed
and another party did not believe.
So We strengthened those who believed,
and they prevailed.

Sūra 62

This is a Medinan *sūra* of uncertain date. It falls into three sections: the first four verses dwell on God's power, with verse 2 focusing on a specifically Arabian context; the middle section, verses 5–6, refers to Muḥammad's Jewish opponents; and finally there is a brief section on the believers and prayer (9–11).

The Assembly

In the name of the Merciful and Compassionate God

1. All that is in the heavens and on earth glorifies God,
    the Holy King, the Mighty and the Wise.
2. [It is] He who has sent among the common people[1] a messenger from among
        themselves,
    to recite His signs to them and to purify them
    and to teach them the Scripture and the Wisdom
    – previously they were in manifest error –
3. And others of them who have not yet joined them.
    He is the Mighty and the Wise.
4. That is God's bounty,
    which He gives to those whom He wishes.
    God is possessed of mighty bounty.
5. There is a parallel
    between those who have been loaded with the *Torah* and then have not carried it
    and an ass carrying books.
    Evil is the likeness of the people who deny the truth of God's signs.
    God does not guide people who do wrong.
6. Say, 'O you who are Jews,
    if you claim that you are friends of God,
    to the exclusion of the people,
    yearn for death, if you speak the truth.'
7. But they will never yearn for it
    because of what their hands have sent forward.
    God is aware of the wrong-doers.
8. Say, 'The death from which you flee will yet meet you;
    and then you will be returned to the Knower of the Invisible and the Witnessed,

---

[1] See the note on 2:78.

518

and He will tell you what you used to do.'

9.　O you who believe,
　　when proclamation is made for prayer on the day of assembly,[2]
　　hasten to remembrance of God and leave [your] trading.
　　That is better for you, did you but know.

10.　And when prayer is ended,
　　disperse in the land and seek some of God's bounty,
　　and remember God much,
　　so that you may prosper.

11.　When they see merchandise or some diversion,
　　they scatter to it and leave you[s] standing.
　　Say, 'What is with God is better than diversion and merchandise.
　　God is the best of providers.'

---

[2] *i.e.* Friday.

Sūra 63

This is another Medinan *sūra*, consisting of two pieces dealing with two different groups: the hypocrites (*munāfiqūn*) (verses 1–8) and the believers (9–11). It is difficult to date the pieces precisely within the Medinan period. Some Muslim authorities think that verse 8 refers to ʿAbdallāh ibn Ubayy following the expedition against the Banū Musṭaliq in 627/8 AD, but that dating may well be too late.

The Hypocrites

In the name of the Merciful and Compassionate God

1. When the hypocrites come to youˢ, they say,
  'We bear witness that you are God's messenger.'
  God knows that you are His messenger,
  and God bears witness that the hypocrites are lying.
2. They have made their oaths a protection,
  and then they have barred [people] from the way of God.
  Evil is what they have been doing.
3. That is because they believed and then disbelieved.
  And so a seal has been set on their hearts,
  and they do not understand.
4. When youˢ see them, their bodies please you;
  and if they speak, you listen to what they have to say
  – but it is as though they are propped-up blocks of wood.
  They think that every shout is against them.
  They are the enemy – so bewareˢ of them.
  May God confound them.
  How are they involved in lies?
5. When it is said to them, 'Come,
  and the messenger of God will seek forgiveness for you,'
  they turn their heads.
  Youˢ see them turning away and being haughty.
6. It is the same for them whether youˢ seek forgiveness or not.
  God will not forgive them.
  God does not guide people who are reprobates.
7. [It is] they who say, 'Do not spend on those who are with God's messenger so
      that they disperse,'
  though God's are the treasuries of the heavens and the earth.

But the hypocrites do not understand.

8. They say, 'If we return to Medina,
the mightier will expel the humbler,'
though might belongs to God and His messenger and the believers.
But the hypocrites do not know.

9. O you who believe, let neither your possessions nor your children
divert you from remembrance of God.
Those who do that – those are the losers.

10. And spend of what We have given you as provision
before death comes to one of you and he says,
'O my Lord, if only You would defer me to a near term,
that I may give alms and be one of the righteous.'

11. God grants deferment to no soul when its term comes;
and God is informed of what you[p] do.

Sūra 64

Some Muslim commentators treat this as a Meccan *sūra*, but its present form appears to be Medinan, reworked to a large extent from Meccan material. It is a short sermon.

Mutual Fraud

In the name of the Merciful and Compassionate God

1. All that is in the heavens and on earth glorifies God.
    To Him belongs sovereignty.
    To Him belongs praise.
    He has power over everything.
2. [It is] He who created you^P.
    Some of you are unbelievers,
    and some of you are believers.
    God is observer of what you do.
3. He created the heavens and the earth with the truth
    and formed you and made fair your form;
    and to Him is the journeying.
4. He knows what is in the heavens and the earth.
    He knows what you^P keep secret
    and what you make public.
    God is aware of what [thoughts are] in [men's] breasts.
5. Have you^P not heard the story of those who did not believe in the past
    and thus tasted the mischief of their affair,
    and who had a painful torment?
6. That was because their messengers used to come to them with the clear proofs,
    and they would say, 'Shall mortals guide us?'
    So they disbelieved and turned away.
    But God had no need of them.
    God is All-sufficient and Laudable.
7. Those who disbelieve assert that they will not be raised [again].
    Say^s, 'Of course you will, by My Lord.
    You^P will be raised
    and then you will be informed of what you did.
    That is easy for God.
8. So believe^P in God and his messenger
    and the light that We have sent down.

God is informed of what you do.'

9.   On the day when He gathers you^P to the day of gathering
     – that will be the day of mutual fraud.
     Those who believe in God and act righteously,
     God will redeem their evil deeds for them
     and admit them to gardens through which rivers flow,
     and they will remain in them for ever.
     That is the great triumph.

10.   But those who do not believe and deny the truth of Our signs
     – those are the companions of the Fire,
     in which they will remain for ever,
     and evil is the journeying.

11.   No misfortune befalls, except with God's permission.
     Those who believe in God, He guides their hearts.
     God is aware of everything.

12.   Obey God and obey the messenger.
     If you turn away,
     it is only for the messenger to convey [the message] clearly.

13.   God. There is no god but Him.
     Let all the believers put their trust in God.

14.   O you who believe,
     among your wives and your children there are enemies for you.
     So beware of them.
     If you^P pardon and overlook and forgive
     – God is Forgiving and Compassionate.

15.   Your^P possessions and your children are a temptation,
     and God – with Him is a mighty wage.

16.   Fear^P God to the best of your ability,
     and hear, and obey, and spend.
     [That is] better for your souls.
     Those who are saved from their own greed
     – those are the ones who prosper.

17.   If you^P make a fair loan to God,
     He will multiply[1] it for you and will forgive you.
     God is Grateful and Prudent,

18.   Knower of the Invisible and the Witnessed,
     the Mighty and the Wise.

---

[1] Or 'double'.

Sūra 65

This is a Medinan *sūra*. It falls into two sections: verses 1–7 expand on the divorce laws set out in 2:226*ff* and must be later than that passage (and also later than the vaguer 4:19–21); and 8–12 carry warning of punishment for unbelievers and blessings for the believers.

Divorce

In the name of the Merciful and Compassionate God

1. O prophet,
   when you men divorce women,
   divorce them at the end of their waiting-period
   – and reckon the period accurately and fear God, your Lord.
   Do not expel them from their houses,
   nor should they leave unless they commit some clear act of immorality.
   These are God's limits.
   Those who transgress God's limits wrong themselves.
   You[s] do not know.
   It may be that God will cause something [new] to happen after that.[1]
2. Then, when they have reached their term,
   either retain[p] them in a way recognized as proper
   or part from them in a way recognized as proper.
   Call as witnesses two just men,
   and set up the testimony for God.
   Those who believe in God and the Last Day
   are admonished to act thus.
   And whoever fears God
   – God will appoint a way out for him,
3. And will provide for him from whence he has not reckoned.
   Those who put their trust in God,
   He will suffice them.
   God attains his command.
   God has appointed a measure for everything.
4. With those of your women who have reached the menopause;
   if you[p] have doubts, their period is three months;

---

[1] To reconcile them.

likewise the barren.
For pregnant women, the period shall be until they give birth.
Whoever fears God
– God will appoint for them ease in their affair.

5.   That is God's command, which He has sent down to you^P.
Whoever fears God, He will redeem his evil deeds for him
and give him a mighty wage.

6.   Lodge^P them where you lodge, according to your means;
and do not harass them so that you make things difficult for them.
If they are pregnant,
bear their expenses until they bring forth their burden.
And if they suckle [the child] for you^P,
pay them their wages
and consult together in a way recognized as proper.
If you find mutual difficulties,
another woman may suckle for him.

7.   Let a man of ample means spend some of those means;
and those whose provision is measured,
let them spend some of what God has given them.
God charges no soul except [according to] what He has given it.
God will grant ease after hardship.

8.   How many a settlement turned in disdain
from the command of its Lord and His messengers;
and We called it to a severe account
and punished it with a punishment unknown?

9.   And so it tasted the mischief of its affair,
and the consequence of its affair was loss.

10.   God prepared for them a severe torment.
So fear God, O men of understanding who believe.
God has sent down to you a reminder

11.   A messenger who recites to you God's signs in clarity,
that He may bring those who believe and do righteous deeds
out of the darkness into the light.
Those who believe in God and act righteously,
He will admit them to gardens,
through which rivers flow,
in which they will remain for ever.
God has made fair provision for them,

12.   God, who created seven heavens and of the earth their like.
The command descends among them,
that you^P may know that God has power over everything,
and that God encompasses everything in [His] knowledge.

Sūra 66

This Medinan *sūra* appears to draw together material of various times, with the latest, that referring to Muḥammad's wives 1–5 and (probably) 10–12, dating from 629–30 AD. There is a considerable amount of background material in *Ḥadīth* connecting verses 3 and 4 with two of Muḥammad's wives, Ḥafṣa and ʿĀʾisha. Though the material is well attested, its authenticity remains very uncertain.

Prohibition

In the name of the Merciful and Compassionate God

1. O prophet,
   why do you prohibit what God has made lawful for you,
   seeking the approval of your wives?
   God is Forgiving and Compassionate.
2. God has made lawful for you[p] absolution from your oaths,
   and God is your protector.
   He is the Knowing and the Wise.
3. [Recall] when the prophet confided a matter to one of his wives.
   Then, when she divulged it and God disclosed that to him,
   he made a part known and turned aside from part.
   And when he told her about it,
   she said, 'Who told you this?'
   He said, 'I was told of it by the Knowing and Informed.'
4. If you two [now] turn to God in repentance,
   your hearts originally inclined [to wrong].
   But if you support one another against him,
   God is his protector
   – and Jibrīl and the righteous among the believers;
   and after that the angels are his supporters.
5. If he divorces you[p],
   it may be that his Lord will give him in exchange wives who are better than you,
   women who have surrendered, believing, obedient,
   devout, travelling [for God],[1] married or virgin.
6. O you who believe,
   protect yourselves and your families against a Fire

---

[1] Or 'inclined to fasting'.

526

whose fuel is the people and stones,
over which are harsh, severe angels,
who do not disobey God in what He commands them
but do what they are commanded.

7. 'O you who disbelieve,
make no excuses for yourselves to-day.
You are being recompensed for what you used to do.'

8. O you who believe,
turn to God in sincere repentance.
It may be that your Lord will redeem your evil deeds for you
and admit you to gardens,
through which rivers flow,
on the day when God will not shame the prophet and those who believe with him.
Their light will run in front of them and on their right hands,
and they will say, 'Our Lord, perfect our light for us and forgive us.
You have power over everything.'

9. O prophet,
strive against the unbelievers and the hypocrites,
and be harsh with them.
Their abode will be Jahannam,
an evil journey's end.

10. God has coined an example for those who disbelieve:
the wife of Noah and the wife of Lot.
They were married to two righteous servants of Ours,
but they betrayed them;
so [their husbands] were of no avail to them against God.
They were told, 'Enter the Fire with those who are entering.'

11. And God has coined an example for those who believe:
the wife of Pharaoh when she said,
'My Lord, build for me a house with You in the Garden
and deliver me from Pharaoh and his work,
and deliver me from the people who do wrong;'

12. And Mary, the daughter of 'Imrān,
who guarded her private parts;
and We breathed into it some of Our Spirit,
and she counted true the words of her Lord and His Scriptures
and was one of the obedient.

Sūra 67

The *sūra* is generally considered to be from the middle Meccan period, and it seems likely that most of the material did originate then. As it stands, the *sūra* falls into four sections: an introductory piece on God's glory (1–4); a punishment passage (5–11) offset by a verse (12) on reward; a passage on God's power (13–22); and finally a series of statements for Muḥammad to make (23–30). The order of the final verses, particularly the positions of verses 27 and 29, has been much discussed, but in recitation they are effective enough. There is only one change in the assonance, after verse 21.

Sovereignty

In the name of the Merciful and Compassionate God

1. Blessed is He in whose hand is sovereignty
   and who has power over everything,
2. Who created death and life that He might try you[p]
   – which of you is better in conduct,
   and Who is the Mighty and the Forgiving,
3. Who has created seven heavens in storeys.
   You[s] cannot see any fault in the Merciful's creation.
   Look again. Do you see any cracks?
4. Look again and again,
   and your sight will come back to you dim and weary.
5. We have adorned the lowest heaven with lamps
   and made them projectiles against the devils;
   and We have prepared for them the torment of the Blaze.
6. For those who do not believe in the Lord
   there is the torment of Jahannam,
   and evil is the journeying.
7. When they are flung into it,
   they hear a roaring from it as it boils,
8. It almost bursts asunder with rage.
   Whenever a troop is cast into it,
   its keepers ask them, 'Did no warner come to you?'
9. They say, 'Yes, a warner came to us,
   but we thought him a liar and said,
   "God has revealed nothing.

You^P are merely in great error".'

10. And they say, 'Had we listened or understood,
we would not have been among the companions of the Blaze.'

11. So they acknowledge their sin.
Away with the companions of the Blaze.

12. Those who fear their Lord in the Invisible
will have forgiveness and a great wage.

13. Keep^P what you say secret or make it public
– He is Aware of the thoughts in men's breasts.

14. Shall He who created not know?
He is the Gentle and the Informed.

15. [It is] He who has made the earth submissive to you^P.
So walk in its sides and eat of His provision.
To Him is the raising.

16. Do you^P feel safe that He who is in heaven
will not cause the earth to swallow you up,
when it is convulsed?

17. Or do you^P feel safe that He who is in heaven
will not let loose on you a sandstorm,
and then you will know how My warning is?

18. In the past those who were before them denied the truth.
And how was My disapproval!

19. Have they not seen the birds above them,
spreading their wings and closing them?
Only the Merciful holds them [there].
He is observer of everything.

20. Or who is this who would be a host for you^P to help you
apart from the Merciful?
The unbelievers are merely in delusion.

21. Or who is this who would make provision for you,
if He withholds His provision?
No, they persist in insolence and aversion.

22. Shall those who walk bent on their faces be more rightly guided
than those who walk upright on a straight path?

23. Say, '[It is] He who produced you^P
and then gave you hearing and sight and hearts.
Little gratitude you show.'

24. Say, '[It is] He who has scattered you^P in the earth
– and to Him you will be rounded up.'

25. And they say, 'When is this promise [to be fulfilled]
if you^P speak the truth?'

26. Say, 'Knowledge [of it] is only with God.

I am merely a clear warner.'

27. When they see it[1] close at hand,
those who have disbelieved will be discountenanced
and they will be told,
'This is what you have been calling for.'

28. Say, 'Have you[p] considered?
If God destroys me and those who are with me,
or if He has mercy on us,
who will protect the unbelievers from a painful torment?'

29. Say, 'He is the Merciful.
We believe in Him and we put our trust in Him.
And you[p] will know who is in manifest error.'

30. Say, 'Have you[p] considered?
If some morning all your water were to have disappeared into the earth,
who would bring you water welling from the ground?'

---

[1] Traditionally taken to refer to the Punishment.

Sūra 68

This *sūra* is usually thought to come from the early Meccan period, though some Muslim authorities consider 17–33 and 48–50 to be Medinan. The material falls into three sections, which were almost certainly separate pieces originally: (*a*) 1–16 offer encouragement to Muḥammad and order him not to obey well-to-do opponents and denigrators; (*b*) a punishment parable told not of sinners and prophets but of the overweening owners of a garden, sharply unfolded and with nice detail (17–34, for a similar passage see 36:13–29); (*c*) a typical piece of Meccan polemic (35–52). My own feeling is that the second section was added to the first, (which may in itself be composite), and then the third added later, all at Mecca.

The Pen

In the name of the Merciful and Compassionate God

1. *Nūn.*[1]
    By the pen and by what they write!
2. Through your[s] Lord's blessing
    you[s] are not possessed.
3. You[s] will have a reward unfailing.
4. You[s] are of a mighty nature.
5. You[s] will see and they will see
6. Which of you[p] is the afflicted.
7. Your[s] Lord is well aware of those who stray from His way,
    and He is well aware of those who are rightly guided.
8. So do[s] not obey those who deny the truth,
9. Who would like both you[s] and them to compromise.
10. And do not obey every contemptible swearer,
11. Backbiter, spreader of slander,
12. Hinderer of good, transgressor, sinner,
13. Greedy, moreover, ignoble,
14. Because he has wealth and sons.
15. When Our signs are recited to him,
    he says, 'Fables of the ancients.'
16. We shall brand him on the snout.
17. We have tried them,

---

[1] On the mystical letters see the note on 2:1.

531

as We tried the owners of the garden
when they vowed that they would pick its fruit next morning,

18. Not making any exception.
19. A visitor from your^s Lord went round it in the night
while they slept.
20. In the morning it was as if picked.
21. They cried out to one another that morning,
22. 'Go early to your field,
if you are going to pick [the fruit].'
23. So they went off, murmuring to each other,
24. 'No destitute person will enter it to-day against your will.'
25. They went early, determined on their purpose.
26. When they saw it, they said,
'We are in error.
27. In truth, we are destitute.'
28. The most moderate of them said,
'Did I not say to you,
"Why do you^p not glorify"?'
29. They said, 'Glory to our Lord,
we have been wrong-doers.'
30. They turned to one another, blaming each other.
31. They said,
'Woe on us. We were insolent.
32. Perhaps our Lord will give us [something] better than this in its place.
We turn towards our Lord.'
33. Such is the punishment.
And the punishment of the world to come is greater,
if they did but know it.
34. Those who protect themselves will have gardens of delight with their Lord.
35. Shall We treat those who submit in the same way as those who sin?
36. What is the matter with you^p?
How do you judge?
37. Or do you have a Scripture wherein you can study?
38. You have in it what you choose.
39. Or do you have oaths from Us,
reaching to the Day of Judgment?
You will have what you judge.
40. Ask^s them which of them will guarantee that.
41. Or have they associates?
Let them bring their associates if they are truthful.
42. On the day when [the] leg will be bared,
they are called to prostration,

but they cannot,

43. With eyes downcast, overtaken by humiliation
    – and they had been summoned to prostration when they were sound.
44. Leave Me [to deal] with those who deny the truth of this story.
    We shall come upon them gradually
    from where they do not know.
45. I shall bear with them for my guile is firm.
46. Or do you⁵ ask them for a fee,
    so that they are weighed down with debt?
47. Or is the Invisible with them,
    so that they can write [about it]?
48. Wait⁵ patiently for the judgement of your Lord
    Do not be like the man of the fish,²
    when he cried out when he was choked with emotion.
49. Had he not been reached by a blessing from his Lord,
    he would have been cast on to a desert
    while he was blameworthy.
50. But his Lord chose him and made him one of the righteous.
51. Those who are ungrateful almost disconcert you⁵ with their glances
    when they have heard the reminder.
    They say, 'He is possessed'.
52. It is nothing but a reminder for all beings.

---

² Jonah.

Sūra 69

The *sūra* is generally considered to be of the late Meccan period, though internal evidence suggests that some material may be earlier. The *kāhin*-style beginning is answered by a brief passage on ʿĀd and Thamūd (4–6 and 8, with 7 probably being added at a later stage). This is followed by an equally brief reference to Pharaoh (9–10), and then, with change of person, to Noah and his family (11–12). There is then an abrupt move to the Day of Judgement (13–18), the reward of the good (19–24) and the punishment of the bad (25–37). The final section is a polemic affirming the truth of Muḥammad's message. It should be noted that the changes in assonance coincide with other breaks only at verses 3 and 12.

The Reality

In the name of the Merciful and Compassionate God

1. The reality.
2. What is the reality?
3. What can give you[s] knowledge of what the reality is?
4. Thamūd and ʿĀd disbelieved in the Smiting.
5. As for Thamūd, they were destroyed by the Overwhelming.
6. As for ʿĀd, they were destroyed by a violent, roaring wind
7. That He imposed on them for seven nights and eight days, consecutively,
   and you[s] could see the people prostrate in it,
   as though they were the stumps of palm-trees that have keeled over.
8. Can you[s] see any remnant of them?
9. And Pharaoh and those before him and the overturned settlements brought error,
10. They resisted the messenger of their Lord,
    and He seized them with a tightening grip.
11. When the waters rose, We carried you[p] in the ship,
12. To make it a reminder for you
    for remembering ears to remember.
13. When there will be one blast on the trumpet,
14. And the earth and the mountains are lifted up
    and crushed with a single blow,
15. On that day the Event will occur.
16. The heaven will be split asunder,
    for on that day it will be frail.
17. The angels will be on its borders,

and above them eight will carry the throne of your^s Lord.

18. On that day you^p will be exposed;
no secret of yours will be concealed.
19. As for him who is given his record in his right hand,
he will say, 'Here you^p are. Read my record.
20. I thought that I should meet my reckoning.'
21. He will be in a pleasing life
22. In a lofty garden,
23. Whose clusters are near.
24. 'Eat^p and drink with relish for what you have done previously in the days gone-by.'
25. But as for him who is given his record in his left hand,
he will say, 'Would that I had not been given my record,
26. And did not know my reckoning,
27. Would that it had been the end.
28. My wealth has been of no avail to me.
29. My authority has gone from me.'
30. 'Take him, and fetter him.
31. Then roast him in Hell-fire
32. Then insert him into a chain whose length is seventy cubits.
33. He used not to believe in God, the Mighty,
34. Nor did he urge the feeding of the destitute.
35. To-day he has no friend here,
36. Nor any food except filth
37. Which none but the sinners eat.'
38. No. I swear by what you^p see
39. And what you do not see,
40. It is the speech of a noble messenger.
41. It is not the speech of a poet
– little you^p believe –
42. Nor is it the speech of a soothsayer
– little you^p are reminded –
43. [It is] a revelation from the Lord of all beings.
44. If he¹ had invented any sayings against Us,
45. We would have seized him by the right hand,
46. Then We would have severed his aorta,
47. And not one of you could have defended him.
48. It is a reminder for those who protect themselves.
49. We know that some of you will deny the truth.
50. It is a sorrow to the ungrateful,
51. But it is the truth of certainty.
52. Glorify^s the name of your^s Lord, the Mighty.

---

¹ Muḥammad.

Sūra 70

This is generally taken to be an early Meccan *sūra*, but that cannot be the case with some parts of it. Verses 4 and 26–33 appear to be later additions, the latter probably Medinan; and verses 36–44 seem to be a separate piece, not from the earliest period. As it stands, the *sūra* falls into three sections: an introductory question and its answer (1–7); an eschatological passage (8–35); and a polemical piece (36–44).

The Stairways

In the name of the Merciful and Compassionate God

1. A questioner has asked questions
   concerning a punishment about to fall
2. On the ungrateful,
   – which none can avert –
3. From God, Lord of the stairways,
4. The angels and the spirit ascend to Him on a day,
   the measure of which is fifty thousand years.
5. So be patient with a fair patience.
6. They think that it is far away;
7. We think it near.
8. On the day when the sky will be like molten copper,
9. And the mountains will be like tufts of wool,
10. No close friend will question his close friend,
11. Though they will be made to see [each other].
    The sinner will long to ransom himself
    from the punishment of that day
    at the price of his sons,
12. And his consort and his brother,
13. And his kin, who gave him shelter,
14. And anyone on earth, all together,
    and [long] to be delivered.
15. No indeed. It is a blaze
16. Eager to roast.
17. It summons those who drew back and turned away,
18. And gathered and hoarded.
19. Man was created anxious,
20. Fretful when evil touches him,

536

21. Grudging when good touches him,
22. Except for those who pray,
23. Who continue at their prayer,
24. And in whose wealth there is a known right
25. For the beggar and the deprived;
26. And [except for] those who believe in the Day of Judgement
27. And who are afraid of the punishment of their Lord
28. – There is no security from the punishment of their Lord –
29. And who guard their private parts
30. Except with their spouses and what their right hands possess.
    Then they are not blameworthy.
31. But those who seek more than that are transgressors.
32. And [except for] those who keep their trusts and their covenant,
33. And who stand by their testimony,
34. And who observe their prayers.
35. These will be honoured in Gardens.
36. What is the matter with those who are ungrateful,
    running towards you^s
37. In groups, on the left and the right?
38. Does every man among them yearn to be admitted to the Garden of Bliss?
39. No indeed.
    We have created them from what they know.
40. No. I swear by the Lord of the easts and the wests.
    We are able
41. To replace them by others who are better than them.
    We shall not be outstripped.
42. Let them plunge[1] and play
    until they meet their day, which they are being promised,[2]
43. The day on which they will come from the graves in haste,
    as if they were hurrying to a mark,
44. With eyes downcast, overtaken by humiliation.
    That is the day which they were promised.[2]

---

[1] See the note on 6:68.
[2] The text varies slightly, in a rather odd way.

Sūra 71

On the surface the *sūra* deals simply with the story of Noah, and one should certainly first look at it in this way. However, it is of composite nature, and it seems unlikely that verse 23, which includes the names of five pre-Islamic gods, could have been part of any original narrative. The present structure is complex. The main narrative basically comprises verses 1–4 and 25, but there are further narratives taking up verses 5–12, 15–20 and 21–24. One might have expected verses 26–28, a prayer from Noah, to precede 25, but they do not.

Noah

In the name of the Merciful and Compassionate God

1. We sent Noah to his people, saying,
   'Warn your[s] people before a painful punishment comes upon them.'
2. He said, 'O my people,
   I am a clear warner to you.
3. "Serve God and fear Him and obey me,
4. And He will forgive you some of your sins
   and defer you to a stated term.
   God's term, when it comes, cannot be deferred
   if you did but know it".'
5. He said, 'My Lord,
   I have summoned my people night and day,
6. But my summoning has increased them only in flight.
7. Whenever I summon them so that You might forgive them,
   they put their fingers in their ears
   and draw their garments over them
   and persist and are full of pride.
8. I have summoned them publicly.
9. I spoke to them openly
   and I spoke to them secretly
10. And I said,
    "Ask forgiveness of your[p] Lord
    – He is Forgiving
11. – And He will loose the sky on you in torrents[1]

---

[1] With abundant rain.

12.	And support you with wealth and sons,
	and will assign gardens to you,
	and will assign rivers to you.
13.	What is the matter with you
	that you do not expect God to have dignity,
14.	When he has created you in stages?
15.	Have you not considered how God has created seven heavens in storeys,
16.	And made the moon a light among them and made the sun a lamp?
17.	It is God who has caused you to spring up as a growth from the earth.
18.	Then He will make you return to it,
	and He will bring you forth [again].
19.	And God has made the earth a carpet for you,
20.	That you might thread ways through its valleys".'
21.	Noah said,
	'My Lord, they have rebelled against me
	and followed him whose wealth and children
	increase him only in loss,
22.	And they have plotted a very great plot,
23.	And said,
	"Do not forsake your gods
	and do not forsake Wadd nor Suwāʿ
	nor Yaghūth nor Yaʿūq nor Nasr."[2]
24.	And they have led many astray.
	Do not increase the wrong-doers except in error.'
25.	Because of their sins they were drowned
	and put into a fire;
	and they found no helpers apart from God.
26.	Noah said, 'O my Lord,
	do not leave a single one of the unbelievers on the earth.
27.	If You leave them, they will lead Your servants astray,
	and beget only dissolute unbelievers.
28.	My Lord,
	forgive me and my parents
	and whoever enters my house as a believer
	and believing men and women,
	and increase the wrong-doers only in ruin.'

---

[2] The names are those of some of the deities worshipped by pre-Islamic Arabs.

Sūra 72

This *sūra* is generally thought to belong to the middle or late Meccan periods. However, attempts to link it to a journey made by Muḥammad from Mecca to the neighbouring town of al-Ṭā'if (c. 620 AD) are unconvincing. The nucleus of the *sūra* is a series of short declarations addressed to Muḥammad and introduced by 'Say' (verses 1, 20, 21, 22, 25). However, the first of these has been extended by a piece (3–19) in which virtually every verse begins with 'and that'.

The *Jinn*

In the name of the Merciful and Compassionate God

1. Say, 'It has been revealed to me that a group of *Jinn* listened and said,
    "We have heard a marvellous recitation,
2. Which guides to righteousness.
    We believe in it,
    and we shall not associate anyone with our Lord.
3. [We believe] that He – may the majesty of our Lord be exalted –
    has not taken for Himself any consort or son.
4. And that the fool among us used to speak an outrageous lie against God.
5. And that we supposed that men and *Jinn* would not speak a lie against God.
6. And that individuals of mankind would take refuge with individuals of the *Jinn*,
    and who increased them in their wrong-doing.
7. And that they thought, as you[P] thought,
    that God would not raise anyone.
8. And that we reached up to heaven,
    but found it filled with strong guards and meteors.
9. And that we used to sit on seats there to hear
    – (but anyone who listens now finds a meteor in wait for him) –
10. And that we do not know if evil is intended for those who are on earth
    or if their Lord wishes guidance for them.
11. And that among us there are the righteous
    and among us there are some who fall below that
    – we have become groups [following] different roads –
12. And that we thought that we could not frustrate God on earth
    nor frustrate Him by flight.
13. And that when we heard the guidance,
    we believed in it

– and the one who believes in his Lord does not fear loss or wrong-doing –

14. And that among us there are those who have surrendered and those who are unjust.
And those who surrender choose a right path.

15. As for the unjust, they are firewood for Jahannam."

16. And that if they were to go straight along the way,
We would give them water in plenty to drink,

17. That We might test them thereby;
those who turn away from remembrance of their Lord,
He will lead them into a grievous punishment.

18. And that[1] the places of prostration belong to God;
so do not call[p] on anyone along with God.

19. And that when the servant of God[2] stood to call to Him,
they were almost on him in swarms.'

20. Say, 'I call only to my Lord
and I do not associate anyone with Him.'

21. Say, 'I do not possess either harm for you[p] or a right way.'

22. Say, 'No one can promise me protection from God,
nor shall I find a refuge apart from Him.

23. [I convey] only a proclamation from God and His messages.
Those who rebel against God and His messenger,
they shall have the Fire,
in which they shall remain for ever.'

24. And then when they see what they have been promised,
they will know who is weaker in helpers
and fewer in number.

25. Say, 'I do not know whether what you[p] are promised is near
or whether my Lord is setting a term for it –

26. The Knower of the Invisible.
He does not disclose His Invisible to anyone,

27. Except to such messengers as He is pleased with.
Then He makes watchers go in front of him and behind him,

28. That He may know that they have conveyed the messages of their Lord.
He encompasses all that is with them
and keeps count of everything.

---

[1] The use of 'and that' here seems to be anomalous.
[2] Muḥammad.

Sūra 73

The *sūra* is a series of commands to Muḥammad, though the believers are also addressed in the final verse. The earliest part appears to be the verses numbered in the text as 1, 2 and 4a. This little piece is very much akin to the beginning of *Sūra* 74 and is thought to be one of the first passages of the Qur'ān to have been revealed. Verses 3, 4 and 5–19 come from later Meccan periods, though recasting has made 1–8 a unit. The final verse is of considerable interest. It is Medinan and has the effect of moderating the rigour of the command in verses 1–3 and 4a and of making the modified injunction applicable to all believers.

Wrapped in a Robe[1]

In the name of the Merciful and Compassionate God

1. You[s] who are wrapped up in a robe,
2. Stay up during the night, except for a little
3. – Half of it or a little less
4. Or a little more –
4a. and be distinct with the Recitation.
5. We shall place on you[s] a weighty word.
6. The first part of the night has greater impression
   and is more certain in speech.
7. In the daytime you[s] have long business,
8. But remember[s] the name of your Lord
   and devote yourself steadfastly to Him.
9. [He is] the Lord of the east and the west.
   There is no god but Him.
   Adopt[s] Him as your trustee.
10. Endure patiently what they[2] say,
    and withdraw from them politely.
11. Leave Me with those who deny the truth,
    though they are prosperous,
    and give them a brief respite.
12. With Us are fetters and the hot fire
13. And food that chokes and a painful punishment

---

[1] The title, taken from the word *al-muzzammil* in verse 1, refers to someone wearing a robe.
[2] *i.e.* Muḥammad's Meccan opponents.

14. On the day when the earth and the mountains shake
    and the mountains become a heap of scattered sand.
15. We have sent to you^P a messenger as a witness against you,
    just as we sent a messenger to Pharaoh.
16. But Pharaoh rebelled against the messenger,
    and so We seized him in an irksome grasp.
17. How will you protect yourselves if you are ungrateful[3]
    on a day that will make children grey-haired,[4]
18. On which the heaven will be split and its promise fulfilled?
19. This is a Reminder,
    and those who wish will take a way to their Lord.
20. Your^s Lord knows that you stay up close to two-thirds of the night
    or a half or a third,
    as do a party of those with you^s,
    for God measures the night and the day.
    He knows that you^P will not count it,
    and He has relented towards you^P.
    Recite^P whatever recitation is reasonable for you.
    He knows that some of you will be ill
    and others will be travelling in the land seeking God's bounty
    and others will be fighting in God's cause.
    So recite what is reasonable of it;
    and perform prayer and pay the *zakāt*,
    and lend a good loan to God.
    Whatever good you forward for yourselves,
    you will find it with God, better and with a greater reward.
    And ask forgiveness from God,
    for God is Forgiving and Merciful.

---

[3] Or 'do not believe'.

[4] *i.e.* old.

Sūra 74

The first verses of this *sūra* (1–7) are thought to be very early, most Muslim scholars considering them to be either the first or the second revelation. They are an exhortation and a warning to Muḥammad. Verses 8–10 form a bridge passage, leading to a polemic against the ungrateful (verses 11–26). Muslim sources usually take the whole piece as referring to one of Muḥammad's most prominent Meccan opponents, al-Walīd ibn al-Mughīra. However, it looks as though verses 11–17 are a general passage, to which 18–26 were later added. (The assonance changes in verse 18). Verses 27–30 are an explanation of 26, and they are followed by a long Medinan verse that is thought to explain verse 30. Verses 32–53 look very much like another short *sūra* in themselves, but they are carefully linked to 26–30 (at least) by the use of *kalla* ('no indeed') in 32 and *Saqar* in 42. Verse 56 seems to be another later addition, but probably not so late as 31. It should also be noted that at various points the material in this *sūra* shows a close affinity to parts of *Sūra* 80.

Wrapped in a Cloak[1]

In the name of the Merciful and Compassionate God

1. You^s who are wrapped up in a cloak,
2. Arise and warn,
3. And magnify your Lord.
4. Purify your clothes
5. And shun abomination.
6. Do not show favours, seeking gain.
7. Be patient for the sake of your Lord.
8. When there is a blast on the trumpet,
9. That is then a difficult day
10. For the ungrateful, not easy.
11. Leave Me with the one whom I created alone,
12. And for whom I appointed extensive property
13. And sons to stand before him,
14. And for whom I made [life] smooth,
15. And who desires that I should give more.
16. No indeed. He has been stubborn towards Our signs.

---

[1] The title, taken from the word *muddaththir* in verse 1, refers to someone wearing a *dithār*, a general word for an outer garment.

544

17. I shall impose a difficult ascent on him.
18. He pondered and determined,
19. May he be accursed. How he determined.
20. Then may he be accursed. How he determined.
21. Then he looked,
22. Then he frowned and scowled,
23. Then he turned away and was haughty.
24. And he said, 'This is merely retold magic, → person says the qur'an
25. This is merely mortal speech.'   isn't true
26. I shall roast him in Saqar.[2]
27. What can give you[s] knowledge of what Saqar is?
28. It does not spare, nor does it leave alone,
29. Scorching the flesh.
30. Over it are nineteen.[3]
31. We have appointed only angels to be masters of the Fire,
    and We have appointed their number
    simply as an affliction for those who are ungrateful,
    that those who have been given the Scripture may have certainty,
    and that those who believe may have greater belief;
    and that neither those who have been given the Scripture
    nor the believers may be in any doubt;
    and that those in whose hearts is sickness
    and the ungrateful ones may say,
    'What did God mean by this parable?'
    Thus God sends astray those whom He wishes
    and guides those whom He wishes.
    No one knows the hosts of your[s] Lord but He.
    This is simply a reminder for mankind.[4]
32. No indeed. By the moon,
33. And the night when it retreats,
34. And the morning when it shines forth,
35. It is one of the greatest things,
36. A warning to mankind,
37. To whichever one of you wishes to go forward or stay behind.

---

[2] It is traditionally agreed that Saqar is one of the names of Hell. However, the phraseology of verse 27 seems to indicate that its meaning was not at all obvious at the time of the initial revelation. Apart from this *sūra*, Saqar is mentioned in 54:48.

[3] Initially the meaning of 'nineteen' would have been vague. The verse that was later inserted to follow it up now links it with angels. Over the years there have been many numerological explanations of the number nineteen, all of them implausible.

[4] This whole verse is Medinan, both in style and in the content of some of its key phrases, *e.g.* 'those who have been given the Scripture' and 'those in whose hearts there is sickness'.

38. Every soul is pledged for what it has earned,
39. Except for the companions of the right.
40. In gardens they will ask one another
41. About the sinners.
42. 'What has brought you into Saqar?'
43. They will answer, 'We were not of those who prayed,
44. Nor did we feed the destitute.
45. We used to plunge with those who plunged,[5]
46. And we used to deny the truth of the Day of Judgement,
47. Till the Certain[6] came to us.'
48. The intercession of intercessors will be of no use to them.
49. Why do they turn away from the reminder,
50. As if they were startled asses
51. Fleeing from a lion?
52. No, each man of them wishes to be given unrolled sheets.[7]
53. No indeed. They do not fear the world to come.
54. No indeed. It is a reminder.
55. Whoever wishes will remember it.
56. But they will not remember unless God wishes.
    He is worthy of awe and worthy of forgiveness.

---

[5] See the note on 6:68.

[6] *i.e.* death.

[7] The meaning of this phrase is uncertain.

Sūra 75

This *sūra* is considered to be early Meccan. It appears to have been drawn together from a number of short pieces: 1–6; 7–13; 14–15; 16–19; 20–25; 26–29; 30–33; 34–35; 36–40. All have typical early Meccan themes.

The Resurrection

In the name of the Merciful and Compassionate God

1. No. I swear by the Day of Resurrection.
2. No. I swear by the reproaching soul.
3. Does man think that We shall not gather together his bones?
4. Of course We shall.
   [We are] able to form his fingers [again].
5. But man wishes to act wrongly before it.
6. He asks, 'When will the Day of Resurrection be?'
7. When the sight is dazzled,
8. And the moon is eclipsed,
9. And the sun and moon are brought together,
10. On that day man will say,
    'Where is the place to flee to?'
11. No indeed. No refuge!
12. On that day the appointment is with your[s] Lord,
13. On that day man will be told what he has sent forward and left behind.
14. No! Man will be a clear proof against himself,
15. Even though he offers his excuses.
16. Do[s] not move your tongue about it to hasten it.[1]
17. Upon Us is its putting together and its recitation.
18. When We recite it, follow[s] its recitation.
19. Upon Us is its explanation.
20. No indeed. You[p] love the fleeting,
21. And you leave alone the world to come.
22. There will be faces on that day that are radiant,
23. Looking on their Lord.
24. And there will be faces on that day that are scowling.
25. They think that holes will be made in them.

---

[1] The Qur'ān.

26. No indeed. When [the departing soul] reaches the clavicles,
27. And it is said, 'Who is a sorcerer?'
28. And he thinks that it is the parting,
29. And leg is entangled with leg,
30. On that day the driving will be to your^s Lord.
31. He did not believe it, nor did he pray.
32. But he denied and turned his back,
33. Then he went to his folk, full of pride.
34. Nearer to you^s and nearer,
35. Then nearer to you^s and nearer.
36. Does man think that he will be left on his own?
37. Was he not a drop of fluid that gushed forth?
38. Then he became a clot;
    and He created and shaped [him],
39. And made of him two kinds, male and female.
40. Is not [He who does that] able to restore the dead to life?

Sūra 76

The majority of commentators think that this *sūra* comes from the middle Meccan period, though a small minority believe that it is Medinan. Much of it is rhetorical and impressionistic, and a number of its vignettes now seem opaque because of out-of-the-way vocabulary. These are features of Meccan rather than Medinan material, though some recasting may have taken place at Medina. After a brief introductory piece on man and creation (verses 1–3), a verse on the ungrateful and their punishment (4) leads into the central passage on the pious and their reward (5–22). This is followed by a typical peroration, addressed in part to Muḥammad.

Man

In the name of the Merciful and Compassionate God

1. Has there come upon man a period of time
   when he was a thing not to be remembered?
2. We have created man a sperm-drop, a mixing, to test him;
   and We have made him able to hear and to see.
3. We have guided him on the way,
   whether he was grateful or ungrateful.
4. We have prepared for those who are ungrateful
   chains and fetters and a blazing fire.
5. But the pious will drink from a cup
   whose mixture is Kāfūr,[1]
6. A spring at which the servants of God drink,
   causing it to gush forth in abundance.
7. They fulfil their vows and fear a day
   whose evil will fly abroad.
8. For the love of Him they give food to the destitute,
   the orphan and the prisoner:
9. 'We feed you[p] for the favour of God.
   We do not wish for any reward or thanks from you.
10. We fear from our Lord
    a day that is frowning and inauspicious.'
11. So God has protected them from the evil of that day
    and granted them radiance and joy.

---

[1] It is not clear whether Kāfūr is a proper name or has its ordinary meaning of 'camphor'.

12. He has recompensed them for their patience with a garden and silk;
13. They recline there on couches
    and see neither sun nor cold.
14. Close over them are its shades,
    and its fruit-clusters are lowered.
15. Cups of silver are brought round to them in turn,
    vessels of glass,
16. Glass [set in] silver, which they have measured;
17. There they are given a drink in a cup,
    whose mixture is Zanjabīl,[2]
18. A spring there, named Salsabīl.
19. Immortal youths circle amongst them
    – when you[s] see them, you[s] will consider them to be scattered pearls.
20. When you[s] see them, then you[s] see bliss and a great kingdom.
21. The clothes they wear will be of green silk and brocade,
    and they are adorned with bracelets of silver;
    and their Lord gives them a pure draught to drink.
22. 'This is a reward for you[p], and your striving is thanked.'
23. Truly We have sent down to you[s] the Recitation.
24. So submit[s] patiently to the judgement of your Lord,
    and do not obey any ungrateful one or any sinner among them.
25. Make[s] mention of your Lord morning and evening
26. And part of the night;
    and prostrate[s] yourself to Him
    and glorify[s] Him through the long night.
27. These people love the [world] that hastens away
    and disregard a heavy day.
28. We it was who created them and strengthened their frame.
    And when We wish We shall exchange them for others like them.
29. This is a reminder.
    Those who wish choose a way to their Lord.
30. But you[p] will wish [so] only if God wishes.
    God is Knowing and Wise.
31. He admits to His mercy those whom He wishes
    – but for the wrong-doers He has prepared a painful punishment.

---

[2] Similarly, it is not clear whether Zanjabīl is a proper name or has its ordinary meaning of 'ginger'.

Sūra 77

The *sūra* is early Meccan. It is one of the group of *sūras* (the others are 37, 51, 79 and 100) that begin with tightly structured *kāhin*-style material, the meaning of whose phrases is uncertain. After the initial *kāhin*-style passage and the warning that rounds it off (1–7), there is a piece in which 'when' clauses lead to a sharp passage on 'the day of decision' (8–14). This is rounded off (15) by the first occurrence of the *sūra*'s refrain, which is used ten times. This seems to be one of the earliest examples in the Qur'ān of a verse being used as a refrain. The refrain is a loose one, but not so loose as that of *Sūra* 55. Next comes a passage on God's signs (16–28), followed by one on heaven and hell (29–45). The *sūra* closes with another brief warning.

Those that are sent

In the name of the Merciful and Compassionate God

1. By those that are sent in succession,
2. And by those that are stormy,
3. By those that scatter,
4. And by those that divide,
5. And by those that offer a reminder,
6. An excuse or a warning,
7. That which you^p are promised will occur.
8. When the stars are effaced,
9. When the sky is split,
10. When the mountains are scattered,
11. When the messengers are brought to their appointed time
12. – For what day is their appointment made?
13. For the day of decision.
14. And what can give you^s an idea of what the day of decision is?
15. Woe on that day to those who deny the truth.
16. Did not We destroy the ancients,
17. Then cause the later ones to follow them?
18. Thus we deal with the sinners.
19. Woe on that day to those who deny the truth.
20. Did We not create you^p from a base fluid,
21. Which We placed in a safe abode,
22. For a known term.
23. We determined

– We are excellent determiners.

24. Woe on that day to those who deny the truth.
25. Did we not make the earth a housing
26. For the living and the dead,
27. And set in it lofty mountains
    and provided you[P] with fresh water?
28. Woe on that day to those who deny the truth.
29. Depart[P] to that which you used to deny.
30. Depart to the shadow with three branches,[1]
31. Which gives no shade
    and is of no avail against the flame.
32. It throws out sparks like castles
33. As if they were light-coloured she-camels.
34. Woe on that day to those who deny the truth.
35. This is the day they shall not speak,
36. Nor are they allowed to make excuses.
37. Woe on that day to those who deny the truth.
38. This is the day of separation;
    We have joined you[P] with the ancients.
39. If you[P] have any trick, try it out on me.
40. Woe on that day to those who deny the truth.
41. The god-fearing are among shade and springs,
42. And such fruits as they desire.
43. 'Eat[P] and drink with relish
    in return for what you have been doing.'
44. Thus We recompense those who do good.
45. Woe on that day to those who deny the truth.
46. 'Eat and enjoy yourselves a little. You are sinners.'
47. Woe on that day to those who deny the truth.
48. When they are told to bow, they do not bow.
49. Woe on that day to those who deny the truth.
50. In what statement will they believe after this?

---

[1] Verses 30–33 referring to Hell contrast with 41–44 referring to Paradise.

Sūra 78

The *sūra* appears to be Meccan, but contains material from different periods. Verses 1–35 seem to be relatively early, but 36–40 have the hallmarks of a later date. After a brief warning in verses 1–5, there is a 'creation' passage (6–16), followed by an eschatological piece containing vignettes of hell and heaven (17–35). The final passage stresses God's might on the Day of Judgement. The sparer use of assonance here appears to indicate material later than the rest of the *sūra*.

The Tidings

In the name of the Merciful and Compassionate God

1. About what are they questioning one another?
2. – About the awesome tidings,
3. Concerning which they differ.
4. No indeed! They will know.
5. Again, no indeed! They will know.
6. Have We not made the earth as a resting-place,
7. And the mountains pegs?
8. We have created you in pairs,
9. And appointed your sleep as a rest,
10. And appointed night as a garment,
11. And appointed day for a livelihood,
12. And built above you seven strong ones,[1]
13. And appointed a dazzling lamp,
14. And sent down water pouring in abundance from the rain-clouds,
15. That We may bring forth thereby grain and plants
16. And luxuriant gardens.
17. The day of decision is indeed an appointed time,
18. The day when there is a blast on the trumpet
    and you come in throngs,
19. When heaven is opened and becomes gates,
20. When the mountains are set in motion and become a mirage.
21. Hell is truly an ambush,
22. A resort for the insolent,
23. In which they will linger for ages,

---

[1] The heavens.

24. In which they will taste neither cool nor drink,
25. Except scalding water and pus:
26. A recompense fit for them.
27. They were not expecting a reckoning
28. And they denied the truth of Our signs.
29. Everything we have numbered in a document.
30. So taste^p.
    The only increase We shall give you will be in punishment.
31. For the god-fearing there will be a refuge:
32. Gardens and vineyards,
33. And maidens as companions,
34. And an overflowing cup,
35. Where they will not hear idle chatter nor claims of falsehood
36. – A recompense from your^s Lord, a gift, a reckoning,
37. Lord of the heavens and earth and what is between them,
    the Merciful,
    from Whom they hold no [right of] address.
38. On the day when the spirit and the angels stand in ranks, not speaking,
    except those to whom the Merciful has granted permission
    and who speak aright.
39. That is the true day.
    Those who wish may take a refuge close by their Lord.
40. We have warned you^p of a punishment that is near,
    on the day when a man will see what his hands have sent forward
    and the unbeliever will say, 'Would that I were dust.'

Sūra 79

This is one of the group of *sūras* (the others are 37, 51, 77 and 100) that begin with a fairly specialized form of *kāhin*-style material. The structure and overall thrust are very similar to *Sūra* 77, though some of the themes are different. The initial *kāhin*-style passage (1–5) moves into one on the Day of Judgement (6–14). This is followed by a narrative referring to Moses and the destruction of Pharaoh (15–26) and a 'creation' passage (27–33). Another 'judgement' passage follows (34–41), and the *sūra* is rounded off by warnings.

The Pullers

In the name of the Merciful and Compassionate God

1. By those that pull to destruction,
2. By those that rove,[1]
3. By those that swim,
4. And by those that outstrip,
5. And by those that manage an affair,
6. On the day when the shuddering shudders,
7. Followed by the one that rides behind,
8. There are hearts on that day that will beat painfully,
9. Their looks downcast,
10. They will say, 'Are we being restored to our original state
11. – when we have become decayed bones?'
12. They will say, 'That will then be a losing turn.'
13. There will only be a single driving,
14. And see, they will be awake.
15. Have you[s] heard the story of Moses?
16. – When his Lord called to him in the holy valley, Ṭuwā,
17. 'Go to Pharaoh. He has been insolent.
18. Say, "Have you[s] [any wish] to purify yourself
19. And that I should guide you to your Lord and you fear Him"?'
20. He showed him the great sign,
21. But he[2] denied [the truth] and acted rebelliously;
22. Then he turned away in haste,

---

[1] Or 'act with energy'.
[2] Pharaoh.

23. And mustered and proclaimed,
24. Saying, 'I am your^p lord, the most high.'
25. So God seized him as exemplary punishment for the next world and for this.
26. In this there is indeed a warning for those who fear.
27. Are you^p stronger as a creation or the heaven that He built?
28. He raised its vault and fashioned it.
29. He made its night dark, and brought out its forenoon.
30. And after that He spread out the earth,
31. And brought out from it its water and its pasture,
32. And anchored its mountains:
33. A provision for your^p beasts.
34. But when the great catastrophe comes
35. – The day on which man will be reminded of his endeavours
36. And Hell is advanced for those who see.
37. As for the one who has been insolent
38. And preferred the life of this world,
39. Hell will be his abode.
40. As for the one who has feared the time when he will stand before his Lord and has forbidden his soul its wishes,
41. The garden will be his abode,
42. They ask you^s about the Hour, 'When is the time of its anchoring?
43. What mention can you^s make of it?'
44. To your^s Lord is its goal.
45. You^s are merely the warner of those who fear it.
46. On the day they see it, it will be as if they had tarried only for an evening or its forenoon.

Sūra 80

The *sūra* falls naturally into five sections: 1–10; 11–16; 17–22; 23–32; and 33–42. The transitions from one section to another are very much like the transitions we see in Arabic poetry: by use of *kallā* 'no indeed' in 11 and 23; the abrupt optative in 17; and *fa-idhā* in 33. The first section is generally taken to be a reproof of Muḥammad. The traditional view of the second section is that it refers to a book written in heaven. It is not clear that this is so, though the explanation seems more likely than Bell's view that the reference is to the books of former revelations. The third section deals with man's ingratitude, with the fourth section, on God's bounty, forming a pointed contrast. The *sūra* ends with a passage on the resurrection and judgement. It appears that all the material in the *sūra* is from the early Meccan period. Some of it is linked with material in *Sūra* 74.

He Frowned

In the name of the Merciful and Compassionate God

1. He frowned and turned away,
2. Because the blind man[1] came to him.
3. What gives you[s] knowledge [about this]?
    Perhaps he will purify himself,
4. Or perhaps he will be reminded
    and the reminder profit him.
5. As for the one who thinks himself self-sufficient,
6. You[s] pay attention to him,
7. Though it is not your concern that he does not purify himself.
8. As for the one who comes to you[s] eagerly,
9. And is in fear,
10. You pay no heed to him.
11. No indeed! It is a reminder
12. – And whoever wishes will remember it –
13. On sheets that are honoured,
14. Exalted and purified,
15. By the hands of scribes,
16. Who are noble and pious.
17. May man perish.

---

[1] Traditionally said to be a poor Meccan named ʿAbdallāh ibn Umm Maktūm.

How ungrateful he is.

18. From what did He create him?
19. He created him and proportioned him from a drop of sperm;
20. Then He made the way easy for him;
21. Then He caused him to die and to be buried;
22. Then, when He wishes, He will raise him again.
23. No indeed!

He has not yet accomplished His bidding.

24. Let man consider his food.
25. We have poured out water in abundance;
26. Then We have split the earth in fissures,
27. And have caused to grow therein grain,
28. And grapes and reeds,
29. And olives and date-palms,
30. And luxuriant gardens,
31. And fruit and pasture –
32. Provision for you^P and your beasts.
33. But when the Crack of Doom comes,
34. On the day when a man will flee from his brother,
35. And from his mother and his father,
36. And from his wife and his children,
37. On that day each man will have business to occupy him.
38. On that day there will be some faces that shine,
39. Laughing and joyful;
40. And on that day there will be faces
41. Covered with dust,
42. Overtaken by blackness
43. – Those are the wicked unbelievers.

Sūra 81

The *sūra* consists of two sections of essentially Meccan material: 1–14, with assonance in -*at*, and 15–29, with assonance first in -*as* and then in the common -*ūn/īn/īm*. The first section is notable as one of the longest in the Qur'ān in which there is a series of tableaux, each introduced by *idhā* 'when' in a style typical of *kāhin*-style material. The thrust of the second section is the truth of the message. Its beginning is a briefer version of 1–14, and this may be why they have come together. Verses 20–23 carry echoes of the beginning of *Sūra* 53. The last verse is probably a later addition.

The Enveloping

In the name of the Merciful and Compassionate God

1.   When the sun is enveloped,
2.   When the stars are scattered,
3.   When the mountains are moved,
4.   When the camels ten months pregnant are untended,
5.   When the wild beasts are driven together,
6.   When the seas are made to boil,
7.   When souls are paired,
8.   When the baby girl that was slain is asked
9.   For what sin she was killed,
10.   When the sheets are unrolled,
11.   When the sky is stripped,
12.   When Hell is set ablaze,
13.   When the Garden is brought near,
14.   A soul will know what it has produced.
15.   No! I swear by the [stars] that retreat,
16.   Moving and setting,
17.   By the night when it closes,
18.   By the morning when it breathes,
19.   It is indeed the speech of a noble messenger,[1]
20.   Powerful, secure with the Occupant of the Throne,
21.   Obeyed and to be trusted,

---

[1] Traditionally thought to be Gabriel.

22. Your^p companion² is not possessed.
23. He did indeed see Him on the clear horizon.
24. He is not niggardly about the Invisible.
25. This is not the word of a devil that should be stoned.
26. So where are you^p going?
27. It is nothing less than a reminder to all beings
28. – for whoever of you wishes to follow the straight path.
29. And you will not wish [to do] so
unless God, the Lord of all beings, wills so.

---

² Muḥammad.

Sūra 82

The *sūra* is early Meccan. It falls into two sections: 1–8, pointing to the coming resurrection and warning of man's ingratitude; and 9–19, on the judgement, paradise and hell. It is possible that 17–19 are somewhat later than the rest of the *sūra*, but still Meccan.

The Rending

In the name of the Merciful and Compassionate God

1. When the heaven is rent asunder,
2. When the stars are scattered,
3. When the seas are caused to pour forth,
4. When the graves are overturned,
5. A soul will know
    what it has sent before
    and what it has kept back.
6. O man, what has deceived you concerning your generous Lord,
7. Who created you and formed you and shaped you,
8. Constructed you in whatever form He wished?
9. No, indeed!
    You[p] deny the judgement.
10. Over you[p] are guardians,
11. Generous, recording,
12. Who know what you do.
13. The pious will be in bliss.
14. The profligate will be in Hell;
15. They will roast in it on the Day of Judgement
16. And they will not be absent from it.
17. What will give you[s] knowledge of what the Day of Judgement is?
18. Then what will give you[s] knowledge of what the Day of Judgement is?
19. The day when no soul will have anything to help another soul,
    The affair on that day will be God's.

Sūra 83

This *sūra* is usually thought to be early Meccan. However, some Muslim authorities claim that it was the last to be revealed at Mecca, and still others claim that it was wholly or partly revealed at Medina. There is a good case for arguing that some of the verses (8–9, 19–20, 26) are later Meccan additions, but nothing looks Medinan. Natural breaks in the mixture of polemical and eschatological themes come after verses 6, 17 and 28.

The Skimpers

In the name of the Merciful and Compassionate God

1. Woe to the skimpers!
2. Who, when they measure for themselves against people, take full measure;
3. But cause them loss if they measure for them or weigh for them.
4. Don't those men think that they will be raised
5. For an awful day?
6. – The day when men will stand before the Lord of all beings.
7. No, indeed!
   The record of the reprobates is in Sijjīn
8. – And what will give you[s] knowledge of what Sijjīn is? –
9. An inscribed record.
10. Woe on that day to those who deny,
11. Those who deny the truth of the Day of Reckoning.
12. No one counts it false
    except for every sinful transgressor,
13. Who, when our signs are recited to him,
    says, 'Fables of the ancients.'
14. No indeed!
    What they have been earning has rusted on their hearts.
15. No indeed.
    On that day they will be excluded from their Lord.
16. Then they will roast in Hell.
17. Then they will be told,
    'This is what you[p] used to deny.'
18. No, indeed!
    The record of the pious is in 'Illiyyīn.
19. – And what will give you[s] knowledge of what 'Illiyyīn is? –

20. An inscribed record,
21. Which those who have been brought near[1] will witness.
22. The pious are in bliss,
23. Gazing on couches,
24. You[s] will recognize in their faces the radiance of bliss.
25. They drink from a pure wine, sealed,
26. Whose seal is musk
    – let those who strive strive after that –
27. And mixed with [the water of] Tasnīm,
28. A spring at which those who are brought near[1] drink.
29. Those who sin used to laugh at those who believed
30. And wink to one another when they passed them,
31. And when they went back to their own people, they went back jesting.
32. And when they saw them they said, 'These men have gone astray.'
33. But they were not sent as watchers over them.
34. On this day those who believe who will laugh at the unbelievers,
35. Gazing on couches.
36. Have not the unbelievers been given as a reward
    what they used to do?

---

[1] Near to God.

Sūra 84

The *sūra* is generally agreed to be early Meccan, though verses 2, 5 and 25 may well be later. The initial oaths and statement (1–6) are followed by an eschatological passage (7–15) and then a polemical one (16–25).

The Splitting

In the name of the Merciful and Compassionate God

1. When the heaven is split asunder,
2. And listens to its Lord and is disposed [to Him],
3. When the earth is spread out,
4. And casts out what is in it and is empty,
5. And listens to its Lord and is disposed [to Him],
6. O man, you will be labouring towards your Lord
   and you will meet Him.
7. As for him who is given his document in his right hand,
8. He will receive an easy reckoning,
9. And he will go back happy to his family.
10. As for him who is given his document behind his back,
11. He will call for destruction,
12. And he will roast in a blaze.
13. He used to be happy among his family.
14. He thought that he would never return.
15. Yet his Lord was observing him.
16. No, I swear by the twilight,
17. And by the night and what it envelops,
18. And the moon when it is full:
19. You[p] will ride layer after layer.
20. What is the matter with them that they do not believe,
21. And that they do not bow down
    when the Recitation is recited to them?
22. No! Those who are unbelievers deny [the truth of the recitation];
23. But God knows well what they hide.
24. So give[s] them the tidings of a painful punishment –
25. Though that will not be so for those who believe and do good deeds.
    They will have an unfailing reward.

Sūra 85

Most of the *sūra* is early Meccan. It starts with three verses of a *kāhin*-style material, with verse 4 providing the main statement, a not infrequent pattern in early *sūras*. Verses 5 and 6 may or may not have been part of this passage. Verses 7–11 have every appearance of being later than the rest of the *sūra*. Neuwirth (*Meccan Sūras*, pp. 223–24) argues that they form three different additions to an earlier version consisting of 1–6 and 12–22: 7, explaining 3; 8–9 a further explanatory flashback; and 10–11 explaining verse 8.

The Constellations

In the name of God, the Merciful, the Compassionate

1. By the heaven that holds the constellations,
2. By the promised day,
3. By what witnesses and what is witnessed,
4. Slain were the men of the pit
5. – the fire fed with fuel –
6. When they sat over it,
7. And they were witnesses of what they did with the believers.
8. They took vengeance against them
only because they believed in God,
the Mighty, the Laudable,
9. To Whom belongs the kingdom of the heaven and earth,
for God is witness over everything.
10. Those who persecute believing men and women and do not repent
– theirs will be the punishment of Jahannam;
theirs will be the punishment of the burning.
11. Those who believe and act righteously
– theirs are gardens through which rivers flow.
That is the great triumph.
12. The power of your[s] Lord is severe.
13. It is He who originates and restores,
14. And He is the Forgiving, the Loving,
15. The Glorious Occupant of the throne,
16. The Doer of what He wishes.
17. Have you[s] heard of the story of the hosts,
18. Of Pharaoh and of Thamūd?

19. No, those who disbelieve are [engaged] in denial,
20. While God encompasses them from behind.
21. No. It is a glorious Recitation,
22. Preserved on a tablet.[1]

---

[1] Or 'on a preserved tablet'. Both interpretations are canonical, but see the Commentary.

Sūra 86

The *sūra* is early Meccan. From the parallel sets of oaths (1–3 and 11–12), it looks very much like two short pieces run together to form one *sūra*.

What comes in the night

In the name of the Merciful and Compassionate God

1. By the heaven and by what comes in the night,
2. What will give you^s knowledge of what it is that comes in the night?
3. The piercing star.
4. Over every soul there is a watcher.
5. So let man consider from what he has been created.
6. He has been created from a gushing fluid,
7. That comes from between the loins and the ribs.
8. He is able to bring [men] back.
9. On the day when the secrets are tested,
10. And [they] will have no strength or helper.
11. By the heaven that has the return,
12. By the earth that has the splitting,
13. It is a decisive saying,
14. It is no frivolity.
15. They devise trickery,
16. But I[1] devise trickery.
17. So give^s respite to the unbelievers;
    deal^s with them in a leisurely manner.

---

[1] 'I' refers to God.

567

Sūra 87

This *sūra* is thought to be early Meccan, though verse 7 has the appearance of being a later addition. The *sūra* starts with a piece of encouragement to Muḥammad (1–9). This is followed by a passage contrasting those who accept the Reminder with those who do not (10–15). The final section sharply addresses the heedless, telling them that the next world is better than this and indicating that this message is to be found in earlier scriptures. On the importance of verses 6–7 and 18–19 see the Commentary.

The Most High

In the name of the Merciful and Compassionate God

1.   Glorify^s the name of your^s Lord, the Most High,
2.   Who has created and formed,
3.   Who has determined and guided,
4.   Who has brought forth pasturage,
5.   And then made it withered chaff.
6.   We shall cause you^s to recite,
     so that you do not forget
7.   Except that which God wills.
     He knows what is public and what is hidden.
8.   We shall ease you^s to ease.
9.   So remind^s
     – if the Reminder is useful.
10. He who fears will be reminded;
11. But the most wretched will turn aside from it,
12. The one who will roast in the great fire,
13. In which he will neither die nor live.
14. He who purifies himself will prosper –
15. Who remembers the name of his Lord and prays.
16. But you^p prefer the life of this world,
17. When the world to come is better and more permanent.
18. This is in the ancient scrolls,
19. The scrolls of Abraham and Moses.

Sūra 88

This *sūra* is early Meccan. Like *Sūra* 86 it has the appearance of two short *sūra*s, or at least two parallel passages, put together. The first (1–16) moves from the judgement to hell and then to paradise; the second (17–26) is less homogeneous, dealing with God's signs, Muḥammad's duty to remind, and the punishment of the unbelievers.

The Covering

In the name of the Merciful and Compassionate God

1. Have you[s] heard the story of the covering?[1]
2. On that day there will be faces that are humbled,
3. Labouring, toiling;
4. They will roast in a burning fire,
5. They will be given a drink from a scalding spring.
6. The only food they will have is of thorn shrub,
7. Which does not nourish and is of no avail against hunger.
8. On that day there will be faces that are blissful,
9. Pleased with their striving,
10. In a high garden,
11. Where they hear no idle chatter,
12. Where there is a flowing spring,
13. Where there are raised couches,
14. And goblets set ready,
15. And cushions placed in rows,
16. And carpets spread out.
17. Do they not consider camels and how they were created;
18. And the heaven and how it was raised;
19. And the mountains and how they were set up;
20. And the earth and how it was spread out?
21. So remind[s] [them]. You[s] are only [there to] remind.
22. But you[s] are not an overseer over them,
23. Except over those who turn away and disbelieve.
24. God will punish them with the most severe punishment.
25. To Us is their return,
26. Then upon Us will rest their reckoning.

---

[1] The Day of Judgement.

Sūra 89

Most of the *sūra* is early Meccan. Neuwirth (*Meccan Sūras*, pp. 226–27) has made a plausible reconstruction of a version prior to the present one, by excluding verses 15–16 and 23–24. This, however, leaves unanswered questions about how those four verses were added at some later stage in Mecca. The *sūra* is notable for its brief references to ʿĀd and Thamūd, which have descriptive phrases about the two tribes that are not found elsewhere in the Qurʾān. The cryptic oaths in verses 1–4 are typical of *kāhin*-style material.

The Dawn

In the name of the Merciful and Compassionate God

1. By the dawn,
2. By ten nights,
3. By the even and the odd,
4. By the night when it travels,
5. Is there in that an oath for a man of understanding?
6. Have you[s] not seen how your Lord dealt with ʿĀd,
7. Iram[1] with its pillars,
8. The like of which had not been created in the land,
9. And Thamūd, who hewed the rocks in the *wadi*,
10. And Pharaoh, the man with the tent-pegs,[2]
11. Who were [all] insolent in the land,
12. And caused much mischief in it.
13. Your[s] Lord unloosed on them the scourge of a punishment.
14. Your Lord is in ambush.
15. As for man,
    whenever his Lord tries him and then honours him and blesses him,
    he says 'My Lord has honoured me.'
16. But whenever he tests him and then stints his provision for him,
    he says, 'My Lord has humbled me.'
17. Yet you[p] do not honour the orphan,
18. Nor do you urge the feeding of the destitute,
19. But you devour inheritances rapaciously,

---

[1] Iram is either a sub-tribe of ʿĀd or a place name.
[2] A man of wealth and power.

20. And you love wealth greatly.
21. No, when the earth is pounded to bits
22. And yourˢ Lord and the angels come rank on rank,
23. And on that day Jahannam is brought forward;
    on that day man is reminded
    – but how will the Reminder [help] him?
24. He will say,
    'Would that I had forwarded [some good works] for my life.'
25. No one can punish as He will punish on that day.
26. No one can bind as He binds.
27. 'O soul at peace,
28. Return to your Lord, pleased and pleasing,
29. Enter among My servants,
30. Enter my garden.'

Sūra 90

This is a typical early Meccan *sūra*, starting with a couple of oaths (the first referring to Mecca itself) and then moving on to a number of polemical and eschatological themes that are tangentially related. Verses 8–10 and 17–20 are probably later additions, but probably not much later, with the possible exception of verse 17.

The Settlement

In the name of the Merciful and Compassionate God

1. No! I swear by this settlement[1]
2. – And you[s] are a dweller in this settlement –
3. By a begetter and what he begot,
4. We have created man in distress.
5. Does he think that none shall have power over him?
6. He says, 'I have enjoyed[2] vast wealth.'
7. Does he think that no one has seen him?
8. Did We not assign to him two eyes
9. And a tongue and two lips,
10. And guide him along the two paths?
11. He has not attempted the ascent.
12. What will give you[s] knowledge of what the ascent is?
13. It is the freeing of a slave
14. Or the feeding on a day of hunger
15. Of an orphan near of kin
16. Or a destitute man in misery.
17. Then he becomes one of those who believe
    and counsel each other to be patient
    and counsel each other to be merciful.
18. These are the companions of the right.[3]
19. But those who disbelieve in Our revelations
    – they are the companions of the left.[3]
20. A fire is closed in on them.

---

[1] *i.e.* Mecca.

[2] Or 'consumed'.

[3] On the companions of the left and of the right see *Sūra* 56.

Sūra 91

There is no reason to doubt the generally held view that this is an early Meccan *sūra*. Bell thinks that it was originally two separate sections: 1–10 and 11–15. That is possible – his division certainly reflects a difference in the subject matter, though the rhyme remains the same and there is little change in style, which is largely in the *kāhin* register. After a series of oaths to set the mood, and with the last one (verse 8) longer than the rest, the key point is made in verses 9 and 10: the one who keeps the soul pure will prosper; the one who does not will fail. A moral on the latter is then set out in a brief outline of the Fall of Thamūd, apparently the prototype of the many punishment stories. It appears to be the earliest reference to their fall in the Qur'ān and it is somewhat cryptic. (For the fullest account, see 7:71 *ff.*) As has been mentioned in the Introduction, the earliest narratives in the Qur'ān are Arabian in their origin. The Old Testament stories come later and the New Testament ones considerably later.

The Sun

In the name of the Merciful and Compassionate God

1. By the sun and its brightness in the forenoon,
2. By the moon when it follows it,
3. By the day when it shows it,
4. By the night when it covers it,
5. By the heaven and that which built it,
6. By the earth and that which spread it,
7. By a soul and that which formed it,
8. And inspired it [with knowledge of] what was right and wrong for it!
9. The one who keeps the soul pure will prosper,
10. And the one who corrupts it will fail.
11. In their impiety, Thamūd disbelieved,
12. When the most wretched of them rose up.
13. The messenger of God said to them,
    '[Respect] the she-camel of God and let her drink.'
14. But they called him a liar,
    and they hamstrung her.
    So their Lord punished them for their sin and levelled them.
15. He has no fear of the outcome for them.

Sūra 92

The *sūra* is basically early Meccan, though possibly 19 and 20 were added in the course of a later recitation. After a short passage in the *kāhin* register (1–4), the rest of the *sūra* contrasts the good/generous and the bad/ungenerous and the fates awaiting them. There is a change of person at verse 14 (from 1st plural to 1st singular) that could indicate that the following passage was originally separate.

Night

In the name of the Merciful and Compassionate God

1.   By the night when it spreads its cover,
2.   By the day when it shines in splendour,
3.   And that which has created male and female,
4.   Your[p] effort is truly diverse.
5.   As for the one who gives and is god-fearing,
6.   And believes in the fairest [reward],
7.   We shall ease his way to Ease.
8.   But as for the one who is miserly and thinks himself self-sufficient,
9.   And denies the fairest [reward],
10. We shall ease him to Hardship.
11. His wealth will be of no avail to him when he falls into the Pit.
12. Ours it is to give true guidance,
13. Ours are the last and the first.[1]
14. I have warned you[p] of a fire that blazes;
15. Only the most wretched will roast in it
16. – The one who has denied and turned away;
17. But it will be avoided by the truly righteous,
18. Who gives of his property and purifies himself,
19. And no one has any favour [outstanding against] him that needs to be recompensed
20. – but only through his desire to seek the face of his Lord the Most High;
21. And assuredly he will be satisfied.

---

[1] See the note on 93:4.

Sūra 93

This is an early Meccan *sūra* and possibly a unified piece – the dropping in verses 9–11 of the assonance of verses 1–8 is not necessarily an indication that two pieces have been joined together. The message is one of assurance and encouragement to Muhammad at an apparent time of difficulty. There is no reason for us to take verses 6–8 in anything other than a literal sense. We may therefore assume that Muhammad had been an orphan; had not, before his mission, followed the right path; and at some stage had been relieved of poverty.

The Forenoon Brightness

In the name of the Merciful and Compassionate God

1. By the brightness of the forenoon,
2. By the night when it is still,
3. Your Lord has not said farewell to you nor does He hate you.
4. The last is certainly better for you than the first.[1]
5. Your Lord will give to you, and you will be content.
6. Did He not find you an orphan, and give you shelter?
7. Did He not find you erring, and guide you?
8. Did He not find you destitute and give you sufficiency?[2]
9. As for the orphan, do not oppress him;
10. As for the beggar, do not drive him away;
11. As for the blessing of your Lord, speak of it.

---

[1] This is perhaps the earliest example of the phrase meaning 'the next world is better than this'.
[2] Or 'enrich you'.

Sūra 94

The *sūra* is another message of encouragement to Muḥammad. In my view, there can be little doubt that verses 1–3 are metaphorical, but various legends have grown up about them. Typical of the more restrained accounts is the following piece from Ibn Isḥāq's *Sīrat Rasūl Allāh*, as translated by Guillaume:[1]

> Some months after our return he and his brother were with our lambs behind the tents when his brother came running and said to us, 'Two men clothed in white have seized that Qurayshī brother of mine and thrown him down and opened up his belly, and are stirring it up.' We ran towards him and found him standing up with a livid face. We took hold of him and asked him what was the matter. He said, 'Two men in white raiment came and threw me down and opened up my belly and searched therein for I know not what.' So we took him back to our tent.

This is followed by a much more flamboyant account, put into the mouth of Muḥammad himself:

> He said: 'I am what Abraham my father prayed for and the good news of Jesus. When my mother was carrying me she saw a light proceeding from her which showed her the castles of Syria. I was suckled among the B. Saʻd b. Bakr, and while I was with a brother of mine behind our tents shepherding the lambs, two men in white raiment came to me with a gold basin full of snow. Then they seized me and opened up my belly, extracted my heart and split it; then extracted a black drop from it and threw it away; then they washed my heart and my belly with that snow until they had thoroughly cleaned them. Then one said to the other, weigh him against ten of his people; they did so and I outweighed them. Then they weighed me against a hundred and then a thousand, and I outweighed them. He said, "Leave him alone, for by God, if you weighed him against all his people he would outweigh them."

It is easy to be dismissive about such stories, but they do show us something of the growth of popular Islam as it is reflected in mainline early Arabic sources.

Have We not eased?

In the name of the Merciful and Compassionate God

1. Have We not expanded for you your breast,
2. And removed from you your burden
3. Which weighed down your back,

---

[1] *The Life of Muhammad*, pp. 71–72.

4. And raised for you your reputation?
5. With [all] the hardship there is some ease,
6. With [all] the hardship there is some ease,
7. So when you have ended your task, labour on,
8. And seek after your Lord.

Sūra 95

This short *sūra* has more than its share of difficult phrases. The first three verses are oaths indistinguishable from those in *kāhin*-type fragments. They were probably originally followed by verses 4–5 and 7–8, with verse 6 being added during a later recitation. Apart from verse 6, the *sūra* is early Meccan.

Figs

In the name of the Merciful and Compassionate God

1. By the figs and olives,
2. By Mount Sinai,
3. By this secure territory,
4. We have created man in the fairest stature;
5. Then We have rendered him the lowest of the low,
6. Except for those who believe and do righteous deeds
   – they will have an unbroken reward.
7. What will henceforth declare you[s] false concerning the judgement?
8. Is not God the most discerning of judges?

Sūra 96

Verses 1–5 are regarded by most Muslim scholars as the first passage of the Qur'ān to be revealed. Regardless of whether this is true or not, both 1–5 and 6–8 appear to be very early. However, verses 9–18 (and to some extent 19) deal with opposition to Muslim worship. They cannot therefore be contemporary with verses 1–5, if that is the first revelation, though they are likely to have been added to 1–5 + 6–8 relatively early in the Meccan period. The phraseology of the Arabic indicates section breaks at the beginning of verses 6, 9, 15 and 19. The phrases used at these points occur sporadically elsewhere in the Qur'ān and in early poetry to indicate transitions.

The Blood-clot

In the name of the Merciful and Compassionate God

1. Recite[s] in the name of your Lord who created,   *proclaim*
2. Created man from a blood-clot.[1]
3. Recite[s],
   for your Lord is the Most Generous,
4. Who taught by the pen,[1]   *written scriptures.*
5. Taught man what he did not know.
6. No indeed! Man is impious,   *people dont believe.*
7. Because he thinks that he is self-sufficient.
8. Yet to your[s] Lord is the return.   *death is certain*
9. Have you[s] considered the one who forbids
10. A servant when he prays?
11. Have you[s] considered if [that man] has guidance
12. Or is ordering what is pious?
13. Have you considered if he does not believe and turns away?
14. Does he not know that God sees?
15. No indeed!
    If he does not desist,
    We shall seize him by the forelock,
16. A lying, sinful forelock.
17. Let him call his host

---

[1] It would appear that the words *'alaq*, used to round off verse 2, and *qalam*, used to round off verse 4, are used with the sort of effect that is found in *kāhin*-style material, with catching sound but somewhat Delphic meaning.

579

18.   – We shall call on the myrmidons of Hell.
19.   No indeed!   *servants*
      Do[s] not obey him,
      but prostrate yourself and draw near.   *Heading towards hell*

Sūra 97

The traditional Muslim view is that this is an early Meccan *sūra* and that 'the Night of Power', mentioned in verses 1 and 3, refers to one of the last nights of Ramaḍān, on which Muḥammad received his call. Despite the strength of this tradition, there is nothing in the text of the *sūra* to support it (and nothing against it for that matter). Bell would treat it as early Medinan, but my own guess is that is Meccan.

Power

In the name of the Merciful and Compassionate God

1. We sent it[1] down on the Night of Power.
2. And what can give you[s] knowledge of what the Night of Power is?
3. The Night of Power is better than a thousand months;
4. The angels and the Spirit descend during it,
   by permission of their Lord in every matter.
5. Peace it is until the rising of the dawn.

---

[1] 'It' probably means 'a recitation'.

Sūra 98

This is always regarded as a Medinan *sūra*, and clearly most of the material comes from that period. However, verses 2 and 3 could well originally have been a Meccan piece.

Clear Proof

In the name of the Merciful and Compassionate God

1. The unbelievers among the people of the Scripture
   and among the polytheists
   did not desist until clear evidence came to them:
2. A messenger from God reciting purified pages,
3. In which are true records.
4. Those who were given the scripture
   diverged only after clear proof came to them.
5. They were ordered only to serve God,
   devoting their religion solely to Him as men of pure faith,
   and to perform prayer and to give alms.
   That is the true religion.
6. The unbelievers among the people of the Scripture
   and among the polytheists
   will be in the fire of Jahannam,
   where they will stay for ever
   – those are the worst of creation.
7. Those who believe and do righteous deeds
   – those are the best of creation.
8. Their recompense is with their Lord:
   gardens of Eden through which rivers flow,
   in which they will stay for ever.
   God is pleased with them, and they with Him.
   That is for those who fear their Lord.

Sūra 99

This is generally taken to be an early Meccan *sūra*. Bell thinks that verses 7 and 8 may be later than the rest, but it is very difficult to see any basis for his view.

The Earthquake

In the name of the Merciful and Compassionate God

1. When the earth is shaken with its final[1] earthquake,
2. And the earth brings forth its burdens,
3. And man says, 'What is happening to it?'
4. On that day it will tell its news
5. That your[s] Lord has inspired it.
6. On that day people will come forward in scattered groups to see their works.
7. Whoever does an atom's weight of good will see it.
8. Whoever does an atom's weight of evil will see it.

---

[1] Or 'great'.

Sūra 100

This is one of the group of *sūra*s (the others are 37, 51, 77 and 79) that begin with a particular form of *kāhin*-style material. Here, however, there is no development, merely a couple of short statements with quite different assonance patterns.

The Runners

In the name of the Merciful and Compassionate God

1. By the runners that snort,
2. By the strikers of fire,
3. By the raiders at dawn,
4. When they leave a track of dust,
5. When they engage a host,
6. Man is ungrateful to his Lord,
7. And he[1] is a witness to that,
8. And he is violent in his love of good things.
9. Does he not know?
   When what is in the graves is poured out
10. And when what is in [men's] breasts is made apparent –
11. On that day their Lord will be fully informed about them.

---

[1] Sometimes taken as referring to God: 'He'.

Sūra 101

This seems to be a very early Meccan piece, though verses 10 and 11 have the appearance of being a later explanation of 9. Such expansions are not uncommon (see, for example, 85:5–9 for a complex build up), and I can see no justification for the suggestion made by some western scholars that the verses are spurious.

The Smiter

In the name of the Merciful and Compassionate God

1. The smiter![1]
2. What is the smiter?
3. What will give you[s] knowledge of what the smiter is?
4. On the day on which men are like scattered moths,
5. And the mountains are like carded wool,
6. The one whose balances are heavy
7. Will have a pleasant life.
8. But the one whose balances are light
9. – His mother will take possession.[2]
10. What will give you[s] knowledge of what she is?
11. A blazing fire.

---

[1] Traditionally explained as the Day of Judgement.

[2] Or 'will be childless'. *Hāwiya* cannot be translated by phrases such as 'the bottomless pit' because it is indefinite.

Sūra 102

This is a brief early piece, addressed to Meccans – the second person plural is used throughout – though which group of Meccans is intended depends on the interpretation of verses 1 and 2. It seems to be a unity, despite a change of assonance after verse 2.

Rivalry in Worldly Gain

In the name of the Merciful and Compassionate God

1. Rivalry in worldly gain has distracted you,
2. Until you have come to the graves.
3. No, indeed! You will know.
4. No, indeed! You will know.
5. No, indeed! If you knew with the knowledge of certainty,
6. You will see Hell.
7. Then, you will see it with the eye of certainty,
8. Then, on that day, you will be asked about bliss.

Sūra 103

This short *sūra* consists of two markedly different fragments: verses 1 and 2 have the ring of early Meccan material; while verse 3 appears to be a Medinan verse, exempting the believers from the previous statement. Despite its short length some important variants have survived – these are dealt with in the Commentary.

The Afternoon

In the name of the Merciful and Compassionate God

1. By the afternoon,[1]
2. Man is indeed in a [state of] loss
3. – Though that will not be the case with those who believe and do good works
    and who counsel each other to truth
    and counsel each other to patience.

---

[1] Or 'time'.

Sūra 104

This short piece is considered to be early Meccan. The attack on rich unbelievers recalls the tone of early Arabic satirical poetry.

The Backbiter

In the name of the Merciful and Compassionate God

1. Woe to every slandering backbiter
2. Who has gathered riches and counted them.
3. He thinks his riches have made him immortal!
4. No indeed! He will be flung to the insatiable.
5. What can give you[s] knowledge of what the insatiable is?
6. – The fire of God, kindled,
7. Which rises over the hearts [of men].
8. It is closed over them
9. In outstretched columns.

Sūra 105

This brief piece from the early Meccan period offers encouragement to Muḥammad. It is thought to refer to a failed expedition by Abraha, the Abyssinian governor of Yemen, against Mecca about the time of Muḥammad's birth.

The Elephants

In the name of the Merciful and Compassionate God

1. Have you[s] not seen how your Lord dealt with the men with the elephants?
2. Did He not cause their mischief to go astray?
3. He sent on them birds in swarms,
4. Which pelted them with stones of baked clay,[1]
5. And made them like devoured ears of corn.

---

[1] The meaning of verses 3 and 4 is very uncertain.

Sūra 106

This short piece appears to be an appeal to Quraysh, the tribe who lived in Mecca, to worship God, as being the Lord of the Ka'ba. Other details at the beginning of the *sūra* are not clear. They are traditionally linked with Meccan caravan trade, but this is not entirely convincing.

Quraysh

In the name of the Merciful and Compassionate God

1. Because of the keeping by Quraysh,
2. Their keeping of the journey of winter and summer,
3. Let them serve the Lord of this house,
4. Who has fed them against hunger
   and given them security against fear.

Sūra 107

This short *sūra* is generally considered to be early Meccan, though Bell thinks the whole piece Medinan, and others think so of verse 7. Certainly the first three verses appear to be characteristic of early material, but there may have been some modification in 4 and 5 during either the Meccan or the Medinan period. On the other hand, the use of the strange word *mā'ūn* in verse 7 is likely to be early. The *sūra* has received a certain amount of attention from western scholars, in particular Harris Birkeland, *Muslim Interpretation of Surah 107*, Oslo 1958.

Assistance

In the name of the Merciful and Compassionate God

1.   Have you[s] observed the one who deems religion false?
2.   That is the one who repulses the orphan,
3.   And does not urge the feeding of the needy.
4.   Woe to the worshippers
5.   Who are heedless of their prayers;
6.   Who make a show,
7.   But withhold assistance.[1]

---

[1] Or 'small kindnesses'. The exact meaning of *mā'ūn* is not known.

Sūra 108

This brief *sūra* is an early fragment, addressed to Muḥammad. It is traditionally taken as encouragement to him after he had been mocked for having no son.

Abundance

In the name of the Merciful and Compassionate God

1. We have indeed given you[s] abundance.
2. So pray to your[s] Lord and sacrifice.
3. The one who hates you[s] is the one cut off.

Sūra 109

This is traditionally thought to be an early Meccan piece, and there is no reason to challenge this view. It is in the form of a command to Muḥammad.

The Infidels

In the name of the Merciful and Compassionate God

1. Say, 'O infidels,
2. I do not serve[1] what you serve,
3. Nor do you serve what I serve.
4. I am not the servant of what you serve,
5. Nor are you the servants of what I serve.
6. You have your religion and I have my religion.'

---

[1] Or 'worship'.

Sūra 110

Muslim tradition places this brief piece late in the Medinan period, revealed at Mecca during the 'Farewell Pilgrimage' in March 630 AD. This interpretation links 'victory' in verse 1 with the Conquest of Mecca. This is not certain. The *sūra* might possibly be earlier, but verse 2 seems to rule out Bell's suggestion that the piece might be from after the Battle of Badr.

Help

In the name of the Merciful and Compassionate God

1. When God's help and victory comes,
2. When you[s] see men entering God's religion in throngs,
3. Glorify your[s] Lord by praising Him and seek His forgiveness.
   He is always ready to relent.

Sūra 111

This short piece is normally taken to be a curse on Abū Lahab, the nickname of Muḥammad's uncle, ʿAbd al-ʿUzzā b. ʿAbd al-Muṭṭalib. This traditional view may well give us a proper understanding of the piece, but it is dependent on the way the verbs in verses 1 and 2 are interpreted, a matter discussed in the Commentary. One may also wonder when the nickname was bestowed and under what circumstances. The piece is typically early Meccan, and I see no merit in the suggestions that it dates from after the time when Abū Lahab became leader of the clan of Hāshim, thought to be in 619 AD, or that it is a factual piece dating from the time of Abū Lahab's death (after the battle of Badr).

Palm-fibre

In the name of the Merciful and Compassionate God

1. The hands of Abū Lahab will perish and he will perish.
2. His possessions and gains will be of no avail to him.
3. He will roast in a flaming fire,
4. And his wife, the carrier of firewood,
5. With a rope of palm-fibre on her neck.

Sūra 112

There has been considerable discussion among western scholars whether this *sūra* is directed against Christian doctrine or the pagan view that there were goddesses who were the daughters of Allāh. I do not see why it should not be directed against both. As noted in the Commentary on 2:116, the claim 'God has taken to himself a son', or any equivalent phrase, is always made anonymously.

Sincerity

In the name of the Merciful and Compassionate God

1. Say, 'He is God, One,
2. God, the Eternal,
3. Who has not begotten nor has been begotten.
4. There is no equal to Him.'

Sūra 113

This *sūra* and *Sūra* 114 are known in Arabic as *al-mu'awwidhatāni*, 'the two formulas of protection against magic'. They were omitted from the Qur'ān by one important early authority on the text, Ibn Mas'ūd. Both knots and blowing on objects featured in the sorcery of the time, as can be seen in various verses that occur in pre-Islamic poetry.

Daybreak

In the name of the Merciful and Compassionate God

1. Say, 'I seek refuge in the Lord of the daybreak
2. From the evil of what He has created,
3. From the evil of a darkness when it envelops,
4. From the evil of the women who blow on knots,
5. From the evil of an envious man when he is envious.'

Sūra 114

See the Introductory Note to *Sūra* 113. Both pieces seem to be early Meccan, though Bell assigns this one to the Medinan period.

Men

In the name of the Merciful and Compassionate God

1. Say, 'I seek refuge with the Lord of men
2. The King of men,
3. The God of men,
4. From the evil of a slinking whisperer,[1]
5. Who whispers into the bosoms of men
6. – of *Jinn* and men.'

---

[1] Normally interpreted as Satan.

General Index

---

[1] The three phrases given here are the most common for describing the Day of Judgement/ Resurrection, but there are various others that cannot easily be indexed, such as ʿthe day when they are raisedʾ etc

Index of Legislation[1]

Ablution 4:43; 5:6
Adultery *see* Fornication
Alms, almsgiving 2:263–4, 271; 9:60, 79,
    103; 57:18; 58:12–13
Arbitration 4:35

Bequests 2:180, 240; 4:7–9, 11–12a, 176
Blood-money 4:92
Booty *see* Spoils
Bribery 2:188

Calendar 9:36
Charity 2:215
Children
    suckling of 2:233; 4:23; 65:6
    adoption of 33:4, 37
    killing of 6:137, 140; 17:31; 81:8
    daughters 16:58–59
Cleanliness 2:222
Contracts, covenants 2:282–3; 4:33; 8:72b;
    9:1, 7–13

Debts 2:280 ff
Divorce 2:226–232, 241; 33:4, 49; 58:2–3;
    65:1–2
Dowries 4:4, 20, 24a, 25; 33:50

Fasting 2:183–5, 187, 196; 5:95
Fighting 2:216–17; 3:13; 4:74–77; 22:39–
    40; 47:20; 73:20
Food, regulations concerning 2:172–73;
    5:1a, 3; 6:119–121, 146; 16:114–15;
    22:34, 36
Fornication 4:15–16, 19; 17:32; 24:2–3;
    25:68; 33:30; 60:12

Gambling 2:219; 5:90–91
Guardians, duties of 4:2–6

Inheritance 4:19, 176; 89:19

Killing 4:29, 89a, 92–93; 5:32; 6:137,
    140; 9:5; 17:33; 60:12

Marriage 2:221–1a, 232, 235; 4:3–3a, 22–
    25; 24:32; 33:49; 60:10
    prohibited degrees of 4:22–24
    of fugitives 60:10–11
Menstruation 2:222

Oaths 2:224–25; 5:89; 16:91–92
    absolution from 66:2
    expiation of 5:89
Offerings 2:196; 5:2, 95; 9:75, 99
Orphans 2:83, 177, 215, 220a; 4:2–3a, 6–
    10, 36, 127; 6:152; 8:41; 17:34; 59:7;
    76:8; 90:15; 93:9; 107:2

Pilgrimage 2:158, 189, 196–200; 3:97a;
    5:2, 95, 97; 22:27
Prayer 2:3, 238; 4:43, 101–03a, 142; 5:6,
    58; 6:92; 11:114; 17:78, 110; 29:45;
    62:9–10
Purification
    4:43; 5:6–6a

Qibla 2:142–5, 150

Retaliation 2:178–9, 194; 5:45; 17:33

Slander 4:112; 24:4, 23; 33:58
Slaves
    freeing of 2:177; 4:92; 5:89; 58:3;
        90:13
    marriage of 4:25; 24:32
Spoils 8:1, 41; 48:20; 59:6–8

Trading 2:275, 282; 4:29
Theft 5:38; 60:12
Treaties *see* Contracts, covenants

---

[1] General injunctions, such as 'Perform prayer and pay the *zakāt*' are not included.